THE MAN IN
THE ARENA

ADST-DACOR Diplomats and Diplomacy Series

Series Editor
Margery Boichel Thompson

Since 1776, extraordinary men and women have
represented the United States abroad under widely
varying circumstances. What they did and how and why
they did it remain little known to their compatriots.
In 1995, the Association for Diplomatic Studies and
Training (ADST) and DACOR, an organization of foreign
affairs professionals, created the Diplomats and
Diplomacy book series to increase public knowledge
and appreciation of the professionalism of American
diplomats and their involvement in world history.
Rodger McDaniel's recounting of Gale McGee's three
careers—as a university professor, U.S. senator, and
ambassador to the Organization of American States—
is the 64th volume in the series.

THE MAN IN THE ARENA

The Life and Times of U.S. Senator Gale McGee

RODGER McDANIEL

Foreword by Alan K. Simpson

An ADST-DACOR Diplomats and Diplomacy Book

Potomac Books | *An imprint of the University of Nebraska Press*

Library of Congress Cataloging-in-Publication Data

Names: McDaniel, Rodger E. (Rodger Eugene), 1948–,
author. | Simpson, Alan K., writer of introduction.
Title: The man in the arena: the life and times of U.S.
Senator Gale McGee / Rodger McDaniel; foreword by
Alan K. Simpson.
Description: [Lincoln]: Potomac Books: University of
Nebraska Press, [2018] | Series: ADST-DACOR diplomats
and diplomacy series | Includes bibliographical refer-
ences and index.
Identifiers: LCCN 2018009199
ISBN 9781640120013 (cloth: alk. paper)
ISBN 9781640120884 (epub)
ISBN 9781640120891 (mobi)
ISBN 9781640120907 (pdf)
Subjects: LCSH: McGee, Gale W. (Gale William), 1915–
1992. | Legislators—United States—Biography. | United
States. Congress. Senate—Biography. | United States—
Politics and government—20th century.
Classification: LCC E748.M1482 M33 2018 |
DDC 328.73/092 [B]—dc23 LC record available at
https://urldefense.proofpoint.com/v2/url?u=
https-3a__lccn.loc.gov_2018009199&d=Dwifag&
c=Cu5gl46wZdoqVuKptnsyhefx_rg6kWhlklf8eft
-wwo&r=Qxk-cj_QrVzflu7b7vxqTw&m=
jb7flbsKytkhqqKyewuhhfDpe9jskm34x-tnux4l440&s=
AuMl_34wqgisKamrDng3bFdavgFbx2yy9zjk0jNaktg&e=

Set in ITC New Baskerville by Mikala R Kolander.

For Robert McGee and Elizabeth Strannigan
as well as my loving wife, Patricia

"It is not the critic who counts; not the man who points out how the strong man stumbles, or where the doer of deeds could have done them better. The credit belongs to the man who is actually in the arena, whose face is marred by dust and sweat and blood; who strives valiantly; who errs, and comes short again and again, because there is no effort without error and shortcoming; but who does actually strive to do the deeds; who knows the great enthusiasms, the great devotions; who spends himself in a worthy cause; who at the best knows in the end the triumph of high achievement, and who at the worst, if he fails, at least fails while daring greatly, so that his place shall never be with those cold and timid souls who know neither victory nor defeat."

From Theodore Roosevelt's "Man in the Arena" speech, *Paris, April 23, 1910*

Contents

ALAN K. SIMPSON

This is the splendid second book Rodger McDaniel has written regarding U.S. senators who served the people of Wyoming. He is a fine author and friend. I am most pleased to share some thoughts as I introduce this biography of Senator Gale W. McGee.

I was a sophomore at Cody High School when I first met Gale. He and his wife, Loraine, were often guests in my parents' home. Back then, my dad, Milward L. Simpson, was president of the Board of Trustees of the University of Wyoming. Dr. McGee was a young, vigorous, vital and energetic history professor. The two spoke of university matters and state politics and enjoyed many a pheasant hunt.

Over the years these two men were, from time to time, great adversaries. But they were always greater friends. In spite of their partisan differences, which were not insignificant, they maintained a high degree of respect for one another. That is the way it was then. Two people could vigorously disagree about politics and still tramp along together down a row of corn stalks hoping to kick up a pheasant or two! Theirs was one of those relationships that made Wyoming politics unique. Their lifelong friendship proved that everything in Wyoming is politics except politics. Politics is personal!

From Gale's earliest days at the university, there were those who worried he was a little too far left. They called him a "progressive," a word that in the context of the McCarthy years had a rather sinister meaning. That image coupled with the first rumors that this outspoken professor had designs on seeking public office as a Democrat led some to the conclusion that he should be fired and run off the campus.

Gale was always true to himself. Even though he was unprotected by tenure, he did then what he did his whole life. He walked into the middle of the arena to fight the good fight soon after his arrival in Laramie, boldly leading the charge against censoring textbooks. He was outspoken when others might have been more cautious. A small clump of people, a world apart from the mainstream, thought McGee should go, and they had just the plans to make that happen.

The matter came to a head when presented to the University trustees chaired by my father. The vice chairman was newspaper publisher Tracy McCraken, a delightfully witty man, a Democrat of great wisdom and good common sense. He and my father were dear friends from their days as ATO fraternity brothers at the University of Wyoming, one a conservative Republican, the other a liberal Democrat. They reached the same conclusion: that canning a popular and capable professor because of his political beliefs was un-American, a violation of the 1st Amendment, and a blow to academic freedom. They'd have none of it. Individually each was persuasive. Together they were dominant. They powerfully persuaded a majority of the trustees and Dr. McGee kept his job.

I arrived at the University of Wyoming as a student in 1950. I can assure you of this. Gale McGee's history classes were the most popular on campus. Every student wanted to be in his classes. Townspeople came to hear him lecture. Every seat was taken. If you wanted one, you had best get there early. I never missed a class even though it meant rising early (for me!) in the morning from the rumpled sack in my humble garret at the "Ape House," as the athletic dorm was so described!

All of us were inspired by this man. His lectures were thorough, witty, and filled with marvelous anecdotal material of the kind that makes it fun to study history. This professor stood each morning before an overflowing classroom, bursting with his own contagious enthusiasm, gesturing and using his almost lyrical voice to hold our attention to every single word. Gale McGee loved teaching and he loved history, and he embedded that same love in his students.

He also loved his students, and they in turn loved him. Dr. McGee paid enough attention to our lives that one day he visited with me, asking whether I was paying attention to my studies or just the lovely young girl from Greybull. I allowed as to how it might have been the latter. Gale had the great good fortune to have a wife with whom he was a full life partner. He and Loraine were always a team, always shared their lives and all of their hopes and dreams. I think he was very happy for me that I was smitten with Ann Schroll, that young woman from Greybull whom I married more than sixty-one years ago and who has shared my life as Gale and Loraine shared theirs.

I graduated in 1954 and went off for a couple of years to Germany in the U.S. Army. When I returned to Laramie for law school, we would see the professor often. Ann had begun her teaching career at the University School on the campus. One of her most engaging students was Robert, one of Gale and Loraine's fine children.

By then it was 1958. Gale ran for the U.S. Senate and my dad ran for reelection as governor. Gale won. Pop lost. Before long, Dad joined Gale in Washington when he was elected to the U.S. Senate in 1962. Thus, these two longtime friends were once again joined in the common cause they so often shared, representing the state they both loved. It's true. They didn't always vote alike, but they always maintained a great wellspring of respect and affection for one another.

One of the oft-told jokes of their days together held that a young Wyoming high school student wrote a paper touting Wyoming as "the Equality State." He also said that was borne out because we were proud to have two women representing us in the U.S. Senate, "Gail McGee and Mildred Simpson." True story.

Gale's eighteen years in the Senate were more than a little eventful. He found himself in the arena where the battles were fought on major issues ranging from civil rights to environmental protection, Medicare and Medicaid, Watergate, battling the extremists of the John Birch Society, and, of course his support of the war in Vietnam. He held his own and did so with integrity and courage, never swerving even as the clouds gathered and others sought political shelter.

As the years rolled on, I practiced law in Cody as Gale continued his work in the Senate. I'd receive frequent letters and calls from him asking about Ann and my family and about my work in the courtroom and the Wyoming State Legislature. Two years after Gale left the Senate, I was elected to it and began my eighteen years in Washington, the same duration as his service. When Ann and I arrived, among the first people to greet us were Gale and Loraine. I will always treasure his advice, guidance, and counsel especially during those first years when he helped smooth my transition in dealing with a Democratic president, House, and Senate. It's when you are in the minority that you really learn how to govern. No choice!

Gale took his 1976 defeat in stride and went on to several more years of public service. I would look forward to our lunches in the Senate dining room when he would speak enthusiastically about his work as ambassador to the Organization of American States. In that capacity, he was able to use his vast and considerable skills and knowledge of foreign affairs to further the good of the nation. Had it not been for his eloquent gifts as an orator and historian, the Senate would not have eventually ratified President Jimmy Carter's proposed Panama Canal Treaties.

After Ronald Reagan was elected president, Secretary of State George Schultz called on him once again to serve his nation. He was appointed a member of a panel doing the important work of finding solutions to the problems the United States faced with relocating the tens of thousands of Indo-Chinese refugees following the end of the Vietnam War. His fine efforts there gave the two of us another opportunity to work together, for then I was a senior member of the Senate Judiciary Subcommittee on Immigration and Refugee Policy embroiled in all of the difficult issues surrounding immigration and refugee reform, and Gale took time to brief me and assist me greatly through some of that work. I indeed could never thank him enough.

Being asked to prepare and present this foreword of Gale McGee's biography permits me to give full voice to the gratitude I feel for the man who helped me with his loving concern, interest and honest counsel during many of the formative stages of my life. These pages have allowed me some rare and dear moments to gratefully recall the contributions he made to my successes.

Gale McGee was indeed an extraordinary person. He had three distinct careers and loved them all equally. As a professor, a United States senator, and an ambassador, his powerful intellect and eloquence reached the young minds in his classroom and extended across the globe where he shared his energy, knowledge, and brilliance—all to the common good.

Gale leaves a marvelous legacy, chronicled in the pages ahead. Enjoy!

Author's Note and Acknowledgments

Most books are the offspring of many parents. This one is no different. The list begins with Gale and Loraine's children. Special thanks are due Robert McGee, Gale and Loraine's youngest son, without whose support this book could not have been written. He believed knowing his father's story had value beyond the family. Robert's collection of papers and writings and his recollection of significant events were central to completing this project. He and his wife, Mary Lou, were a source of encouragement as I plodded through the writing. Their sons Kirk and Scott provided invaluable research assistance, able to locate documents and other useful information beyond my grasp.

Daughters Mary Gale and Lori Ann contributed important memories of their parents' lives and were willing to share deeply personal recollections that give the story a depth it might not otherwise have.

Equally deserving of my gratitude is Elizabeth Strannigan. Liz worked for Gale McGee from the time he first ran for the Senate in 1958 until his death in 1992. With respect, I refer to Liz as "the keeper of the flame." She served the senator and Loraine faithfully and has worked tirelessly to keep his memory alive.

Other former McGee Senate staffers contributed as well, people like Jim Burridge, Dick McCall, Jan Stoorza, Betty Cooper, Irma Hanneman, Andy Manatos, and Phil Riske.

Personal thanks are extended to Alan Simpson. Like McGee, Simpson served three terms in the Senate. He appreciated the historic value of telling McGee's story and joyfully offered up memories of times his family and the McGees shared over many years. The foreword he wrote for the book was a product of his personal friendship with Gale McGee.

Thanks go to the American Heritage Center at the University of Wyoming, where McGee's official papers are housed along with several other collections to which I referred. It is an extraordinary resource for writers and researchers. Don Ritchie, the retired U.S. Senate historian, was immensely helpful as were the folks at the Wyoming State Archives office in Cheyenne and the Library of Congress.

When friends like Kathie Lowry, Mary Guthrie, Marion Yoder, and Lynn Simons offered to proofread drafts, I took them seriously. Their work is deeply appreciated.

My gratitude is given to Margery Thompson, the publishing director and series editor at the Association for Diplomatic Studies and Training. She believed in the value of this book and worked to make sure it was published. Working with the staff at the University of Nebraska Press/Potomac Books was a pleasure. Thanks as well to Elaine Durham Otto for improving the book through the contribution of her copyediting skills.

I am blessed with a wife who is bright, well read, and patient. Patricia has endured the hours I have isolated myself in my basement office or was on the road as this book developed. She listened patiently as I recounted every little nugget I found. After reading the manuscript aloud to me, Pat said, "As I was reading it, I forgot that you were the writer." I took that as a compliment.

Writing Gale McGee's story has been a wonderful journey. Thanks to all of you who took it with me.

THE MAN IN
THE ARENA

Prologue

No one saw it coming. Nobody. Neither a pollster nor a pundit. Certainly no one who failed to think about how much America had changed since Gale McGee was first elected in 1958. Even the new senator-elect seemed stunned when the senator called to concede. But it was over. McGee had lost his third bid for reelection.

Boxers say the punch that hurts the most is the one you didn't see coming. It wasn't like 1958, when the McGees waited all night and into the next day to learn they had narrowly won. In 1976, the punch no one saw coming came early in the evening. CBS news legend Walter Cronkite called it first. The polls hadn't been closed for more than an hour. Not many votes could have been counted. The margin was that big. The punch was that hard. McGee had three distinct and distinguished careers. As a professor, he taught for more than two decades, most of those years at the University of Wyoming. As a U.S. senator, he served three terms in the greatest deliberative body on earth. For eighteen years, he served with five presidents: Dwight Eisenhower, John F. Kennedy, Lyndon Johnson, Richard Nixon, and Gerald Ford. After the Senate, McGee became the ambassador to the Organization of American States (OAS) under President Jimmy Carter.

Kennedy called him "an asset and a leader of his country."[1] Lyndon Johnson attempted to persuade McGee to accept a presidential appointment as ambassador to the United Nations. He told the Wyoming senator it could put him on track to becoming secretary of state. Nixon thought McGee was "a courageous statesman who always put his country above partisan politics."[2] McGee was on President Ford's short list to become the director of the Central Intelligence Agency. Carter tasked him with spearheading his signature initiative, the ratification of the Panama Canal treaties.

McGee joined the Senate as a part of the Class of 1958. Another of its members was West Virginia senator Robert C. Byrd. Byrd earned a reputation as the Senate's historian in part because of a series of Senate speeches he gave, recognized as "the most ambitious study of the United States Senate in our history."[3] Byrd conducted an ongoing seminar for his colleagues on the history of their institution. His speeches were published as a major collection. Volume 1 includes a tribute to the Class of '58.

Byrd said the "relatively stable political climate" previously existing in Washington was changed by the election of 1958. That election altered not only the political balance in the Senate but also the fundamental characteristics of the body. The new senators were younger and more liberal. Their election shifted power from the South to the West and the North, and an unusually high number were, like McGee, not lawyers. Nor were they establishment senators. Byrd said the Class of '58 "set out to bridge that gap, to break down the inner club and the Senate establishment."[4]

William S. White was a longtime Senate observer. In a 1957 book he wrote that "when one enters the Senate, he comes into a different place altogether. The long custom of the place impels him, if he is at all wise, to walk with a soft foot and to speak with a soft voice and infrequently."[5] The Class of '58 didn't get the memo.

McGee was a vital part of what many historians believe was one of the golden periods of Senate accomplishment. Among the sixteen freshmen were men whose names quickly became well known across the nation. They included Edmund Muskie of Maine, Phil Hart of Michigan, Hugh Scott of Pennsylvania, Frank Moss of Utah, Kenneth Keating of New York, Thomas Dodd of Connecticut, Eugene McCarthy of Minnesota, and Gale McGee of Wyoming.

Several became larger-than-life figures in their own right. They were activists who believed government could be a force for good. They believed strongly that the voters had not made such a wholesale change in the makeup of the Senate by accident. The voters wanted something different from government.

University of California professor Barbara Sinclair studied the historic transformations of the U.S. Senate, concluding the sheer size of the Class of 1958 meant the old-timers could not impose some of the Senate traditions on them. The freshmen were not required to serve the apprenticeship normally imposed on newcomers. Sinclair noted that the Class of 1958 was "extraordinarily well treated" with committee assignments.[6] These assignments, which included prestigious seats on the Finance and Appropriations Committees, positioned the new guard to spearhead an era of action. Members of the Class of 1958 put their fingerprints on much of the most significant legislation of the century. The historic civil rights laws of the 1960s were part of their accomplishments as were Medicare, Medicaid, the National Environmental Protection Act, the Clean Air Acts of 1963 and 1965, and the Water Quality Act of 1965.[7]

Senators McGee, Byrd, and Dodd were the first freshmen ever to receive appointments to the Senate Appropriations Committee. McGee's other committee appointment didn't excite him nearly as much. And yet it was during these years that the Senate Commerce Committee spurred "the greatest single period of concentrated consumer activity in the history of the nation."[8] It also crafted legislation that became a major part of the Civil Rights Act of 1964 protecting blacks from discrimination in public accommodations. The war in Vietnam created harsh divisions and generated some of the most powerful and courageous debates to have taken place among U.S. senators since the Civil War.

Gale McGee was precisely the kind of senator Wyoming voters wanted when they elected him in 1958. But that was then. Eighteen years had come and gone. Something had changed Wyoming and America.

On election night in 1976 McGee's staff and friends gathered in two places two thousand miles apart. One group met at the Laramie home of Dick and Marty Brown. Dick was Gale's right-hand man in Wyoming. McGee joined them in his hometown, the place where he ended each of his four campaigns. The other group gathered in Washington at his Senate office.

The senator's Washington staff arrived early that evening in Room 344 of the Russell Office Building, named for the powerful Georgia senator who had been helpful to McGee in the early days of his career. The walls of the long, rectangular room were painted a light shade of blue. Polished wood trimmed the walls. Cream-colored drapes were embossed with the U.S. Senate seal. Two brass lamps and a giant back-lit panoramic of the Teton Mountains provided subdued lighting.

Along one wall was a large, old-fashioned fireplace. Above its mantel hung a display of the pens used by presidents to sign into law the bills Senator McGee played a key role in shepherding. There was the one Lyndon Johnson used to sign the Civil Rights Act of 1964 and another he used to sign the Voting Rights Act of 1965. Above them was the pen John F. Kennedy used to sign legislation creating the Peace Corps. There were also pens used to sign the bills creating Medicare, the Elementary and Secondary Education Act, and Food for Peace.

Missing from the collection was the pen Johnson used to sign the document that would largely define McGee's career as well as LBJ's. Perhaps the president didn't hand out souvenir pens when he signed the Gulf of Tonkin Resolution.

The pens decorating his office were souvenirs of his relationship with the times, evidence of a career of public service well spent on the Senate's frontlines. McGee wasn't simply a spectator or a critic. He wasn't what Teddy Roosevelt called "the man who points out how the strong man stumbled." He was one of those people Roosevelt would have recognized as "the man in the arena" whose face was, from time to time, "marred by dust and sweat and blood."[9]

His life's story cannot be only about him. McGee's story is that of America during the times in which he lived. The more than two decades in which he served in the Senate and as ambassador to the Organization of American States witnessed a major transition in American politics. McGee was one of those late 1950s liberals who inherited the successes of the New Deal. FDR's liberalism was credited with saving the nation from economic disaster and the world from international fascism. Even in Republican Wyoming, liberals had won the state's electoral votes in four of the five presidential contests prior to McGee's first Senate run. As a candidate in 1958, Dr. McGee had no hesitancy in claiming the liberal label.

The political scientist James Piereson captured the political reality of the times, declaring that "liberalism was without doubt the single most creative and vital force in American politics."[10] McGee firmly believed in the institutions created by liberals and the theories of government they espoused by such achievements as the Marshall Plan, the United Nations, the U.S. Agency for International Development, and the Peace Corps. He was equally convinced that American capitalism and democracy were keys to a peaceful world. In 1958, Wyoming voters agreed. By 1976, they had changed their minds.

Piereson identified the time and the place when American liberalism began its decline: November 22, 1963, in Dallas. Henry Kissinger agreed. "Roughly coincident with the assassination of President John F. Kennedy," he wrote, "the national consensus began to break down."[11]

Another astute observer saw it coming earlier. Dr. Hans Morgenthau was one of the twentieth century's most astute thinkers and one of McGee's professors at the University of Chicago. Several months before Kennedy's murder, Dr. Morgenthau sensed the changes. He wrote to his friend Dean Acheson, who had served as secretary of state under Harry Truman.[12] Morgenthau lamented,

What I find so disturbing in the Washington scene today is the dearth of men who are capable of thinking in political terms. It is not so much a question of evaluating Cuba, Berlin, or de Gaulle one way or the other as it is the congenital inability to bring political categories to bear on these issues. It is as though people were asked to judge paintings, not in terms of their intrinsic aesthetic value, but in terms of, say, the cost of their production, the chemical composition of the paint, or their physical relationship to each other.[13]

Morgenthau described what Senator McGee called "the folly of trying to destroy an idea with a name or trying to destroy a proposal with a slogan," telling his colleagues, "It is time that we face an idea with an idea."[14] But, as would be more and more the case as time went by, slogans and buzzwords increasingly trumped ideas and thoughtful debate.

Whereas many Americans were once willing to engage in meaningful dialogue about the larger social, economic, and political issues of the day, by 1976 they had become more interested in the micro issues immediately in front of them. What's more, the majority of voters no longer trusted the government that had given them reforms like collective bargaining rights, Medicare, civil rights, Social Security, and environmental and consumer protection. They feared the same government planned to take their guns and overregulate the way they lived. The middle class that once asked government to protect it from big business worried that in the process the government itself had become too big. Many citizens now felt they needed protection from the government.

That McGee lost his Senate seat on the same day that the Democratic Party's 1976 presidential nominee won says a great deal about the changes in American politics. In 1976, Jimmy Carter campaigned against Washington. So did McGee's opponent.

Historian and McGee confidant Dr. T. A. Larson analyzed the election's outcome. "Like [Wyoming senator Joseph C.] O'Mahoney in 1952, McGee in 1976 had become 'too big for Wyoming.'"[15]

Larson's assessment appeared to coincide with the views expressed by the editor of the *Green River Star*. His words, published the following day, seemed to reflect the sentiments of many voters that year. Wyoming had become more interested in itself than in the larger world. "I used to justify McGee's role in the Senate. There wasn't much going in Wyoming and we didn't have as many giant problems as other states. We could no longer afford to donate one Senator for national and foreign affairs."

In the immediate aftermath of his defeat, McGee's loss seemed easy to comprehend. Some said he had lost touch with the state. Others said he paid too much attention to foreign affairs. A few blamed the length of his hair and the loud sport coats and ties he wore. It is now clear that something much bigger was at work in 1976. Almost half a century has passed since McGee won a third term and became the last Democrat elected to the U.S. Senate from Wyoming. With the advantage that decades of hindsight afford, this book attempts to view Gale McGee's career and his defeat in the context of a larger picture.

Both the Green River newspaper editor and Dr. Larson were correct, each for different reasons. If McGee appeared to have become too big for Wyoming, perhaps it was because Wyoming's and the

American consensus about the nation's role in international matters had gotten smaller. The more influence he acquired in national and international affairs, the less Wyoming voters wanted to know about anything beyond their borders. As disdain for the federal government fully blossomed in Wyoming, the bloom was off the rose. McGee's "clout" was no longer appreciated.

Regardless of the reason, the campaign was over. The senator had lost his seat. An analysis of the causes could wait. McGee picked up the telephone. He had a concession call to make. He telephoned Senator-elect Malcolm Wallop and graciously congratulated him. The day ended and, with it, McGee's time in the Senate.

Lori Ann McGee had an exam the next day. As she crossed campus, a fellow student asked, "Didn't your dad used to be Gale McGee?" Lori Ann replied with defiant pride, "He still is."

1

From the "Sons of the Mist" to the Plains of Wyoming

On New Year's Day 1649, King Charles still had his head on his shoulders. That soon changed.

January 30 was extraordinarily cold. Charles asked his executioner to permit him to wear two heavy shirts. He didn't want to shiver in the cold and appear to be afraid.[1] Surprisingly, the man with the axe agreed. His Majesty obediently stretched forth his hands. After a dramatic pause, the man with the axe severed Charles's head from his body. He held the king's head high above his own, triumphantly exhorting, "Here is the head of a Traitor."

Charles and his supporters including the McGee boys "believed God put him on the throne." However, Oliver Cromwell "believed he was chosen by God to stop Charles."[2] Having beheaded the king, Cromwell set out to do the same to the McGee boys.

The surname McGee wasn't used then. It evolved steadily from its seventeenth-century Ulster form. The name has a long and lofty history. In Irish, the name is Mag Adoha. Ulster McGees are actually of Scottish extraction.[3] Patrick MacGregor of Albrech was the 3rd Chieftain of the Clan. Some of the younger members of the MacGregor clan of the Scottish Highlands were known in the early 1600s as the MacEagh, or "sons of the mist," because of the stealth with which they disappeared into, and emerged from, Scotland's dense mountain fog.

The MacGregors fought alongside King Charles. After the war ended with Charles's defeat, Cromwell issued an edict proscribing the name MacGregor. The "sons of the mist" were outlawed. Their property was confiscated and a bounty put on their heads.

As they went into hiding in Ulster and later fled across the Atlantic to the American colonies, the MacGregor and MacEagh names gave way to new spellings and new pronunciations. From MackGayhe and MackGehee to McGhee, it was the nineteenth century before it settled on McGee.

Genealogical irony is attendant to this history. It was English royalty that chased the MacGregors from their homeland in the mid-1600s. Three centuries later Malcolm Wallop, born of English aristocracy, chased their descendant Gale McGee from the U.S. Senate.

Gale McGee came from ordinary working people. Harvey McGhee, Gale's great-grandfather, was the first of the clan born in the New World. It was 1820 in Monroe County, Virginia. Sometime later he and his family headed west, eventually settling on Iowa farmland. McGee's grandfather, Joel, was born in 1857 in Wapello County.

Joel was fifteen years old and Diana was fourteen when they married in 1872. They raised eleven sons and daughters altogether. Garton, Gale's father, was their firstborn. They started their family at Lick Creek in southernmost Iowa. They moved often, finally settling in the small town of Humeston, a small farming community of little more than five hundred people, nestled in the gently rolling fields of Iowa, sixty miles due south of Des Moines.

If you had known Gale McGee early in his Senate career, you would have been able to pick Garton out of a lineup. Garton was a handsome man of medium build with brown eyes and dark brown hair. He was a farm worker until 1910, when the McGees became a part of the extraordinary national migration from rural to urban America. They moved to Lincoln, where Garton found work as a department store shipping clerk. There he met Frances McCoy. The two married at high noon on December 16, 1913, in the home of the bride's parents. The local newspaper called Frances "one of our most charming and accomplished young ladies." They didn't know Garton, but assured readers that "he is alright or he wouldn't be here."

Gale William McGee was born at home on St. Patrick's Day 1915. He was Garton's fortieth birthday gift just as Garton had been a

March 17 birthday present for his father.[4] During the spring before the assassination, Garton and Frances arrived at the White House to meet John F. Kennedy. Their son escorted them into the Oval Office. The handsome young president, wearing a smart green tie, smiled broadly and acknowledged the St. Patrick's birth date Garton shared with his son. To Gale's surprise, his father responded to the president, "Who's Irish? We're from Scotland."

Kennedy wrote to Garton, saying, "You have a special claim to the watchfulness of the great saint of Erin, and I hope he obtains for you many more years of health and happiness."[5]

Though perhaps Scots-Irish, a St. Patrick's Day birthday was, nonetheless, special to Senator McGee. He kept a list of every Wyomingite and others he knew to celebrate that day with him. Each year he sent a special greeting to every one of them.

Gale was three years old when brother Max was born. A year later, the family moved to a smaller community. Norfolk, Nebraska, is 125 miles north of Lincoln. In 1866, a small group of German immigrants settled along the banks of the north fork of the Elkhorn River where they made a life for themselves and their descendants. The original 250 Norfolk settlers had grown to about 6,000 by the time the McGees arrived in 1919.

The McGee family moved into a comfortable two-bedroom white clapboard house in Norfolk. It was there in 1921 that Frances gave birth to a third son, Dean. The family was now complete. The three brothers all did well with their lives. Gale became a college professor, a U.S. senator, and an ambassador, Max a successful merchant and mortician, and Dean a physician.

In Norfolk, Garton sold cars and trucks. Soon he knew almost everyone in the county, because nearly all of them drove a car or truck they had bought from Garton. Frances remained in the home to care for their three boys. For many years household income was supplemented by taking in boarders. Frances was just old-fashioned enough to believe that idle hands were the devil's workshop. She was a busy woman who made certain her boys' hands were not idle. Gale played organized youth baseball and belonged to the Boy Scouts. He and his brothers had paper routes. Gale took piano lessons until he was fifteen. He was ten years old when he took his first job as the cleanup boy at Bogue's Grocery Store, and he always had a job thereafter whether sweeping floors at Montgomery Ward or taking out groceries for Norfolk neighbors who shopped at one of the three local grocery stores.

Gale also found plenty of time to hunt pheasants and to go fishing with his father and brothers, developing a lifelong love of the outdoors.

During these years, Frances was as heavily committed to the community as she was to her children. She and Garton and their sons found their pew every Sunday morning at the Norfolk Methodist Church. At one time or another, Frances held most of the lay positions in the church. She visited shut-ins for eleven years. She passed a driver's test on her eightieth birthday, renewing her license, determined to continue her visitation duties.

She was a stalwart member of the Madison County Republican Party. Mrs. McGee headed its women's division for three and a half decades. A foot soldier for the party, she went door-to-door organizing voter registration and get-out-the-vote drives. Her son recalled his mother was "a button-holer and a doorbell ringer, and a stamp licker."[6] Frances taught Gale the value of registering voters and making certain each went to the polls. When he was old enough, Gale drove the family car, following his mother as she walked through every precinct. She knocked on the doors of each Madison County Republican until the last one voted.

His mother's influence led Gale to establish a Young Republicans Club while he was in college. He loved his mother deeply, calling her weekly even while in the Senate. But her political influence didn't survive his college education. Frances admitted as much in January 1959, with CBS cameras rolling. On screen was the new senator from Wyoming with his proud family. The moderator of "Meet the New Senators" turned to Frances. Neil Strauser asked her in all good humor, "Mrs. McGee, I've learned you and Mr. McGee are Republicans. Just what happened to Gale?" Frances was quite comfortable in her first appearance on national television. "Well," she replied deadpan, "Daddy and I have often talked about it. We decided that we made our mistake when we sent him to college where he learned to read."[7]

Gale graduated from Norfolk High in 1932. As a graduation gift, a close family friend took him to Washington, DC. It was Gale's first trip east of Omaha. One morning he walked into the ornate chamber of the U.S. Senate. Nebraska senator George Norris, whom John Kennedy called "one of the most courageous figures in American political life," was speaking at just that moment.[8] "I was inspired by George Norris's example," McGee said years later. "He was a symbol of what I thought was good, clean political responsibility."[9] That may have been the moment McGee decided he wanted one day to serve in that chamber.

Gale wanted to be a lawyer. But it was the height of the Great Depression. Money was scarce. Finances would not permit such a lengthy course of college studies. Instead he enrolled at what was then called State Normal School and Teacher's College at Wayne in the northeast corner of Nebraska. The rather odd name "Normal School" comes from a sixteenth-century French concept, *école normale.* In France, "normal" schools provided expositional classrooms where student teachers came together with students to learn model-teaching practices. Normal schools were popular in American education circles, including the University of Wyoming, from the mid-nineteenth to the early twentieth century.

In 1949, the school's name changed to Nebraska State Teachers College. Since 1963, it has been known as Wayne State College. The school produced a number of notable alumni. James Keough was an assistant managing editor of *TIME* magazine before becoming the director of the U.S. Information Agency under President Richard Nixon. John Kyl, one of McGee's students, was a member of Congress from Iowa. John Neihardt wrote *Black Elk Speaks.* Several played professional sports. Among the best known is Byron Chamberlain, a member of two of the Denver Broncos' Super Bowl winning teams. Others became best-selling authors or noted Nebraska political figures. One became a United States senator.

Gale McGee was on the campus from 1932 until he graduated in 1936. He thrived in college, maintaining excellent grades while engaged in extracurricular activities. He was a leader in the campus Young Republicans Club. He won the Nebraska intercollegiate oratorical championship in 1936, foreshadowing a lifelong rhetorical ability that contributed greatly to all of his future successes. McGee's first-place entry was an oration entitled "Forgotten Men." Demonstrating his early flirtation with isolationism, the speech was designed "to ring the bells against the new 'warmongers' on the loose in the world around us."[10] Gale was a member of the Literary Society and the "B" basketball squad and served as student body president. He studied history, political science, and speech.

During his college years, Nebraskans worried about the Dust Bowl and the near daily "black blizzards." The only time Nebraska lost population was between 1930 and 1940.[11] These were times when folks couldn't see the top of the state capitol building in Lincoln. Streetlights were turned on at midday. Exceedingly high temperatures and wind-driven dirt caused hardship.

However, international problems invaded their homes even more than the wind-borne dirt. The daily news was tainted with stories of the threat posed by Hitler, Mussolini, and Tojo. Those images revived another one from his childhood. He was three years old when his parents took him to a 1918 Armistice Day parade. Among the bands and marching soldiers, a fire truck dragged a stuffed shirt and pants made to appear like a headless body through the streets strung with a sign reading, "Kaiser Wilhelm." McGee recalled years later how terrified he was by that horrible image.

While in college, "the girl of my dreams" came into Gale's life.[12] Loraine Baker was the daughter of a country doctor who was also mayor of Pierson, Iowa. She was the only child of deeply religious parents who raised her in a small town that enforced a strict code. Dancing and drinking were forbidden. Although her parents agreed with the community on the matter of alcohol, they often pulled down the shades, rolled up the rug, turned on the Victrola, and danced in the privacy of their own home. Dancing with them led Loraine to a lifelong love of dancing, especially with Gale.

In that part of the country there were unwritten rules about courting. Gale and Loraine strictly adhered to them. On warm Midwest evenings, the young couple could be seen visiting on her parents' porch. From the beginning, Gale was not particularly welcome when he visited Loraine at her home. Her parents seldom, if ever, invited the young man in. The two got to know one another on that porch.

Loraine was initially uneasy about this fellow whose name seemed to pop up everywhere on campus. He was president of this and that and seemed to be on everyone's "most likely to succeed" list. Contemporary photographs show a young man who was handsome, exhibiting a confident and persuasive appearance. She tired of hearing about how great everybody thought he was. Like her parents, Loraine initially thought Gale was arrogant, even snobbish. Unlike her parents, Loraine gradually overcame that feeling as she got to know him better. Gale concentrated on persuading her. He didn't need all three votes. He didn't even need a majority. The only vote he needed was Loraine's. Eventually he got it.

Gale wrote in Loraine's yearbook "on the last Saturday of the last year of college life." "Bake," as he and others called her, "it would seem futile to attempt to recount in this small space all of the perfectly grand times we've had the past few months. They represent the happiest part of my life because I spent most of my time with the nicest girl I have ever known." He apologized for being "a rather disagreeable individual to get along with" and closed by referring to himself as very lucky. "For a number of years now I have been told that I could never find a girl who didn't drink or smoke, but I fooled them."

This is as close as we'll get to reading love letters from their courtship. It's not that there weren't others. Likely the other letters were as old as those long-ago days in college and later when Loraine taught in Holdrege and Gale was 235 miles away in Crofton. On a snowy afternoon at their ranch in the Dunoir valley near Dubois some years after he left the Senate, Gale and Loraine put on some Big Band music and stoked a warm blaze in the fireplace. They took turns reading the old letters to each other. Then they lovingly tossed them into the fire. When daughter Mary Gale asked her why, Loraine said, "Because they weren't for our children to read."

With college degrees in hand, they took separate paths. Loraine left to teach in Holdrege in the far south central part of Nebraska and Gale to teach at Crofton, a tiny town to the north, on the Nebraska–South Dakota border. They were miles apart, but that didn't keep them from seeing one another frequently and writing those love letters.

McGee began his teaching career with Crofton's first-grade class of 1936. He was paid $80 a month for the eight-and-a-half-month school term. He complied with his contract, which demanded he "not attend public dances on school nights."[13] Later he taught history and speech and coached the girls' basketball team before moving to Kearney in 1937. There he taught history, speech, and debate for three years. His salary increased to $100 a month.

He found time to visit Holdrege often enough to keep the romance alive. The *Holdrege Citizen* newspaper carried a brief announcement in its "About Town" column telling the world when "Loraine Baker, elementary school teacher, was visited by Gale McGee, Kearney."

It was the afternoon of June 11, 1939. The song "Deep Purple" rang through the neighborhood from the backyard of Gale's parents' Norfolk home as Gale and Loraine were wed. Loraine's mother attended, but her father, Howard, had died three months earlier, following a massive stroke suffered while crossing a street in Pierson. Madge Baker died nine months after the wedding.

Loraine told her adult children that she always felt her parents' early deaths were brought on in part by their deep unhappiness over her decision to marry Gale. Likely their unhappiness had less to do with Gale than with the fact that Loraine was their only child. Her parents held even more tightly to Loraine because of the circumstances of a miscarriage Madge suffered with her first pregnancy. Howard was the only doctor in town, and so it fell to him to deliver the dead fetus. Understandably, Madge and Howard were reluctant to lose their little girl to marriage.

After their wedding, Gale earned a living teaching so he could attend the University of Colorado during the summer. After writing his thesis on "Economic Aspects of the Stamp Act," McGee received a master's degree in 1939. He was ready to teach at the college level. The success of his high school speech and debate teams came to the attention of a legendary speech professor at Nebraska Wesleyan University in Lincoln. Professor Enid Miller earned a reputation for her formidable speech and debate teams winning tournaments across the country. She was nearing retirement and fervently desired to leave the school's team in good hands. Gale McGee was recruited for the job, and in 1940 he became the university's debate coach and assistant professor of speech.

During his tenure at Wesleyan, McGee edited the *Nebraska Social Studies Bulletin*. A March 1941 issue may be the first time he ever mentioned Wyoming. In an editorial about the need to teach tolerance, McGee referred to an incident in Rawlins, Wyoming. In June 1940, a mob of more than a thousand men and boys attacked members of the Jehovah's Witnesses. One, called a "pioneer Rawlins businessman," was dragged from his home, forced to kiss an American flag, and then severely beaten. Others were beaten, and their property was burned.[14] When they demanded protection, they were put in jail.

McGee used the tragic incident to teach his fellow social studies teachers. "The Social Studies teacher should ever bear in mind the real objective, that of inculcating in youth a spirit of tolerance." The following year, he had an opportunity to teach by his own actions.

That year a group of twenty Nisei, that is, second generation Japanese Americans, were admitted to Nebraska Wesleyan. Most completed high school in one of the internment camps to which Japanese Americans were "evacuated" under the orders of President Franklin Roosevelt in February 1942, a few weeks following the attack on Pearl Harbor. Given the level of fear and anxiety during those dark days, it was not a simple process for Nisei students to move from high school graduation to college. They weren't welcomed in many communities. It was even complicated to enroll at schools in communities that were more tolerant. In the summer of 1942, the National Student Relocation Council worked with the president and military authorities to create a system under which at least some of the interned students could continue their education during the war.[15]

They agreed on a classification system, taking into account a student's scholastic accomplishments and personal characteristics including "loyalty." Some schools added other barriers including church affiliation and ability to pay tuition and costs. Military officials imposed even stricter barriers. Nisei students petitioning for enrollment had to "be recommended by one or more responsible citizens" willing to attest to the applicant's "character and loyalty."[16] Schools, as well as potential students, were required to have military clearance before enrollment. Colleges and universities qualified only if they were not engaged in military research and were located more than twenty-five miles from "important power installations, defense factories, or railroad terminal facilities."[17] In addition to military requirements, federal officials demanded evidence of the willingness of the local community to accept these students. An application had to be accompanied by a statement from a local official such as a mayor, police chief, sheriff, or district attorney, assuring that the community was welcoming. Many communities were not able to provide such assurance.

Much more than soliciting letters from community leaders was asked of colleges and universities willing to take Nisei students. Under federal law, the Japanese Americans were under what was termed "protective custody" of the military, which didn't extend to meeting the actual needs of the students. Many of these students looked to the schools for help in finances, housing, counseling, employment, and relocation.

Not many schools around the country met these conditions. The requirement that the school be distanced from militarily sensitive facilities alone precluded most from participating. It's no coincidence that most of the 402 Nisei students in the first group to transfer from an internment camp to a college campus went to schools in the Rocky Mountain and midwestern regions of the United States, including Nebraska Wesleyan. "NWU to Take Jap Students," read the October 23, 1942, headline in the student newspaper, the *Wesleyan*. One of the first to arrive was Kazuo Tada. He started at NWU in January 1943. There he met his future wife, but he met none of the racism frequently found in other communities.

"Oh gosh," Tada reported years later, "I tell you, we were accepted. I'll never forget one incident in which a sorority girl (American) invited me to a dance. And that really shook me up. The main thing that shook me up was that I possibly should not go. So I asked the public relations man—that wasn't his title but he was responsible for seeing we got along all right, and I went in to see him, and what he said was, 'Of course, go!' So I did go."[18] That man was Professor Gale McGee.

Why were these students accepted so readily at this school and not at others? Some attribute that success to the McGees. Betty Cooper was a McGee student at Wesleyan during these days. "They smoothed the way," she said, and took it upon themselves to make sure not only that the students were comfortable but also that others could accept them. Cooper recalled, "During those days of wartime biases, Gale and Loraine McGee were outstanding examples of tolerance and warm hospitality when several Nisei students enrolled at Wesleyan."[19]

During their time at Nebraska Wesleyan, Loraine and Gale welcomed their first-born child. After suffering a miscarriage, they celebrated all the more with the birth of a healthy David Wyant on November 13, 1942 in Lincoln. Loraine suffered two more miscarriages and bore three more children over time.

Before Pearl Harbor, McGee exhibited a reluctance to support the buildup to World War II. He voted for Norman Thomas in the 1940 presidential election. Thomas was not only a Socialist but also a leading antiwar voice. He formed the "Keep America Out of War Congress." Professor McGee proposed inviting Thomas to speak on the Wesleyan campus. The idea quickly evaporated in the heat generated by local clergy.[20] Thomas and McGee shared the views of the America First Committee, one of the nation's largest antiwar organizations. Charles Lindbergh was one of that committee's best-known spokesmen. McGee was one of 100,000 traveling to Chicago on August 4, 1940, to hear Lindbergh rally antiwar sentiment. Lindbergh told the gathering, "We have participated deeply in the intrigues of Europe, and not always in an open democratic way. There are still interests in this country and abroad who will do their utmost to draw us into the war. Against these interests, we must be continuously on guard."[21]

McGee's concerns about "warmongers" and his former "militant isolationist" beliefs motivated him to seek a deferral from the military draft.[22] The college professor wrote to his draft board seven months before the Japanese attacked Pearl Harbor. "After deep study and much careful consideration, I find it impossible to support this present war in its current form. Therefore, except in case of attack against the Continental United States, I conscientiously object to serving in the armed forces of this country. Realizing that this brief statement cannot fully explain my position, I will be glad to submit a detailed statement of my beliefs at the discretion of the board."[23]

McGee sought advice on how to handle his request for a deferment. Maj. Dwight Williams of Station Hospital at Ft. Riley, Kansas, responded. He lauded McGee for seeking conscientious objector (CO) status. Major Williams told McGee that if drafted and assigned to a combat unit, he could appeal through a chaplain. He further advised McGee to contact his own minister for assistance. The McGees were Methodists, a denomination known to support conscientious objectors. "In your case," wrote Williams, "I should think the church would be a powerful aid in seeing that justice is done."[24]

And then came December 7, 1941. Pearl Harbor changed everything. The America First Committee dissolved three days later. Norman Thomas reluctantly became a supporter of the war. The country was at war whether the isolationists liked it or not. As soon as Congress declared war on Japan, Italy, and Germany, Americans lined up to enlist. As a result, college enrollments immediately dropped precipitously. Some colleges began planning to close their doors for at least the duration of the war. The V-12 program changed those plans for some schools. The program was initiated in July 1943 in order to quickly supplement the ranks of Naval and Marine Corps officers needed for the war effort. College enrollment increased because the V-12 program allowed officer candidates to obtain a bachelor's degree in their chosen fields of study. The curriculum was augmented by military courses. Naval officer candidates were then sent to a four-month course before joining the fleet. Upon college graduation, Marines went to boot camp followed by a three-month officer candidate school before being commissioned and sent to the front as platoon leaders.

Professor McGee left Wesleyan to teach at Iowa State College in Ames. There he was assigned classes filled with young Navy cadets preparing for deployment. The following year McGee joined the Navy's V-12 program at Notre Dame. As an instructor in a significant military program, he was deferred from the draft. However, his earlier letter to the draft board now came back to haunt him.

When the head of the Nebraska Selective Service System learned that someone who had sought a CO deferment was an instructor in the military's V-12 program, he complained bitterly to the president of Notre Dame. McGee was immediately summoned. On January 17, 1944, the professor was relieved of his duties because "it had been reported to them I was a CO."[25]

Anxious to resolve the matter, McGee quickly wrote to the draft board. "My opposition to the European war in May 1941 was based on purely academic grounds. In other words, I felt that more would be gained by delay and education than by war." He explained the attack on Pearl Harbor "took the question out of the realm of academic speculation. I have never advocated pacifism in any form, in fact I have been a longtime proponent of strong, forceful action in order to keep the peace."[26]

That letter was followed by another three days later. "A few days ago, I submitted a detailed explanation of a statement made in May 1941, relative to my opposition to the war *at that time.*" McGee explained he "would not oppose induction." Within three weeks the draft board obliged him. He received a new draft card. McGee was reclassified I-A and reinstated at Notre Dame, now considered "available for unrestricted military service."

In May, McGee applied for a commission so that he could become a Navy pilot. The application required Notre Dame to release him from his teaching responsibilities in the V-12 program. Already shorthanded, they refused. On September 11, 1944, McGee received an "Order to Report for Induction." He departed from the Lincoln train station at midnight to take an induction physical. He was certified "Physically fit, accepted by Navy, including Marine Corps, Coast Guard." However, his induction depended "on results of blood tests." The blood tests disclosed he had a serious health problem that followed him for the remainder of his life. Gale McGee first learned he had "diabetes mellitus" in a March 5, 1945, letter from the Selective Service Board. He was disqualified for military service. The war went on without him. He and Loraine got on with their lives.

Earlier Gale and Loraine had made the hard trudge to obtain Gale's master's degree from the University of Colorado. He taught during the school year and took classes all summer. The time had come when he knew that further advancement in the teaching profession required a doctorate. Gale had already earned some credit hours toward a PhD attending summer school at the University of Chicago. That was a slow grind. Faced with a dilemma about how best to complete the degree, the couple's optimism about their future won out.

He and Loraine decided "not to go on for a hundred more summers to finish in Chicago, but to borrow the money, go into debt, and to get it done."[27]

Life in Chicago wasn't easy. The neighborhoods surrounding the university were becoming slums, populated by undesirable and dangerous characters. "Students, especially young ladies, risked their purses, their jewelry, their virtue, and even their lives if they ventured on the streets after dark." It was said that reputable academicians from around the country refused to come to the University of Chicago because of this environment.[28]

Loraine not only cared for three-year-old David while Gale spent most of his day in class or studying. She was also Gale's helpmate through the entire process of earning a PhD. She typed his dissertation, proofread it, and then retyped it several times over. The two earned the degree as a team.

They lived in the Deronda apartments on Chicago's Southside. It was a small, unpleasant apartment as congested as the streets below. The apartment was affordable but barely, as was all housing near the noisy El train. The train dragged passengers and tumultuous racket across the metal rails and concrete platform as it passed near their bedroom window day and night all year long. Those who could afford to live elsewhere did. Those who couldn't simply turned up the radio.

The weather taunted them winter, spring, summer, and fall. During torrid Chicago summers, windows were left open. More flies entered than cooling breezes. Summers included long periods of especially stifling hot days, which meant unbearable nights in that confined space. Gale and Loraine hauled a mattress to the rooftop where they slept more comfortably under the stars. During bone-chilling winters, closed windows could not ward off the Chicago winds. The cold found its way through the walls and the windows. But the McGees did what they had to do.

The three years at the University of Chicago proved pivotal in forming Gale's political philosophy. His rhetorical skills were honed through his undergraduate work and teaching experiences. His political convictions were evolving as the world around him evolved. His earlier flirtation with isolationism no longer made sense to him in a world where the Nazis had nearly won a world war. The combination of his not insignificant rhetorical skills and firm political convictions created a path Gale McGee would travel to the world stage during the difficult days of the Vietnam War.

The moment he walked through the doors of that revered academic institution, he began to develop a worldview that served him through his career in academia and public service. It was a hard-earned worldview, perhaps aided by his ability to focus entirely on his studies. Previously, by financial necessity, his academic pursuits were interspersed with work requirements. Now he focused time and thought to explore what he really believed and why. He spent hundreds of hours reading and researching. He wrote dozens of scholarly papers on subjects ranging from "The Signing of the Declaration of Independence" and "French Colonial Policy" to "Problems in British Imperial History" and "Contemporary Diplomatic Issues."[29]

The beginnings of his transition from isolationism can be observed in McGee's doctoral studies. During the summer of 1940, in the waning days of his experimentation with isolationism, McGee wrote "A Survey of Foreign Efforts to Ally with the United States, 1789–1919." Having spent fifty-eight pages reviewing dozens of foreign attempts "of all shapes and sizes" to entangle the United States in their affairs, McGee concluded that "they point to the futility of the term 'isolation,' as well as indicate the need for defining a new course which takes into account the complicated way of international politics."[30]

As he came to believe isolation was futile, he searched for an alternative to fit his new understanding of those complications. He made the transition under the tutelage of an isolationist. Professor J. Fred Rippy was a historian of national repute, a Tennessean born in the nineteenth century, who revered the memory of Robert E. Lee. He and McGee had something in common. Rippy had been drawn to the outdoor wonders of Wyoming in 1914, when he spent a summer as a hired hand at Yellowstone National Park. Young Rippy was expert enough at handling a horse that rumors grew he was actually "a Panhandle cowboy in disguise" or a professional rodeo cowboy from Cheyenne.

Rippy was an isolationist who openly worried through the days of Woodrow Wilson into the presidency of Franklin Roosevelt that America would "destroy itself in its repeated efforts to save the world."[31] In spite of Dr. Rippy, Gale McGee rejected isolationism by 1947, and his transition from being an isolationist to believing the United States was obliged to engage in world politics was complete. His doctoral dissertation, "The Founding Fathers and Entangling Alliances," acknowledged that the "annals of the Republic, during the first generation, abound with declarations against meddling in European affairs." He argued, "Past scholars seem to have been satisfied that those idealistic protestations constituted an accurate photographic record of the deeds and advice of the Founding Fathers."[32] He set out to earn his doctorate by proving those scholars wrong.

His 265-page treatise thoroughly surveys not only the words but also the deeds of leaders such as Washington, Adams, and Jefferson. The Founding Fathers, McGee concluded, exhibited a disposition to achieve a balance of power in order to protect America's security. "It was a disposition that had constantly been in evidence since the birth of the Republic, and thus perhaps it better represents a 'tradition' in American policy than the so-called pole-stars of aloofness, isolation, and non-entanglement."[33] McGee's research built a solid case for international engagement in order to achieve a balance of power among nations.

His conclusions about the role of the United States in world affairs were first defended before a University of Chicago dissertation committee. Later he defended his ideas as a member of the U.S. Senate during the most trying days of the Vietnam War.

The two professors before whom he was required to defend his dissertation could not have been more daunting or different. The first was Dr. Rippy. The other was one of the twentieth century's leading experts on international politics. Dr. Hans Morgenthau made landmark contributions to international law and international relations theory. He wrote extensively for national publications such as the *New Republic*. In his seminal text, *Politics Among Nations*, published shortly after the end of World War II, Morgenthau advanced the argument that became the center of his analysis of U.S. involvement in Vietnam, a war he opposed.

Morgenthau argued that good motives don't necessarily produce good results.

We cannot conclude from the good intentions of a statesman that his foreign policies will be either morally praiseworthy or politically successful. Judging his motives, we can say he will not intentionally pursue policies that are morally wrong but we can say nothing about the probability of their success. How often have statesmen been motivated by a desire to improve the world, and ended up making it worse?[34]

When Gale McGee sat across from these intellectual giants to defend his dissertation, he could be excused for feeling intimidated. But Rippy and Morgenthau were so diametrically opposed in their philosophies that, according to McGee, they spent most of his time arguing between themselves. "Fred Rippy and Hans Morgenthau got to fighting over how isolated the hemisphere was, Morgenthau arguing that the hemisphere was another linkage in the chain that wraps the whole world together. Rippy was arguing, 'Thank God, America First. We're isolated from the embroilments of the old world.' And they argued for a substantial portion of the two-hour orals period. I slipped through between their disagreements, one with the other."[35]

Humility aside, McGee proved to be a match for the intellect of both Rippy and Morgenthau. The strength of his research not only earned him a doctorate but also set the course for his significant role in crafting the foreign policy of the United States in the middle of the twentieth century. Ironically, while Morgenthau's views aligned more closely with McGee's dissertation, the two became adversaries as Americans debated the nation's role in Southeast Asia in the 1960s and 1970s.

It wasn't long before suitors from the University of Wyoming came calling. More than a decade later, when McGee sought political office, detractors claimed he came to Wyoming as a carpetbagger, planning to take advantage of a small state to win a Senate seat. Not so, said McGee. He came to hunt and fish.

Some of his fondest memories were of those days fishing and hunting with his father and brothers along the Elkhorn River near Norfolk. His love affair with the trout streams and pheasant fields of Nebraska readily transferred to Wyoming.

If anyone doubts this was why he came to Wyoming, they didn't know Gale McGee. His obsession with fishing later landed him the job as captain of the Laramie fly-fishing team that won Wyoming's 1951 fishing derby. Another of those competitions ended with McGee driving away in the first prize, an old car with a rumble seat, "worth at least $50."[36] His obsession with hunting was so great it later led him to accept the invitation to take part in an unusually dangerous pheasant hunt. During a trip to South Korea as a member of the Senate Foreign Relations Committee, a South Korean general escorted the senator to a field outside Seoul. As they loaded their shotguns, he warned McGee to stay on the path marked with white flags. "We were instructed not to chase down any of the pheasants we might shoot." They were hunting in a minefield laid purposefully to keep North Korean soldiers from crossing into the South. They shot eighteen pheasants that day. Each time "either the general or one of his colonels would pick his way between the mines to retrieve the birds."[37]

In May 1951 the *Denver Post* published a newspaper supplement heralding Wyoming as a fisherman's paradise. Most Wyoming fishermen and women don't like Coloradans packing their favorite fishing holes. McGee sent the newspaper "An open letter to unwary Colorado fishermen who may have read the *Denver Post.*" Protecting his favorite fishing holes from an onslaught of Coloradans, he warned, "While there may be 700 miles of streams, you will have to walk nearly that distance to reach them and upon arrival discover them to be the birthplace of mosquitoes and abounding with ticks. The annual list of tick fever victims reads like a Korean casualty report."[38]

When Dr. Ottis Rechard, the dean of the Liberal Arts College at the University of Wyoming, went to Chicago to recruit professors, he found Dr. Gale McGee. They talked about the possibility of the young professor coming to teach at the University of Wyoming. McGee had never been to Wyoming but expressed interest. Aware of the extent to which Laramie's isolation and the long, harsh winters contributed to the premature decisions of others to leave the school, Rechard suggested he first speak to someone who knew what life in Laramie was like before deciding.

McGee went to see a colleague who once lived three years in Laramie. "It's a very interesting place," he told McGee, "but I don't think you'll like it there." McGee asked why. "Well, there's not a legitimate supper club within a hundred miles. There's not a legitimate theater within a hundred fifty miles. All the local folks do is catch trout and shoot deer."[39]

That's all Gale McGee needed to know about Laramie. "I signed up the next morning." The McGees headed west.

2

Nothing to Lose but a Little Self-Respect

"Let's go fishing!"[1] Those were the first words "Doc" Larson recalls
Gale McGee saying as he arrived in Wyoming in the early summer of
1946. Larson, a uw history professor, welcomed his new colleague.
The two were fellow Nebraskans who both earned master's degrees
at the University of Colorado. They were destined to become lifelong
friends and compatriots, a relationship they solidified during hundreds of hours walking along trout streams near Laramie.

Descending the steep mountain pass along the old Lincoln Highway at the crest of the mountains just east of Laramie, one could see
why fishing might have been the first thing that came to McGee's
mind. More than a thousand feet above Laramie, travelers get a first
glimpse of the geologic bowl in which the town sits. As the blacktop
straightens and moves west, the Laramie valley opens. On the horizon, the Snowy Range forms a long, white-capped wall. Below are the
lush grasslands of the valley.

The Laramie River flows through the town after a journey along
the east side of the Medicine Bow Mountains. Leaving Laramie and
headed north, it transcends the Laramie plains. The mountains,
punctuated with peaks rising nearly thirteen thousand feet, stand in
the background to the west. It wouldn't have taken much to imagine
the hundreds of miles of trout streams that lay within reach. Finding
a place to fish proved far less difficult than finding a place to live.

Housing was at a premium in the days following the war. Students
and faculty competed with one another for what little was available.
Loraine, expecting a second child within a few months, remained

behind in Norfolk with little David until Gale located housing adequate for the family. In the meantime, he found a room within walking distance of the university and went fishing.

The university had hired him to begin teaching in the fall 1946 semester. However, History Department head F. L. Nussbaum wrote to Dr. McGee in April asking him to come earlier. "The prospective registration in summer school is larger than we had expected and if your situation makes it possible we would like to have your services for both terms."[2]

As the fall semester ended, Gale finally found a house that would accommodate his family. Loraine and David joined him a few days before their second son, Robert, was born on December 15, 1946.

Loraine quickly grew fond of the community's informality. She told a friend that while women in the Midwest could wear shorts in the afternoon and evening on very hot days, women in Wyoming could wear shorts only during the daytime. "For more formal evening activities, you changed into jeans."[3] The four made their home in a small, rented white house with black trim on Eighth Street. Gale made an appointment with a Denver doctor to assess the progress of his diabetes. The specialist predicted McGee had a life expectancy of only twenty to twenty-five years.[4] He lived another forty-six.

The McGees set about getting to know the town and their new neighbors. For a history aficionado like Gale, Laramie was a fascinating place. A short walk from their house to First Street and they were downtown. They shopped at the Lovejoy Novelty Shop owned by the family of Elmer Lovejoy, who built the first automobile west of the Mississippi River.[5] Twenty-three-year old Elmer "sped around Laramie at the incredible velocity of eight miles an hour in this carriage resembling a beer wagon." He patented the first electric garage door opener before dying in 1960.[6]

Nearby was the J. C. Penney Building. In 1868, three outlaws were publicly hung there. On that same block was the Holliday Opera House and the Frontier Hotel built in 1868. The entire block burned to the ground a year and a half after the McGees came to town.

The next block over was one of Laramie's two movie theaters and the building where Bill Nye opened the *Boomerang*, a newspaper named for one of his cantankerous mules. Nye published the newspaper from an office above the stable, and this location proved to be a problem. The "fumes from the stable came up through the floors, and we all smelled too strong most of the time to go into respectable society."[7] Just around the corner was the Elks Lodge, where a dozen years later Gale McGee would announce his candidacy for the U.S. Senate.

A couple of blocks up the street and around the corner on Ivinson Avenue, they found Laramie's first jail. Its cramped and musty cells once held Jesse James, Calamity Jane, and Jack McCall, the man who murdered Wild Bill Hickok. Along the way, a careful look at many of the buildings would reveal the colorful facades of the original ornate architecture.

Laramie's centerpiece was then, and it has always been, the University of Wyoming. Wyoming was still four years away from statehood when its territorial legislature created the University of Wyoming on March 4, 1886. The first building, Old Main, rose four stories above what was then little more than prairie. The architects were intentional about not imitating eastern campuses. They achieved a uniquely western design relying on native stone. The rough sandstone defining much of the building is trimmed by smoother sandstone, providing a beautifully contrasting texture. Its Romanesque design is characterized by the symmetry of the right and left facades originally divided by a large spire, later removed because of structural safety concerns. The arched entryway invites visitors up a wide stairway and through the main doors. Old Main opened in time for the first students to walk through the doors on September 6, 1887. When Professor McGee arrived in 1946, the four-story building was much the same as it had been when it first opened.

A new president was installed at UW the year before McGee came. George Duke Humphrey would earn his place in history as one of the school's giants. Duke gave his first address to the university community on the day that World War II ended. As with most colleges and universities in those days, the war's end gave birth to demanding increases in student enrollment at the University of Wyoming. Enrollment promptly tripled, as did the challenges of meeting the immediate needs of so many students. UW's 1946 yearbook cleverly described the faculty and deans as "haunted by the expanding future and maltreated by the shifting present." Humphrey quickly hired new faculty members including McGee. Housing students was as big a challenge as teaching them. The Laramie Chamber of Commerce donated fifty trailers, adding capacity to the new dormitories built expeditiously by the school. "Even a water tower behind Dray's Cottage where Washakie Center is now located was remodeled and occupied."[8]

Near the end of McGee's first year, he nearly accepted an offer to leave Wyoming. Moorhead State Teachers College offered him more money if he would go to Minnesota. McGee told President Humphrey he wanted to remain at UW, but "I have not been able to meet the expenses of my family with my present salary." He asked for a raise to an annual paycheck of $3,700.[9] Humphrey agreed, and McGee stayed. But it didn't take long for the new professor to find himself in hot water.

In early October 1947, the National Association of University Governing Boards sponsored a conference at the University of Michigan. It was nearly three years ahead of Senator Joseph McCarthy's Wheeling, West Virginia, speech when the Wisconsin demagogue claimed to have a list of known Communists employed by the U.S. State Department. As early as 1947, President Harry Truman had issued an executive order requiring loyalty reviews of federal employees. The national hysteria about communism was percolating.

One of the speakers at the University of Michigan conference titled his presentation "The Little Red Schoolhouse Is Redder than You Think." He warned university board members that subversive, anti-American books were finding their way into the libraries of the schools for which they had responsibility. He cited two authors in particular, Valery Yakovlevich Tarsis, a Russian dissident, and American education reformer and political activist George Counts. Tarsis and Counts were certainly controversial. Neither was anti-American. What's more, neither of their books could be found on bookshelves at the University of Wyoming until after the textbook controversy alerted educators and students to their existence.

In the audience that October day at the University of Michigan conference were UW board president Milward Simpson and trustee

Harold Del Monte. They returned from Ann Arbor with a great deal of angst about what they had heard. The topic was immediately placed on the agenda for the next board meeting. On the morning of October 25, 1947, the trustees joined Humphrey in the boardroom of Old Main. Simpson called the meeting to order promptly at 10 a.m., and the meeting seemed routine for a time. The minutes of the previous meeting were approved, a list of students upon whom degrees were being conferred was read, some faculty appointments were approved, bids for remodeling Old Main were rejected because they exceeded the appropriation, and the board granted Dr. Humphrey's request to attend a conference in Denver.

Then with no sense of the furor he was about to unleash on the campus and throughout the country, "Dr. Cunningham moved that President Humphrey appoint a committee to read and examine textbooks in use at the University of Wyoming, in the field of social sciences, to determine if such books are subversive or un-American. The motion was seconded by Mr. Del Monte and carried."[10] The meeting adjourned, and the trustees left to watch the University of Wyoming play a football game against the University of Utah.

UW was one of the first U.S. institutions of higher learning to conduct a "Red Scare" investigation of textbooks. The outcome was an avalanche of negative attention. Criticism came from far and near. Historian Arthur Schlesinger said it was a "crude" investigation by "ill-informed trustees."[11] The *St. Louis Post Dispatch* called the trustees' action "an insult to the good sense and patriotism of the faculty" and "an affront to the intelligence" of the students.[12] Newspapers in at least twenty communities around the United States followed suit.[13] The criticism was even greater at home.

Even so, in November Dr. Humphrey complied with the board's resolution. He named a panel headed by UW Law School dean Robert Hamilton, who in turn demanded department heads submit a list of required texts. A political tornado touched down on the Laramie plains. The faculty voted overwhelmingly to send a delegation to meet with the board. Dr. Larson was named chair, and McGee and Nussbaum were among the members.

Of the fifteen-member committee, fourteen were protected from arbitrary discharge by tenure. Professor McGee alone was subject to being discharged without cause. Even so, he did not wither. He was not shy in his criticism of the board. He said the investigation was a "gratuitous insult to faculty who seemed viewed by the board as incompetent to select and interpret their own course reading materials."[14] The untenured professor found himself in the crosshairs. One member of the UW board immediately went fishing for evidence to support McGee's firing. He paid the tuition of several students who agreed to attend Dr. McGee's classes and report back to him on what he was certain was subversive, anti-American teaching.[15] "The fellow on the board leading all of this was John Reed, a banker from Kemmerer," McGee later claimed.[16] McGee believed that of the six to eight "spies," one was the child of Joe Budd, another of Frank Mockler, Republican state legislators. A third student, he thought, was the daughter of trustee Harold Del Monte.[17] It all came to naught. The students reported back only that McGee's classes were filled and that most students enjoyed his teaching. They said they had heard nothing subversive or anti-American.

That didn't stop the plotting to rid the university of the professor who so openly criticized the administration at the height of the textbook controversy. It was proposed that the board hold a meeting outside of Laramie, purposely to avoid the pressure from the faculty of a Laramie meeting. The plan was to meet in Sheridan, three hundred miles from the campus. There, it was felt, they could quietly deal with the McGee problem.

But the chairman and the vice chairman of the board had other ideas. Milward Simpson, a Cody Republican who later served as governor and as one of McGee's Senate colleagues, and Tracy McCraken, the powerful Democrat who published several Wyoming newspapers, intervened. Simpson told fellow board members, "I will have none of this. This is what an institution of higher learning is all about, expressions of divergent views, the First Amendment, academic freedom."[18] Their objections caused the board to reconsider. No meeting was held in Sheridan, and McGee was not terminated.[19] John Reed let it go until a more opportune time.

By now everyone was looking for a dignified way out of the textbook controversy. It was McCraken and Simpson who found it. The board saved face by agreeing with the idea of appointing a small group of professors to review some books and report back. Among the book reviewers were T. A. Larson and Gale McGee. They read sixty-four books and assured the board they found no anti-American or subversive information in any of them. "That's fine," said McCraken. "Now the people of Wyoming will know that even though subversive teaching may be practiced at other schools, there is none of it in Wyoming."[20] It was over.

The controversy took a toll on the McGees. As the matter was hotly debated on campus and sides were taken, some of his colleagues accused McGee of being a Communist. A few of their wives were so consumed in the controversy that they told Loraine that she and her children were no longer welcome in their homes. For his trouble, McGee received a letter from Ralph Conwell, a fellow professor at UW, thanking him for his role in resolving the matter. "This department appreciates the courage and intelligence which you displayed as a member of the faculty committee, many thanks."[21] A decade later, it was the same Conwell who led the charge to paint McGee as too far left to serve in public office.

It was one of those spring days that makes a person glad to live in Laramie. Quarrelsome winds are often a part of a Laramie spring day, as the warm air from the valley collides with the cold air off the mountains. Not that day. Only a slight breeze tweaked the leaves on the aspens in the front yard. Gale woke, started the coffee, and retrieved the *Laramie Republican* from the porch.

He grabbed his morning cup of black coffee and sat down at the kitchen table. Awaiting him was his usual fare. There was a plate of bacon and eggs and a hot bowl of his favorite Zoom oatmeal. When he became a senator and found Washington area grocers didn't sell Zoom, he special ordered it regularly. Zoom was important enough to the senator that during a 1959 four-week congressional trip to Africa, his personal secretary sent him a letter assuring him all was well in the office and with his children and, oh yes, the shipment of Zoom had arrived.[22]

That morning in the spring of 1950, he thumbed through the paper. A front-page story quoted Harry Truman. The president doubted it could be possible to libel Joe McCarthy. Turning the pages, he found that Penney's was celebrating its forty-eighth anniversary by offering men's dress shirts for $1.75. The Fox Theater was showing Ernest Hemingway's *Under My Skin.* The ad promised, "Nothing left out. Nothing held back."

Then he got to the editorial on page 4. Smiling broadly, he called to Loraine, pointing to "An Open Letter to Gale McGee" at the top of the page. She read it aloud. "These very times in which we live cry out for leadership."[23] The editor wanted her husband to run for the U.S. House of Representatives. "That you have become recognized nationally for your grasp of problems of American foreign policy makes it imperative in these days of the Cold War that you accept the challenge of representing your state and your people in Washington."[24] The state's largest newspaper, the *Wyoming Eagle,* joined the Laramie paper in encouraging McGee to make the run. "It can be said of Mr. McGee that he possesses every qualification that could be demanded for a representative in Congress." The Albany County Democratic Central Committee then passed a resolution urging the professor to enter the race.

Friends from around Wyoming and elsewhere were excited about the prospect and joined the chorus. Letters filled McGee's mailbox. They came from new friends in Wyoming and from old friends on the many campuses where he had either studied or taught. Party activist and fellow professor John Hinckley of Powell urged him to run with a starkly candid but characteristically humorous assessment of what was at stake. "I say, give us a chance to stand and be counted. Hell! You've nothing to lose but your shirt and perhaps a little self-respect. Both can be recovered."

That was enough for McGee. He headed for the starting line. A family portrait was taken for a campaign brochure. The UW professor asked the school's president about the employment consequences of seeking public office. At the time, there was no policy. A handful of Republican members on the board got wind of the possibility that a Democrat on the faculty might run. They believed university employment was not compatible with seeking public office. Humphrey asked the director of the Association of University Governing Boards for advice on "the problem of staff members of state universities running for public office."[25] At a May meeting of the university board, a decision was made to require any employee seeking office to resign. But Tracy McCraken was absent, and at the following month's meeting he raised an objection to the policy. The board then rescinded the policy and voted to conduct further study.[26]

In early May, McGee told the press, "It is more and more likely I will enter the race." A few days later, he spoke to a Casper meeting of the faithful "where I received considerable encouragement to file for the seat in Congress." The Wyoming Democratic Party Central Committee gave him a warm welcome. He would learn later that these partisans were less like oddsmakers and more like the crowds in the ancient Roman coliseum. They were thrilled to see a new gladiator enter the ring regardless of the inevitable outcome.

Returning upbeat from Casper, McGee wrote to Senator Joseph O'Mahoney. McGee was so new to Wyoming he had yet to meet the state's senior senator. Gale asked to meet with him for a discussion of his candidacy. The two sat across from one another for the first time. McGee expected the iconic senator to add his voice to those who thought he should run. After all, the popular four-term incumbent congressman Frank Barrett was vacating the seat to run for governor. A grandson of a president, William Henry Harrison, a Republican who had, like McGee, recently come to Wyoming from somewhere else, was his likely opponent. The Democrats were having a difficult time fielding a candidate. McGee was ready to fill the void. All he needed was a nudge from O'Mahoney.

By then, O'Mahoney had been through three statewide campaigns.[27] Although he had won them all, the senator knew how tough it could be, especially for a Democrat and especially this year. Making it even tougher were polls showing that Truman's popularity wasn't likely to improve by November. Across the country, the party would most likely lose a great number of congressional seats. O'Mahoney believed that Wyoming would not buck that trend. He poured cold water on the idea and advised the young professor to wait for a more opportune time.

McGee's excitement waned as he heard the same analysis from others he trusted, those he called his "kitchen cabinet." Among them were Cheyenne businessman Bill Norris and future Sweetwater County sheriff George "Mac" Nimmo. They were unanimous. He needed more time to get to know Wyoming and for Wyoming to get to know him. The timing wasn't right in 1950, but they were confident his day would come. They were also confident that O'Mahoney would mentor the young man and do what he could to help position McGee for a successful run in the future. Exhibiting a degree of patience not evident in many ambitious politicians, Gale McGee listened. Then he walked away.

With McGee sidelined and no other candidate coming forward, Democratic Party chairman John B. Clark of Cheyenne fell on his sword for the party. Harrison's campaign foretold what Gale McGee would later face. Harrison accused the Democrats of compromising with the Communists and sacrificing American interests.[28] Clark objected. He said he hoped the day would come when Wyoming Republicans "actually run through an entire campaign on a level of intelligent discussion instead of hysterical name-calling." Harrison assured Clark and the voters that he would "continue to cry socialism and communism until the Democratic administration wakes up to the dangers in which they are placing the country."[29]

In November Clark lost to Harrison by a 55 to 45 percent tally. McGee luckily dodged a bullet that might well have ended any hope for a political future. Years later, McGee described bowing out in 1950 as the right choice. "The guardian angels were watching over me or I'd have been murdered."[30] Harrison went about his political work in Washington. Gale McGee bided his political time in Wyoming.

3

The Good News from Foggy Bottom

In the 1950s, Americans were a fearful lot. Indeed, some might have said they had reason to fear while others worked to exploit those fears. Americans volleyed between those who thought war with Russia was inevitable and the isolationists who wanted no part of it. Chinese Communists drove Chiang Kai-shek and his followers from the mainland of their country. The United States was fighting a brutal war in Korea.

President Truman's advisers at the National Security Council convinced themselves a military conflict with Russia was inevitable. The Soviet threat grew as Stalin developed more and bigger weapon systems. The Council told the president the United States needed to engage in a massive buildup of conventional and nuclear arms and be prepared for what was to come.[1]

Senator Joseph McCarthy was invited to Wheeling, West Virginia, to give the annual Lincoln Day speech in February 1950. Before a gathering of the Ohio County Women's Republican Club, the Wisconsin Republican claimed to have a list of Communists working in the State Department. A special subcommittee later investigated McCarthy's charges and rejected them as "a fraud and a hoax."[2] But in the context of the times, Americans were highly susceptible to his brand of demagoguery.

One of the early victims of "Red Scare" hysteria was McGee's mentor, Joseph C. O'Mahoney, who had been in the Senate since 1934. The popular Democrat was a mainstay in Wyoming politics. That changed in 1952 when Joe McCarthy brought his "red-baiting" band-wagon to the Cowboy State. O'Mahoney was locked in a tough bat-tle with Frank Barrett, a former governor and Wyoming's current member of the U.S. House of Representatives. McCarthy was there to support Barrett. In Riverton, he spoke to one of the largest polit-ical gatherings in the state's history, telling the cheering partisans their longtime Democratic senator was a member of the "Commie-crat" party and no longer deserved to represent "loyal Americans."[3]

In November, O'Mahoney lost to Barrett and McGee lost his men-tor. Las Vegas oddsmakers wouldn't have given McGee much of a chance of winning an election in Wyoming anytime soon.

The UW professor, still hoping for a political career, faced a deci-sion. He could adjust to the times or teach others to resist them. McGee, always the optimist, believed that while demagogues might hold sway on American thinking for a while, a rational conversa-tion would eventually take hold. Likewise, he was always a teacher. McGee kept in his desk drawer a clipping of a January 23, 1949, *New York Times* article titled "Teaching Today's History: A Vital Task." Its premise was that "if high school and college students are to be good citizens, they must study current issues."

The professor firmly believed that if voters understood America's role in the world, knowledge could overcome both the demagogu-ery of McCarthy and a knee-jerk reaction toward isolationism. As a history professor, McGee told the university administration his goal was to expand the "study of American foreign policy."[4] He published scholarly articles targeting policymakers and educators, and in the spring of 1950, the *American Scholar: A Quarterly for the Independent Thinker* published an article titled "A Debate Resumed: American Foreign Policy." It featured the opposing views of Gale McGee and William G. Carleton, a history professor at the University of Florida.

McGee's contribution, "Using the Past to Move Forward," argued there is a set of premises that explain American foreign policy. First, World War II didn't change the world. "Whether we like it or not, ours is still a jungle world of sovereign nations and international anarchy." Next, he said, the political balance upset by the war must be restored before "a system of peace can be expected to evolve." A third premise was "Russia is bent on a course of dynamic expansion and cannot be trusted to keep her pledges." Soviet agitation, he foresaw, would long be a factor.

In the past, Americans have enjoyed the luxury of choosing sides. Now they have found themselves one of the two sides. For the first time in its history, the United States is striving to live up to *the responsibilities of world power.*[5] This is the single most important fact in the world today. Remembering a national tradition of isolation and non-entanglement that carried through nine wars and the peace, which followed each, the significance of such a change of policy cannot easily be exaggerated.[6]

McGee concluded, "This suggests a fourth premise of American foreign policy. The United States should strive to fulfill the hopes it represents in the eyes of the rest of the world by strengthening the concept of collective security whenever possible and, by example, encouraging a universal faith in liberty and democracy." His writings caught the attention of thoughtful people around the country. Yet the most compelling "classroom" in which the professor engaged the public was the University of Wyoming's Institute on International Affairs.

The institute began in 1945, the year before McGee arrived. It started as a four-year "experiment in international education and the study of the problems of world peace."[7] McGee became heavily involved in this initiative from his first day on campus. He felt the institute filled an especially important role in the "isolationist" Rocky Mountain region, an area he described as "more or less out of touch with the international scene." It was designed as a multiweek educational experience built around lectures accompanied by substantial reading assignments and course work. Lectures were delivered by important national and international figures. Conflicting points of view were integral to the institute. Some evenings were devoted to public town meetings. The institute endeavored to attract teachers in order to "stimulate better teaching especially in secondary schools, encourage student research, and raise awareness and understanding of international issues."

The faculty was composed of academics from major U.S. and foreign universities and high-level political leaders from several nations. Initially it relied on the good graces of UW administrators for funding. As its reputation grew, the Carnegie Foundation provided a $40,000 grant allowing the institute to attract even more important national and international figures.

Participants included Sidney Hook, a leading American philosopher, and Vaclav L. Benes, the highest-ranking Czechoslovakian government official to escape Communist captors. Professor McGee invited Alexander Kerensky, who fled the Russian Bolshevik regime in 1917. The onetime member of the Social Revolutionary Party and "only democratic premier" Russia had to that time told the participants, "If only I had shot 3,000 Bolsheviks, I would have survived."[8]

The annual conference attracted Eleanor Roosevelt in 1954. Mrs. Roosevelt arrived in Laramie in time for a luncheon at UW's Knight Hall attended by a large, enthusiastic crowd. Afterward she spoke to a standing-room-only audience at the Liberal Arts auditorium. In all, more than 3,000 people were able to hear her during a short stay in Wyoming. That evening, Loraine hosted a small dinner for Mrs. Roosevelt in the McGee home. Afterward Professor McGee drove Mrs. Roosevelt to Denver to catch a 3:00 a.m. flight back to New York. The road time afforded the two an opportunity to get to know one another. Mrs. Roosevelt found Dr. McGee to be an engaging conversationalist and well informed on foreign policy issues. It was a fortuitous meeting for McGee that would have far-reaching consequences in his bid for the Senate four years later.

When Norman Thomas made an appearance at the institute, the American socialist challenged an attendee who questioned whether he was a Communist. "Anyone who hasn't been a Communist for at least a few minutes in his life hasn't thought very deeply."[9]

The 1957 institute theme was "Foreign Policy in a Nuclear Age." It featured a debate between Henry Kissinger and Hans Morgenthau over U.S. nuclear and foreign policy. In the end, the two agreed the United States wasn't well prepared to match the Soviet challenge. Morgenthau declared the United States couldn't demonstrate technological superiority over the Russians. It must now show, he said, "it has the determination and organizational ability to close the gap quickly and thoroughly." For his part, Kissinger told the institute audience, "The power and speed of modern weapons have ended our traditional invulnerability, and the polarization of power in the world has reduced our traditional margin of safety."[10] Kissinger's appearance led to a lifelong friendship with McGee, whereas he and Morgenthau became adversaries as the debate over U.S. involvement in Southeast Asia reached a crescendo in the 1960s.

Over time, the institute grew in popularity, attracting hundreds of teachers and other professionals from around the world who came to learn from a predictably impressive faculty. Gale McGee served as the institute director from 1952 until he took a leave of absence to run for office in 1958.

During this time, McGee continued to write on the subject of U.S. foreign policy. In an acclaimed essay, "A China Policy for the U.S.," he echoes what would be heard years later in his opponents' views on the war in Vietnam, McGee argued the United States, unlike the Soviet Union, failed to recognize the powerful "new forces of genuine revolution and nationalism at loose in Asia." He concluded that as a result, as to China and the rest of the Far East, "Russia is in and we are out."

McGee advised readers that the close Russian-Chinese relationship made it impossible to resolve Cold War issues that threaten free world nations such as India and Southeast Asia. American policy must "aim at the separation of the Chinese from their Russian allies." In Asia "the West already possesses a legacy of hatred and resentment," McGee wrote. "It ought to become an essential of American policy not to underrate Asia's fear of Western domination." McGee believed the two Communist governments were not as close as many feared. He accurately predicted cracks would eventually form in the Sino-Soviet relationship. "The foregoing estimates suggest a belief that Mao Tse-tung may be for sale or that, at least, he is not a Soviet stooge." He exhibited a strong understanding of Russian history, including the negative impact Stalin's demands had on Mao's views. McGee rejected the idea that Mao "is a Soviet puppet," arguing Mao seems to "maintain an independent position parallel to and coincident with that of Moscow."[11]

This and other essays he wrote were well received around the country and published in serious intellectual journals, securing a national reputation for the young Wyoming professor. As a result, McGee was invited to serve as a visiting fellow with the Council on Foreign Relations during the academic year of 1952–53.

The Council was founded in 1921, following the 1919 Paris Peace Conference. U.S. diplomats, academics, retired generals, and others believed Americans needed to be better informed on matters of foreign policy. The CFR was created to "afford a continuous conference on international questions affecting the United States, by bringing together experts on statecraft, finance, industry, education, and science."[12]

In August 1952 the McGees rented out their Laramie house on Sheridan Street. They loaded their Dodge Coronet with a few belongings and their two sons and headed east.

During his fellowship, McGee specialized in Soviet policy. His work meant rubbing elbows and sharing ideas with President Eisenhower, John Foster Dulles, Dean Rusk, and Dean Acheson among other notables. McGee worked with a group of experts discussing Russian policy issues with heads of state in Europe and Asia as well as learning from key participants in the deliberations of the United Nations on the Korean truce process.

While there, he wrote a working paper, "Prospects for a More Tolerable Co-existence with the Soviet Union," which suggested Cold War emphasis had shifted. While the center was once Europe, McGee said it was now Southeast Asia. A longtime U.S. policy of keeping China independent of other powers changed with Mao's victory and his alliance with Moscow. McGee cited the new juxtaposition of the United States and Russia. While the Russians were prodding the Chinese to front for them in Korea, the Americans were backing the losing Chiang Kai-shek forces. McGee's 1953 essay suggested an approach based on his conviction that Mao was not beholden to Stalin.[13] It was a bold assertion at a time when most experts saw international communism as homogeneous.

His CFR fellowship afforded opportunities to meet with American and foreign leaders in intimate, conversational dinners. In those settings, he visited with Israel's ambassador to Washington, Abba Eban, and Anthony Eden, then the British secretary of state for foreign affairs who soon followed Winston Churchill as prime minister. McGee also enjoyed time with Averill Harriman and George Kennan, American ambassadors to Russia, Konrad Adenauer, the future head of Germany, and Dr. J. Robert Oppenheimer, the "father of the atomic bomb."

Likewise, the UW professor met people with whom he would later have a great deal of involvement in America's foreign policies. These included Ellsworth Bunker, ambassador to Italy, and Chester Bowles, ambassador to India. A British journalist made an impression on McGee when he discussed Southeast Asia. Richard Goold-Adams of the *London Economist* said presciently, "In Asia we must answer the question whether we are fighting China or the Soviet Union or communism." It was a mistake to believe China and the Russians always "saw eye-to-eye."[14]

While at the Council on Foreign Relations, McGee was encouraged to think about policy toward the Soviet Union after Stalin's death. McGee did so in an unpublished essay, "The American Hunger for Sudden Performance."[15] The title came from a phrase used by Ralph Waldo Emerson to describe "an unfortunate American trait." Said McGee, "More so during the years of the Cold War than at any other time in our history has the pressure of popular impatience burdened the statesmen who shape foreign policy." McGee felt a meaningful relationship with Russia required a shift in the balance of power away from the Soviet Union and toward the West. The current imbalance, he asserted, resulted from Soviet domination of Eastern Europe and the Sino-Soviet alliance.

McGee worried that the "Red Scare is an example of a lack of American confidence." He agreed with the suggestion made by Granville Hicks, a onetime American Communist who later bitterly denounced communism. Hicks said, "The United States should make less of how much communism there is in this country and more of how little there is."[16]

In a treatise on American-Chinese relationships, Dr. McGee posited that Mao's victory over Chiang Kai-shek had "so enhanced the Russian position in the Far East" as to give credence to what Henry

Adams called a "dire threat." Adams, the American historian and descendent of two presidents, asserted in 1903 that such a level of threat was posed "if Russia organizes China as an economic power." In that event Adams believed "the overthrow of our clumsy Western civilization" would inevitably follow.[17]

McGee traced U.S.-Chinese relationships from the "Open Door" policy articulated by Secretary of State John Hay in 1899, which became American policy in the Far East through the first half of the twentieth century.

> But the China question of 1954 is not the China question of a bygone era. The new forces of revolution and nationalism in Asia, which the Soviets were smart enough to recognize and direct to their own advantage, but which the United States ignored and as a result was swept out of China, have been caught up in the struggles of the Great Powers, currently manifested in the Cold War.

He demonstrated a prescient knowledge of that part of the world, suggesting there was "a fair chance to split the Communist bloc in the Far East." He encouraged the administration to avoid "unnecessary aggravations of Chinese-American differences."[18] McGee cited Representative Ralph W. McGwinn (R-NY), who questioned American Cold War policy, saying, "We have violated every precept of George Washington, every faith he made for himself, for his children or his fellow countrymen." McGee asserted that McGwinn failed to accurately read history. The UW history professor had written his PhD dissertation on this very subject. He retorted, "To believe that American policy in 1950 marks a complete departure from 'tradition' is to ignore the precepts and deeds of the Founding Fathers." Concepts such as "the balance of power" and foreign alliances were among those historic precepts. "When George Washington, who is yet today quoted as advising against foreign entanglements, was faced with threats from England and Spain in 1792, he said the time had come to form an alliance with France."[19]

All of that supported his premise that "if confronted by the diplomatic problems of today, it is difficult to imagine that the Founding Fathers would have failed to promote the equivalents of the Truman

Doctrine, the Marshall Plan, and the North Atlantic Pact. One might be moved to wish, in fact, that a few of those statesmen were available now for executing the responsibilities implicit in our foreign policy."

Upon returning to Wyoming, McGee was a highly sought-after speaker. Between 1954 and 1956, McGee gave at least fifty-six speeches throughout the country. On the speakers' list of the Knife and Fork Club, he spoke in every region of the United States. The club provided organizations with lists of interesting speakers for their meetings and conventions. Speakers were paid a small stipend and travel expenses. McGee was invited to give after-dinner talks in cities like Pine Bluff, Arkansas; Enid and Muskogee, Oklahoma; Palestine, Texas; Brigham City, Utah; Topeka, Kansas; Appleton, Wisconsin; Ontario, Oregon; Mount Vernon, Illinois; Stockton, California; Roanoke, Virginia; and Seattle, Washington. Often the title of his speech was "The Good News from Foggy Bottom."[20]

The stock speech was decidedly optimistic. Addressing problems the country was experiencing, Dr. McGee said America "is not lost; nor are we helpless or hopeless." He concluded, "We are committed by our history to world leadership."[21]

In 1954, he and Loraine were recruited to lead an American tour group through eight European nations during which he provided lectures on the history and politics of the region. He was later contracted to deliver lectures on the Cold War to tourists cruising around the world on Sitmar Steamship Lines.

By this time, Joe O'Mahoney was back in the U.S. Senate. Following the suicide of Senator Lester Hunt in June 1954, O'Mahoney was elected to a final term that November. In May 1955, McGee's mentor invited him to spend time on his Washington staff. "The best part of the offer," said George Nimmo, a close confidant, "is the rigid FBI check you will have to undergo before your appointment can be affirmed. This should be the very thing to put down all the rumors concerning your so-called radical views."[22]

The UW professor obtained a leave of absence from the university to serve as "research counsel to the Senate Judiciary Committee" from September 1955 until June 1956.[23] McGee's few months with Senator O'Mahoney were fruitful. O'Mahoney made certain the young professor had quality time with people like Lyndon Johnson, John Kennedy, and Montana senator Mike Mansfield. In the process, McGee established close relationships with the three men who could do the most to help his political future.

Professor McGee also spent time working on an antitrust investigation that the Judiciary Committee conducted against General Motors. He was assigned to work on water issues impacting Wyoming and to assist in studying monopolistic practices in agriculture.

McGee returned to Laramie and resumed his writing and teaching in 1956. Despite having studied and written at length about the Soviet Union, he and other American citizens were unable to actually visit that country until 1956, when he led the first nongovernment contingency of Americans on a 5,000-mile tour behind the Iron Curtain.

4

Behind the Iron Curtain

"An informant who has furnished reliable information in the past, advised on May 4, 1956, that Gale William McGee, 1421 Sheridan, Laramie, Wyoming, has been making arrangements through Cosmos Travel Bureau, New York, New York, for a visa to visit the Soviet Union."[1] FBI director J. Edgar Hoover filed this report in Gale McGee's FBI file, taking note of McGee's plan to lead a tour through Russia. His political advisers suggested he not take this trip, but being one of the first Americans to venture behind the Iron Curtain was an opportunity he was unwilling to miss.

The trip had begun when the group gathered in New York City on August 16, 1956. They departed for Europe the next day from Idlewild International Airport, renamed John F. Kennedy International Airport after the 1963 assassination. Their route took them across Nova Scotia to a refueling stop in Gander, Newfoundland. Air traffic control routed the plane above Hurricane Betsy, by then a weakened tropical storm that had wreaked havoc in Puerto Rico just a few days earlier.

Arriving in Hamburg, the Americans were treated to an unscheduled tour of the German port. Huge scars from World War II bombs still pocked the face of the city. They walked on the stones of a narrow Hamburg street and then ducked down an alleyway. There they found a small club tucked away inconspicuously from the view of most travelers. Entering through the weathered door into a rather dark room, they spotted a jukebox in the corner. Delighted to find it included "The Man from Laramie" and "Ragtime Cowboy Joe," they dropped a Deutsche Mark in the slot and cheered the welcome reminder of home.

The next stop was Berlin. Recently constructed modern buildings couldn't hide the decade-old destruction. They toured West Berlin before crossing into the Soviet sector. "It is like driving into a ghost town," Loraine wrote home. "The streets are mostly deserted. There are few vehicles. Where people do appear, they seem to be extremely serious—or perhaps sad." The differences between the East and the West sectors of the German city gave witness to Soviet failures. "Millions of words could not as effectively advertise that difference as did this, our first visit behind the Iron Curtain."[2]

Heaps of rubble were everywhere they looked. More surprising, the huge portraits of Stalin they anticipated would be ubiquitous were not to be seen. A group of young Bulgarian students laid wreaths on the graves of Russian soldiers at a nearby memorial. Afterward they visited with the Americans. A late night visit to a Russian nightclub was memorable for great food and music. They toasted the trip with "Robar" cocktails made of unmeasured mixtures of champagne, blackberry juice, and a tasty liqueur. They attended a water ballet, ending the long evening in "little Hamburg," where they were treated to late night hors d'oeuvres of liver, bacon, and onions on skewers. After two days, the group gathered at the Berlin airport for the final leg of their long-anticipated trip to the Soviet Union.

Customs officials carefully searched passenger bags. They then determined that the American group exceeded the capacity of the aircraft scheduled to take them to Moscow. The Americans learned that Russian bureaucrats found it difficult to deal with surprises and changes. Gale was no stranger to bureaucracy, but he wrote, "The negotiations themselves required patience. All officials were friendly and tried to be helpful. Even so, it took two hours to receive the necessary clearances." The wearisome discussions culminated in a simple solution. The group would be split up. The Americans boarded two aircraft for the six-hour, 1,600-mile journey.

The Lusinov Li-2 lumbered down the long runway in West Berlin. Loraine felt the wheels lift as the plane gained altitude. Looking out the smudged and scratched window, she noticed that the aircraft seemed to level out too soon. She waited impatiently for the Soviet version of a DC-3 to gain elevation the way planes did in the United States. It didn't. The Aeroflot passenger plane barely cleared the treetops. Cattle, calmly grazing moments earlier, scattered in the wake of the airplane's loud engines.

Loraine asked an attendant if there was a problem. Why was the aircraft not flying higher? The attendant explained that Aeroflot's commercial airliners were not pressurized and as a result could fly at an altitude of no more than 1,200 feet. The explanation didn't calm her anxiety, but she and the others were given a close-up view of East Germany, Poland, and Belarus before they crossed into the Soviet Union.

There were no seatbelts. Passengers moved around freely. Gale and Loraine passed time in the plane's "tea room." Gale thought the long black velvet curtain hung to separate the main cabin from the tea room gave "the effect of the quarters of a Gypsy fortune-teller." Seated round the small table, those fortunate enough to share the tea room with Dr. McGee were treated to a lively discussion of the politics and history of Berlin and the Soviet Union.

"It is a curious sensation," Loraine wrote home, "when you learn your plane is landing in Moscow, the political center of the Russians and the hub of the Soviet empire." As they deplaned on August 21, they were surprised to see faces from "nearly every land," travelers from Turkey, Niger, India, China, Japan, and other parts of Asia.

Boarding a modern tour bus, they headed to the sprawling campus of Moscow State University. At the center of the school, which was established in 1755, was a towering skyscraper of more than twenty stories. "This imposing institution rises directly from the prairie floor on the western outskirts of the city," Loraine noted in her journal. Writers Anton Chekhov and Ivan Turgenev are among its alumni. Mikhail Gorbachev is a graduate. If any in the group were inclined to view Russian education as second-rate, they were quickly disabused of the notion.

Next stop was their hotel in the heart of Moscow. The twenty-one-story Hotel Leningradski had served its first guests just three years earlier. Their four days in Moscow included a visit to the Lenin-Stalin Mausoleums, the Agricultural Exhibition, the Kremlin, art galleries, an evening at the Bolshoi, as well as visits to other cultural events, concerts, and historical sites, including those recalling the heroic defense of Moscow during World War II, what the Russians called "the Great Patriotic War."

Among the most pleasant surprises was the friendliness of the Russian people and the comfortable Moscow subways. Colorful mosaics framed subway tunnel walls. Large decorative arches appeared throughout. The trains were new and very clean, "a notable contrast with our own subways." Given anti-American attacks in the Russian press, the visitors girded themselves for hostility on the streets. "We were not prepared for the handshaking and backslapping from total strangers in the Moscow subway or the throngs that surrounded us on the streets or the peasants who actually shed tears of joy over our presence." Cashiers chased after Americans to return change to those who miscounted their rubles. People in the subway went to extraordinary lengths to overcome the language barrier and to help the Americans find the right train. Russians attending the ballet insisted on giving up their seats to the tourists.

A subway ride across the city took them to the Moscow Agricultural Exposition. One of its most striking displays was the "Worker and Kolkhoz Woman," a statue twenty-five meters high depicting a man and woman holding the Soviet hammer and sickle. The most popular exhibit was the Atomic Energy Building, where they saw a life-sized atomic reactor. To Gale the exhibit represented a "sobering reminder" that the United States no longer had a monopoly on atomic know-how.

McGee was deeply impressed with Moscow. He worried that others from around the world might be as well. McGee found the numbers of foreign visitors, especially the formal delegations, a cause for concern. "From the lobby of the Hotel Leningradski in Moscow, we observed during a single afternoon the arrival of sizeable groups from East Germany, Bulgaria, Poland, Czechoslovakia, Red China, Japan, India, Indonesia, Niger, and Indo-China." He added, "Enough 'show pieces' exist in Moscow to stir the imagination of those who go there. The subways, a few apartment house districts, skyscraper hotels, Moscow University, the Lenin Library, and of course the great Agricultural Exposition." McGee worried these impressive sites might "crowd the rest of what goes to make up Russia out of the minds of the newcomers, especially those from Asia and Africa." It is an image that would remain in Gale McGee's thinking after he became a senator and one of the leaders in helping his government craft a policy for dealing with the Soviet Union and the Cold War.

A Chinese tourist told him that what the United States had accomplished is far beyond the ability of his country. "But in Russia we see a great country that not too long ago was as backward as we, but which in much less than a lifetime has literally hurdled several centuries of time. We figure that what Russia has done we can also do." That was the future senator's epiphany on the nature of competition for Third World hearts and minds.

Looking across the Moscow River, the American tourists first glimpsed the Kremlin. When a light rain ended, the McGees took note of the visual effect of the raindrops as the sun began to set. The light "played on the rich yellows of the palaces and the golden domes and gilded minarets of the cathedrals. The bulbous cupolas and towers glistened in the sky as so many balls of fire." The Russian word "kremlin" means "fortress inside a city." Bordered to the south by the Moskva River and by Saint Basil's Cathedral and Red Square to the east, the Alexander Garden provides a beautiful western boundary. Inside are five palaces, four cathedrals, and the Kremlin Towers. It was the object of Russian pride and the center of the Russian government.

The McGees' trip diary eloquently reflects awe at seeing the fortress. "Still preserved inside the Kremlin is one of the richest collections of treasure in all the world. It represents the personal accumulation of gold, silver, precious stones, jewelry, crowns, robes, thrones, carriages, glass, carved ivory, porcelain, arms, and armor of the Tsars and Tsarists." One entire ballroom was filled with gold and silver.

All Russian tour guides proudly made certain their groups were taken to the Stalin-Lenin tombs. In 1956, the bodies of the two Russian leaders lay side by side in refrigerated glass showcases. As the McGee group arrived, thousands stood "in a line, two abreast, that stretched across Red Square, back along the towering walls of the Kremlin for at least a mile." They were, for an unspoken reason, given VIP status and taken to the front of the line, placed second only behind delegations from Red China and Central Asia who carried wreaths to place at the base of the tombs.

Lenin had died thirty-two years earlier, Stalin only three. Gale and Loraine found the bodies of the paragons of communism in surprisingly good shape. Gale wrote home, "Looking into the faces of these two Soviet heroes, one gets a queer feeling of standing in the middle of the stream of history. The length of that twisting line outside the tomb, which is a daily phenomenon, suggests that the final chapters of the history of Lenin and Stalin are still being written."

It wasn't clear whether so many people came to the mausoleum because they revered these men or because they wanted to make certain they were actually dead. Lenin had initiated the "Red Terror," a campaign that included the torture and mass murder of his enemies after he seized power in 1917. Stalin, one of the most ruthless dictators of the twentieth century, was responsible for killing at least twenty million of his people.

The group headed for Stalingrad on August 25. Once again, the size of their group required separate flights. McGee's group flew on the first plane out of Moscow. Although it was a smooth flight at the worrisome 1,200 feet above ground, when the aircraft landed in Stalingrad, it felt as though they had landed not on any runway but on prairie not unlike that between Cheyenne and Laramie. Startled by the rough landing, they peered out the windows, trying to figure out where they were. The only nearby structure was a Quonset hut. It was the Stalingrad airport.

The experience of the second group was not nearly so pleasant. They flew through severe storms, "not at treetop level but at corn stalk level." Their plane landed roughly in what appeared to be a plowed wheat field. It was actually an airport serving the 200,000 people of Lipesk. After refueling, the pilots needed three attempts to extricate the craft from a mud hole.

The second group arrived harried at around 10 p.m. The reunited Americans headed for their hotel, one of the few prewar buildings to have dodged German bombs. When Loraine saw the hotel, she whispered to Gale that it might have been better if the building had been bombed.[3] The following morning, they toured Stalingrad and the surrounding area. They found the landscape much like parts of eastern Wyoming, treeless and flat for miles. "More than any other city we have seen so far, Stalingrad still shows the scars of World War II." The group listened intently as Gale offered an off-the-cuff lecture on the Battle of Stalingrad.

He explained that the city was the site of one of the "most heroic sagas of World War II." On this city, he told the Americans, rested the hopes of the world to stop Nazi Germany. "We all remember those anxious days in the autumn of 1942 and the early winter of 1943. Der Fuehrer had already secured Europe and was trying to destroy his only remaining enemy to the east." At the summit of Mamayev Kurgan, the Americans stood reverently overlooking the city as the history professor described the bloody battle. Different sides, Germans then Russians and then Germans again, repeatedly took control of the dominant hill. It went that way a dozen times back and forth before the gruesome battle ended.

It was said there was so much gun and rocket fire aimed at the hilltop that when the dust settled, there remained nearly 1,200 metal fragments in each square meter of the hallowed ground. More than 200,000 soldiers were buried on the site in the wake of the Russian victory. McGee described the horror in terms reflecting his great respect for the sacrifice of the Russian people.[4]

Gale and Loraine wanted to get a glimpse of the religious life of Soviet citizens. Their request to visit a church "turned out to be a diplomatic operation of major proportions." Their young guide tried to dissuade them. The biggest problem seemed to be not so much political as bureaucratic. A church visit was not on the schedule. "To change any part of the schedule usually shook the bureaucracy to its foundations." A chance meeting with Senator Henry Jackson, whom McGee had come to know while with the Council on Foreign Relations, opened the door. Jackson, also touring Russia, told McGee's guide that he had been permitted to visit the church. And so the guide relented.

The church's white interior and Byzantine architecture included walls and ceilings decorated with the kind of colorful murals characterizing the ornate cathedrals of Europe. There were no pews. Congregants stood during the service. The large sanctuary was filled, and hundreds of worshippers were jammed shoulder to shoulder. Mrs. McGee recalled, "It was these people who made the experience one which will not be soon forgotten." Older women were the more numerous. Each woman covered her head with a scarf. There were few men, about as many as would be found in an average American congregation on a hot summer Sunday. However, there were more young people than the Americans usually saw in their churches back home. There were lots of babies and small children. By their clothing, it appeared most were Russian peasants who had walked miles to be there. "The music was outstanding." Crying babies lent a familiar air to the occasion. But parishioners with tears streaming from their eyes were even more numerous. As the worship service ended, led by the Russians, the Americans joined in, singing, "God Be with You till We Meet Again."[5]

When the services were completed, our tour group was accorded such a reception as none could remember. Every Russian, or so it seemed, wanted to shake the hand of each Americanski. Gifts of flowers, vegetables, and religious objects were thrust upon us. Kissing and weeping accompanied it all. One very old lady pointed to the miles of Stalingrad ruins, which lay in every direction, and said, "Americanskis, no more wars, no more wars.

That evening they dined at a local club, enjoying a bottle of what was labeled "No. 6" wine. Loraine danced with a couple of Russian patrons. Afterward Gale and Loraine took a walk through the city center.

An altogether different mode of transportation took them on to the next stop. Gale and Loraine recalled a 1928 Russian novel written by Mikhail Sholokhov, *And Quiet Flows the Don,* as they floated from Stalingrad to Rostov on the river Don. What the McGees observed had not changed much from what Sholokhov had described more than three decades earlier.

The frogs were croaking beyond the riverside willows. The sun streamed over the hillside across the rapids. The cool of evening was soaking into the village of Sietrakov. Enormous slanting shadows cast by the huts fell athwart the dusty road. The village cattle were straggling slowly back from the steppe. The Cossack women drove them on slowly with wattles. The barefoot and already sunburnt children were playing leapfrog in the side alleys. The old men were sitting in rows on the ledges of the hut walls.[6]

Along the 400-mile route were herds of cattle, sheep, and goats but almost no machinery. Animal and human labor provided any necessary locomotion. The slow float afforded them time to appreciate the beauty of the Russian countryside, which looked to them much the same as Iowa or Illinois farmland. The time sitting aboard the gently rocking boat also provided an opportunity to get to know Russian travelers. At each port, Russian sailors gathered round Americans with questions about life in the United States.

The group disembarked at way stations, meeting farmers strolling through marketplaces and learning a great deal about their lives. Each belonged to a collective but was allowed to own a few geese or chickens and a cow. In addition to raising crops for the state, they were permitted to farm a small plot for their families.

As their boat docked at Rostov-on-Don, several citizens of that historic city greeted the Americans. Rostov, then a city of half a million, was always of strategic importance. With its river port and rail junction accessing the oil and mineral rich Caucasus region, it was often contested during wars and other conflicts. It was not long before the McGee group arrived that the city had been restored after the World War II bombing and tank attacks of the Nazi armies.

The Americans had traveled by plane, bus, and boat. Departing Rostov, the group set out on the 1,000-mile journey to Kiev, boarding a train organized especially for the Americans. It had a "private" car, albeit without much privacy. In each of eight compartments were four bunks. "Among the four occupants of each compartment," noted Mrs. McGee, "no secrets could be hidden!"

Without air-conditioning, the windows and doors were kept open. A small coal-burning stove sat at one end of the compartment. An attendant brewed tea for the passengers. At the other end was a single toilet. A dining car was attached specifically for the American tourists at the opposite end of the train, upfront and next to the engine. Getting there meant walking through nine or ten of what the Russians called "hard cars," those in which ordinary Russians could afford to travel.

Dinner hour approached, and Loraine and a few others headed for the dining car, crossing over the open-air couplings between cars and entering the hard cars. The difference between their cars and these was stark. Wooden slats replaced padded seats along each side of an aisle that divided the congested cars. Russian passengers had to lie down on the uncomfortable slats because there wasn't enough vertical room for even the smallest person to sit upright.

The tight compartment had no ventilation. The American tourists were ambushed by "a distinctive aroma such as we'll never forget." The bare, unbathed feet of some of the Russians reached into the aisle. The Americans politely dodged and weaved their way through the car. As they sat for dinner and realized they would have to run this same gauntlet en route to each meal, Loraine lamented, "For so long we had been saying we wanted to get close to the Russian people. On the train between Rostov and Kiev we succeeded with a vengeance."

As the train made its way, Gale and Loraine shared time with an English professor from Moscow State University. Albert Dneipetrovsky's language skills enabled the three to enjoy a rich conversation. Dneipetrovsky loved Stalin, confiding, "He was like a god to me." Gale asked about Khrushchev's recent denunciation of Stalin. Khrushchev's words had floored him, Albert admitted. He stared out the window as he wondered aloud how much more had not been told. Quite a lot, he suspected.

Since 1947, it had been illegal for Soviet citizens to be seen with, much less talk to, foreigners.[7] That had changed recently. "A year ago," the Russian professor said, "I would have not taken a seat next to an American under any circumstances. Lots of things might have happened to me then but not now."

The hours they shared on the train gave the uw professor a feel for the dilemma faced by Russian citizens trying to navigate the history and the politics of their own country. McGee began to understand what it was like for people to be caught between a dark past, which was not far behind them, and a hopeful future. McGee wrote home, "Diplomats of both governments would do well to get the 'feel' of the people of Russia. To miss it may be the last and biggest opportunity for discovering a basis of understanding between the two giants of the atomic age."

Finally, the train arrived at the station in Kiev. They were greeted and given small gifts by smiling Russians. People asked for autographs. Most of the Americans wished to see a collective farm. The 7,000-acre Lenin Victory Farm was a 50-mile bus ride to the south of Kiev. The poor condition of the roads imposed a grueling four-hour trip over rutted and rough roads. It was harvest time, and grain was piled on the narrow pathway to dry. The bus driver swerved through the ditches alongside the road to avoid the harvested crops.

These were the first Americans the farmer-peasants had ever seen. There were official greetings and a picnic lunch. Then they toured the farm, which raised livestock, wheat, corn, and beets. Farmers worked eight-hour days, six days a week, for which they were paid two kilos of grain, a bit less than four and a half pounds, and eight rubles, then about thirty-two U.S. dollars.

Ending their time in the Soviet Union, the Americans completed the tour of Kiev. They saw the Museum of Ukrainian Art and the State Museum of History and eagerly visited religious sites like the Kiev-Pechersk Monastery, known as Kiev Monastery of the Caves. Later they went to the Sophia Cathedral, a preeminent center of Eastern Orthodox Christianity dating to 1051. The Cathedral displayed religious icons, frescoes, and other religious art. Russians filled the pews for worship services, causing McGee to note, "It would be a mistake to underestimate the role of religion in this Communist state. Not only has the Communist Party failed to stifle religious interest, it has not dared to destroy the church itself."

The Americans had traveled more than 5,000 miles inside the Soviet Union by plane, train, boat, bus, and automobile. Upon returning to Laramie, Gale reflected on what he had seen in Russia. "It's a sobering experience to see firsthand the bigness and massive bulk that is the Soviet Union. Some tourists miss the larger point. There is a tendency to compare Russian consumer goods with our own and to judge therefore that their country is backward, even illiterate. Indeed, their clothing is quite shoddy, but it keeps them warm; their housing is woefully inadequate, but it keeps out the weather; women do heavy labor on the streets and in construction projects, but the streets and buildings get built. Factories are dirty and crowded and lack safety devices, but they turn out heavy industrial goods. That Russia has come so far in such a short time seems to be the inspirational focus of her people."

One member of the group, Venita Kelly, a writer for Scripps-Howard Newspapers, reported that on the streets Russians offered to buy McGee's coat, trousers, watch, and shirts.[8] That led McGee to believe the Russian people would be more inclined to reject communism if they met more Americans, having an opportunity to "feel our clothing, smoke our cigarettes, and observe our shoes." "It is the fear of averse comparison that prompts severe [Soviet] restrictions on foreign travel by the Soviet people."

The standing joke around Washington went like this. "The U.S. need not fear a 'suitcase bomb' because the Soviets have not been able to perfect the suitcase." McGee came home feeling as though Americans were discounting Soviet determination at their own risk. "The Russians are grimly determined to close the remaining gap between their production capacities and those of the West. To achieve that dream they are willing to forego personal comforts, luxury goods, and even individual freedoms." *Sputnik*'s launch was a little more than a year away.

5

Drunkards Can't Do That

London, Oct. 4 (AP)—Moscow radio said tonight that
the Soviet Union has launched an earth satellite.

The day before *Sputnik* was launched, life in America was fairly rou-
tine. The Braves beat the Yankees 4–2 in the second game of the
1957 World Series a day earlier. The Series evened at a game apiece.
Jimmy Hoffa was elected president of the International Brother-
hood of Teamsters. People read *Alley Oop* on the cartoon page. Nine
Negro students integrated Little Rock High School accompanied by
National Guardsmen and protected by paratroopers from the 101st
Airborne Division. An editorial reported, "The faces of the mob in
Little Rock have, in a sense, constituted a rude awakening to north-
erners, and they are certain to react accordingly."

But the rudest awakening for Americans was the A-flat chirp coming from outer space. Like fingernails on a chalkboard, *Sputnik*'s beep
sent chills down American spines. The McGees were in Norfolk visiting Gale's parents. They, like millions of Americans, watched the
reports on a grainy television screen. The adults in the room were
unable to hide their concern from the McGee children, who watched
with them.

An NBC radio announcer called it "the sound that forevermore
separates the old from the new."[1] The "old" could be characterized
as the "Red Scare." It was a time of demagogic-fueled hysteria when
Wisconsin senator Joe McCarthy held court. Wyoming senator Frank
Barrett saddled that horse and rode it into the U.S. Senate in 1952 at

the height of the Red Scare. Barrett conveyed the same hysteria about *Sputnik*: "A manned satellite in orbit could serve as a laboratory from which one could learn the secrets of controlling the weather and harnessing new sources of energy, or it could be a space weapon carrying missiles which could be dropped with unerring accuracy upon any point on earth."[2] The Wyoming senator claimed that "Christian civilization" was at stake.

Certainly Barrett wasn't the only politician peddling *Sputnik* fear, but the president seemed calm and calming. Eisenhower assured Americans that their country would follow the Russians into space quickly. Administration officials promised that "as soon as the weather clears," the United States planned to launch a rocket "higher than the Russian satellite." It would be a while before "the weather cleared." On December 6, a Vanguard rocket, America's initial response to *Sputnik*, exploded while yet on the ground. Senator O'Mahoney believed the country had failed to commit adequate resources to the space program and had made unwarranted cuts in the nation's research and development budget. He wisecracked that "the Eisenhower administration would meet the invading Russians at the shore with a balanced budget."[3]

Nonetheless, an October 7 editorial in the *Wyoming State Tribune* acknowledged that most people were calmed by Eisenhower's response. "We haven't run into anyone around Cheyenne who has been moved to alarm, or even depression, by Russia's feat in winning the race to outer space." The editor echoed Professor McGee's post-Russian trip reflections. Too many Americans were guilty of "looking down our noses" at the Russians. The complacency of many American leaders was uncalled for in retrospect. What was called for "in retrospect," said the column, "was an immediate indication that America was responding to the threat." Shortly after *Sputnik*, the U.S. Defense Department announced a $65 million facility would be built at Francis E. Warren Air Force Base near Cheyenne. It would house "the 5,500-mile range Atlas missile."

If *Sputnik* separated the old "Red Scare" from the new, the "new" was best described as the "Red Curiosity." Fourteen-year-old Ronnie Rounds, a Cheyenne newspaper boy, exemplified the nation's curiosity. As Ronnie delivered newspapers before 5 a.m. in 20 degree temperatures, he stopped to search the sky for the Russian satellite. There was enough curiosity in the community that when he said he spotted it, the paper printed his story.[4] That same day, the WYO movie theater in Cheyenne advertised *Satellite in the Sky*, calling it "the first space-shattering" film about "the man-made satellite that could rule the earth." This basketball-sized artificial moon grew larger in American imaginations as it circled the earth every ninety-six minutes. People reevaluated what they had been told about the Soviet Union.

Two years later, Gale McGee was a U.S. senator, and although he was not yet a member of the Senate Foreign Relations Committee, its chairman, J. William Fulbright, was aware of McGee's interest in Soviet affairs. He was invited to join the committee when it met with Russian premier Nikita Khrushchev. The senators and the Russian leader shared tea during a September 17, 1959, gathering in the committee's historic meeting room at the U.S. capitol. Khrushchev joked about how difficult it was to speak while drinking tea. Fulbright jocularly suggested he could arrange for some vodka to be served. "It is a misconception to think that the Russians have such a proclivity for vodka," Khrushchev responded with a sly smile. "If they only drink vodka, they would not have time to launch rockets to the moon. Drunkards can't do that." After a dramatic pause, the Russian added, "But that is a joke."[5] The American politicians got the joke. They were the butt of it.

Americans needed an explanation. If it was true that theirs was a backward nation of automatons who drank too much vodka, how did the Russians win the first round of the space race? Was America asleep or just complacent? It was a fair question. It had to be one or the other. Americans knew their scientists were brighter than any in the world. Now they were forced to admit that, despite pre-*Sputnik* assumptions, the United States didn't have the corner it thought it had on scientific knowledge. They began to wonder, who are these Russians? How did they accomplish such a major feat? There was a University of Wyoming history professor upon whom they could call to help them find answers.

Not everyone was impressed that McGee had actually been to the Soviet Union. Just as a confidential informant reported McGee was planning to travel to the Communist nation, another now reported

McGee's Russian trip to FBI director J. Edgar Hoover. Hoover ordered the Denver Division of the FBI to investigate. Agents found "no derogatory security information identifiable with either Mr. or Mrs. McGee."[6] Later another "source" reported a speech McGee gave discussing the Soviet Union with an Adult Education Forum in Laramie. It wasn't the last time someone attempted to convince Hoover that Gale McGee was a security risk.

By now a number of University officials were nervous about McGee's political ambitions. They saw his speeches as not so much for educating people about Russia as setting himself up for a run at public office. McGee was receiving invitations from all four corners of Wyoming to talk about Russia and *Sputnik*. He was aware his activities were being scrutinized. Few doubted he was gearing up for a political campaign. Still, Wyoming people wanted to know more about Russia. Most knew about the trip Dr. McGee had taken to Russia the previous year. His and Loraine's regular dispatches were published in most Wyoming newspapers on a regular basis. What people may not have known is how much deeper his knowledge of the Soviets was than what he acquired on that journey alone. He had written numerous scholarly articles about U.S.-Russian relations in journals around the country. McGee's fellowship at the Council on Foreign Relations and his chairmanship of UW's Institute of International Affairs had brought him into close contact with some of the brightest thinkers of the day on matters pertaining to the Soviet Union.

McGee had been on the speech-making circuit since his return from Russia. In September 1956 he spoke to a crowd of 500 in Rock Springs. A few days later, "2,000 students and townspeople packed our university auditorium" to hear an account of his Russian trip. At a teachers' convention in Worland, McGee warned against what he saw in Russia, attempts to make conformists of children. "Conformity in ideas is but one step removed from the totalitarian state."[7] During a 1957 Fourth of July celebration in Evanston, McGee impressed the audience with his rhetorical skills and knowledge of international issues. "As a public speaker, Dr. McGee has few equals anywhere in the country," wrote the editor of the *Laramie Daily Boomerang*. "In all parts of Wyoming Dr. McGee has told of what is going on behind the Iron Curtain, and he speaks from actual knowledge."[8] By the end of the month during which *Sputnik* was launched, he had accepted more than seventy invitations to talk to groups about Russia.[9]

Even Wyoming's Republican governor was a fan. Milward Simpson told McGee, "I have been fascinated with your reports on 'Inside Russia.' You and Loraine are to be congratulated on this significant presentation. Lorna and I have read every one with avid interest. We have been enthralled by the account of this land which to us seems so strange."[10]

McGee went to great lengths to assure UW administrators he was tending to his university responsibilities even as he traveled the state. Whenever he had a speaking appointment, he departed Laramie after his last class of the day. Accompanied by his wife, they drove for hours to make the engagement. After each speech, Loraine drove home while Gale typed press releases on a tiny typewriter in the backseat. He would then sleep a few hours so that he would be refreshed for his 8 a.m. lecture the next morning. Weekends were spent traveling to Saturday evening speeches and Sunday morning pulpit calls in churches. It was during these days that Gale and Loraine began a lifetime habit of collecting the names and addresses of everyone they met. Throughout their lives, the two would send a note or a card to those folks as they maintained friendships across the state and over the years.

Gale McGee's official papers include a three-inch-thick file of invitations for Russia-related speeches. He spoke at Jaycees Boss Night in Newcastle, Business and Professional Women's Clubs, civic clubs of all sorts, community colleges, chambers of commerce, labor union meetings, the Third Annual Eagle Court of Honor for Boy Scouts in Cody, the YMCA, the Wyoming Farm Bureau, the Wyoming Certified Public Accountants state convention, and countless high school commencement ceremonies.[11] His voice was a constant presence on radio stations across the state with reporters clamoring to interview him about Russia.

He spent most Sunday mornings in the pulpit of churches of almost every denomination in 1957 and early 1958. At the Community Church and the First Methodist Church in Thermopolis, McGee gave a sermon entitled "Christianity as It Lives in Russia." The Rock Springs Congregational Church heard a sermon called "Religion Lives in

Russia," as did the Presbyterians in Worland and the Methodists of Rawlins. After he preached at Union Presbyterian in Evanston, the congregation sang spontaneously, "In Christ There Is No East or West." When he spoke to the United Church Women of Wyoming at its 1957 Sheridan convention, the local newspaper praised his comments. "Dr. Gale McGee named religion as a major force in combating Communism." The editorial discussed McGee's 1956 trip. "And on the basis of that observation along with his knowledge of the history of America and the world he sees in the Christian religion is a force which he is confident may check the Red menace."[12]

He wasn't always welcomed. When a planned Sunday morning talk at the Christ Episcopal Church in Cody was announced, some members of the congregation complained. They compared McGee to Paul Robeson, a singer and actor who had been blacklisted for alleged Communist leanings during the McCarthy era. It was Milward Simpson, a future governor and a future Senate colleague of McGee's, who then, as a member of the church's governing board, stepped in to say McGee would be allowed to speak.[13]

Following their return from the Soviet Union and the subsequent launch of *Sputnik,* Gale and Loraine traveled thousands of miles throughout Wyoming. There is little question these trips and speeches were a part of McGee's 1958 political plans even as they served to educate Wyoming about such an important contemporary matter as U.S.-Soviet relations. Gale told Senator Mike Mansfield, "I have been following your advice on campaign tactics, speaking after hours and on every weekend. Loraine and I traveled 55,000 Wyoming miles in 1957, making 240 speeches and, what is more important, shaking 51,000 hands. In addition, we kept going a weekly newspaper column and a weekly radio broadcast."[14]

Unlike when he considered running for Congress in 1950, he was ready now. As 1958 rolled around, no candidate in American history may have been more prepared to run for a seat in the U.S. Senate than Gale W. McGee.

6

Not Even a Dark Horse but a Hopeless One

The man who wanted to become Wyoming's next U.S. senator walked along a Laramie street toward the Elks Club that warm June evening in 1958, leaving behind more than two decades of a successful teaching career and all the security afforded a tenured professor. He was trading it for the unpredictability of a political campaign.

An excited crowd of supporters gathered, exceeding the hall's capacity. Many had driven long distances from all parts of Wyoming to hear Gale W. McGee announce his candidacy. He was a Democrat in a heavily Republican state. He was an eggheaded professor among rough-edged ranchers and oilmen. He had lived in Wyoming for only a dozen years among fourth- and fifth-generation Wyomingites who routinely distrusted newcomers. Yet Gale McGee gave not one of the 350 supporters gathered in that hall any reason to doubt his confidence. He was an extraordinarily optimistic man in general, and he felt certain he would win come November, a confidence cultivated by the hard work he and Loraine had put in over the last eight years.

Dr. McGee was joined by a very pregnant Loraine and sons David and Robert. Four-year-old Mary Gale remained at home. Lori Ann was born three days later. Newspaper reporters scribbled on small notepads. Radio station reporters carefully positioned their reel-to-reel recorders. A television camera whirred to record the event for the Cheyenne station's newscast later that night.

McGee began by assuring listeners that, while he was a Democrat, he valued the two-party system. He said both parties were honorable. Both "believe in our people." The world was on the "crest of a new future" when it will "look to the U.S. for leadership." McGee insisted that the nation's security was in jeopardy and that his GOP opponent was part of a group in Washington that had dealt ineffectively with the crisis.[1]

He paraphrased newspaperman James Reston: "We are in more than an arms race. We are in a race with the pace of our own history, and the pace is so swift that our habits of mind and our institutions are lagging behind." Dr. McGee said both parties were sending younger men and women to Congress. "The states with younger representation in Washington will reap the fruits of the future." McGee, who was forty-three, suggested that sixty-four-year-old Senator Frank Barrett was unable to keep up with current events. "The twentieth century has brought to Wyoming and the world new problems of an entirely new age in human history. Men born in the nineteenth century have not been able to keep the pace which modern history has set. It's time we turned the twentieth century over to youth."[2]

The crowd was on its feet, worked up as the candidate concluded, "It's time we in America stood up and let the people of the world know why we believe in America." The campaign distributed bumper stickers, buttons, and posters with the words "McGee for Me" emblazoned in gold with a brown backdrop, the colors of the University of Wyoming athletic teams. The design branded every McGee Senate campaign thereon.

The *Laramie Daily Boomerang* editor wrote a column titled "Professor Politicians." He said McGee is a "brilliant, young professor of history at the University of Wyoming" and "is extremely well qualified" to serve in the Senate. "Congress continues to run rather thick with lawyers." Finally, he acknowledged that voters around the country had recently nominated or elected a large number of university professors. Neither Wyoming nor McGee would be alone.

Gale McGee was youthful and exhibited a flair and eloquence not before seen in a Wyoming politician. A newspaper serving a predominately Republican area of the state quickly jumped on board. A *Powell Tribune* editorial published the day McGee officially announced predicted, "It's going to take a lot of doing to keep him [McGee] from unseating Mr. Barrett." The editor cited McGee's 1956 trip to Russia, the thousands of Wyoming people he had spoken to, the thousands of miles he had driven throughout the state, and Gale and Loraine's regular columns printed in thirty-five newspapers as well as numerous radio and TV broadcasts. "Gale is perhaps one of the best speakers to appear in a long time on the Wyoming scene, which, incidentally, as everyone knows, is a prime requisite for a politician."[3]

The pollsters were not nearly so gushing. "If the election were held today," a Democratic Party analyst said, "it seems likely the Republican candidate would win reelection as U.S. senator." A poll taken in the early spring of 1958 showed the incumbent with an all but insurmountable 51 percent to 33 percent lead.[4] Earle Clements of Kentucky, chairman of the Democratic Senate Campaign Committee, sent the report to McGee. Clements added a handwritten note urging the candidate to not "let this material discourage you."

It didn't. The poll was no surprise. Senator Barrett was one of Wyoming's most beloved public servants. McGee himself regarded Barrett as a "very able person."[5] There was another significant factor. It's not uncommon in any state for members of the House to seek a Senate seat. However, those from Wyoming have a unique advantage when they decide to do so. In most states, members of the U.S. House of Representatives have to expand their campaign from a small House district to a statewide contest. They haven't yet faced all the voters in their state. But the entire state of Wyoming is but a single House district. Candidates run for the Senate in the same district in which they got elected to the House and, in the case of Frank Barrett, also to the governorship and a term in the U.S. Senate. Barrett is the only Wyoming politician to have served in so many statewide offices. He had been elected to the Wyoming Senate and served on the university board of trustees. He was elected to the U.S. House of Representatives in 1942. He served four terms in the House, leaving it to become governor in 1950, and was then elected to the Senate in 1952. Prior to 1958, Barrett had unprecedented success, winning six statewide elections, earning a favorable impression across the state. On the other hand, the report noted, Gale McGee cast "no particular image." The McGee campaign pollster, Elmo Roper and Associates, prepared a memorandum titled "A Survey of the Present Political Climate in Wyoming." It cited the "favorable image" Barrett had among Wyoming voters and warned, "It has to be cracked."[6]

Although McGee's campaign strategists knew their ultimate opponent was Frank Barrett, they were forced to deal with a primary contest first. Hepburn T. Armstrong, the president of Wyoming Uranium Corporation, announced his candidacy in July. Armstrong issued a letter to Democrats touting his Democratic Party connections. Included among Armstrong's supporters were several party members. Former Wyoming Democratic Party chairman Robert Chaffin was on the list, as were two state legislators, several labor union leaders, and a few prominent businessmen and ranchers. Ed Herschler, a popular rancher and attorney who would become governor sixteen years later, and Don Anselmi, a wealthy Rock Springs businessman, who became a powerful state party chairman during McGee's Senate tenure, added their names.[7]

Armstrong's campaign said the choice was between a candidate who "served the Democratic Party faithfully" and one "who has never been associated with the Democratic Party." Armstrong campaigned with vigor, but McGee was the darling of the media and most organizational Democrats. Newspapers decried Armstrong's "crude attacks on McGee."[8] Armstrong said McGee was a "self-styled, misguided amateur" on Russian matters. He accused him of "insulting the intelligence of the people of Wyoming" by bringing "a Communist" to speak at the university.[9] Armstrong's closing attack was designed to take advantage of the whispering campaign long under way.

In the August 19 primary McGee defeated Armstrong by 20 percentage points, with 24,532 votes to Armstrong's 15,025. A University of Wyoming student cast one of those votes. Jim Burridge set out to make a statement about the importance of voting, walking the twenty-four miles along the highway from Glenrock to the Casper courthouse on his twenty-fourth birthday to cast a ballot for McGee.[10] Burridge later served on Senator McGee's Washington staff.

Republicans were appalled to learn that not as many of them journeyed to the polls that day. For the first time since 1938, more Democrats voted in a primary than did Republicans.[11] It was a bad omen for Barrett.

With the primary behind him, McGee took a few days off from shaking hands to cast flies near Jackson Hole. That late August morning felt like the fall days that so often come early to that part of the state.

The sky was clear as the sun rose over the mountains. Temperatures were in the 40s headed for the mid-70s. McGee was stealing a few hours from his political campaign to relax. Relaxation didn't come as easily that morning as it most often did along a stream, casting a fly. His mind focused on what was going on below the surface.

As an accomplished fly fisherman, McGee was keenly aware of what was happening below the surface of the water. That's where the fish feed. The fisherman has to know what they're feeding on. If the fisherman doesn't know whether it is larvae, nymphs, worms, leeches, or minnows, he or she will fail in one of the most critical elements of fly-fishing, what's termed "matching the hatch." The fly one chooses to attach to the line must resemble whatever it is the fish are eating on that day and in that stream.

The professor who had never campaigned for any public office was about to learn the similarities between fly-fishing and politics. The difference between one who succeeds and one who doesn't is the ability to know what's going on below the surface and to "match the hatch."

McGee expected the political attacks, especially those below the surface. His mentor Joe O'Mahoney warned him with anecdotes from his 1952 campaign. His adversaries launched a below-the-surface campaign. Joe was too old, they whispered, too left, and perhaps too pink. McGee recalled what they did to John Clark in 1950, how subtly they connected him with the Communists. Democratic Party chairman Teno Roncalio told McGee he had been in Cody trying a lawsuit. He ate dinner with a group of what Teno called "a few of the extremely reactionary, black-hearted Republicans who are the big boys at that end of the state. Oh, how they hate Democrats and you particularly!"[12] A *Denver Post* editorial was already referring to McGee as "one of the most talked about and controversial figures to aspire to public office in Wyoming's modern history."[13]

His political campaign invoked more campus politics. Adversaries threatened to go after his job when he considered running for Congress in 1950. Even before he became an official candidate in 1958, Republican activists were demanding his resignation. James Griffith Jr. was a former McGee student. His father was the Wyoming Republican Party chairman who recruited Frank Barrett to run for the U.S. Senate. Jim Griffith Jr. was now the editor of the *Lusk Herald*, an influential conservative newspaper. Griffith said McGee should resign from his professorship because of his impending candidacy. "What logical reason is there," Griffith asked rhetorically, "that the people of Wyoming should pay the salary of a candidate for the United States Senate?"[14]

Cliff Hansen was a prominent Republican who later served in the Senate with McGee. In 1958 Hansen was the president of the UW board of trustees. He responded to Griffith. The university already had a policy requiring employees seeking office to obtain a leave of absence without pay beginning the day they file for office. That wasn't good enough for Griffith. He warned the legislature would ask tough questions about whether the school was financing McGee's political trips around the state.[15] Hansen conducted his own inquiry. He reviewed UW class attendance records and reported to his fellow trustees. Of all history department faculty members, Professor McGee had, by a wide margin, the greatest number of students: 358 were registered for his classes. The second highest class load totaled 198. McGee, Hansen said, was in compliance with university requirements with regard to off-campus speaking engagements.[16]

Confident that McGee would lose the election, some wanted to make certain he didn't return to the university after November. The Federation of Republican Women of Lincoln County passed a resolution calling on UW to "permanently remove from the payroll" any professor "found to be engaged in any political campaign."[17]

UW trustee John Reed had long but unsuccessfully urged university president Duke Humphrey to investigate McGee. Dissatisfied with the outcome, he undertook his own investigation. Before the August primary, Reed told Governor Milward Simpson, "I am gathering all of the records together and before this is over I am going to find some way to use it as he is the biggest liar I have yet to come in contact with."[18]

Fellow UW professor W. E. Kuhn sent a letter to GOP chairman Harry Thorson attacking his colleague McGee as "dishonest." Kuhn suggested Professor Ralph Conwell was one of a few "whom you should enroll as collaborators in the anti-McGee campaign on the campus." Thorson forwarded Kuhn's letter to Governor Simpson, who passed it along to others, including John Reed.[19]

Although Conwell expressed gratitude to Dr. McGee for challenging the UW trustees during the textbook controversy in 1947, the two hadn't seen eye to eye since. Professor Conwell may have opposed a "Red-scare" review of textbooks, but he was adamant that anyone he thought might be too far left ought not to be allowed to speak at the university. In 1954, Dr. Conwell complained loudly when McGee's Institute on International Affairs invited the one-time socialist Sidney Hook to speak. Referring to statements Hook made in earlier years, Conwell claimed Hook was a Communist. Conwell wasn't satisfied when Dr. McGee provided evidence that while Hook was once a socialist, in recent years he had become "one of our country's most militant anti-Communists." Hook had achieved national notoriety in 1939 when he called on academia to "rid itself of Communists." Hook argued then that the failure to do so would fuel people like Conwell.[20] In spite of Conwell's protest, Hook spoke on the UW campus in 1955, and Conwell still held a grudge.[21]

When Reed received the Kuhn letter from Simpson, he promised the governor he would "try and see Ralph Conwell myself and as I told you before, I have a man coming over to do some 'ghost-writing.'"[22] Conwell, like Reed, stalked McGee throughout the campaign.

It was unusual for a Senate candidate not to have personal wealth. At the very least, they nearly always had access to someone else's wealth if they didn't have their own. It wasn't like that for Gale McGee. The McGees, like most families, relied on monthly paychecks to pay the bills. Now they were tasked with gathering "start-up" funds for a state-wide campaign. Worse, they had to do so as Gale was given a leave of absence without continuing pay. Nonetheless, Gale assured the Democratic Senate Campaign Committee there would be adequate funding to run an effective campaign. "If our own sources here in the state do not produce sufficient totals, I will of course borrow personally, or if necessary, mortgage my house in order that our time-table shall not be interrupted for want of money."[23] Accordingly, Loraine and Gale boldly borrowed $3,500, the equivalent of nearly $30,000 in today's value. A Laramie bank made the sizeable loan in exchange for a mortgage on their home. The note was due November 25, 1958, payable in full whether he won or not. In addition, Gale's parents gave them $2,000, and the candidate cashed out a life insurance policy for another $600.[24]

Longtime ally Joe Davis of Cheyenne was named campaign manager. The slim campaign operation orchestrated everything out of a small back room at Davis's Texaco gas station in Cheyenne. The professor's former students lined up to volunteer. A professor who was once a McGee student said, "For those of us who knew him in his academic prime at UW, McGee remains a nearly mythical figure."[25] Thus dozens and then hundreds rushed to help. McGee estimated there were some five thousand of his former students around Wyoming by 1958. "My fortunate beginnings as a senator were influenced rather considerably by my former students."[26] McGee said the former students, "none of whom I flunked," saturated "every cubbyhole and remote corner" of Wyoming stumping for his election.[27]

The campaign was also greatly aided by the highly regarded former First Lady Eleanor Roosevelt. Her 1954 trip to Wyoming afforded her the opportunity to meet Dr. McGee. She remained impressed in 1958, employing her considerable influence to raise money for him. She worked with an organization called the National Committee for an Effective Congress. Its Republican opponents, like Senator Herman Welker of Idaho, called the committee "a clan of pinks and punks."[28] Using its vast mailing list, the committee successfully encouraged contributors across the nation to send checks to McGee. "Don't pass the buck," read the solicitation. "Give a buck." They did.

In addition to fund-raising, Mrs. Roosevelt publicly endorsed McGee and personally attacked Barrett. She said the Republican was an isolationist and a "silent non-entity." Using a double-barreled insult, she called the incumbent "one of the least articulate but most faithful acolytes of the late Joe McCarthy."[29] Barrett called foul. "The Committee for an Effective Congress has poured money into the coffers of my opponent's campaign fund in a lavish and reckless fashion enabling the professor to monopolize the newspapers, the radio networks, and the television every hour of the day."[30]

Over the preceding few years, McGee had successfully established his credibility on foreign affairs, particularly U.S.-Soviet relations. Senator Clements and others, however, worried he would be viewed as "an internationalist" who didn't understand Wyoming issues. Jim

Griffith Jr. thought this might be McGee's Achilles' heel. Writing in the *Lusk Herald*, Griffith said, "Should the people of Wyoming be duped into electing Dr. McGee, then Wyoming will have only one Senator because Afghanistan, Pakistan, or the Mongolian Republic could rightfully claim Dr. McGee as their Senator."[31]

Undeterred, McGee never backed off what he felt was a necessary dialogue about foreign policy. Telling audiences that America was on the "frontline of the world," McGee challenged Barrett's isolationist views, saying, "The Sputniks have placed us closer to the Russian frontier than at any other time in our history."[32] All the while, he exhibited a command of state issues important to Wyoming voters.

McGee's sons accompanied him on many campaign trips. Their responsibility was spotting fence posts on which he could staple a campaign sign. One afternoon as they made their way from Dubois to Lander, Robert spotted a likely fence post near the roadway. The station wagon screeched to a stop. Robert opened the rear hatch and retrieved a "McGee for Me" sign. Gale grabbed the staple gun, and they all walked through tall grass to the post. David held the sign in place as the candidate swung the staple gun around and fired. He missed the sign but shot a staple through his thumb. Fortunately, he said, the injury was not to his "handshaking" hand. He wasn't so fortunate on another occasion.

It wasn't uncommon for McGee to wake in the early morning hours when he would leave his motel room and jump in a friend's truck for a couple of hours of hunting or fishing. One morning he returned to the Sheridan motel where his staff waited. His right hand was wrapped but still bleeding. McGee had severely cut his hand on a barbed wire fence chasing down a wounded deer he had hit. He joked it was the worst injury that could happen to a politician. He was unable to shake hands for a couple of days.[33]

At the end of May, Gale was invited to speak to the American Legion's Boys State. A young Dick Cheney was in the audience. It was one of dozens of speeches the candidate gave in a frenzied effort to cover every one of the state's 97,818 square miles.

As the campaign wore on, McGee continued to hammer on Barrett, trying as his strategists encouraged to "crack" the favorable Barrett image that kept McGee at bay. He charged Barrett was a part of "the bankrupt leadership in Washington threatening American security against the Reds." The Democratic Party nominee called Barrett an isolationist. "We cannot afford representatives in Congress who must be dragged, protesting, into the Atomic Age." McGee said Barrett consistently supported large, out-of-state corporations seeking to "take control of our resources and rule the state." By contrast, the Democrat supported "legislation to balance prices and wages, increase social security payments, cut taxes for small businesses, aid for education, and a farm aid program based on parity."[34]

Barrett had enjoyed a great deal of support in rural Wyoming in prior campaigns. Historian T. A. Larson called Barrett "the idol of the cattlemen and woolgrowers."[35] So when Barrett said farm income was up, McGee was quick to draw a distinction. The Democrat said Barrett "is playing recklessly with statistics" and telling only half the truth. Gross farm income was up, McGee acknowledged. "But net farm income is down more than $87 million among Wyoming farmers in the last five years." As cracks began to appear in Barrett's image, McGee repeatedly asked Barrett to explain why he voted against the interests of his constituents, holding out Barrett's votes against "the interests of the Rural Electrification Administration," against increased funds for school lunches, and against investigating price fixing "that harms farmers and ranchers."

Barrett's campaign criticized McGee for being an outsider, a carpetbagger who came from Nebraska. The sources of the charge were apparently unaware of their own candidate's roots. An anonymous caller informed the McGee campaign that Frank Barrett was originally from Omaha, Nebraska. He came to Wyoming for a career in law and politics. The carpetbagging charge evaporated in Wyoming's summer sun.[36]

Barrett unwisely claimed to know more about the "defense of our nation than my opponent will ever know." That charge moved the debate to McGee's strongest ground. Barrett, a member of the Senate Armed Services Committee, said America "need not worry" about national security, that the nation was only a "trifle behind" the Russians. McGee was happy to show his superior knowledge of the Russians. He branded Barrett "woefully uninformed" for someone who should be aware given his committee membership. He called his opponent "complacent" and said, "We must not bury our heads in the sand when faced with the threat of Russian superiority."[37]

All the while, Gale and his family received gushing treatment from the press corps. The day after Labor Day, a photograph in the *Wyoming Eagle* showed the young father changing his baby daughter's diaper. The caption read, "A heavy schedule of campaigning hasn't excused Gale McGee, Democratic candidate for the United States Senate, from his home chores."[38]

McGee continuously challenged his Republican opponent to debates. Like most incumbents, Barrett refused. Late one afternoon a horse-drawn hay wagon pulled up in front of the Student Union at the University of Wyoming. Sitting on the bales was a straw-filled shirt and pair of pants with a sign hung around its neck. "Senator Frank Barrett," it read. Soon McGee appeared to the cheers of the growing crowd. "The United States Senate is the greatest debating body in the world," said the Democrat. "Why then does the incumbent U.S. senator refuse to debate me?"[39]

Barrett was feeling the heat. A Democratic Party stalwart told McGee she attended a September GOP rally in Sheridan. When the Republican candidates for governor and the U.S. House complained to the crowd about the problems their opponents were causing them, Barrett spoke up. "My two fine colleagues think they have troubles from their opponents? They ain't seen nothing yet!"[40]

As September gave way to October, two familiar opponents faced off against one another. Whitey Ford and Warren Spahn were named starting pitchers in the 1958 World Series opener between the Yankees and the Braves. At the same time, Frank A. Barrett and Gale W. McGee headed into the final innings of their face-off.

In the final month of the campaign, John Reed's effort to recruit Professor Ralph Conwell paid dividends. McGee's UW colleague wrote weekly opinion pieces, published in several Wyoming newspapers. In mid-October, he went after McGee on economic issues. Conwell called him Doc Magic, claiming McGee's "'give away' philosophy is dangerously inflationary."[41]

A group of forty other UW faculty members took out an ad, assuring voters that not many of his colleagues shared Professor Conwell's opinion of Gale McGee. Still, Conwell continued his blasts.[42] In the final week of the campaign, he hit the "McGee may be a Red" theme. Conwell bootstrapped the fact that McGee invited Alexander Kerensky and Norman Thomas to speak at UW into an assertion that McGee was "proposing a Communist on the university faculty."[43]

McGee was hounded by whispers that he leaned too far left, that he might even be a Communist. Joe O'Mahoney and others like Tracy McCraken predicted the GOP strategy. They had warned him two years earlier not to go to Russia. They felt conservatives would use that trip to bolster rumors about McGee's loyalty. O'Mahoney was certain that kind of undercurrent had caused his own loss to Frank Barrett in 1952. In the closing days of the 1958 race, the McGee team decided to hit the issue head on. A large newspaper ad signed by the state's Democratic illuminati announced, "The Big Smear Is Here." The signatories called the whispering campaign about McGee's loyalty a "pitiful attempt at slander."[44]

Dr. Larson, at first reluctant to involve himself in a partisan manner, placed "An Open Letter to the People of Wyoming" in several newspapers. Describing his work with McGee on the UW faculty, Larson said McGee was "slightly to the right of Senator O'Mahoney." He reminded voters they had elected O'Mahoney four times. "He has not destroyed Wyoming, nor will Gale McGee do so."[45]

Wyoming's hot Senate contest attracted big-name politicians from both parties. A future president was the first to come. One afternoon, shortly after he announced his candidacy, Professor McGee received a phone call from Massachusetts senator John F. Kennedy. He wanted to know whether McGee could meet him the following day at the Laramie airport. Kennedy diverted his plane to Laramie as he headed for an event elsewhere. As the *Caroline* banked and approached the runway, McGee told his sixth-grade son, Robert, who accompanied him to the airport, "This man may well be the next President." Kennedy "slipped me five one-hundred dollar bills and wished me well."[46] It turned out to be one of the most significant investments Kennedy made toward his 1960 nomination for president.

Vice President Richard Nixon came to tout Barrett. In mid-September, national GOP strategists were telling one another the Wyoming Senate seat was safe. By the end of that month, the GOP was beginning "to grit its teeth" for November losses.[47] By October

17 when Nixon arrived in Wyoming, Republicans feared the worst. Although the headline in the Cheyenne newspaper reported a "Large Audience Greets Nixon," the story that followed displayed their pessimism. Nixon pleaded, "If Republicans fight hard till November 4 we can turn what appears to be almost certain defeat into one of the greatest victories in our party's history."

Others came as well. Senator Roman Hruska of Nebraska campaigned for Barrett, as did Senators Everett Dirksen of Illinois and Karl Mundt of North Dakota. Former Minnesota governor Harold Stassen and Agriculture Secretary Ezra Taft Benson also stumped for the Republican nominee.

McGee's list of outside advocates was just as impressive. Former president Harry Truman came. Maine governor Edmund Muskie interrupted his own campaign for the Senate to make a trip to Wyoming on McGee's behalf. Others coming to boost McGee included George Smathers, Estes Kefauver, New Jersey governor Robert Meyner, and New Mexico congressman Joseph Montoya. McGee's mentor, Joe O'Mahoney, worked nearly as hard as the candidate himself in the closing weeks of the campaign, traveling the state and talking to large and small crowds about the man he hoped to serve with in the next Congress.

In late October, the White House made an announcement. It seemed innocuous at the time. President Eisenhower nominated Atomic Energy Commission chairman Lewis Strauss to be secretary of commerce. If candidate McGee even noticed the story, he would have had no inkling of how personal it would become a few short months later.[48]

Leaves began falling from the giant cottonwoods, and daylight hours shortened. The hours both candidates spent driving between small Wyoming towns lengthened. Each was desperate to find something that might make a difference in Wyoming's 1958 Senate contest as the gap between the two men narrowed. Two outsiders made that difference in those closing days. One came to Wyoming to help McGee. Another tarnished Barrett's image in a popular nationally published column.

TIME was prepared to run an election eve story predicting Barrett would win. The influential magazine's analysis was based on the perception that the incumbent had exceptional support among the state's oil and mining interests.[49] Texan Lyndon B. Johnson was then the powerful majority leader of the U.S. Senate. Senator O'Mahoney, who had gotten wind of the *TIME* story, prevailed on Johnson to make a trip to Wyoming to boost McGee's chances. Johnson called McGee and told him to gather as many Wyoming oilmen as possible. LBJ could speak their language. He knew that in the absence of some persuasion, those oilmen were likely to use their considerable influence to support Barrett. Shortly before Election Day, McGee assembled a large room full of the wealthiest and most influential oilmen who would accept his invitation to meet Johnson at the Townsend Hotel in Casper.

Politely removing his ten-gallon hat, Johnson strolled into the packed room, bantering with the group about the price of oil. He got their full attention when he raised the sensitive issues surrounding the oil depletion allowance, a controversial provision in the tax code allowing them to charge off huge amounts of income avoiding millions in federal income taxes. Congressional liberals planned to make another run at closing the loophole. LBJ assured them McGee could be counted on to oppose those efforts.

The powerful Texan then got down to business. He started with a quick refresher course on how important the Senate Appropriations Committee was to Wyoming. Members write the legislation allocating federal funds to government agencies and programs. No freshman member of Congress had ever been permitted membership. Where seniority rules, its members were inevitably senior senators. Each waited years to accrue enough seniority to have even a chance to serve on the committee. States fortunate enough to have one of their senators sitting on the Appropriations Committee are assured a lavish flow of federal dollars.

Quick learners all, his audience got it. These were politically savvy people who knew that what was good for Wyoming business was especially good for them. Then Johnson dropped the bomb. He pledged that if they would get Gale McGee elected to the Senate in November, he would use his considerable power to make McGee the first freshman to fill a seat on the Appropriations Committee. "That isn't the way you do these things," Johnson told the Wyoming oilmen referring to the hide-bound Senate seniority system. "But this is my commitment out of my respect for Joe O'Mahoney and for your state."[50] It was a stunning promise from one with the authority to keep it.

The other outsider to have an outsized impact on the 1958 election was Drew Pearson, a nationally syndicated columnist. His column, Washington Merry-Go-Round, appeared in 650 newspapers, reaching 60 million readers each week including thousands in Wyoming. His style of investigative reporting meant finding scandals among politicians and embarrassing them.

On October 30, the Washington Merry-Go-Round headline read, "Barrett Helped Compromise a Senator's Tax Case."[51] The column alleged former one-term Wyoming senator E. V. Robertson sold his Cody ranch to millionaire oilman H. L. Hunt. The IRS scrutinized the transaction. The result, according to Pearson, was a $900,000 tax bill that Robertson couldn't pay. "However," Pearson claimed, "ex-Senator Robertson had a friend in Washington, namely Senator Barrett." The columnist charged that Robertson's problems were dissolved as a result of Barrett's implied unethical intervention.

Initially, Robertson refused to respond. "I am no longer a public official," he told Pearson. "This is my own private business." Barrett, however, realized the story had the potential to do serious harm. Within hours, both he and Robertson denied the column's allegations. Barrett called Pearson a "notorious hatchet-man" and claimed the columnist "has been trying to drive me out of public life for the last 16 years."[52] Robertson bought last-minute newspaper ads with the heading "A Vicious, Malicious Lie." The responses motivated Pearson to issue another last-minute attack.

On election morning as Wyoming voters headed for the polls, a second Pearson column raised the ante by challenging Robertson to make his tax files public. Pearson said the release of Robertson's tax records would "clear up any doubts about Senator Frank Barrett's intervention in the case."

Jack Anderson was Pearson's investigator. After Pearson's death in 1971, Anderson's name appeared on the column's byline. The following year he was awarded a Pulitzer Prize for his reports on secret deals between Pakistan and the United States. It was Anderson who uncovered the information Pearson used in his October surprise. A week before the column ran, Anderson told Pearson he had "established to my satisfaction that Senator Frank Barrett intervened with the Justice Department to save Robertson from criminal prosecution." He added a warning. "We would have some difficulty proving it." Much of the evidence was hearsay. Senator O'Mahoney's administrative assistant, Mike Manatos, told Anderson what he had been told by his boss about Robertson "trolling the Senate" looking for a former colleague to intervene with the IRS. Senator Eugene Millikin, a Republican from Colorado, relayed that information to O'Mahoney, who passed it along to Manatos, who provided it to Anderson. At the moment Millikin was telling this to O'Mahoney, O'Mahoney claimed Millikin "made a gesture towards Robertson and Barrett who were huddling."[53] The $900,000 figure also came from Millikin.

Anderson vouched for Manatos. "Of course, I didn't talk to O'Mahoney directly about the incident, but I have found that Manatos is extremely reliable." Anderson's memo provided additional assurances about the veracity of the story. He had verified Barrett's intervention through confidential IRS sources. "I have enough confidence in my source to believe the story is true. However, it is secondhand." John Raper, the U.S. attorney in Wyoming, allegedly told the investigator he "had heard reports which agreed with what we have learned."

Armed with the information Jack Anderson collected and his assurances of its accuracy, Drew Pearson went forward with his October 30 column. Soon after the election, Barrett hired a Washington lawyer to go after Pearson. The lawyer persuaded Pearson to issue a retraction. Exactly one year after the Anderson memo, attorney David G. Bress advised Pearson that his "letter of retraction of this date, addressed to Honorable Frank A. Barrett, is satisfactory."[54] The retraction, sent to Frank Barrett and later published in the Washington Merry-Go-Round, recounted the earlier allegations made against the former senator. "However," Pearson admitted, "I now find that I was wrong. And in fairness to Mr. Barrett, I take the opportunity of setting the record straight and offering apologies."[55]

There was no allegation that the McGee campaign had any role whatsoever in the publication of the story. The official papers left by Pearson provide no information about what brought about the retraction, which seems at odds with Anderson's documentation.

The author of Barrett's *Lusk Herald* obituary, likely his friend James Griffith Jr., said, "The last-minute attack upon him in that campaign by Columnist Drew Pearson was the greatest hurt of his career."[56]

On election night, the McGees and a few close friends pulled an all-nighter at the home of UW art professor Robert Russin. Vote counting in those days was painfully slow as the paper ballots were counted by hand in more than six hundred precincts. Local radio stations were always aggravatingly behind in reporting returns. Most of them and the two Wyoming television stations went off the air after the 10 p.m. news, long before results could be determined.

As the McGees waited nervously, Robert Russin had an idea to take some of the edge off of what was a nerve-wracking vigil. Russin was a New Yorker who found his way to Laramie and the University of Wyoming around the same time McGee arrived. He taught art at UW for the next four decades. His sculptures are displayed all over the world and include the thirteen-foot-high, 4,000-pound bust of Abraham Lincoln commemorating the old Lincoln Highway from a perch high above what is now Interstate 80 between Cheyenne and Laramie. A small replica was later installed at Ford's Theater in Washington, DC, at the behest of Senator McGee.

Russin's idea that November evening was to create a bronze bust of Gale W. McGee.

It was around 3 a.m. "Get on that table, Gale," commanded Russin, pointing to the corner of the room where the sculptor kept his tools. Russin placed a block of wood under the candidate's head as he applied a thin coat of baby oil to McGee's wavy brown hair and Vaseline to his skin to prevent the plaster of Paris from adhering to either. Russin soaked strips of cheesecloth in the plaster as Doc Larson and Bill Steckel made phone calls, calling out what they learned from each contact. Barrett's lead, they said, was about two thousand votes. Russin distracted McGee by applying more Vaseline along the sides of his head, carefully avoiding the ears and nostrils, which were protected by small soda straws protruding from each opening. McGee was preoccupied with what those on the phones were reporting. He didn't give a thought to how silly he looked.

Larson got off the phone with someone from Casper who told him his UW colleague was still behind by a couple of thousand votes. Gale was unable to speak now as the plaster hardened. Loraine glanced at her husband, giggled quietly, and asked Larson to check with Sweet-water County.

Larson dialed State Senator Rudy Anselmi's phone number in Rock Springs as additional pieces of wet cheesecloth were placed over McGee's face strip by strip. Russin lightly tapped each into place until the professor's entire face was covered. McGee waited uncomfortably for information as Russin brushed a coat of plaster atop the cheese-cloth. By the time the mold hardened, McGee had learned the crit-ical Sweetwater County votes, likely to go heavily his way, weren't yet a part of the total reported count. Barrett's lead, he figured, would dissolve as they were tallied. Soon the mold and the straws were removed, and the Vaseline and baby oil were washed away. Only the tension remained. Hours more would have to be endured before the vote count was completed. The sculpture is on display today in the American Heritage Center at the University of Wyoming.

Gale and his friends spent all night on the phone. They called county clerks, newspapers, radio stations, and campaign supporters trying to learn anything about the count. Most of the night's sparse reports had McGee trailing. Gradually the margin narrowed. Vote totals were teasingly slow in coming, and it wasn't until just before sunrise that campaign manager Joe Davis called from Cheyenne. Joe was sitting in the offices of the *Wyoming Eagle* where for hours he had been staring at the Teletype. Finally, the bells that announce bulletins began ringing. "You're in, Gale. Now go get some sleep."[57]

On election night, the count was incomplete by the time the *Laramie Daily Boomerang* reached its final extended deadline. On Wednesday morning, the paper told readers Barrett had a close lead. By Thurs-day morning, the *Boomerang* could safely print a large black headline, "McGee Wins." To the right of the headline was a photograph evoca-tive of the one showing Harry Truman holding a copy of the *Chicago Tribune* prematurely announcing a 1948 Dewey victory. This time it was Gale and Loraine with huge smiles, holding aloft the November 5 *Rocky Mountain News*. Its headline? "GOP Win Seen in Wyoming."

On the day before the election, a reporter asked McGee to predict the outcome. He refused but did say he thought that a good turnout favored Democrats. He suggested that if 115,000 Wyoming people voted, he would likely win. On November 4, 116,230 voters went to the polls. McGee won by a 1,913-vote margin, receiving 50.8 percent of the total to Barrett's 49.2. McGee credited his former students and the Wyoming Democratic Party chairman. "The luckiest thing for us was that Teno Roncalio was the state chairman. Teno had bounce and fire. I was not even a dark horse. I was a hopeless horse," McGee remembered. "But he got the party mechanism put together, and that made the difference."[58] *Sheridan Press* columnist Dick Redburn added a touch of Wyoming levity. "Republicans, although saddened by the McGee victory, now realize they must grin and Barrett."

Political campaigns are grueling ordeals. Long months are spent covering thousands of miles, answering hundreds of questions as candidates and their families are put under a microscope. North Carolina political science professor Donald R. Matthews published a landmark study of the Senate as it was in the years before Gale McGee arrived. Matthews said it is impossible to understand senators, "how they act and why, without considering what happens to them while running for office."[59] Matthews believed campaigns change the people who run.

The 1958 campaign for the U.S. Senate also changed Wyoming. In six short years, the voters went from being moved by fear, wishing the United States were more isolated from the world, to cultivating a genuine curiosity about the world and Wyoming's role in it. They transitioned from a time when they hoped the world would go away to understanding the dangers of isolationism in the atomic age. By a whisker, it's true, but still they chose an optimistic young "egghead" to speak for them in the U.S. Senate.

7

A Name to Be Reckoned With

The U.S. Senate was not designed to be an institution open to people like Gale McGee. Its model was the Roman Senate, which was strictly limited to the nobility. West Virginia's Robert Byrd, an erudite member of the Senate known for his expertise in the history of these things, described their Roman counterparts. "Not the swiftest of the swift, not the strongest of the strong, but the wisest of the wise."[1] The wealthier, the wiser. Romans did not become senators unless they held vast sums of wealth. Neither did most U.S. Senate candidates.

The word "senator" is derivative of the Latin *senex*, meaning "old man." In Rome, the working definition was "rich old man." Gale McGee was neither. The average age of those serving in 1958 was over sixty. The incoming 1959 freshmen averaged around fifty. McGee was forty-three. He certainly didn't enjoy the wealth of many of his colleagues.

Delegates to the Constitutional Convention spent countless hours sculpting the Senate. It was, as McGee later observed, not intended to be representative but rather deliberative.[2] It was designed to protect the interests of the smaller states and the landed class. Alexander Hamilton proposed senators be elected by a small group of six to twelve electors, each a large landowner. Eventually they compromised on a plan that allowed the commoners, at least the white males among them, to vote for members of the House of Representatives. However, members of state legislatures would choose senators. Thus the moneyed interests in individual states controlled the Senate. The characteristics of senators changed little even after 1913, when the

Seventeenth Amendment to the Constitution deprived state legislators of the right to elect senators and gave it to the voters. In the years
before the youthful Wyoming professor of middle-class origins arrived
forty-six years later, "the 'typical' senator was a late middle-aged or
elderly white Protestant, native-born man with rural or small town
and upper-class origins, a college-educated lawyer, and a 'joiner.'"[3]

Of the tens of millions of Americans who have come and gone over
the almost 230 years that have passed, fewer than two thousand, mostly
men and a few women, have taken the oath to become U.S. senators.
Gale William McGee joined that select group on January 3, 1959.

The McGees arrived in Washington a few days before Christmas 1958.
Their lives were about to undergo enormous change. Not many
families easily make the transition from private to public life. The
move from Laramie to Washington, from university professor to
senator, is more than geographic and professional. It is earthshak-
ing emotionally and personally. Countless books about the lives of
notable people, especially politicians, include the almost inevitable
regrets about how they raised their children or that they wish they
had spent more time with family. Senator Hubert Humphrey served
with McGee. At one point the two were working long hours to gain
passage of the Civil Rights Act of 1964. The debate lasted sixty days,
longer than any before it. As it wore on through the hot summer
months, an afternoon came when McGee told a Humphrey aide he
wouldn't be able to stay late that night. "I have dinner plans with my
family." When Humphrey learned of McGee's absence, he barked,
"He better make up his mind whether he wants to be a senator or a
father. He can't be both."[4]

Sometime after their children were grown, Gale visited with Humphrey at a social gathering. The former U.S. senator from Minnesota
and vice president spoke of the joys and accomplishments of his life
in the public arena. He said there was "almost nothing" he would do
differently if given the opportunity. Almost. But he stopped short and
said, "There is one thing I would do over." He regretted not having
made more time for his children.[5]

Not so for Gale and Loraine McGee. "We decided in the early
years," Mrs. McGee told an interviewer, "that our family was the most

important. If we gave them up, all was down the tube."[6] It was that simple. Family came first. Their approach was tested a few years later when their eldest son, David, wrote a controversial piece of fiction for a national magazine. His work was a satirical account of the 1958 Wyoming campaign. Titled "A Family Affair," it lampooned a few well-known Wyoming Democrats. One example is David's irreverent assessment of the 1958 Democratic candidate for governor and his wife:

Dad's partner was to be the candidate for governor, J. J. Hickey, a gentleman who would have been far more comfortable as a Republican, except that in 1958, it was not the 'in' thing to be. His wife could never quite understand how a woman of her position—she was a member of a sheep ranching dynasty—had been thrown headfirst into the muck of a political campaign. She once confessed that she had never found her way into a voting booth. Perhaps she mistrusted its resemblance to an outhouse.[7]

The magazine's editor called McGee and suggested he might want to preview the article prior to publication and make some changes. David's father refused. "I'm not going to look at it until after it's in print for everyone to read. It's David's thing, not Gale's."[8] When they learned of David's essay, the senator's staff warned him there would be political fallout. They were right. There were some angry folks back home. One was Winifred Hickey, whose husband was elected governor the same night McGee was elected to the Senate. She wrote a letter to the publication's editor. As might have been expected, David's attempt at parody was not appreciated by its target. "The article is so full of untruths I could not expect you to publish a letter citing all of them," Mrs. Hickey wrote.[9] Journalist Theodore H. White saw it differently, albeit from a personally removed perspective. "David McGee's article was as neat and a happy and an effective story of American politics as I have read recently anywhere."[10] Many years later, McGee admitted he found the article humorous and honest. "Well," said David's father, "he made the mistake of calling some fuddy-duddies 'fuddy-duddies.' He really was quite on target."[11]

From the beginning, Gale and Loraine established a pattern for their family's new life in Washington. Congress didn't take many days off back then, and so vacations to Wyoming were not feasible. In the summer, they went to the beach at Fenwick Island, Delaware, north of Ocean City in Maryland. Staff members and other senators including Frank Church, Ed Muskie, and Clair Engle joined the McGees.

McGee came to the Senate at the end of an age when being a member of Congress was a part-time job. He believed the invention of air-conditioning was the evil that made it possible for Congress to meet through long, torrid Washington summers and into the fall. Those schedules made family vacations impossible, particularly if the family wanted to go back to Wyoming for a few weeks when school was out. Over time McGee became increasingly unhappy with the extent to which Senate schedules crowded out family time.

A senator couldn't do anything about his children's school calendar. So Gale went about changing the Senate's calendar. In March 1961, he introduced a resolution "to bring the work of the Senate in step with the rigidity of the schedule that Members with children must adhere to."[12] Senator Muskie quickly added, "The Senator has four and a half additional votes from the Muskie family." Thirty-one other senators joined the cause, but a generational split among elders and young reformers in the Senate as well as House opposition prevailed until the Legislative Reorganization Act of 1970 became law. The McGee family finally had an August recess.

The ceremony began at noon. Outside, winter clouds hung low over the U.S. Capitol. Inside, the gold trim and crimson edging of the historic chamber seemed especially resplendent. As McGee walked through the door of the Senate chambers, he noticed the inscription above the door. *Annuit Coeptis*. "God has favored our undertakings." Mahogany desks dating to 1819, when there were but twenty-two states and forty-four senators, sat beside more recent replicas of those artifacts, copies necessitated by the fact that there were now ninety-six senators, soon to be one hundred. Spittoons and snuffboxes sat on either side of the presiding officer's dais. Vice President Richard Nixon gaveled the session to order.

Wyoming's senior senator, Joseph C. O'Mahoney, escorted the new senator to the podium. Loraine and the children along with Gale's parents looked down from the family gallery of the Senate balcony. The new senator placed his right hand on the Holy Bible, and Nixon asked him to repeat after him as he recited the words of the oath of office.

The November 1958 midterm election produced the widest swing from one party to the other since 1866. The nation's high unemployment rate resulting from the 1958 recession along with *Sputnik* were blamed for the unprecedented size of the GOP losses. The Democratic Party gained sixteen seats, boosting it to a 65–35 majority once Hawaii and Alaska sent their members to Washington. Among McGee's fellow freshmen were several who would make history, including Ed Muskie of Maine, Philip Hart of Michigan, Eugene McCarthy of Minnesota, Frank Moss of Utah, and Robert Byrd of West Virginia.

By the time McGee became a senator, he had earned a PhD from the University of Chicago and had already demonstrated he could hold his own in discussions of world affairs and current events with the likes of John Kennedy, Lyndon Johnson, Eleanor Roosevelt, and Henry Kissinger. Through extensive travels, he was thoroughly acquainted with much of the United States and with much of the world. He was one of the first Americans allowed behind the Iron Curtain after World War II, traveling extensively throughout Russia and the Soviet-bloc nations. He had been an adviser to the Council on Foreign Relations on issues dealing with Russia and China. He wrote acclaimed scholarly articles on foreign policy for major academic journals and delivered well-received speeches all over the United States. One could search long, and likely in vain, to find another freshman as well prepared to serve in the Senate as Gale McGee.

Before McGee moved into his office, the Senate leadership had to persuade Frank Barrett to move out. Calling him "the worst loser in the 1958 election," his old nemesis Drew Pearson wrote a column claiming, "Republican Barrett was so bitter over his defeat last year that he locked himself in his office on his last official day and brooded alone long after all other defeated Senators had packed off."[13] While McGee and his new staffers waited to move in, Lewey Caraway, the Senate office superintendent, urged patience. New Mexico's Democratic senator Dennis Chavez finally borrowed the custodian's key to get into Barrett's office and eject the former senator.[14]

Seniority was the way the system disciplined newcomers and rewarded longevity. It was something freshmen learned to accept. When McGee came in 1959, the Senate had ninety-eight members, and he ranked ninety-seventh on the seniority list. Understandably, he may not have liked the seniority system then. After he won a third term in the Senate, however, he experienced a change of heart. "When I first got to Washington, I hated the seniority system," he said in 1970. "But, you know, the longer I'm there, the more I like it."

Seniority was gauged using a complicated system providing significant benefits to those who had been there the longest. But many came at the exact same time. That year alone, there were eighteen new members. The seniority system scored highest those with prior congressional service. Of the incoming senators, eleven had previously served in Congress, including Robert Byrd, Hugh Scott, and Eugene McCarthy. The next tiebreaker was given to those who had served as governors of their states. Ed Muskie of Maine and Ernest Gruening, Alaska's first senator, received those points.

There remained a five-way tie for last place. The deciding factor was the population of their states. Among those five, Philip Hart of Michigan ranked highest, followed by Vance Hartke of Indiana and Frank Moss of Utah. In 1959 Wyoming had double the population of Nevada. Howard Cannon was, therefore, relegated to ninety-eighth place. Gale McGee was a single rung ahead of him. Hawaii soon sent numbers ninety-nine and one hundred.

Seniority, or the lack thereof, is the reason no freshman senator had ever served on the Appropriations Committee without at least having served in the House first. It was considered the most powerful of all Senate committees. Congress, it is often said, has the "power of the purse." The Appropriations Committee is ground zero for the exercise of that power. Its members have direct access to a legislative process enabling them to bring home considerable funding for projects and programs important to their states. Senators use their seniority to win a seat on this committee.

In 1959 two other senators petitioned for a seat. Both outranked McGee. John F. Kennedy of Massachusetts and Stuart Symington of Missouri had been in the Senate a full term before McGee came. They made their case to the majority leader. It was a relatively easy decision for Lyndon Johnson to award the prizes to freshmen senators McGee, Thomas Dodd, and Robert Byrd. LBJ had promised those freshmen seats during their Senate races, and both Kennedy and Symington had designs on the 1960 Democratic Party presidential nomination, as did he. The Texan wasn't about to give such a cherished assignment to rivals who would use it as a platform for their presidential campaigns.[15]

One of McGee's first orders of business was to organize his staff. Joe Davis of Cheyenne, McGee's former campaign manager, was named administrative assistant, a position known today as "chief of staff." Elizabeth Strannigan of Reliance became McGee's personal secretary, a post at which she faithfully remained until his death in 1992. Dick Cook of Lance Creek was appointed press secretary, and Chuck Whittemore of Laramie, Ira Whitlock of Worland (who served on Senator Lester Hunt's staff), Margaret Brennan of Newcastle, Vona Osmond of Afton, and James Fagan of Casper were among the first staff members.[16] The senator established a rule: no one from outside of Wyoming could serve on his staff. He later made an exception for an old friend and former student from his days at Nebraska Wesleyan when he hired Betty Cooper, but visitors were told she was from "east of Cheyenne."

Staff selection says a great deal about a senator. His or her relationship with staff says even more. These opinions, offered anonymously by some Senate staffers, are not uncommon. "They are like 100 princes. I'll tell you one thing, their staff members are all terrified of them." Another said ruefully, "They can't tell their constituents to go to hell. But he can give his staff a very hard time."[17]

That's not how former staff members remember Gale McGee. Out of respect, they all referred to him as "the senator." He returned their respect in the way in which he treated them. The senator personally greeted staff members by name each morning. On a staffer's birthday, he always took him or her to the Senate Dining Room for lunch. Others recalled having ready access to McGee and having their opinions considered in policy discussions. They all remembered Gale's bad jokes.

While staff members for some senators viewed their jobs as temporary, many of McGee's remained in his employ for several years.

Dick Cook and Liz Strannigan were onboard for the entire three terms he served.

Reflecting McGee's priorities, he didn't recruit longtime, well-placed Washington professionals. His focus was to be on Wyoming and its issues alone. The onerous workload was distributed among a small staff, each of whom was required to spend extraordinarily long days answering mountains of letters from back home. Constituents called or wrote asking for information, seeking to know their senator's position on every imaginable issue, asking for help in dealing with federal agencies, applying for jobs, or complaining about a vote McGee made or a position he took. From Wyoming came dozens of requests for the *1959 Agricultural Yearbook,* the senators' statements on the oil depletion allowance or a range of other issues, and complaints about the color of the stripes on the highway. Constituents sought his help in getting a son an appointment to a military academy. Some clipped "coupons" from their organization's newsletter and sent them to McGee to share their position on matters before the Senate.

Paul Jones wrote from Otto, Wyoming, requesting "all available information on adobe and rammed earth walls." Mary Lippincott Swartz of Casper wrote angrily on February 24, 1959, about an airman who appeared on the TV game show *Tic-Tac-Dough.* She felt the senator should make certain the airman's contest earnings were "confiscated and given for the benefit of his comrades who have been sweating it out the hard way."[18] A constituent who had been drafted wanted help in getting an assignment in the Army permitting him to devote time to practicing his piano.[19] On June 17, 1959, McGee received a handwritten letter from Glen Hagen of Jackson. "Can our military defense use better missiles and aircraft?" Hagen asked. "My design ideas are far superior to any we have now. Please advise source for evaluation of these ideas and proof that I am not a crackpot. Evaluation authority should be security minded, high rank, and honest, if possible."[20]

A letter came from Joseph Payne of Laramie, complaining that McGee was suffering from "spenditis" and asking, "Just how dumb can you get?" Mr. Payne added a postscript. "But, after all, what more can one expect of a college professor given too much rope?" Even that letter received a prompt reply.[21] McGee insisted that each letter be answered, each request be filled if possible, and that any problems his constituents had with federal agencies be thoroughly investigated. The senator and Loraine also took time to clip notices of any significant event in the life of a constituent. They would write a congratulatory note on a wedding or graduation announcement or a story of an achievement of any sort and send it to the person being honored. Many people kept those notes for a lifetime. Forty-hour, five-day-a-week work schedules were long lost memories for anyone choosing to serve on McGee's staff.

Gale hadn't received a paycheck since beginning his leave of absence from the University of Wyoming in June 1958. His first Senate paycheck wouldn't be deposited until the last Friday of January 1959. After taxes, group insurance, and retirement contributions, his take-home pay on a $22,500 annual salary was about $1,250 per month, more than tripling his UW salary.[22] Even so, the costs of moving family and furniture to DC had drained what little remained in the bank.

The McGees called a real estate agent to help them find a Washington area home in December 1958. Oklahoma senator Robert Kerr gave the newcomers some helpful advice. Don't worry about how much the house costs, he said. Few of us will be here long enough to pay one off anyway. Just make sure you can handle the monthly payment. The agent apparently figured any senator could afford an expensive house. She began showing him homes priced from $50,000 to $90,000. The senator asked to see something far less expensive. They finally found one they could afford but had no money for the down payment. The sale had to wait until the McGees could arrange a loan. The agent said, "It's nice to know that a man without a bank account can be elected to the United States Senate."[23]

Their first house in Washington was a Dutch Colonial built in the late 1920s. It had three bedrooms, two bathrooms, and a small nursery upstairs. There was a large backyard with a goldfish pond. A tree produced edible cherries. A screened porch overlooked the yard. The bedroom and bath in the basement, known in DC as the maid's room, became Frieda's room. Referred to them by Gale's brother Dean, Frieda Maier came to live with the McGees in Laramie during the 1958 campaign. Frieda took care of the children and the Laramie house while Loraine and Gale campaigned. After the election, Frieda moved to Washington with the family. She was a constant companion for the McGee children. Once they were raised and out of the home, Lori Ann and her husband invited Frieda to live with them and help raise their children. She did so until her death in 2007.

The popular magazine *Pageant* published an article about Wyoming's new senator in its May 1959 issue. Alvin Toffler, author of the 1970 best seller *Future Shock*, wrote "A Freshman's Washington Merry-Go-Round" after following McGee in his first days in Washington.[24] McGee was open about his family's financial hardships in the wake of the campaign. Truthfully, the McGees never had much money. Some found that hard to explain. A confidential FBI informant once told J. Edgar Hoover falsely that McGee's personal debts had been paid off by the Kennedys as a part of a deal to get his vote for JFK's test-ban treaty with the Soviet Union.[25]

Toffler followed when Joe O'Mahoney accompanied McGee to the office of the secretary of the Senate, Felton Johnston. If anyone knew his way around the Senate it was "Skeeter" Johnston. He had already had this job for fourteen years and would go on to serve another fifteen before retiring. Skeeter gave McGee bad news when he asked for an advance on his first check. Then he reviewed the privileges McGee received as a member of the Senate. He didn't have to buy stamps to mail official letters, there was an allowance for long-distance phone calls, free haircuts, funds for staff and offices in DC and Wyoming, and two paid trips a year back home. Doctors remained on duty at all times to provide medical care for senators. Nonetheless, he would still have to wait until the end of the month for his first paycheck.

O'Mahoney then took McGee to the Mayflower Hotel's Presidential Suite for a courtesy meeting with former president Harry Truman. Truman, himself a former senator, told McGee, "If you're like the rest of us, for the first six months, you'll walk around asking, 'How'd I ever get here?' After that, you'll walk around asking yourself, 'How'd the rest of them get here?'"

McGee was the first freshman that year to be assigned the role of presiding over the Senate in the vice president's absence. It was expected to be a brief hour in the chair on a mid-January afternoon. Instead, it became a nearly six-hour assignment as Wayne Morse of Oregon engaged his colleagues in a filibuster.

Toffler asked McGee when he actually began to feel he was a U.S. senator. It was that night, McGee said. As he was leaving the chambers at 10:30 p.m., a small group of lobbyists approached him in the hallway as he boarded an elevator. He withheld a commitment to vote as they wanted on some bill. One of them warned McGee, "You'll be sorry. We have ways, you know." Wrote Toffler, "After that, McGee said he knew he was really a member of the United States Senate."[26]

McGee threw himself into the work of the Appropriations Committee. The room in which the committee did its work was inspiring. A lunette, a half-moon shaped painting, filled the space between the door and the arched ceiling. This 1875 fresco by Constantino Brumidi depicted an enthroned female figure symbolizing authority. The ceiling included rinceaux and rosettes, ornamental floral motifs in shades of green. A border of tromp l'oeil was designed to give a three-dimensional illusion. Nineteenth-century mosaic portraits of Abraham Lincoln and James Garfield painted by Antonio Salviati were hung on the walls.

Despite the historic nature of the hearing room, Gale McGee found the committee work "dullsville."[27] But it took no time for him to recognize how important it was, especially to the people of Wyoming. The lawmaker mastered the work of the committee well enough to channel "more federal appropriations to Wyoming than anyone else had ever done."[28]

McGee easily made friends of his fellow senators. Regardless of their party, the Wyoming senator reached out, learning about them and their families. It is unlikely there was a more thoughtful member of the Senate. Each year Gale sent birthday wishes to each one of his ninety-nine colleagues. On Mother's Day, he sent a letter to the mother of every member of the Senate, regardless of political party. "Dear Mrs. Allott," went the note to Colorado Republican Gordon Allott's mother in Pueblo. "As people all over the country prepare to pay tribute to their mothers this weekend, it made me realize how doubly fortunate are those of us serving in the Senate of the United States, to have our mothers with us to share those memorable experiences. And I felt you too would enjoy knowing how highly your son is regarded by his colleagues and how justly proud you should be." Each of them, from Senator Barry Goldwater's mother to Russell

Long's and Edmund Muskie's, twenty-four mothers in all, received a letter. "I don't know what you did to my mother," wrote Senator George Smathers, "but she wrote me a letter singing your praises."[29]

McGee promptly reconstructed his thoughts about politicians and their work. He acknowledged that from outside the Senate, "the solutions to the world's problems seemed easy. In the classroom, I had a lot more pat solutions to the problems of mankind than I have now in the United States Senate."[30] He surrendered to his new reality. "As a teacher, I had often approached questions as either black or white, when in truth most are a shade of gray."

He quickly tasted the hard work of finding the right shade of gray on vital matters. The first matter facing the Senate was a civil rights battle disguised as a Senate rules fight. Journalist William White said the filibuster, which was at issue, was "the South's unending revenge on the North for what happened at Gettysburg."[31] The bell rang signaling yet another round early in 1959.

The civil rights movement was gaining strength, but the cause wasn't a significant issue in the 1958 Wyoming Senate contest. However, it became significant immediately after McGee's election. The first of his new colleagues to talk to him about this matter was Hubert Humphrey. Long before Election Day, Humphrey and Illinois senator Paul Douglas wrote to McGee to brief him on the cloture matter. Eleanor Roosevelt followed up with a mid-October letter of her own urging the candidate to take the Humphrey-Douglas overture seriously.[32] Less than a week after McGee's victory, Humphrey congratulated him and again alerted him to the coming battle over Senate rules limiting debate. Humphrey expected the Wyoming liberal to join his cause.

The controversy over Rule 22, which preserved prolonged debates or filibusters routinely used by southern senators to block civil rights legislation, came quickly as the 86th Congress convened. In the early years, the Senate had no procedure for ending debate. Unlimited debate was honored. In 1917 President Woodrow Wilson complained loudly after debates prevented the Senate from voting on critical war-related measures. "The Senate of the United States," Wilson said, "is the only legislative body in the world which cannot act when its majority is ready for action. A little group of willful men, representing no opinion but their own, have rendered the great government of the United States helpless and contemptible."[33] The Senate responded by adopting a rule. However, its longtime tradition of unlimited debate was preserved. The new rule put the burden on those wishing to bring closure, or cloture, to the debate. Debate could be limited only if those wishing to do so could muster a two-thirds majority of senators actually present and voting. In other words, the two-thirds requirement was levied not against all one hundred senators but only those who showed up for the vote. Senators would, thereafter, be limited to one additional hour's debate each.

In 1949 Georgia senator Richard Russell succeeded in tightening the rule. His amendment imposed a two-thirds majority of all elected senators whether they came to the floor or not, what opponents called "a super majority." A decade later, liberals like Humphrey thought they had found a way around the stringent cloture rule. The Senate had the authority to change its own rules at the outset of each Congress by a simple majority vote. Therefore, they argued, they could amend Rule 22 to end the two-thirds vote requirement with just fifty-one votes.

Southerners worried their last weapon to stop civil rights bills was seriously threatened. But their biggest weapon proved to be the Senate majority leader from Texas. Lyndon Johnson cobbled together a compromise. He would allow the liberals their wish to return the two-thirds requirement to only those present and voting. In exchange, the two-thirds rule would also be made applicable to amending the Senate rules.

McGee and the other Democratic Party freshmen were caught between a rock and a hard place in the first week of their Senate careers. For McGee, the rock was LBJ. He had campaigned for McGee and had named McGee to the Appropriations Committee. The hard place was Eleanor Roosevelt. She had raised large amounts of campaign cash for McGee's campaign, and she fervently wanted a rule that would stop the use of the filibuster against progress toward civil rights.

The Wyoming senator pleased LBJ as much as he displeased Mrs. Roosevelt when he joined O'Mahoney and seventy-one others. By a 72–22 vote, LBJ's proposal was adopted. Civil rights activists were deeply discouraged. They felt the best opportunity to end civil rights filibusters had faded into history.

Many of the liberals they helped elect just two months earlier disappointed activists on this vote. Ray Robinson, managing editor of *Pageant,* the magazine that published such a flattering piece about Gale McGee, was unhappy. He had responded to Mrs. Roosevelt's request the previous summer by sending a check to the McGee campaign committee. "I must confess," he advised McGee, "your support of Lyndon Johnson's clique during the opening round of the anti-filibuster fight has left me disappointed and confused."[34]

The senator admitted to Robinson that siding with some of the others left him uneasy and wondering, "What am I doing on the same side as so-and-so?"[35] In a personal note to friends Mike and Claire Leon of Story, Wyoming, the senator said he regretted having to part ways on the issue with "great liberals whom I admire."[36] McGee was asked during a radio interview about an accusation made by columnist Drew Pearson. Pearson said McGee had "been roped and branded with an LBJ iron."[37] The accusation ruffled the Wyoming senator, who defended the vote as necessary "to protect the unpopular and the unpopulous." McGee was convinced that restricting the circumstances under which Senate debate could be limited was an especially important safeguard for the interests of smaller states like Wyoming. He said westerners should understand his position, adding, "I felt it was morally wrong to change long-standing rules merely to get at integration."[38] As Gale McGee's education on civil rights continued, he came to feel differently.

Journalist William S. White observed, "Not all of [the Senate's written rules] have one tenth the force of simple tradition, that tradition that some things are done and some are not."[39]

Senate tradition held that new members were to be seen and not heard for a long period of apprenticeship. "That period once ranged from several months to several years."[40] The tradition ceased to exist before McGee rose to give his "maiden speech." However, for decades there had been a not so subtly enforced unwritten rule that new members should refrain from speaking on the floor for many months. Violators were shunned. Robert La Follette was a freshman senator in 1906, with a prior career of more than twenty years as Wisconsin's governor and as a member of the U.S. House of Representatives.

Even so, as he rose to speak after several months as a senator, nearly every other member got up and walked off the floor. La Follette's wife watched from the gallery. "There was no mistaking that this was a polite form of hazing."[41]

On February 19, 1959, just six weeks had passed since McGee had taken the oath of office. That morning McGee walked confidently through the door and took his seat at the rear of the Senate chambers. John F. Kennedy introduced his colleague. "Mr. President, I wonder if a quorum might be obtained before the senator from Wyoming speaks. I know there are a number of senators desirous of hearing him."[42]

McGee stood, his right foot slightly in front of his left. There wasn't a note in his hand or a piece of paper on his desk. His voice betrayed not a bit of the nervousness he felt in his stomach. "In ordinary times," he began, "I think I would be interested in continuing my education without breaking silence. But these are not ordinary times." He acknowledged that he and other freshmen had been given extraordinarily important committee assignments. McGee felt that alone gave them "the responsibility" to raise their voices. He also said the voters, by electing so many new members, expected them to "act in certain ways in regard to the future."

He spoke of the challenges posed by the Soviet Union and the nation's fiscal situation. He felt "the urgency of a fresh, new look at some of the questions which bear upon us in these times." Calls of others for a balanced budget led him to reflect on what he thought was the need, not for a balanced budget, but for "a totally necessary budget." Citing Khrushchev's threats, he raised both arms, his left hand stretched out with his index finger pointed to the sky. "It is time that we present to the people a war budget, not a peace budget." The Wyoming senator told his colleagues of the vast array of resources his state was able to contribute to the well-being of the nation and its efforts to defeat communism. The United States, he said, should be "mobilizing capitalism" to solve social problems. The nation must create full employment to prove to the world the value of our system over communism.

McGee earned immediate credentials as one of the Senate's premier orators. Edmund Muskie of Maine said, "As a freshman senator, I wish to say how proud I am to be associated with one who can express himself as [McGee] has this afternoon."[43] Kennedy, possessed himself of not insignificant oratorical skills, was astounded by his Wyoming colleague's ability to speak publicly. Kennedy told the Senate that McGee's was the first maiden speech delivered in modern times with no manuscript. It was a skill McGee would frequently exhibit over the course of his long career. A rhetorician no less renowned than Edward R. Murrow told McGee much later how he regretted he could not "extemporize as skillfully as you."[44]

McGee's official papers, donated to the American Heritage Center at the University of Wyoming, include dozens of requests from people all over the world for copies of his speeches. To each request a staffer responded something like this: "I'm sorry I can't provide you with a copy of the Senator's speech. He seldom prepares a manuscript and most always speaks without notes." McGee's oratorical skills were legendary. The speeches of the onetime college debate coach were widely reprinted in periodicals like *Vital Speeches* and included in books like *Representative American Speeches, 1964–1965,* a publication containing speeches the editor said deserved to be kept in the "public remembrance."[45] A decade later, *Esquire* devoted a lengthy essay to a discussion of the great orators of the U.S. Senate. Much of the article focused on Gale McGee. The writer, William H. Honan, said McGee's colleagues were "dazzled" by the senator's maiden speech, and he referred to McGee as the Senate's most brilliant speaker.[46] McGee's "dramatic pose with right foot forward and both arms outstretched" reminded Honan of Henry Clay pleading with the Senate to pass his Compromise of 1850.

A few months later, the editors of *Talamac Magazine* polled members of Congress, asking them to name the most effective congressional leaders and newcomers with the most potential. Topping the two lists were Kennedy and McGee. The magazine quoted words used by colleagues to describe the Wyoming lawmaker: "brains and guts, deep interest in domestic and foreign problems; one of the best informed; outstanding capacity to speak eloquently on many subjects, and brilliant, scholarly."[47] In his column, Three Names to Reckon With, William White told readers the West was slowly replacing the South "as the holder of the balance of power in the Senate." White gave credit to what he called the "real eggheads of the Democratic Party." They were Eugene McCarthy, Frank Church, and Gale McGee. "These will be three names to reckon with in the Senate, and in the country, for decades to come."[48]

To be certain, not everyone admired McGee. J. Edgar Hoover received a letter from Wyoming, written on the official letterhead of the Lincoln County Federation of Republican Women. The signer's name was blocked out when the FBI files were released, but the letterhead named, among others, Mrs. John Reed Jr., wife of the UW trustee who sought to have Professor McGee discharged when he ran for the Senate. The writer of the April 25, 1959, letter was deeply concerned "over the ever-smothering flood of Communism in our country." She added, "I understand you have our Terrible Gale McGee (U.S. Senator) under your watchful eye, thank heavens for that." An FBI agent drafted a suggested response for Hoover telling him, "This letter [drafted for Hoover to sign] has been couched in terminology to avoid giving correspondent any ammunition for what appears to be the onset of a political campaign on her part." The agent reminded Hoover that McGee was a supporter of both Hoover and the FBI.[49]

The Appropriations Committee came with a great deal of status and a steep learning curve. It was his other committee assignment that provided the senator with a political baptism. He wanted a seat on the Foreign Relations Committee, but there were no openings and the majority leader had already pushed the system to its limits by putting McGee on Appropriations. Johnson put him on the Interstate and Foreign Commerce Committee instead. Eisenhower's nomination of Lewis Strauss (pronounced "Straws") to be secretary of commerce was referred to that committee on January 17, 1959. McGee had been a senator for all of two weeks.

The highest level of formal education attained by Admiral Strauss was a high school diploma. That misled many because he was accomplished in both the public and private sectors. Strauss's government service began in 1917. He served with Herbert Hoover, then U.S. food administrator and chairman of the Commission for the Relief of Belgium. A Navy officer during World War II, Strauss was promoted to the rank of admiral. He was highly decorated, receiving the Distinguished Service Medal and the Legion of Merit. Eisenhower chose Admiral Strauss to head the Atomic Energy Commission in 1953. In 1958 he awarded Strauss the Medal of Freedom. Strauss was also a successful businessman.[50]

He certainly appeared well qualified to serve as secretary of commerce. What's more, the Senate had not rejected a president's cabinet appointee since 1925, when Warren Harding's nomination of Charles Warren to be attorney general was denied. Troubling signals appeared early. The Commerce Committee chairman delayed hearings to accommodate those being held down the hall by the Joint Committee on Atomic Energy. Clinton P. Anderson was the chairman, and he represented New Mexico and the people working at Los Alamos National Laboratories. Strauss was the director of the Atomic Energy Commission during Anderson's tenure as committee chair, and the two clashed. Anderson had scores to settle with Strauss.

Since his early days developing the atomic bomb, J. Robert Oppenheimer was routinely scrutinized because of the nature of that work. His FBI file was more than four feet thick. They tapped his phones, followed his footsteps, opened his mail, skimmed his trash, and quizzed acquaintances. He accepted it as a part of his job. As he put it, "The government paid far more to tap my telephone than they ever paid me at Los Alamos."[51] The conflicts originated with a letter to J. Edgar Hoover alleging that Oppenheimer was "an agent of the Soviet Union."[52] Such accusations long swirled around Oppenheimer. His wife and brother were former Communist Party members. He had given money to the Party and joined several left-wing organizations. Eisenhower knew. Hoover knew. The Joint Committee knew. Maj. Gen. Leslie Groves, the military supervisor at Los Alamos, knew. The media knew. But in the McCarthy era, no one wanted to admit that they knew.

Another person who was aware was Lewis Strauss. He was charged with the responsibility of reading the FBI's information and signing off on Oppenheimer's loyalty, which he did routinely. Now, instead of supporting Oppenheimer with his knowledge of the massive amount of exculpatory information, Strauss ordered a security hearing. Oppenheimer, despite all he had done for his country, was deemed "a bad security risk." Senator Clinton Anderson was outraged.[53]

And then there was the Dixon-Yates contract, named for Edgar Dixon, president of Middle South Utilities, and Eugene Yates of the Southern Company, a utility holding conglomerate. The New Deal's Tennessee Valley Authority (TVA) was always a matter of disagreement between those who thought it was socialism and those who believed it was necessary to provide the public with access to affordable power. The contract was conceived in an effort to avoid conflict with Congress over the question. The purpose was to use the two private utilities to provide power without having to ask Congress for public dollars.[54]

Strauss's involvement in negotiating the contract, which was characterized by alleged blatant conflicts of interest, proved problematic when he sought to be confirmed as commerce secretary. The contract was a thorn in the side of Wyoming's senior senator. Joe O'Mahoney's opposition went back to 1954. He raised objections before the Securities and Exchange Commission. As an expert on monopolistic practices, he studied the contract and concluded, "The Atomic Energy Commission has actually entered into a contract with what to all intents and purposes was a non-existent corporation."[55] He thought the Dixon-Yates contract created a "monopolistic merger."[56]

A month before the Commerce Committee voted on the nomination, O'Mahoney took his complaints to the full Senate. Noting Strauss's role in Dixon-Yates, he called the admiral "a leading figure in bringing about" the contract. After reciting his lengthy list of objections, O'Mahoney proclaimed, "No person associated, as Admiral Strauss was associated, with this plan would be qualified to be Secretary of Commerce."[57] He undoubtedly brought his concerns to McGee, a member of the committee that would conduct the inquiry into the Strauss nomination.

Chairman Warren Magnuson gaveled the Commerce Committee to order on March 17, 1959. It was St. Patrick's Day and Gale McGee's forty-fourth birthday. McGee was in a celebratory mood until he began to ask questions of the nominee. If Strauss was hoping for an easy ride, he didn't help himself when the freshman senator asked about the Dixon-Yates contract. Strauss had not made McGee's acquaintance and replied arrogantly: "I don't respond to questions from staff members." McGee politely replied that he was a senator and that he would appreciate some answers.[58]

Lyndon Johnson arranged a meeting between McGee and Anderson to alert McGee to the majority leader's strong interest in the defeat of this nomination. Anderson asked McGee to slow the proceedings. He expected that a more deliberate pace would result in others coming forward with damning information. Anderson's hunch proved correct.[59]

After the first two days of committee testimony, McGee told his staff he would likely vote to confirm Strauss. But as the hearings dragged out, Anderson revealed Strauss had withheld critical information from both the Joint Committee on Atomic Energy and the AEC.[60] Dr. David Inglis, a former AEC employee, testified, accusing Strauss of being "vindictive and sometimes unethical."[61] The nominee was later accused of trying to obtain classified files to impeach Inglis. Strauss categorically denied the allegation. "I never asked for anything on Dr. Inglis in my life." Within days, Strauss's successor as AEC chairman, John McCone, acknowledged Strauss had indeed called the agency, asking specifically for such information.

The Commerce Committee voted 9–8 to recommend approval of the nomination. McGee was one of the "no" votes. He said, "Mr. Strauss failed to inspire in me confidence in his dealings with Congress.[62] He was now determined to defeat Strauss's nomination. Bobby Baker, Lyndon Johnson's right-hand man and vote counter, told Johnson that his nose count revealed a majority was prepared to vote against the nomination.[63] McGee wasn't so sure. He hadn't yet learned the fine art of "nose counting," but felt in his gut the result would be close and that Eisenhower could well prevail.

Years after leaving the Senate, McGee looked back on the Strauss affair and his involvement. He called it "an accidental event of rather considerable proportions."[64] He was one of the few members of the Commerce Committee with virtually no prior political experience. Yet with the suddenness of a train wreck, McGee found himself standing between a president and what that president wanted.

One of those who had been around the Senate long enough to recognize the dangers of sending a freshman to the frontlines for a battle like this was Richard Russell of Georgia. The Southern Democrat came to the Senate in 1932, and many considered him to be second only to the president in influence and power. During the Strauss hearings, the Georgian was a member of the Joint Committee on Atomic Energy. Having the background on the facts that led many to question Strauss's fitness to serve and knowing the depth of the pit that potentially awaited McGee, Russell visited his young colleague. He gave McGee his personal assurance that the Wyoming senator would not get hurt politically as a result of his leadership in this fight.[65]

As the battleground shifted from the Commerce Committee to the Senate floor, its outcome was in doubt. Bobby Baker's earlier vote count became shifting sand, and McGee's earlier worries were confirmed. The White House did its own count, and Eisenhower was told that Strauss would win the nomination by at least five votes.[66]

The midnight oil burned in McGee's office. Robert Oppenheimer was brought secretly into McGee's office at night to assist in preparations. Knowing how much was at stake, he and his staff worked days, nights, and weekends preparing for the epoch floor fight. Each was aware that a confrontation with the president on a cabinet appointment was no small matter. *TIME* called it a "blood feud."[67] McGee's rhetorical skills could get him only so far. He knew he must master a lengthy list of complicated facts before taking the floor to ask his colleagues to reject Strauss.

On the morning of June 9, 1959, McGee rose to address the Senate. "Mr. President, I move that the Senate proceed to the consideration of executive business and take up the nomination of Mr. Lewis B. Strauss to be secretary of commerce." A raucous debate followed. As the final vote approached, the drama heightened. On June 12, Johnson called for a vote. He was now confident he had the necessary majority. At 12:35 a.m. the roll was called. The nomination was defeated 49–46. Anger boiled over on the GOP side of the aisle. Barry Goldwater of Arizona charged at his Democratic colleague George Smathers of Florida, who Goldwater expected to vote for Strauss. Goldwater's fists were clenched, and Smathers thought he was about to find himself in a fistfight. "What's the matter with you?" he asked Goldwater. "Do you want to step outside?" Goldwater demurred and strode brusquely from the Senate floor.[68] Dwight Eisenhower called it "one of the most depressing official disappointments I experienced in my eight years in the White House."[69]

It was a great political victory for the freshman from Wyoming, but it was bitter and sweet at the same time. Senator O'Mahoney, though ill and quite tired, had answered the call. Looking gray and frail, he came to the floor for this critical vote. Once the results were announced, he was taken home, where he suffered a serious stroke later that morning.[70] Hospitalized for several weeks, O'Mahoney decided against seeking another term. On August 26, 1960, Senator Wayne Morse wheeled the iconic senator into the chambers, and O'Mahoney gave a final speech. He died two years later at the age of seventy-eight.[71]

Less than six months into his first term, McGee had been baptized with fire. He was an accomplished orator and a respected member of the greatest of all debating clubs. He was a historian working with people determined not to make the mistakes of the past. He quickly earned the admiration of people who enjoyed the respect of others. Having come from academia's "ivory tower," where he enjoyed ample time to read, reflect, and write, the senator had but one complaint. "In the Senate," he reminisced later, "you still don't have a chance to read and reflect or to just sit on a mountaintop, or in a quiet bay somewhere on somebody's sloop, and think big. We all came to the Senate with a whole barrel full of ideas that we had generated ourselves over a long period of time, and you finally empty that about your first term in the Senate, but you don't ever quite get a chance to read a book again."[72]

It was a sign of either the time he actually found to read or perhaps proof that he no longer had time enough to do so. The Library of Congress sent a notice on October 30, 1959. A book he had checked out was overdue. It was Allen Drury's Pulitzer Prize–winning *Advise and Consent*, the fictional account of Senator Lester Hunt's 1954 suicide.[73]

8

Give Me Four More Votes

Martha Aasen's father was a Mississippi delegate to the Democratic National Convention in 1960. Martha decided to come along late, and the only accommodation Martha and her husband, Larry, could find was a room in a rundown Spanish-style hotel in a seedy area on the outskirts of LA. As they checked in the morning before the convention opened, she and Larry noticed a large, seemingly out-of-place black limousine. Senator John Kennedy got out and walked through the front door of their "crummy hotel."[1] Martha asked Kennedy why he was there of all places. Kennedy replied that he had come to meet with the Wyoming delegation.

Tracy McCraken was incensed when he learned about the hotel the Democratic National Committee had assigned the Wyoming delegation. As chairman of the delegation, he complained bitterly. Wyoming had exceeded its contribution goals and deserved better lodging in a better part of town. The arrangements committee offered no explanation. Perhaps assignments had been made in alphabetical order. While the alphabet may have been responsible for putting the delegation in that "crummy hotel," it was also responsible for putting Wyoming in the history books a couple of days later.[2]

JFK was not Gale McGee's first choice. He preferred Lyndon Johnson.[3] Both played pivotal roles in McGee's election. From the beginning of the 1960 presidential contest, McGee knew he would be required at some point to make a tough call.

Kennedy was the first national figure to endorse McGee in his 1958 campaign. Kennedy flew to Wyoming, McGee said, "the moment I announced."[4] Just a couple of weeks after McGee's announcement in June 1958, Kennedy's private jet, the *Caroline,* landed at the Laramie airport. Before leaving Wyoming, Kennedy handed McGee five hundred dollars, a huge campaign contribution, the largest McGee had received from any individual that year.[5]

The two senators occupied offices not far from one another in the Old Senate Office Building, and they and their staffs spent time working together on a variety of matters. The Wyoming senator developed close friendships with many of JFK's inner circle. He came to know Larry O'Brien, who headed Kennedy's Senate campaign and later became national director of his presidential run. Kennedy speechwriter Ted Sorensen was an old friend dating back to their debating days in Nebraska. Likewise, McGee had known top JFK adviser Arthur Schlesinger for many years as a result of his friendship with Schlesinger's father when the elder Schlesinger was a distinguished historian at Harvard.

McGee liked Kennedy. He found the wealthy Bostonian warm and easy to visit. Kennedy and his wife, Jackie, invited the McGees to their Georgetown home for dinner. While the men talked politics, Jackie gave Loraine a tour of the home, including Caroline's nursery.

People noticed similarities between the two. Kennedy was born two years after McGee, and both campaigned on the promise of their youth. There were striking similarities in physical appearance as well. One afternoon as McGee stepped from the elevator in the Old Senate Building, a young woman mistook him for Kennedy. She told him how much she admired him and asked for an autograph. Rather than disappoint her, McGee obliged and forged JFK's signature. They both walked away smiling with stories to tell.[6]

Kennedy and McGee shared mainstream Democratic Party views. Kennedy was pilloried for not being a "true liberal." He responded much as McGee did when facing the same condemnation: "I'm a realist."[7] The liberals and the "realists of the Democratic Party" distanced themselves from one another mostly on the question of how to handle the Soviets. Politicians like McGee and Kennedy separated their positions from the far left by taking a tough line against the

Russians and communism. The two senators agreed on a cautious approach to civil rights, supporting the goals of the movement but not its aggressive strategies. They were painfully aware of how difficult it was to make progress. Above all, they feared that losing brutal fights over civil rights would negatively affect their other goals.

Given their friendship and the significance of all they had in common, Kennedy had reasons to expect McGee's help in winning the 1960 Democratic Party nomination for president, as did Lyndon Johnson.

From the moment Joe O'Mahoney introduced McGee to Johnson in 1956, the two hit it off. Lady Bird became so fond of Loraine and Gale McGee that as First Lady, she made special seating arrangements at formal White House dinners to have Gale seated at her side. "I couldn't have asked for better company," she recorded in her diary after one dinner. She considered both McGees "charming and highly intelligent."[8]

Judging the two men on the surface, their relationship might not have been predicted. McGee was formal in appearance and speech. The strongest word his children ever heard him say was "damn." Johnson, on the other hand, enjoyed the looks on faces when he used colorful language. It might have surprised the Wyoming senator to know Johnson thought he was "my type of a man."[9]

Below the surface these two had a great deal in common. "Lyndon and I struck it off rather well only in the sense that we could talk the same language, that is, Texas oil and the Texas plains and the Texas cowboys. All this sort of quick imagery imitated or was paralleled by those precise images in Wyoming."[10] They represented patriots who drilled for oil, raised cattle, and settled some of the harshest land on the continent. Those kinds of folks were initially leery of both of these liberals. Each won his first race by a razor-thin margin. "Landslide Lyndon" won his first campaign by eighty-seven votes. McGee won his first by eight-tenths of a point over 50 percent. Johnson told McGee he was aware of "what it's like for a Democrat in Wyoming. It's a bit like Texas," he said. "You're always swimming upstream."[11] Johnson had a reputation for leaning hard on senators when he needed their votes. But McGee said LBJ never asked him for a vote if Johnson thought it would hurt him back home.[12] LBJ understood what it took to earn the confidence of conservative voters, and McGee learned from him.

Though they expressed themselves quite differently, both men were savvy politicians. LBJ's promise to put McGee on the powerful Appropriations Committee was more than an impromptu political gimmick. Johnson had known McGee for a few years, and the two had engaged one another in discussions of significant national issues. The candidate from Wyoming earned the respect of the Senate majority leader long before winning a seat in the Senate. Gale McGee, Johnson said, exhibited "a little of the mold of a Wilson and Lincoln combination, a little of George Marshall and Sam Houston." He considered McGee someone who pulled himself up by his bootstraps, high praise from one who had done the same.[13]

The powerful Texan took the newcomer under his wing in those early days. Johnson was aware of the traps into which an eyes-wide-open freshman might fall unknowingly, and he helped McGee avoid them. Bobby Baker was a confidant of the majority leader who ran political errands for Johnson and ended up skating too close to the legal edge. Likewise, Baker attached himself to other Senate Democrats. When Baker learned of a large fund-raising dinner the Wyoming senator planned, he offered to help. The dinner was set for Cheyenne. A dozen of McGee's colleagues agreed to make the trip as a show of his respect in Washington, and so Baker told McGee he would arrange for a private jet to ferry them.

LBJ got wind of Baker's offer one day as he sat in the Senate chamber listening to a debate. When McGee entered, he took his seat. Looking up, McGee saw Johnson's long bony finger beckoning him. "Do I understand correctly that Bobby's offered to get you a plane?" McGee acknowledged the offer. "Well," Johnson snapped, "for God's sake, don't do it. Don't ever do that. They'll kill ya if you all fly in there with a bunch of senators on a private jet. Just tell Bobby no."[14]

Kennedy decided to run for president in 1960 shortly after losing the Democratic Party's 1956 vice presidential nomination. He campaigned in all fifty states before his January 2, 1960, announcement. Kennedy set the stakes high. "I believe that the Democratic Party has a historic function to perform in the winning of the 1960 election, comparable to its role in 1932." He had "an image of America as fulfilling a noble and historic role as the defender of freedom in a time of maximum peril and of the American people as confident, courageous, and persevering."[15]

During the summer before Kennedy's announcement, campaign operatives and the candidate's family spent considerable time in Wyoming. After a July visit, organizer Bob Wallace wrote a long memorandum to Kennedy, saying that Governor J. J. Hickey "is for JFK." He counted several other key Democrats as supporters. The list included two of Senator McGee's staff members. "Because of his two fine trips to Wyoming, most of the Democratic sentiment has been definitely pro-Kennedy." Wallace told his boss that state Democratic Party chairman Teno Roncalio and McGee were "committed for all practical purposes." Still, the Wallace memo betrayed a certain amount of ambivalence. Wallace's first recommendation to Kennedy was that "Hickey and McGee should be committed in blood as soon as possible." If they commit, Wallace said, "Wyoming's delegation can be lined up solidly."[16]

Kennedy received conflicting reports on McGee's support. During Wallace's Wyoming trip, Roncalio asked McGee whom he backed. "My frontal attack on Gale McGee," Teno told JFK, "was met with a massive resistance of pure silence."[17]

By November 1959, the Kennedy organization achieved certainty that McGee was "leaning very strongly for Senator Johnson."[18] The candidate's brother Ted reminded McGee supporters of JFK's trip to Wyoming to help elect him. The comeback was a reminder that LBJ had also come and that he had awarded McGee a seat on the Appropriations Committee. Wyoming Democrats told the young Kennedy brother that McGee "owes Johnson a debt which he is going to pay off at this time." Nonetheless, Ted was able to find a number of likely delegates strongly backing Kennedy. His search took him to a rodeo in Lander, Wyoming, where he somehow managed to stay atop a bucking bronco for almost the required eight seconds to the cheers of a bipartisan crowd.[19]

Roncalio continued working on McGee. He called McGee "a young, bright bushy-headed man" whose 1958 victory he had predicted. "Today, Gale, I suggest similarly to you that the bushy-headed counterpart of yours from Massachusetts will be nominated at Los Angeles." Teno wanted McGee on the bandwagon. "As soon as it is possible, without injuring your own career, your state chairman will be happy to welcome you on board."[20] Two weeks following Kennedy's formal announcement, Teno no longer held out any hope that McGee would join the team. He told Ted that McGee "will attempt some Humphrey activity and will not meet with success."[21]

Teno came home late from a party meeting, exhausted but buoyed. He reported that Bobby Kennedy's speech in Wyoming that week "took all the steam out of Johnson's efforts here." He then told JFK, "Wyoming now looks as though what was a strong possibility of fifteen full votes [for Kennedy] is now a reasonable certainty provided there are no slips in Wyoming between now and then."[22]

Spring came and Lyndon Johnson had yet to make a formal announcement. *TIME* surmised LBJ was waiting until Kennedy fell "on the lances of the old professional bosses."[23] He made an April 1960 trip to speak in Cheyenne, and at the time, the Johnson folks were quite sure McGee was behind LBJ.

Larry L. King was "a reporter, a Capitol Hill aide, a raconteur, a brawler, and a full-time Texan" who "helped define the freewheeling New Journalism of the 1960s and 1970s." He was also the playwright of *The Best Little Whorehouse in Texas.*[24] King volunteered to help in the Johnson-for-president office in Washington. When he complained that the campaign seemed to be chaotic and directionless, he was exiled to the West. His responsibility was to persuade Wyoming Democrats to adopt what was called "the unit rule." The rule was devised to give party bosses control over unruly, unpredictable delegates. The adoption of a "unit rule" meant all delegates would be required to vote for the candidate the party endorsed. LBJ figured that with McGee's help, imposition of the unit rule would give him all of Wyoming's fifteen votes.

"Go see Gale McGee," King was ordered. "He'll cooperate one hundred percent." To prove their case, the LBJ team gave King a recent copy of *TIME* that quoted McGee speaking about the Texan. McGee was "glowing" when he said, "He'd make a honey of a President."[25]

King found McGee in Casper, and the two had a pleasant conversation. The senator told him to go see Jim Fagan, McGee's top state operative. When King tracked down Fagan, he was told the senator had instructed staff not to take sides. King was flummoxed. Washington had misjudged LBJ's Wyoming friend. "Almost everyone," King reported, "favored Kennedy, including state chairman Teno Roncalio, who would control the delegation's fifteen votes."

King's marching orders were quickly reversed. He was now in Wyoming to make certain the unit rule was not applied. King was instructed, "Rather than seeking to 'solidify and harmonize' delegates under the unit rule, we should fight to 'preserve the independence' of the individual delegate." By stopping imposition of the unit rule, they hoped to escape with at least four of Wyoming's votes.

King reported McGee was determined to remain neutral. He cornered McGee as he left a downtown restaurant. McGee "said smoothly that all the delegates were his friends, that his friends were split up among the numerous good men seeking the nomination, and that he just couldn't find it in his heart to disappoint any of his friends."[26] The senator was merely telling them what they had known if they had taken his earlier words at face value. He had told the *Christian Science Monitor* that he had no plans to endorse anyone prior to the convention.[27]

One of LBJ's top staffers was Walter Jenkins. Upon learning that McGee was not as solid as his boss thought, he called the Wyoming senator. He no longer expected an endorsement. His more modest request was for help in avoiding the unit rule. Jenkins then called King and told him not to worry. McGee would help them.

Shortly before the Democratic National Convention began, the press learned McGee had turned down a request to second the nomination of "a major candidate." McGee cited Wyoming's decision not to impose the unit rule. He didn't want to violate the "spirit of that decision" by taking sides. When Governor Hickey seconded Lyndon Johnson's nomination, McGee felt Hickey had betrayed that agreement.[28] Speculation was fueled that there was now a rift between Johnson and McGee.

Johnson didn't formally announce until July 5, less than a week before the National Convention opened in Los Angeles. Without naming Kennedy or any of the other senators seeking the presidency, the majority leader criticized colleagues for missing "hundreds of votes" while campaigning. "Someone had to tend the store," Johnson said, referring to himself. Now that Congress was adjourned, he entered the race. LBJ believed the odds were strongly against a first ballot victory by anyone. Hickey told LBJ he figured Kennedy would be about a hundred votes short at the end of the first ballot. Johnson felt he could win on the second or third ballot. Because of Senator Gale McGee, it never got that far.

Paul M. Butler, the chairman of the Democratic National Committee, called the 1960 Democratic National Convention to order on Monday, July 11. There were 1,521 delegates, and Wyoming had 15, slightly less than 1 percent. Day one was spent settling rules and other technical matters. Senator Frank Church of Idaho delivered the keynote address: "Ours is an awesome age." Church sounded like a preacher when he decried "conspicuous consumption," saying, "Our lives are cluttered with gadgets. Yet we have cared so little about our public responsibilities that both young and old have been neglected." Church pleaded with delegates to "give us a leader whose stature will match the dimensions of this atomic age."[29]

On the second day, they listened to more speeches and adopted a party platform. It pledged to oppose armed Communist aggression, support noncommunist nations in the Third World, and affirmed an "Economic Bill of Rights," which among other guarantees sought to make certain that workers' wages were adequate and farm prices high enough to provide rural families a "decent living." The platform strongly supported civil rights legislation.

The third day was that for which most delegates came to Los Angeles. At 3:00 p.m. Rabbi Max Nussbaum gave the invocation. "Mankind finds itself living in an endless fear of uneasiness and discontent." He prayed for leaders who could "remember tomorrow what they pledged today." The national anthem was played, and delegates recited the Pledge of Allegiance. The convention clerk, Emery Frazier of Kentucky, began the call for nominations as he had during each of the previous seven Democratic National Conventions.

MR. FRAZIER: "Alabama?"

MR. ALMON: "Alabama yields to Texas for the purpose of placing in nomination a candidate for President of the United States."

The Speaker of the U.S. House of Representatives, Sam Rayburn, nominated Lyndon Jonson. Wyoming's governor, Joe Hickey, seconded the nomination. "I am pleased to second the nomination of the Majority Leader of the U.S. Senate, who by his proven ability as a leader selected by the Senators of Wyoming and all the other Democratic states, and . . . will be the winner in November and the next President of the United States of America."[30]

Frazier next called on Alaska. Its chair yielded to Minnesota governor Orville Freeman, who strolled briskly to the podium to place Kennedy's name in nomination. He said JFK "could provide the kind of leadership our land needs." Florida senator George Smathers was nominated next. Missouri senator Stuart Symington's nomination followed. After a couple of other "Favorite Sons" were nominated and declined, Eugene McCarthy placed Adlai Stevenson's name on the ballot. Eleanor Roosevelt seconded the nomination of the man who had been chosen the Democratic candidate twice before. The next nominee was Robert Meyner, the governor of New Jersey, who had campaigned for Gale McGee in 1958. The final name placed in nomination was that of the Mississippi segregationist governor, Ross Barnett.

According to news accounts, "It had taken about six and a half hours to place the nine candidates in nomination and to allow their supporters to shout and parade around the hall in wild, but well-organized demonstrations."[31] Then began the main event. Frazier asked, "Will the chairmen of the delegations kindly give your attention?" He asked them to give their votes in the order in which candidates were nominated. Johnson, Kennedy, Smathers, Symington, Stevenson, Meyner, and Barnett.

MR. FRAZIER: Alabama—29 votes.[32]

Alabama gave twenty of those votes to LBJ. Three and a half went to Kennedy. The rest were spread among the field. Senator Kennedy received 9 of Alaska's votes and all of Arizona's 17. LBJ got the entire slate of Arkansas's 27. Next came California. "Mr. Chairman, California casts 7.5 votes for Johnson, 33.5 for Kennedy, 8 votes for Symington, 31.5 for Stevenson, and 0.5 vote for our favorite son for whom we would all like to vote, Pat Brown." Senator Kennedy went over the 100 mark as Illinois cast its votes. Iowa put JFK over the 200-vote mark. He topped 300 with his own state of Massachusetts. New York had 114 votes and gave Kennedy all but 9.5 of them. When the roll call got within one state of Wyoming, JFK had 735 votes, LBJ 405, Stevenson had 79.5 votes, Symington 86, and Ross Barnett 23, all that Mississippi had to give. West Virginians then brought Kennedy to the cusp of the nomination. He received 15 of their 25 votes. Wyoming was the only state left. Kennedy needed 11 of their 15 delegates to win the nomination on the first ballot. LBJ needed the process to move to a second ballot to have any chance of winning.

All eyes shifted to the Wyoming delegation, including those of the writer of *The Best Little Whorehouse in Texas.* Ted Kennedy was in the middle of a Wyoming huddle. He knew his brother had slightly less than half the state's delegate votes, not enough to win. Johnson had six. If it held, his brother would be deprived of a first-ballot nomination and would be at risk of losing if the question went to a second or third ballot. JFK needed four more Wyoming votes and it would all be over. King heard someone standing next to Teddy hollering, "Give me four votes. We can put him over the top. Please give me four more votes."[33]

An Associated Press photograph shows a broadly smiling Ted Kennedy standing next to the chairman of the Wyoming delegation, his right hand tightly grasping the "Wyoming" placard. Tracy McCraken suddenly grabbed the microphone and cried out gleefully, "Mr. Chairman, Wyoming's vote will make a majority for Senator Kennedy."[34] All 15, which ostensibly included the vote of delegate Joe Hickey, who had just seconded LBJ's nomination, went to the young senator from Massachusetts. It was over on the first ballot. John F. Kennedy won the Democratic Party nomination for president of the United States. The crowd exploded.

Larry King's eyes followed that one man, "the man who had begged for four votes. He was jumping up and down, slapping a beaming

Ted Kennedy on the back, apparently beside himself with joy. I recognized him as our old friend Senator Gale McGee."[35]

Campaign operatives trying to figure out which candidate Gale McGee supported didn't understand Wyoming. If they had taken him at his word, none would have been disappointed. The Wyoming senator later acknowledged that it took LBJ "a long time to forgive."[36] That's understandable, though Johnson the politician surely understood. In those days, Wyoming politicians knew that the worst characteristic a small state could exhibit was predictability. Large state politicians have the luxury of endorsing candidates early. They have such meaningful numbers of votes that they remain relevant for the duration of the process. Small states hold the interest of major aspirants only so long as there is a question of where they might land. As McGee, Hickey, and others kept them guessing, Kennedy, Johnson, and Symington courted the delegates. They came to the state repeatedly, something they would not have needed to do had McGee endorsed one or the other earlier.

As if to prove this theory, once JFK won the nomination, he made no plans to return to the state during the general election campaign. LBJ came to Wyoming for a Cheyenne Frontier Days rodeo a few weeks after the ticket was nominated, calling it the "highlight of my year."[37] That was high praise for "the Daddy of 'em All" Cheyenne rodeo from a man who had just been nominated for vice president of the United States. But Kennedy felt he needed to spend his time elsewhere. Why spend valuable and limited campaign hours in a state where there was so little chance he would win in November? Kennedy's mind was changed, but it took a lot of grousing from Tracy McCraken, then Wyoming's member of the National Democratic Party's Central Committee.

Before being told Kennedy would not campaign in Wyoming, McCraken told Senator Henry Jackson, the chairman of the Democratic National Committee, that "both Jack and Lyndon must make not less than three or four speeches each in Wyoming."[38] When McCraken learned there would be none, he telegrammed the candidate. "Fully appreciate how crowded and rugged your schedule is and that Wyoming has no large electoral vote." But, said McCraken, those three Wyoming votes in the Electoral College might prove helpful in a close election.[39] Then he called on Senator McGee. "No need of my telling you why I think this is not only bad for our chances in Wyoming but also for our senatorial and congressional candidates. Our people would feel downright slighted, and I don't think they could be blamed."[40] McGee's intervention persuaded JFK to make one last stop in Wyoming.[41]

September 23, 1960, was one of those glorious fall days that Wyoming often enjoys. Skies over Cheyenne were cloudless, and the temperature was on its way to the upper 60s. Senator Kennedy began by acknowledging his audience included many who had driven hundreds of miles from the other three corners of the state. Then he reminded them of what a big thing it was that their small state did in Los Angeles. "I know that Wyoming is a small state, relatively, but it is a fact that Wyoming, which was not talked about as a key state in the days before the convention, when they were talking about what California and what Pennsylvania and what New York and Illinois would do at the convention, not many people talked about what Wyoming would do, and yet, as you know, Wyoming did it."[42] Turning dramatically, looking pointedly at Tracy McCraken on the dais behind him, the witty Kennedy quipped, "As Gale said, I have been to this state five times. My brother Teddy has been here ten times, and I think that the Kennedys have a high regard and affection for the State of Wyoming. Bobby has been here, I guess, several times. We have been here more than we have been to New York State."

The Democratic Party nominee used considerable time demonstrating knowledge of Wyoming issues such as natural resource development. "What we do here, what we fail to do, affects the cause of freedom around the world. Therefore, I can think of no more sober obligation on the next administration and the next president and the next Congress than to move ahead in this country, develop our resources, prevent the blight which is going to stain the development of the West unless we make sure that everything that we have here is used usefully for our people."

The handsome young candidate looked out across the crowd, smiled broadly, and said, "I don't know whether it is going to be that close in November. I don't know whether Mr. Nixon and I will be three votes apart, but it is possible we will be. If so, Wyoming having gotten us this far, we would like to have you take us the rest of the way on November 8."

Kennedy won without Wyoming's electoral votes. Nixon received all three, though it mattered little as he lost by a margin of 303–219.

On the day before the general election, Senator McGee was feeling overwhelmed. He was exhausted having pushed himself hard campaigning for Kennedy all across the country. He sat at his desk staring at the calendar. His recent schedule had kept him away from home and time with his children more than he was accustomed. Now, he saw, there was an upcoming trip to Africa. Long ago, when it seemed like a good idea, McGee agreed to join Frank Church, Eugene McCarthy, and Ted Moss on a journey requested by Carl Hayden, chairman of the Appropriations Committee. That morning he announced a change of mind. He would not participate in a thirty-two-day African fact-finding trip scheduled to depart in less than two weeks.

When Hayden heard of McGee's cancellation, he telephoned to remind McGee how significant this mission was to the committee. Kennedy was president-elect, and Africa would receive additional focus. Citing Kennedy's "strong concern about these emerging countries," Hayden assured McGee that JFK would be "deeply interested in your findings."[43] As the chairman of the Foreign Relations Committee's African subcommittee, Kennedy took a special interest in the continent, especially in the developing independence movements. He and McGee recognized the strategic advantage the continent held during the Cold War.

McGee and Loraine quickly packed for the grueling monthlong tour of sixteen African nations. Kennedy called McGee, asking that the senators take his brother Ted along for the education.[44] The young Kennedy's presence excited the crowds throughout Africa.

The Defense Department assigned Col. Edwin J. Witzenburger to be the escort officer for the four senators and their wives.[45] It was a nice coincidence for Gale and Loraine. Witzenburger had old Wyoming ties. A highly decorated airman, he was shot down by the Japanese in 1945 but rescued by the French Foreign Legion. He flew fighter jets over China in World War II and fought in Korea and

Vietnam. He had attended the University of Wyoming and married into a Wyoming ranching family. After retiring from the military in 1971, Witzenburger returned to Wyoming and was later elected state auditor and treasurer. Along with Witzenburger, the party set out for Africa on November 20, 1960.

As World War II ended, international attitudes toward European colonization were changing. Still, as time passed, it became increasingly certain that the Europeans were not going to grant independence to the Africans easily. Since the Berlin Conference of 1884, when the European powers sat around large maps and divided Africa among themselves, they had enjoyed the fruits of African resources.[46] They weren't excited about giving them up now. But that dangerously outmoded policy was unraveling quickly as Kennedy prepared to take office in 1961. As for many African nations, these were days of revolution and celebrations of independence. Independence didn't come without a challenge. As Africans freed themselves from Europe's yoke, they were caught between the West and the Soviets as pawns of the Cold War.

As the "CODEL," military shorthand for "Congressional Delegation," flew from New York to London and then on to Mali, Witzenburger briefed the senators on each of the sixteen African nations they planned to visit. Many of the issues centered on Cold War tensions. The United States had deep concerns, for example, that Mali "would follow the pro-Soviet course of Guinea."[47] The briefings given on the status of each African nation they visited in the coming month explained whether they were friends of ours or of the Reds.

Ghana, the West African nation colonized by Britain nearly a century and a half earlier, achieved independence in 1957. There the senators encountered the influential prime minister, Kwame Nkrumah. He was largely credited with leading the Pan-African independence efforts. "By the mid-1960s, over 30 African countries were independent and many had charismatic leaders, including Jomo Kenyatta in Kenya, Julius Nyerere in Tanzania, and Kenneth Kaunda in Zambia."[48]

The State Department was wary of leaders like Nkrumah. They were more comfortable with those like Nigeria's prime minister, Alhaji Sir Abukabar Tafawa Balewa, who had been knighted by the queen of England the previous January. Comparing his style with America's friends in Nigeria, the State Department memo said, "Kwame Nkrumah's anti-colonialism has more appeal to the African masses than the moderate statements of Nigerian leaders. But few decisions are made by the masses."

The long journey went through Brazzaville, Republic of the Congo, and Leopoldville, DRC in the Congos. At Leopoldville, they walked under kapioka trees lining the streets. Their nine-foot-diameter trunks permitted them to tower more than 150 feet. The trees' creamy white and pale pink flowers offered a sweet aroma almost overcoming the smell of mildew created by dead leaves and garbage piled in the steamy hot streets. Rounding a corner and turning instinctively toward music they heard, they found a hotel terrace to watch the street below. Suddenly a wagon appeared, "one in which there was a black man with a chain around his neck, on his knees, with his hands tied behind his back." It was Patrice Lumumba.[49] Lumumba, the first prime minister of the newly independent nation, had been arrested and imprisoned. A little more than a year after McGee and the others visited the Congo, Lumumba was executed, allegedly with the assistance of the American CIA.

After the Congos, the party went on to Johannesburg, South Africa; Nairobi, Kenya; Khartoum, Sudan; Tripoli, Libya; Tunis, Tunisia; and Algiers, Algeria. During a stop in Ethiopia, Emperor Haile Selassie unexpectedly boarded their plane, demanding use of their radio because rebels had cut off his communications. As they traveled the countryside, the senators met poor farmers using ancient less-than-productive techniques to grow crops. Young children without schools spent their days in the stifling heat collecting scraps such as the fallen fruit of the karite trees to take home for food. Others trudged miles carrying heavy jugs of water on their heads so that villagers might have reasonably clean water that day. McGee also met enthusiastic young revolutionaries, men and women who either had the technical skills necessary to develop their country or were anxious to learn them. In larger cities teachers and students crowded into bookless schools trying to learn English. Given the opportunity, they were hungry for the knowledge needed to move their newly independent nation into the future. Knowing JFK planned to propose the Peace Corps, McGee took notes and readied himself for that debate.

The delegation flew back to the United States in time to celebrate Christmas with their families. Soon thereafter, McGee met with the new president. Kennedy was eager to hear about the trip and to receive McGee's recommendations. The Wyoming senator urged JFK to make clear his new administration would give credence to the independence movement and distance itself from the colonial policies to which some Europeans still clung.[50]

While in Johannesburg McGee learned the sad news of the sudden death of Keith Thomson, the Republican who would have become Wyoming's junior senator in another month. When Senator O'Mahoney decided not to seek reelection in 1960, Thomson ran. He defeated former senator Frank Barrett and UW basketball legend Kenny Sailors in the GOP primary. The three-term congressmen won an easy November victory over Democrat Raymond Whitaker on November 8. However, Thomson died of a massive heart attack on December 9, 1960.

Now it fell to Democratic governor Joe Hickey to appoint a senator. Democratic Party central committees in at least ten counties and the University of Wyoming Young Democrats Club asked the governor to appoint Teno Roncalio. Ray Whitaker, the Democrat who lost to Thomson, nominated himself. Thomson's widow, Thyra, quietly lobbied for the job. Republican power broker James Griffith and Roy and Bob Peck, Republicans and publishers of the *Riverton Ranger*, encouraged the governor to appoint Tracy McCraken.

Governor Hickey implored McCraken to accept the appointment. On December 23 McCraken declined. "I know that when . . . I advised you of my decision against acceptance I was declining one of the highest honors and privileges that could be accorded one."[51]As fate would have its way, Tracy McCraken never would have served in the U.S. Senate had he accepted Governor Hickey's offer. He suddenly became seriously ill on Christmas night and died the next day.

After first telling reporters he would not take the seat, Hickey resigned the governorship so that Democratic secretary of state Jack Gage could succeed him. Governor Gage then appointed Hickey to the Senate.

Kathy Karpan, who would be elected Wyoming secretary of state in 1986, wrote a brief biography of Jack Gage. She recounted Hickey's decision, saying, "The political ramifications were enough to handicap, almost beyond redemption, any hopes of either Hickey or Gage winning election in 1962."[52] Two years later, Milward Simpson defeated Hickey, and Cliff Hansen, the UW trustee who had defended Professor McGee, defeated Gage and became governor.

In a brief span from 1960 to 1962, McGee's Wyoming Senate colleagues went from Joe O'Mahoney to Keith Thomson to Joe Hickey and finally to Milward Simpson. Through it all, McGee became Wyoming's senior senator and would remain so for the next sixteen years.

9

Searching Souls, Minds, and Spirits

Gale McGee ran for the U.S. Senate in 1958 because "the twentieth century has brought to Wyoming and the world new problems of an entirely new age in human history." As he announced his candidacy, he declared, "Men born in the nineteenth century have not been able to keep the pace which modern history has set. It's time we turned the twentieth century over to youth."[1] He was elected two years ahead of the first American president born in the twentieth century. In his inaugural address, Kennedy said, "The torch has been passed to a new generation of Americans born in this century." Yet it was a man born in the preceding century who would, in large measure, define both men's political careers as well as that of Kennedy's successor.

Ho Chi Minh was born a quarter of a century before McGee and Kennedy. Politicians like JFK and McGee summoned the heights of optimism. Ho mined the depths of nationalism. Had these men been able to understand the hopes and fears of the others, the world might have avoided a mid-twentieth-century catastrophic clash.

It is understandable that many U.S. leaders failed to perceive the aspirations of this Vietnamese revolutionary. He was a Communist at a time when American politicians were not permitted to "understand" Communists. Yet Ho declared the independence of his country using words familiar to Americans. "All men are created equal," he wrote in the September 2, 1945, Declaration of Independence of the Democratic Republic of Vietnam. "They are endowed by their Creator with certain unalienable Rights; among these are Life, Liberty, and the pursuit of Happiness."[2]

Ho traveled the world as a mess boy on a French ocean liner going ashore in the major ports of the Mediterranean and Africa. As a youthful expatriate in Paris, he knocked on Woodrow Wilson's hotel door during the 1919 Versailles Peace Conference. Ho sought recognition from the president for basic liberties of his colonized countrymen, but he was "unceremoniously shown the door." Before Kennedy or McGee learned to tie their shoes, Ho Chi Minh had "served out his apprenticeship in life, politics, and revolution."[3]

In the end, the United States saw Ho as simply another Communist. The calculation led to a conviction that, like dominoes, other nations would fall to the Communists if either China or Ho were permitted to upset the balance of power in Asia.

The evening before Kennedy's inauguration, the snow was unusually heavy. The Washington temperature was 10 degrees below freezing. In the brisk wind, it felt much colder. That evening McGee suffered a diabetic episode, and en route to the Georgetown hospital, he drove his car into a snowdrift. An ambulance was summoned to complete the trip, and he spent the night in the hospital for observation.[4]

As the morning sun spread its rays, the DC snowscape warmed only a bit. On January 20, there was considerable doubt that the McGees or anyone else would make it through the snow-clogged streets to the Capitol. McGee misplaced confidence in the family's giant 1958 Plymouth station wagon. He was certain it would go anywhere in that snow. It would not. However, the senator's administrative assistant, Joe Davis, drove an old Volvo that, with the help of National Guardsmen directing traffic and extricating stuck vehicles, made it to the senator's parking place outside the Old Senate Office Building. From there the McGees walked to the east side of the Capitol, where they joined twenty-two thousand shivering but proud Americans to witness one of our great national rituals. McGee went to his place among seating reserved for senators behind the podium where Kennedy would take the oath. Loraine and Robert sat in front of the platform in seats reserved for Senate family members. President and Mrs. Eisenhower arrived with Vice President and Mrs. Nixon. Earl Warren, the chief justice of the Supreme Court, took his place. Vice

President-elect Lyndon Johnson and Lady Bird were seated. President-elect John Kennedy and his wife, Jacqueline, followed.

Poet Robert Frost was having difficulty reading a poem he had written for the occasion. The bright sun blinded his aging eyes as cold winds whipped about his manuscript. Johnson walked to the podium and offered him a top hat to shield the sun. As the appreciative crowd applauded, the eighty-seven-year-old Frost rejected the hat, saying, "I'll just have to get through it the best I can."[5] And he did.

As Kennedy repeated the words "So help me God," the torch passed from the oldest executive to ever serve to the youngest ever elected. The twentieth century now belonged to younger leaders.

John Kennedy and Gale McGee had known one another for more than five years. They had been Senate colleagues for two years. The McGees enjoyed a comfortable friendship with the president and Mrs. Kennedy, what McGee once called an "old shoe" relationship.[6] They worked together at a time when that relationship was social as well as political. Just as the McGees had been guests in the Kennedy Georgetown home then, so it was now in the White House.

McGee enjoyed Kennedy's emphasis on physical fitness. Many of McGee's constituents joined in the craze JFK created for fifty-mile hikes, taking the trek from Cheyenne to Laramie. A number of senators joined a congressional softball league, McGee among them. In a June 18 game between the congressional and press corps teams, McGee went 2 for 2 with a double and a home run, driving in four runs before "running out of gas."[7]

Some members of Congress were put off by the lifestyle the Kennedys instilled in the White House. A Tennessee congressman complained about "all that Mozart string music and ballet dancing down there [in the White House]. He's too elegant for me. I can't talk to him."[8] That wasn't a problem for either Gale or Loraine.

The president frequently sought out McGee for conversations about issues confronting his administration. They discussed "lots of things starting to loom on the world stage."[9] Among the topics occupying their time were Vietnam and Laos, Cuba and the Soviet Union, civil rights, and the John Birch Society. McGee viewed Kennedy as an ally in moving ahead on issues that mattered to Wyoming, such as water projects, oil, gas, and coal development, controlling agricultural imports, and public land use reforms. In February, his relationship with the Kennedy team was further strengthened when his friend Mike Manatos, a former top aide to Senators Lester Hunt and Joe O'Mahoney, was appointed to JFK's White House staff to manage congressional relations.

Within a few weeks of assuming the presidency, Kennedy received a "top secret" report from Gen. Edward Lansdale. Kennedy considered Lansdale an American James Bond. Attorney General Robert Kennedy assigned him to Operation Mongoose, the spectacularly unsuccessful attempt to rid the world of Fidel Castro. The 1958 best seller *The Ugly American* portrayed a Lansdale-like figure as one of the few Americans who understood Vietnam.[10] "The novel was a warning that the United States was losing the cold war because of its ethnocentrism and arrogance."[11] Lansdale was written into the storyline as "Colonel Edwin Hillandale," someone savvy enough to know what it would take for the United States to win the war by winning the hearts and minds of the Vietnamese people.

Lansdale returned in December from an Eisenhower-requested trip to review the state of affairs in Vietnam. When Lansdale's report landed on the new president's desk, it revealed "the Viet Cong hope to win back Vietnam south of the 17th parallel this year if at all possible and [they] are much further along towards accomplishing this goal than I had realized from reading the reports received in Washington." Lansdale added an ominous comment. "The Viet Cong crowded a lot of action into the year 1960. They infiltrated thousands of armed forces into South Viet Nam, recruited local levies of military territorials and guerrillas, and undertook large-scale guerrilla and terroristic operations."[12] Kennedy was discouraged. He told an adviser that the Lansdale report was "one of the worst we've got."[13]

McGee had become familiar with Vietnam earlier than most of his colleagues. Before JFK's election, McGee burnished his Southeast Asia credentials during a visit to Vietnam and demonstrated his knowledge in a widely acclaimed Senate speech. Fewer than two years in the Senate, and McGee was already chairman of the Appropriations Committee's Subcommittee on Foreign Aid. In that capacity, he and Albert Gore Sr. (D-TN), a member of the Foreign Relations

Committee, toured the rugged northern plateau jungles as well as the Mekong River delta of Vietnam. They visited villages and talked with political leaders, farmers, and refugees. Afterward they held two days of hearings in Saigon in December 1959.[14]

Gore and McGee each saw the same things, but they didn't see things the same. Years later, Gore was on the board of directors of Occidental Petroleum, the company for whom McGee's son Robert worked. Gore told Robert he always thought it was interesting that he and Gale went on the same trip and had the same briefings, but came away with totally opposite conclusions about the war.[15]

The following February, McGee addressed the Senate, telling colleagues that "because of [South Vietnam's] resources and its key position in the vast continent of Asia, it continues to cause a critical concern in the minds of all free men." He explained the hurdles facing the new government. Dividing the nation between the north and the south resulted in nearly all of the nation's manufacturing capacity falling into the hands of the Communists. Most of the region south of the 17th parallel, the dividing line, was agrarian. McGee said South Vietnam's "achievements in crisis" should be recognized. President Ngo Dinh Diem, he believed, had brought stability and promise to the south. McGee judged American criticism of Diem as "impatient," and he implored the senators to engage in "a soul-searching study of our goals, intents, purposes, targets, and hopes in Southeast Asia."[16]

McGee's February 1960 speech received notoriety both inside and outside the Senate chambers. The day following the speech, J. William Fulbright, chairman of the Foreign Relations Committee, told McGee, "I was deeply impressed and heartened by your vigorous affirmation of what has been accomplished in Vietnam."[17] Elbridge Durbrow, then U.S. ambassador to Vietnam, sent a copy of McGee's speech to Diem, telling McGee, "I am sure [Diem] will be most appreciative of your sound analysis of the problems he and his government have to face."[18] In May, retired general John W. O'Daniel, national chairman of American Friends of Vietnam, invited McGee to join the organization's advisory committee. O'Daniel had served in Vietnam during the French occupancy. The organization he headed lobbied members of Congress for sustained U.S. involvement in Vietnam, and McGee accepted O'Daniel's invitation.[19]

McGee had taken another major step toward becoming the Senate's most effective spokesman for America's Vietnam policies, a role he would fill through the next three administrations.

McGee long advocated a Cold War strategy of employing nonmilitary strategies for winning the hearts and minds of people in the Third World. As he campaigned for Kennedy, McGee addressed a large student assembly at the University of Dallas. Following up on Kennedy's call for a Peace Corps, McGee told the audience, "We have a reason to search our souls, minds, and spirits by asking ourselves what it is we stand for, where it is we ought to be going, and how can we get there."[20] The new administration was barely a month old when McGee called for an end to the military draft. He told a convention of school administrators, "We found a way to get 12 million young Americans around the world with guns on their shoulders. Is not America big enough, strong enough, wise enough, dedicated enough, to get a million young Americans a year around the world with ideas in their heads?"[21] He wanted the draft replaced with a "Manpower Resources Board" to engage young men and women in international humanitarian work. McGee called for a "massive educational assault" in the developing world equal to the military assault of World War II.

McGee was thrilled when, on March 1, 1961, JFK signed the executive order creating the Peace Corps. Kennedy termed it "a pilot project" pending authorization and funding by Congress. On April 20, McGee addressed a crowd on the campus of Georgetown University. The title of his speech was "Africa and the Peace Corps." He told the audience that the two greatest U.S. resources are "our historic tradition of ideas and the vigor and dynamism of our youth."[22] By June, McGee and several colleagues had drafted and introduced the legislation creating the Peace Corps.[23]

The president appointed his brother-in-law, Sargent Shriver, to head the Peace Corps, asking him to lead a task force to study the idea's feasibility. Shriver accepted the position, asking for no salary. Upon being told of Shriver's appointment, McGee was ebullient. "If we had ten Sargent Shrivers, we could conquer the world."[24]

"The purpose of the Peace Corps," said Shriver to the Senate Appropriations Committee, "is to make available a pool of trained Americans to help other countries meet some of their urgent needs for skilled manpower.[25] Shriver was candid about what was being asked of the volunteers. "The work will be hard. It may be frustrating. It could be dangerous. But it will also be exciting and rewarding." It quickly proved to be dangerous. Philip Maggard was a twenty-two-year-old Peace Corps volunteer from Buffalo, Wyoming, one of the first to be sent to the Philippines. Philip taught in a small Filipino school on the Isle of Mindanao. He was killed near there in the crash of a small airplane on March 2, 1963. McGee announced the death to his Senate colleagues, saying that Maggard "exemplified a new and dedicated grade of young Americans who are giving of their best to extend the variety and strength of our free way of life to the far corners of the earth."[26]

Largely because of his responsibilities to the Appropriations Committee, McGee visited more Peace Corps sites around the world than anyone except Shriver. McGee never gave up his firm commitment to the lofty principles upholding international service, urging his fellow Americans not to allow those principles to "die on the vine." He said they were "inspired by our Founding Fathers on July 4, 1776, the most exciting, explosive idea in all of human history."[27]

New Deal Democrats like Kennedy, Johnson, and McGee brought to public office a sense that the world could be developed, nations democratized, and international economies saved just as the United States had done with programs like the Tennessee Valley Authority. Massive projects along rivers in the southern United States brought low-cost electricity, creating jobs, political and social stability, and economic development. It could be done, they believed, along the Mekong River delta of Vietnam or the Amazon of South America. After all, the Marshall Plan and its combination of loans and grants had saved postwar Europe just as the U.S.-led Government and Relief in Occupied Areas program (GARIA) had restored Japan, Germany, and Austria. The political ramifications were as important as the human benefits. Massive U.S. aid held Stalin at bay in the early years of the Cold War in South America.

Financial aid to South America was not a new idea. For the previous two decades, the United States had operated a small technical assistance program there. As a candidate in 1960, JFK spoke often of his concern about the plight of South Americans. He felt the United States had ignored their poverty, which drowned the hopes of millions while we bankrolled corrupt dictators. Remembering FDR's Good Neighbor Policy, Kennedy asked speechwriter Ted Sorensen to come up with a name for a new South American initiative. Sorensen included the phrase "a new alliance for progress" in Kennedy's inaugural address.[28]

At the urging of the White House, McGee and fellow senators Frank Moss of Utah, Clair Engle of California, and Stephen Young of Ohio went to South America at the end of the year "to gauge the conditions in Latin America which would be underpinning the President's new 'Alliance for Progress' and to evaluate the attitudes of local people toward the program." The senators visited eight countries, becoming fully aware of the Cold War implications of the Alliance. McGee bemoaned the amount of Communist literature at bookstands in marketplaces and an increasing number of "Communist Party agents whose primary tasks, skillfully carried out, are aimed at preying upon unhappiness, suffering, and hopelessness." McGee reported to the president that there were "great expectations" for the success of the Alliance for Progress, what the South Americans called in Spanish "Alianza." He felt there was a possibility that "Latin American can develop through evolution, not revolution." He cautioned, "The people of Latin America have heard these words before." He urged JFK to promptly fund projects that could demonstrate early progress.[29]

McGee's growing influence on foreign policy was exhibited in 1963 when he undertook a study of America's beleaguered foreign aid efforts. The Agency for International Development (USAID) was under constant attack from conservatives who could point to its fiscal problems and administrative failures. They argued that these problems justified ending all foreign aid.

In late 1963, McGee led the Appropriations Committee's inquiry into foreign aid at the request of committee chairman Carl Hayden. According to John A. Sanbrailo, a former USAID mission director who has been involved in foreign assistance efforts since serving as a Peace Corps volunteer in the 1960s, McGee's study was the first comprehensive review of USAID. Sanbrailo considers McGee's 1963 report one of the truly important documents in the history of foreign aid.[30]

The McGee report acknowledged both the "severe criticism" and the "monumental tasks" facing the agency. At the time, USAID employed more than 18,600 persons working on projects in seventy countries with an economic development budget of $2.6 billion and $1.3 billion in its military assistance budget.[31] Only 4 percent of a total federal budget of $92.5 billion in foreign aid was, nonetheless, a huge political target.

McGee admitted much of the criticism was warranted. However, he concluded, "In spite of the numerous headlines chronicling disappointments in our foreign-aid efforts, there are many indications that substantial additional benefits to the gains already made will accrue to the United States and to the free world from such efforts."[32]

McGee attributed congressional and public unhappiness to a combination of factors including the failure of beneficiary nations to appreciate the assistance, the inherent difficulty in measuring success, and insufficient public knowledge of what had been accomplished. "It is a well-published fact that we have spent over $100 billion in foreign aid," he reported, "but too little is known about what has been received in return." Twenty-five percent of the total provided in the form of loans had already been repaid. One-third was used to purchase military equipment "to serve well the needs of our allies" who no longer fully depended on U.S. armed forces. Ten billion dollars bought agricultural products, saving "tens of millions of people from hunger or starvation." U.S. aid permitted many nations to expand foreign trade to the benefit of American companies. Technical assistance programs improved public health, education, and the standard of living throughout the world. Finally, McGee's report noted, "Most of these countries are our allies. They are free and strong," and "the free world has maintained a comfortable balance of power against Communism and its ambitions."[33]

McGee's USAID report was released a week after Kennedy's assassination. Although JFK did not have an opportunity to act on McGee's recommendations, the Kennedy years were the source of several key developments in international affairs. USAID was initiated by JFK in 1961, as were the Peace Corps and the Alliance of Progress. McGee's fingerprints can be found on the history of each, which was one reason that the John Birch Society detested him.

Who was John Birch? Like most mortals whose stories are used posthumously for a cause, it is difficult to know what is true and what is

myth. The "biography" employed by Robert Welch to inspire followers claims Birch was the son of missionaries, born in India in 1918. He
graduated from a Baptist seminary in Fort Worth, Texas, and served
as a member of Gen. Claire Lee Chennault's World War II "Flying
Tigers." Days after v-J Day, Birch was carrying out a mission in China
when he was discovered by a group of Communist guerillas. He was
shot and then bayoneted. Welch's story takes on the characteristics of
myth when he "quotes" Birch's dying words, which Welch, of course,
did not hear personally: "It doesn't make much difference what happens to me, but it is of utmost importance that my country learns
now whether these people are friend or foe." Welch considered the
martyred Birch "the first American casualty of World War III."[34]

The John Birch Society (JBS) was not organized well enough to
mobilize nationally before McGee's 1958 Senate race. By 1961 he and
JFK anticipated that would change by the time each sought reelection in 1964.

It seems odd JBS would target Gale McGee. The senator consistently
spoke against communism, warning of the threat before and after his
1958 election victory. He balanced social liberalism with a strapping
anti-Soviet position. But that doesn't account for a key Birch tenant.
It was Welch's "principal of reversal." Welch was convinced that "in
the conspiracy of history, things are never what they seem, and are
often the opposite."[35] For example, Welch warned JBS followers against
trusting Richard Nixon, despite his reputation as one of the country's
strongest Communist foes. They scorned the men Gale McGee most
admired, including journalist Walter Lippmann, Martin Luther King,
Chief Justice Earl Warren, and the president of the United Automobile
Workers Union, Walter Reuther. It was, therefore, easy for the Birchers to distrust a liberal like McGee. As McGee spoke more often and
more fiercely against them, they painted a larger target on his back.

McGee decided to do unto them before they did unto him. As
Bircher influence grew in Wyoming, the senator was among the first
national figures to challenge them. The media, alerted to the issue
by McGee's speeches in the Senate and around the country, began to
scrutinize Welch and his tactics. The *New York Times* called McGee "a
leading foe of right-wing extremism."[36] Drew Pearson said McGee was
a "two-fisted former professor who is hitting back" at the Birchers.[37]

The host of a new television program was impressed with McGee's knowledge of the JBS and his willingness to talk openly about it. David Susskind, famous for his flowing silver hair and baritone voice, was far enough to the left of American politics that the FBI routinely monitored him. Susskind interviewed guests ranging from presidents and prime ministers to actresses and paupers. When he learned of McGee's willingness to do battle with the JBS, Susskind invited him to appear on *Open End*, a combative talk show so named because it had no scheduled ending time. It continued until that night's discussion ran its course. A single evening of *Open End* could last for hours as Susskind intentionally pitted guests against one another.[38]

Four were on the "fight card" that night. It was three against one. In one corner were JBS founder Robert Welch, Congressman John Rousselot of California, an outspoken Bircher, and Tom Anderson, a conservative known as "the Will Rogers of the right." In the other corner was the liberal Gale McGee. As they waited to go on that night, Susskind asked McGee if he felt the program had been loaded against him. The senator replied, "Well, I wouldn't think so. They probably think it takes that many of them to keep up with one of us."[39] It was the first of several debates between McGee and the JBS lineup.

On April 12, 1961, just a few days before the *Open End* debate, McGee had gone to the Senate floor to make an *ad hominen* attack on the JBS founder. He quoted Welch: "Protestant ministers do not become Communists, but Communists do become Protestant ministers." He called Welch's statement "a reckless slur and smear" and told his colleagues, "It is time that we bring squarely to the mat the issues between our society and these twisted, distorted, sick people who seek to charge with conspiracy all who disagree with them."[40]

In the early 1960s McGee first noticed "the hardening of lines" and the "emergence of name-calling." John Birch chapters were popping up across Wyoming, and Robert Welch trained followers to find their way into every community through existing civic structures. "Join your local PTA at the beginning of the school year, get your conservative friends to do likewise. And go to work to take it over. When you get your local PTA group straightened out, move up the ladder as soon as you can to exert wider influence."[41] It wasn't long before Birch disciples in Wyoming followed that advice. Former governor

Milward Simpson spoke to the PTA in Cody, his hometown, about the need for mental health services, saying the statistics show that one in six people need mental health services. The local John Birch Society members erupted, asserting that the governor was claiming they were mentally ill. They heckled Simpson until he ended the meeting.[42]

The Birchers ran full-page ads soliciting Wyoming members and saturated local radio stations with right-wing programming. With little television coverage across much of the state and only weekly newspapers in most communities, radio provided most of what little electronic entertainment and news were available to most people. If all they had was that one radio station, the radical right was determined to dominate what people could hear. And they did. Most station owners offered it to their listeners as "a public service." A few radio stations were paid to run the programming.

The Reverend Carl McIntire is an example. A "fire and brimstone" radio preacher, he used the Bible to make his case against communism, mixing of the races, fluoride treatment of water, sex education in the schools, and liberals in general. *The Twentieth Century Reformation Hour* could be heard on more than 600 stations nationwide, including a few in rural Wyoming that paid him a thousand dollars a month for his taped program.[43] Another was H. L. Hunt, a billionaire who owned the Hoodoo Ranch near Cody.[44] Hunt peddled a fifteen-minute daily radio show called *Life Line* to hundreds of radio stations, including several in Wyoming. The program warned Americans daily of the threat posed by communism. At one time he was "the largest, single cattleman" in Wyoming.[45]

McGee told the president, "It would be difficult to exaggerate how the concentration of these programs in limited population areas ultimately captures the public mind, even among well-meaning citizens."[46] He raised his complaints about the constant barrage of right-wing programming to Wyoming broadcasters. One disagreed. "Senator," he objected cluelessly, "you're unfair in accusing Wyoming broadcasters of carrying too much right-wing material. Some of us make a conscious effort to balance it with more liberal content. I, for example, carry Paul Harvey on my station six days a week."[47] Excerpts of a broadcast entitled "If I Were the Devil (A Warning for the Nation)" show the kind of programming the radio station owner thought "balanced" the "right-wing material" his station otherwise ran. "If I were the Devil," said Paul Harvey, "I should set about however necessary to take over the United States." Harvey saw the devil in the decisions of the Supreme Court, saying that if he were the devil, "I would evict God from the courthouse, and then from the school house, and then from the houses of Congress."[48]

McGee was the most outspoken member of Congress engaging Birchers in debates around the country. Often it was the same lineup as the Susskind show. He debated Rousselot, Welch, and Anderson in Boston, Chicago, St. Louis, and Kansas City.[49] McGee intended to place himself directly in their crosshairs, and conservative groups including the Wyoming chapters of the John Birch Society set a goal to defeat McGee in 1964. In an article titled "Conspiracy USA," published in *Look* magazine, one of McGee's colleagues, Frank Church of Idaho, described the confrontations his Wyoming colleague experienced. "In Wyoming, Sen. Gale McGee, an outspoken critic of the Radical Right, found youngsters in Laramie and Cheyenne on a house-to-house canvas distributing mimeographed leaflets. They were instructed to say, 'This man is an enemy agent. Here are the facts about Communist McGee.' The Senator's wife, Loraine, had her husband's campaign cards grabbed from her hands, torn into pieces, thrown at her feet, and then spat upon."[50]

The JBS state president, whom McGee did not name in an interview recalling this incident, was an old duck-hunting friend. Although they had spent hours together in duck blinds, his friend now refused to accept McGee's phone calls. After McGee's 1964 reelection, the fellow apologized to him. "I was sure taken in by those rascals. I thought they were good Americans trying to find spies and Communists and I was helping. They just took me in and I want to apologize."[51] Others weren't nearly so kind as to simply refuse to take his phone calls. In Big Piney, a JBS member spat on him, and things were stolen from his car. On a freezing Halloween night in Douglas, while McGee spoke to a local gathering, someone squirted shaving cream on his station wagon. "Our car was absolutely covered, totally." It froze, and they had a hard time removing it from the windows so that he and Loraine could drive on to the next rally.[52]

Kathy Karpan, Wyoming's secretary of state from 1987 to 1995, was a cub reporter for the *Cody Enterprise*. She recalled the time McGee came to speak to a gathering of Park County businesspeople in the early 1960s. When word got out that McGee was coming, a group of Birchers, mostly local ranchers, planned to confront him. They were angry about McGee's support for social programs they believed amounted to socialism. McGee supporters told him to be prepared for a tough outing. He was. No sooner had he been introduced than several in the crowd began stomping their feet and creating a disturbance. McGee asked them to relax, assuring them he would take their questions and hear them out. But he wanted to make a few remarks first. The crowd settled down as McGee pulled a stack of papers from his briefcase.

"I have here some public records. No secrets here. All of these are open to anyone who wants to see them. What I have is a list of Park County folks who are receiving money from the federal government, agricultural subsidies." McGee began reading names and the amounts received, and he spoke of the hypocrisy of the Bircher claims that the federal government was interfering too much in people's lives and wasting tax dollars, while many of their members "were usually the first in line to get federal funds." Several of those on the list were in the room preparing to verbally attack McGee for his "socialist" votes. Many of them quietly left, and the threatened protest dissipated.[53]

On another occasion in Cody, a group of Birch supporters threatened physical violence. "Several of my former students in the audience, three or four of them had been football players at Wyoming . . . put together a flying wedge . . . in order to get me out of there safely." In the lobby of Casper's Henning Hotel, the senator was grabbed "by some husky cattlemen. They were very threatening." They raised their voices and clenched their fists. McGee's staff intervened "and made sure there was no violence, but it was sure a hairy moment."[54]

Incidents like that led McGee to warn the president of what he thought was the insidious nature of the right wing's appeal to "our population in the West [who] already believe the extreme right-wing line before the current group of extremists invented it."[55]

In 1963, he cautioned JFK not to sideline the extremists too early. McGee thought the issue "may well turn out to be the winning issue for 1964."

One of the most difficult issues of the time was civil rights. "In 1953, John Kennedy was mildly and quietly in favor of civil rights legislation as a political necessity consistent with his moral instincts." That's how his biographer, Ted Sorensen, described JFK's early relationship with the issue. "In 1963, he was deeply and fervently committed to the cause of human rights as a moral necessity consistent with his political instincts."[56]

James Farmer headed the Congress for Racial Equality (CORE) and organized the Freedom Rides of the early 1960s. He felt Kennedy was "ignorant on civil rights in particular and blacks in general at the time he became president." Farmer remembered that in the 1960 campaign, JFK said to Jackie Robinson, the first African American to play Major League Baseball, "I don't know any Negroes. Would you introduce me to some?" Close friend and adviser Arthur Schlesinger, who served inside the Kennedy White House, was kinder but equally revealing. "I think we all underestimated the moral dynamism that the civil rights movement was acquiring by the early 1960s."[57]

Gale McGee was similarly unaware of the centrality of the issue and its "moral dynamism" in his pre-Senate days. He was born in Lincoln, Nebraska, and by 1930, 90 percent of Nebraska's black population had moved to Lincoln or Omaha. Only a handful of African Americans lived in Norfolk, Nebraska, at the time the McGees did. The same was true as McGee moved to Crofton and Kearney to teach. It was no different in Wyoming. Peruse the University of Wyoming yearbooks from the time Dr. McGee arrived in Laramie in 1946 until he left in 1958. The number of African Americans at the university in those years can be counted on one hand. At the time the 1950 census was compiled, less than 1 percent of Wyoming's population was black. That number actually decreased before 1960.[58] Though they were few and the discrimination they faced was seldom publicized, African Americans living in Wyoming felt its sting even if many whites failed to notice.

Should Gale McGee have been more aware of the civil rights problems in Wyoming by the time he was elected to the U.S. Senate? He was hardly the only Wyoming politician to be unaware in those days. In 1961, the Wyoming Advisory Committee to the U.S. Commission on Civil Rights held a hearing on discrimination in the state, but no one bothered to show up.[59] That same year, the Cheyenne branch of the NAACP invited sixty-three community leaders to a forum to discuss what could be done to reduce the level of race-based discrimination in the capital city. Only eight attended.[60]

Charles C. Diggs, a member of the U.S. House of Representatives from Michigan, wrote to Wyoming governor Milward Simpson in 1957, describing a survey undertaken by the Committee on Human Rights for the Western States. "Places of public accommodation in Cheyenne and Laramie, Wyoming, discourage and refuse service to Negroes. Repeated complaints have been made by Negro airmen at the Francis E. Warren Air Base near Cheyenne." In response, Simpson assured him that there were only "isolated instances."[61]

The governor's assurances were consistent with the views of Wyoming's political leaders, but they were inconsistent with the experiences of its black citizens. "Many Wyomingites, of whom some 90 percent to 97 percent have always been white, do not remember witnessing racism in Wyoming, and do not believe it existed. But it did and does." Historian Todd Guenther chronicled the horrors faced by blacks in the earlier times. An article he wrote for the Wyoming Historical Society in 2009 documents the extraordinary number of lynchings perpetrated against black men in Wyoming in the early twentieth century. "Some people expected a different reality in Wyoming, which boasted the nickname the Equality State." Guenther asserted, "A black man's life wasn't worth much in the Equality State."[62]

Between 1910 and 1920, five Wyoming blacks were lynched, a per capita lynching rate 62 times higher than the national average and 123 times that of Mississippi. Of the surrounding states, none lynched men of color except Nebraska, where one was hanged. In the 1920s, the Ku Klux Klan organized in several Wyoming communities, including, according to Guenther's chronicles, Sheridan, Casper, Torrington, Riverton, Shoshoni, and Lander. "All across the state, businesses posted signs in their front windows saying, 'No Indians, No Mexicans, No Negroes.'"[63]

In 1949, Harriet Elizabeth Byrd was a twenty-three-year-old college graduate. She was also black. Mrs. Byrd applied for a teaching job in Cheyenne. "The State Superintendent of Public Instruction refused Byrd's application because whites didn't want black teachers disciplining their children, and thus, Wyoming did not hire 'Negro' teachers."[64] Mrs. Byrd couldn't get a classroom teaching job until 1959, the year McGee was first sworn into the U.S. Senate. She later served with distinction in the Wyoming legislature from 1981 until 1992, sponsoring a number of bills targeting discrimination.

The problem finally caught the attention of influential white people in 1957. University of Wyoming historians Kim Ibach and William Howard Moore wrote about the straw that nearly broke the camel's back. "Two prominent Wyomingites watched as an African American serviceman and his spouse seated themselves in the little cafe at Cheyenne's Plains Hotel in 1954. The couple sipped water and read the menus. Suddenly a waitress snatched away the menus. The manager entered the scene and ushered the two African Americans out of the restaurant. Teno Roncalio and Dr. Francis Barrett discussed the shameful incident they had witnessed."[65]

Roncalio, who later served ten years as Wyoming's congressman, was then chairman of the Wyoming Democratic Party, and Dr. Barrett was the son of Senator Frank Barrett. The two reported the story to Governor Simpson. As a result, Simpson proposed a civil rights bill drafted by Roncalio, and Wyoming enacted the law in 1957. "No person of good deportment shall be denied the right of life, liberty, pursuit of happiness, or the necessities of life because of race, color, creed, or national origin."[66]

As Gale McGee prepared to enter the Senate, his education on civil rights began in earnest. Before he took the oath, a December 21, 1958, letter from Mrs. C. T. King of Knoxville, Tennessee, advised McGee that she had relatives in Wyoming. Frank Barrett, she warned, "lost his Senate seat because of his stand on civil rights. He evidently forgot that there had been a great flow of southerners to the Wyoming oil fields and they certainly voted against him. Integration can never be forced on the white people of the South regardless of what the law says."[67] However, civil rights were never an issue in the 1958 campaign between McGee and Barrett.

Will Maslow of the American Jewish Congress wrote in January 1959 seeking McGee's support for civil rights legislation. The Wyoming lawmaker assured Maslow of his support, although he added, "I would not number myself among those who wish to rush headlong toward a rigid enforcement of integration." McGee was clear. He preferred what he called "a calm and orderly process."[68] He found anything but, as the civil rights struggle entered the late 1950s and moved into the decisive battles of the 1960s. Although many hoped there could be a calm and orderly process for integration of schools following the unanimous Supreme Court decision in *Brown vs. Board of Education of Topeka,* it was not to be.[69]

Wyoming promptly repealed its statute "providing separate schools for colored people."[70] Other states, particularly in the South, chose to defy the Supreme Court. The enforcement of *Brown* took the form of continual battles between the federal and state governments. State National Guard units, routinely under the control of governors, were nationalized to force entry of black students into schools across the South. Bus boycotts started in Montgomery, Alabama, to fight "Jim Crow" laws affording front seats to whites only. Blacks and their supporters conducted sit-ins at segregated lunch counters, and the "Freedom Riders" rode commercial buses into the South. Thugs waited with clubs to beat them at bus stops along the way. African American churches were firebombed and black leaders assassinated. Racist policemen turned fire hoses and dogs on women and children who were protesting institutional discrimination. Civil rights leaders made certain these events received maximum publicity. McGee's road to becoming a full-blown activist was paved in part by what he saw on television. His reversal from refusing to number himself "among those who wish to rush head-long toward a rigid enforcement of integration" advanced during the hearings on civil rights legislation before the Commerce Committee.

After receiving considerable criticism from his own party for suggesting weak civil rights legislation, President Kennedy sent a far bolder bill to Congress on June 19, 1963. The bill prohibited most literacy tests for voting, allowed the U.S. attorney general to file suits to integrate recalcitrant schools, and cut federal funding for programs discriminating on the basis of race. The toughest and most controversial provision addressed public accommodations, prohibiting discrimination against people of color by hotels, motels, restaurants, and all other retail businesses. That put the bill within the jurisdiction of the Senate Commerce Committee, where proponents of the public accommodations legislation quoted Kennedy's message. Discrimination in restaurants, motels, and retail businesses, the president said, was a "daily insult" to Negroes.

Secretary of State Dean Rusk testified, calling racial discrimination a matter of national security. Rusk talked about the extent to which the Soviet Union capitalized on American racial problems in their quest to win the Cold War in African nations. But, he said, "It is not my view that we should resolve these problems here at home merely in order to look good abroad." Rusk testified, "We must try to eliminate discrimination due to race, color, or religion, not to make others think better of us but because it is incompatible with the great ideals to which our democratic society is dedicated."

Despite Rusk's concerns, southerners contended the legislation was "Communistic" and "would please Castro and Khrushchev." John Pastore of Rhode Island questioned a southern attorney whom South Carolina senator Strom Thurmond had invited to testify as a constitutional expert. "Do I understand you correctly then that your philosophy implies that Negroes are not first-class citizens?" The witness replied, "Which is superior, a Hereford cow or a Holstein?" The same witness claimed to have proof that "the Negro brain" is smaller than that of a Caucasian.[71]

Listening to the testimony day after day had a profound impact on McGee. He had been a member of the Congressional Country Club since shortly after his arrival in Washington, but he abruptly ended his membership upon learning that blacks were barred from the club.

Ultimately, the Commerce Committee approved the legislation and sent it to the full Senate. On November 22, 1963, the bill was still awaiting a final vote.

In his January 1962 State of the Union address, President Kennedy had ventured into the political quicksand that underlay any president's effort to reform health care. Franklin Roosevelt and Harry Truman had both tried, and each had failed. JFK's proposal was more limited, targeting only the elderly. "In matters of health," he told Congress, "no piece of unfinished business is more important or more urgent than the enactment under the social security system of health insurance for the aged."[72] Two years earlier, McGee had introduced a "Retired Persons Medical Insurance Act" proposing a system of prepaid health insurance for men over sixty-five and women over sixty-two years of age.[73] Senators Kennedy and Humphrey sponsored similar legislation during the same Congress.

Almost immediately after President Kennedy's bill was put forward, the proposal's opponents, including the American Medical Association, called it "socialized medicine." The fact that this proposal was tied to the popular social security system gave the Democrats a defense. McGee, one of the bill's floor managers, spoke to the issue during a lengthy July 9, 1962, debate shortly before a final Senate vote. McGee said the proposal had ignited "one of the most active and acrimonious debates that has occurred in many years."[74] He set out to address what he thought were the misconceptions of the legislation's opponents.

When the notion was raised that the bill constituted "socialized medicine," the former history professor was ready. "To paraphrase a famous historian, history repeats itself when Senators fall for the same scare words over and over." He told his colleagues that doctors in his state were sending people door to door to tell constituents to "write your Senator and tell him you don't want socialized medicine." He urged the bill's opponents to "face an idea as an idea and address the problem at hand to see if we can conquer the problem that threatens to weaken the fiber of our society."

That problem, as McGee defined it, was that most of the nation's 17 million senior citizens could not afford health insurance or hospital care. "We are trying to make it possible for an individual American to hold up his head, knowing that he has a chance to enjoy retirement out of a retirement reserve without that reserve being eroded by the severity of a lengthy stay in a hospital."[75]

The day after McGee's Senate stand, Kennedy staffer Larry O'Brien told the president he thought they could win by a slim 51–49 margin. Instead, Kennedy's Medicare bill died 51–49.[76] McGee was most disappointed when several of his Democratic friends voted against the bill, including Mike Monroney of Oklahoma, George Smathers of Florida, and John Sparkman of Alabama. McGee excused them. "They were under constant threats from very conservative interests in their states, and they had to make a decision to vote against their own judgment."[77]

Ted Sorensen said the president "never got over the disappointment of this defeat." Nonetheless, Kennedy went back to work immediately to get a compromise with the powerful chairman of the House Ways and Means Committee, Wilbur Mills of Arkansas. The two announced they had reached a deal on the morning of November 22, 1963.[78] Medicare would have to wait for the Johnson administration.

It was September 1962, a little more than a month before the world knew the Soviets were placing missiles in Cuba. McGee opened an envelope containing an unsolicited but intriguing letter. A Del Rio, Texas, lawyer claimed he had received a letter from inside Cuba informing him that Russian ships were coming and going from the island, dropping off soldiers and supplies. "We can see a string of cars loaded with tanks, machine guns, and antiaircraft guns, and they hide them along the highway in the brush."[79] McGee's files do not include a response. Perhaps he thought the letter writer was a crackpot, but apparently the Texas lawyer knew something. A month later, Kennedy was shown surveillance photos of missile sites being installed ninety miles from the Florida coast.

McGee had no idea why the Texas lawyer chose to inform him of the letter he had received from Cuba, but likely it was because of McGee's outspokenness on the Cuban Revolution. Earlier in 1962, he had appeared on the *David Susskind Show* to discuss Cuba. McGee was a harsh critic of the Castro regime. He and Frank Church made an inspection of U.S. military facilities at the Guantanamo Naval Base in Cuba at the end of September 1962. During their visit, McGee and Church, more playfully than defiantly, stood at the boundary where each placed one foot inside Cuba.[80] McGee praised security measures, saying, "The U.S. policy of 'watchful waiting' will pay off in the long run."[81]

Thanks to LBJ, McGee avoided the sort of embarrassment experienced by Church when, upon his return, he issued a newsletter to his Idaho constituents assuring them that Cuba posed no threat. The newsletter arrived in mailboxes the same day Kennedy announced the beginning of the crisis.[82] Soon after the president was informed of the missiles in Cuba, his vice president was traveling with McGee in Wyoming. Johnson was there to support the fledgling Senate campaign of his old friend Joe Hickey. During a short flight from Casper to Riverton, Johnson took McGee aside. Johnson was aware of McGee's public statements on Cuba. McGee had once referred to Castro as "a pipsqueak," and he discounted the threat posed by the Cuban dictator. McGee said the hijackings of U.S. airliners to Havana had little if anything to do with the Cuban government. In August 1961, he strongly urged the United States not to allow itself to be provoked into a war with Cuba.[83]

Johnson told McGee to be careful of any further discussion of Cuban issues. Without explanation, he said the nation "may be skirting on the edges of a war" and warned that the Cuban problem was soon "going to blow up."[84] A few days later, on October 22, Kennedy announced the discovery of Soviet missiles in Cuba, making public the Cuban missile crisis. Kennedy also announced a naval "quarantine on all offensive military equipment" headed for the island. McGee returned to Washington the following day for a top secret briefing.[85]

For the next week, the world teetered on the brink of a Russian-American nuclear war. But on October 28, it ended peacefully when Nikita Khrushchev agreed to remove the missiles.

In the summer of 1963, Wyoming and the nation faced the threat of an economy-crippling railroad strike. As many as 4,000 Wyoming rail workers were preparing to be idled and walk a picket line, 1,000 in Cheyenne alone.[86] Warren Magnuson of Washington, chairman of the Senate Commerce Committee, feared such a work stoppage would "paralyze the economy, throw millions of nonparticipants involuntarily out of work, impair the national defense, and have adverse and possibly disastrous effects on public health."[87] The president persuaded the parties to delay a strike so that a "blue-ribbon panel could review the dispute and recommend legislation."[88] Hours ahead of the threatened strike, the Senate grappled with the matter, and McGee found himself in the middle of the battle.

As the clock ticked toward the deadline, it was McGee who found middle ground. He was especially close to organized labor but recognized the fears of both sides that the Senate might impose a solution that would become a precedent and force binding arbitration on future labor disputes. At the eleventh hour, McGee offered a solution. His proposal contrasted with JFK's, which McGee and others worried would set "a precedent for throwing other major labor disputes into the laps of federal boards."[89] He proposed a settlement limiting arbitration to the primary issues and giving the unions and carriers time to cool off and settle the matter through normal collective bargaining procedures. On August 27, and after a lengthy debate during which McGee skillfully defended both collective bargaining rights and the need to resolve this matter without a work stoppage, the Senate voted 75–17 to adopt the McGee amendments. There would be no nationwide railroad strike.

An undated newspaper column clipped so cleanly it doesn't identify the newspaper in which it appeared gathers dust in the "McGee, Gale W." file of the U.S. Senate Historical Office in Washington. The byline is that of nationally syndicated conservative columnist Holmes Alexander. The headline reads, "Sen. McGee Was Rail Hero." Holmes said McGee was a "hard core liberal who seldom gets a hurrah from this corner, but this time he deserves it from the nation. He looked good in there on the railroad dispute. In fact, he looked like a statesman." Despite this success, America's growing involvement in Vietnam was never far in the background.

Carl Hayden, chairman of the Senate Appropriations Committee, looked at the numbers and didn't like what he saw. Without the American people knowing what was going on in Southeast Asia, Congress and the president had spent billions of their tax dollars in that part of the world. Hayden wasn't sure what they had received in return. In late 1962 he asked McGee, Church, and Moss to conduct an inquiry.

The trio left in November for a lengthy trip taking them to Indonesia, Malaya, Laos, the Philippines, Guam, Korea, Taiwan, and Vietnam. McGee came away from a visit to Indonesia "feeling hopeful for her future." He thought that nation, then with the fifth largest population in the world, would guard its independence from communism.[90] In Malaya they visited villages "enclosed in barbed wire and protected by one armored car. This," McGee said, "broke the backs of the Reds." He compared these villages to the "strategic hamlets" of South Vietnam. Gale and Loraine rode an elephant across a large, shallow lake as they toured Angkor Wat and the surrounding temples in Cambodia. He called them and Buddhist monuments they saw "the greatest spectacle in the world," adding, "The ruins in Rome or in Egypt are dwarfed by comparison." The delegation traveled next to the island of Quemoy, a subject of intense debate in the 1960 campaign. They arrived intentionally on an even-numbered day because "the Communists still bombard it on odd-numbered days with 800 guns zeroed in on its tiny area." The McGees met privately with Chiang Kai-shek and Madame Chiang. "We had the feeling of literally sitting with a few pages of history as we talked with them."

McGee met with South Vietnam's president, Ngo Dinh Diem, in Saigon as the trip continued. They talked about one of Diem's methods of reducing Viet Cong (vc) terrorism in rural areas, the "strategic hamlet" program. In order to limit vc access to rural populations, Diem ordered thousands of peasant farmer families to be relocated into villages. There, it was thought, they could be better protected, and the enemy soldiers would have less opportunity to either recruit or terrorize them.

The senators toured a few of the newly created hamlets. Traveling on a new Army Caribou aircraft, they got a good look at the jungle and mountains out of the opened rear hatch. Switching to helicopters and guarded by machine gunners, the group made its way to one of the strategic hamlets where the Montagnard tribes, or "mountain people," lived. "Such dirty, filthy people they are," McGee wrote home. "Scarcely removed from animals, the women were bare from the waist up and the men from the waist down."

The hamlet, with its barbed wire and "pointed sticks" encirclement, reminded the senator "of the old west movie stockades on the frontier." After a brief inspection, McGee reported, "There is no question that the strategic hamlet program is succeeding." However, human rights abuses arising from the strategic hamlet program were at the heart of complaints the senators heard about the Diem government. McGee found the "slowness of fundamental changes in social and economic democracy remains understandable in light of the harassing activities of the Viet Cong."[91]

Finally, the delegation made its way to the Philippines where, at the U.S. embassy in Manila, a woman holding a "McGee for Me" button greeted the party. She was the ambassador's wife, and she had attended a campaign rally when her son-in-law, Governor Robert Meyner of New Jersey, came to Cheyenne to back McGee's election.

Upon their return, McGee wrote the group's final report. Its fundamental finding was that "the shadow of Communist China, which falls across the entire area, is the most dominant single factor today."[92] The size of China's military forces and its ambitions worried the senators and the leaders of each of the nations they visited. Each believed the biggest threat to Southeast Asia, and perhaps the world, was the potential for Chinese expansion. From that time forward, the common thread running through much of U.S. policy in Vietnam was the question of "what will China do?"

More optimistic, however, were the group's findings following a few days in Vietnam. They found that guerrilla warfare in South Vietnam had "hit its zenith." The senators had been persuaded that the counterguerrilla warfare initiated by the South Vietnamese army and its U.S. advisers was "on the right track."[93]

Unbeknownst to the three senators, Kennedy's policymakers were operating with different intelligence. A Special National Intelligence Estimate from August 1960 was dire. It warned that "Viet Cong terrorism had continued to intensify. In the first five months of 1960, 780 government officials and sympathizers were assassinated by insurgents. Since January armed attacking units had been operating over wider areas than at any time since 1954. Support from North Vietnam appears to have increased over the past several months. In particular, senior cadres and military supplies such as communications equipment are believed to be moving south through Laos and Cambodia and by junk along the eastern coastline."[94]

The month before the Senate delegation departed, the Joint Chiefs of Staff urged Kennedy to put combat troops into Vietnam. In their view, "The time is past when action short of intervention could reverse the rapidly worsening situation."[95] The Senate was not aware of the secret conversations being held in the White House.

McGee discussed Southeast Asia at the Pentagon's Defense Strategy Seminar on July 19, 1963. He had already been to Vietnam twice in his first term. He compared the U.S. role with that of a policeman. "A policeman finds it very difficult to go on the offensive. He usually has to wait until a crime has been committed, or is about to be committed, and then he is free to act." He called on those who were advising Kennedy to be more aggressive.

His words reflected the ambivalence of the Kennedy White House. McGee acknowledged a growing U.S. presence in combat situations and predicted heavier costs and casualties. "This has not only cost us dearly in money. More importantly, it is costing us dearly in lives." Even so, he said, "It's important that we take the risk, that we be willing to pay the price to win in this kind of ugly, dirty warfare so characteristic of the jungle of Southeast Asia." McGee said the price that the United States had already paid in Vietnam "ought to haunt us every night."[96]

Soon after President Kennedy died on that awful November day, his successor escalated the war as historians began escalating the debate over what Kennedy would have done if he had lived. David Talbot is one of the historians looking carefully at their question. His 2007 book, *Brothers: The Hidden History of the Kennedy Years*, describes a March 2006 forum at the Kennedy Presidential Library. Former president Jimmy Carter appeared, adding his views. "My understanding, as a young nonpolitician, I was just a peanut farmer then, was that the commitment to go to Vietnam was made basically by the Kennedy Administration. . . . It was initiated by President Kennedy." Ted Sorensen, the former Kennedy speechwriter, was present to hear these assessments of his boss's intentions. He assured the audience that Kennedy had no intention of escalating the war. "JFK listened to his hawkish advisers," Sorensen said, "but he never did what they wanted."[97] Kennedy biographer Robert Dallek quoted presidential adviser Kenneth O'Donnell's account of how annoyed Kennedy had first been with Senate majority leader Mike Mansfield (D-MT) when he publicly said that the United States should withdraw its troops. O'Donnell overheard a conversation between JFK and Mansfield in May 1963.

Kennedy said that he "now agreed with the senator's thinking on the need for a complete withdrawal from Vietnam." However, Kennedy told Mansfield he could not do so until after the 1964 election.[98]

The 1971 release of the Pentagon Papers gave cause to view Kennedy's intentions as far more uncertain, especially when considered in the context of his actions. The Pentagon Papers, a compilation of secret government documents assembled in a study of U.S. involvement in the war, were surreptitiously released by Dr. Daniel Ellsberg in 1971 and published in their entirety by the *New York Times*. The newspaper subsequently published "the definitive edition of the Pentagon Papers" in book form to include the actual documents and commentary from their reporters and editors. A chapter titled "The Kennedy Years: 1961–1963" by Hedrick Smith, a Pulitzer Prize–winning reporter, disclosed, "The Pentagon's study of the Vietnam war concludes that President John F. Kennedy transformed the 'limited-risk gamble' of the Eisenhower Administration into a 'broad commitment' to prevent Communist domination of South Vietnam."[99]

Gale McGee had reached the same conclusion more than three years before the release of the Pentagon Papers and without the benefit of secret documents. While researching his 1968 book, *The Responsibilities of World Power,* he studied presidential documents dating back to the administration of Franklin Roosevelt. He "found a series of statements by each President, by their Secretaries of State, and by a succession of participants in policy-making, all of which add up to the simple fact that the United States was consciously committed to withholding Southeast Asia from the grasp of either China or such other aggressive forces that might prey upon it."[100]

Having been the most outspoken supporter of LBJ's Vietnam policies, McGee seemed especially stung by the post-assassination theory that Kennedy planned a pullout and that Johnson alone was responsible for the escalation that followed. McGee's book, nominated for the prestigious Woodrow Wilson Award given annually in recognition of the best book on government, politics, or international affairs, methodically revisited statements and policies of FDR, Truman, Eisenhower, and JFK. He quoted Secretaries of State Dean Acheson (under Truman), John Foster Dulles (under Eisenhower), and Dean Rusk (under Kennedy) as they made the argument that the United States had a strategic interest in preventing Communist expansion into Southeast Asia generally and Vietnam in particular.

By the time McGee wrote his book, Kennedy had been widely portrayed by historians as a man of peace who, had he lived, would have brought a quick end to the war. McGee saw it differently. His research included a file of pro-war statements made by JFK and his brother Robert.[101] He reviewed the history of the war during the Kennedy years at length.[102] Beginning with JFK's first State of the Union message, the new president warned of the "relentless pressures of the Chinese Communist menace." Speaking to the United Nations in September 1961, Kennedy expressed his belief in the domino theory. He talked about the "smoldering coals of war in Southeast Asia," saying, "For if they are successful in Laos and South Vietnam, the gates will be open wide."

The Wyoming senator pointedly quoted Robert Kennedy, who as a candidate for the presidency was attacking LBJ's policies. McGee revealed, "The President's brother, as Attorney General, joined his voice in the same chorus of appraisal of American goals in Vietnam when he said, 'We are going to win in Vietnam. We will remain there until we win.'"[103] McGee respected Robert Kennedy, calling him "one of the rare ones that was honest about it." According to McGee, Robert Kennedy later said, "I thought it was all for the right reasons in the beginning. I've changed my mind." Years later McGee would say much the same. At the time, he disagreed with Kennedy but admired him for being "forthright."[104]

Leaving no room for the possibility that President Kennedy had veered from the policy before his death, McGee quoted the president from a September 12, 1963, news conference. "I think the Vietnamese people and ourselves agree; we want the war to be won, the Communists to be contained, and the Americans to come home. We are not there to see a war lost, and we will follow the policy of advancing those causes which help win the war."

Those who argue that Kennedy intended to end U.S. involvement in Vietnam point to an announcement that 1,000 American troops would be withdrawn from the country by the end of 1963. Less than a month before his death, Kennedy was asked at an October 31 press conference, "Mr. President, back to the question of troop reductions, are any intended in the Far East at the present time, particularly in

Korea, and is there any speed-up in the withdrawal from Vietnam intended?" Kennedy responded, "When Secretary McNamara and General Taylor came back, they announced we would expect to withdraw a thousand men from South Vietnam before the end of the year. . . . It would be our hope to lessen the number of Americans there by 1,000, as the training intensifies and is carried on in South Vietnam. As far as other units, we will have to make our judgment based on what the military correlation of forces may be."[105]

There were at least 18,000 U.S. troops in Vietnam by then. Withdrawing 1,000 would have meant little. The Pentagon Papers disclosed that the announcement was nothing more than part of a campaign to pressure the unpopular South Vietnamese president into making reforms.[106] President Diem refused and was himself assassinated a few days after Kennedy's press conference.

Less than a week following Kennedy's death, the new South Vietnamese government received assurances from the U.S. State Department that the withdrawal announcement had been made only for show. In the stilted language of a State Department cable, the report said, "Answering Thanh's [Vietnam ambassador and official representative to Kennedy's funeral] query re significance U.S. withdrawal 1,000 men from Vietnam, [Roger] Hilsman [director of the U.S. Department of State Bureau of Intelligence and Research] said withdrawal psychologically important in showing success, encouraging Vietnamese people by showing they can increasingly take over job, and deflating Communist propaganda about American objectives in Vietnam."[107]

Hilsman assured Thanh that President Johnson "not only supports Kennedy policies toward Vietnam, but participated in making them" and that the new president would "give full support to new government in effective conduct of war."[108] When Thanh suggested there had been widespread "misinterpretation" of the troop withdrawal announcement, Hilsman assured him the U.S. government would clarify its intentions.

What was Senator McGee's conclusion? "This, then, is a part of the body of evidence sustaining the conclusion that the United States has had a constant policy of containing China in the large sense and stopping aggression in the more specific cases in order to achieve stability in Eastern Asia."[109]

Judging from remarks President Kennedy prepared for delivery had his motorcade arrived at the Trade Mart in Dallas on November 22, it is difficult to refute McGee's conclusion. Kennedy planned to tell the country, "American military might should not and need not stand alone against the ambitions of international communism. Our security and strength, in the last analysis, directly depend on the security and strength of others, and that is why our military and economic assistance plays such a key role in enabling those who live on the periphery of the Communist world to maintain their independence of choice. Our assistance to these nations can be painful, risky, and costly, as is true in Southeast Asia today. But we dare not weary of the task."[110]

The United States was years away from the unraveling created by President Kennedy's death, the war in Vietnam, and a resulting cultural divide. The nation had yet to be torn by the assassinations of Malcolm X, Martin Luther King, and Robert Kennedy. The Black Panthers, the Weathermen bombings, *Roe v. Wade*, and the break-in at the Watergate Hotel were years away. The fabric would be further shredded by riots in Detroit, Watts, Chicago, and elsewhere. But it was yet intact as the sun rose on September 25, 1963.

The images from President Kennedy's trip to Wyoming that fall are among the last of an optimistic nation. It was the day after McGee and his Senate colleagues ratified the historic Nuclear Test Ban Treaty with the Soviet Union. Spirits aboard *Air Force One* were as high as the sky among those who accompanied the president. With him were Montana senators Mike Mansfield and Lee Metcalf as well as McGee.

September 25 was a glorious early autumn day. The temperature reached a seasonable 75 degrees. There wasn't a breeze in the air or a cloud in the sky as *Air Force One* touched down at the Cheyenne airport. John Kennedy took special note of the big Wyoming sky, telling McGee, "You cannot only see farther out here [than back east], but there is also something more to see." Fifteen to twenty thousand people cheered his arrival at the Cheyenne airport. He gave brief remarks and shook hundreds of hands along the rope line.

The president and McGee boarded *Air Force One* for the short flight to Laramie. Roads leading from the airport were lined with Cub Scouts saluting and several thousand local folks trying to get a glimpse of Kennedy. Photographs memorializing the moment show Kennedy and McGee sitting in the backseat of a convertible not unlike the one the president would ride through the streets of Dallas a few weeks later.

Awaiting them at the University of Wyoming War Memorial Fieldhouse were another twelve thousand or more. Reporters surmised it was "one of the largest indoor gatherings in the state's history."[111] Glenn J. "Red" Jacoby, athletic director at UW, said it was the biggest crowd since the Cowboys' basketball team played Brigham Young University in 1953 in front of 10,580 fans.

Among those in the Fieldhouse that day was a young man who had transferred to the University of Wyoming after two years at Yale. Dick Cheney later said JFK delivered an "eloquent call to public service," which the congressman, defense secretary, and vice president said "inspired us all."[112] With a smiling Senator Gale McGee looking on, Kennedy challenged students to take advantage of opportunities to "be of service to our country." Citing the Greek definition of "happiness" as using your gifts to achieve excellence, Kennedy assured the audience that it also includes bringing happiness to "those whom you serve."

The president mentioned Vietnam only once as he spoke of the American choices about use of resources, fiscal policy, the space race, and the need to develop the resources of the oceans. Americans had choices, he added, to make about "what we should do in the Congo or Vietnam." Kennedy said all of these and more were a part of a long list of "problems far more complicated than any group of citizens ever had to deal with in the history of the world."[113]

President Kennedy left no doubt that day. Americans were fully capable of making the right choices on all of those critical issues. The nation's future was as bright and limitless as the Wyoming sky under which he spoke. But two months later, America veered suddenly off-course and charted a trip to a darker place where optimism became far more elusive, far more complicated. Shortly after noon on November 22, 1963, American liberalism began to unravel as the country steadily lost faith in its government.

10

A Man of Great Faith, Not Dark Fears

We interrupt this program to bring you a special bulletin from ABC Radio.

Here is a special bulletin from Dallas, Texas. Three shots were fired at President Kennedy's motorcade today in downtown Dallas, Texas.

It was shortly before noon, November 22, 1963. Senator McGee, Loraine, and staffer Liz Strannigan were driving through "Radio-Free Wyoming," parts of the state where radio reception is aggravatingly sporadic and static-filled. Deciphering a news story can be nearly impossible.

Leaving Casper, they headed north on old Highway 87 to a campaign event 150 miles away in Sheridan. Driving that route was slower in those days. Between the two towns, fewer than 10 miles of the long-promised four-lane interstate highway were completed. The narrow two-lane road required travelers to slow down as they passed through small towns along the way. One was Kaycee, where they stopped for gas. Only then were they able to make out enough of a radio report to know that President Kennedy had been shot. "Here is a bulletin from CBS News. In Dallas, Texas, three shots were fired at President Kennedy's motorcade in downtown Dallas. The first reports say that President Kennedy has been seriously wounded by this shooting."

In a time without cell phones, McGee was unable to ascertain exactly what had happened in Dallas until he got to Sheridan. There he found a pay phone in the lobby of the Crescent Hotel and learned the president was dead. He made plans to return to Washington immediately. He drove to the small airport at Sheridan. No commercial air service was available, but a local fellow offered to fly them to Denver where they could catch a flight to Washington. "Well," said McGee describing the Denver flight years later, "we hadn't realized at that time what a trip we were in for."[1] The rookie pilot knew how to take off but not how to land. As the plane approached Denver, the pilot fumbled around a compartment near his knees where he found the pilot's manual and handed it to the senator. "He had me hold it on my knees and he'd tell me which page and which paragraph and to read it out loud to him so that he could maneuver his plane in the way to use the instruments to get in the right order of things to land in Denver." Finally they landed. "He made it all the way down to the ground, bounced a few times, but he got us there in time to catch our plane back to Washington for John Kennedy's funeral."

A news photo showed a somber Senator McGee and his family at the front of the crowd, shoulder to shoulder with others paying their respects to the president as his body lay in state in the Capitol Rotunda. Loraine, dressed in black, stares straight ahead at JFK's casket. The senator's hand rests on the shoulder of daughter Mary Gale while young Robert wipes tears from his eyes. Gale and Loraine joined a contingent of congressional colleagues for the president's graveside service at Arlington National Cemetery. As it ended and the McGees departed, they noticed a lone figure standing at a distance under a tree. It was Richard Nixon, who had come to pay his respects.[2]

A quarter of a century after the assassination, Gale McGee summoned his deepest and most eloquent thoughts as vividly as only one who lived through those awful days could. "The awesomeness of the reverence and the sorrow filled the whole setting. It seemed to be a massive, almost impossible to imagine, dimension of sincere regret."[3] The anguish his words conveyed cannot be felt, neither can they be comprehended, by those for whom the Kennedy assassination is but a brief section in an American history textbook. Conversely, those who were in the political arena, deeply engaged in the causes and battles of the day, might not have had the perspective necessary to see how the assassin set in motion a seismic chain of events. In the coming years, the national political consensus unraveled, and American liberalism came undone.

McGee's political career began when liberalism was, according to political scientist James Piereson, "without doubt the single most creative and vital force in American politics." But the American political system is built not unlike Yellowstone National Park, where major geologic fault lines run along the Gallatin, Teton, and Madison mountain ranges. In much the same way, major fault lines are an integral part of the geology of a democracy. Those fault lines are the cause of any number of small earthquakes, but they always have the potential to trigger one of significance. This one did.

The way the popular young president died and Camelot was relinquished to the ambitious, rough-hewn Texan gave rise to conspiracy theories that plagued American politics for decades. Many believed, despite overwhelming evidence to the contrary, that LBJ conspired to murder JFK because LBJ wanted a wider war in Southeast Asia. Many harbored the illusion that their fallen hero would have ended the war, while Johnson, the convenient villain, escalated it. Few accepted the findings of a commission Johnson created to investigate the crime. Half a century later the distrust has only grown, and Americans remain divided over whether Johnson had a role or whether to blame the CIA or the Mafia.[4]

Geologists explain the potential for a destructive volcanic episode in Yellowstone. "Atop a volcano, mountains are pushed up by swelling magma; the subsequent explosion then destroys them and engulfs their remains."[5] Following on the heels of the Kennedy assassination, the escalation of the war in Vietnam begat the swelling of America's political magma. It exploded along the fault lines opened by a racial divide that transitioned from an uneasy treaty between Kennedy, later Johnson, and Martin Luther King into the days of rage. Following King's murder, America witnessed the ascendency of civil rights advocates who saw themselves as leaders not of a movement but of a revolution. Richard Nixon's startling scandals engulfed and then destroyed what remained of America's political consensus. All of that lay in an unpredictable future that day in November when Lyndon Johnson took the oath of office aboard *Air Force One* and flew back to Washington as president of the United States.

McGee and Johnson had been close friends and political allies for years by the time Johnson moved into the White House. On some of those late nights when Johnson couldn't sleep, he called McGee. One evening, the two drove around the darkened city, just talking. "We were quite close," McGee remembered. "Any number of times, he had me down just to talk to him in the Oval Office, or later on down at the ranch a number of times." The two men sometimes talked until one or two o'clock in the morning.[6]

Johnson's loneliness increased with the intensity of the war. He relied more and more on his friendship with a few close allies. "Maybe I was one of the few friends he had left in foreign policy at this stage. But in any case . . . he always gave me the time to listen and particularly when I had just gotten back from Vietnam."[7] The Wyoming lawmaker, one of the Senate's most traveled and best informed on foreign affairs, felt he had a responsibility, not so much to Johnson as to the presidency, "to hold it together on the president's behalf."[8] McGee denied it was because of his personal relationship with Johnson. McGee's position on the war didn't change when Richard Nixon came to the White House. "I can say very frankly this was less out of respect for Lyndon Johnson than it was out of my conviction about the shape of the world."[9]

LBJ last visited Vietnam at Kennedy's request in the spring of 1961. The vice president reported back on May 23: "The battle against communism must be joined in Southeast Asia with strength and determination. We must decide whether to help these countries to the best of our ability or throw in the towel in the area and pull back our defenses to San Francisco and a 'Fortress America' concept."[10] LBJ's memo acknowledged he undertook the trip to Vietnam with "some basic convictions about the problems we faced" and that "many of those convictions sharpened and deepened by what I saw and learned." In late November, Johnson entered the Oval Office with those same sharpened and deepened convictions.

In the beginning, President Johnson was determined not to allow the remainder of his and JFK's agenda to get lost in the jungles of Southeast Asia. As late as it was when Johnson returned to Washington from Dallas on November 22, he arranged to meet with several of his top advisers. They watched as he drew vertical lines on a pad of paper. Using the three columns, he scheduled his immediate priorities, what he hoped to accomplish between that night and the end of what remained of Kennedy's first term and then the objectives of his own full term should he be elected in 1964.[11]

Unlike Kennedy, Johnson was a master politician. He understood Congress and how to transform an agenda into law. He was also a serious liberal with a commitment to continuing the successes of the New Deal. He and McGee were old-time New Deal liberals. They trusted in the power of the federal government to improve people's lives. Both had been frustrated by the failures of the last three years. The legislative wreckage of his predecessor's New Frontier included civil rights and health care reform. But the new president recognized that the stack of unfinished business dated back much further than Kennedy. He told an adviser, "You know, almost all the issues now are just about the same as they were when I came here in Congress nearly thirty years ago."[12]

President Johnson was determined that his administration would address a long-delayed social agenda. JFK died with health care reform and civil rights legislation imprisoned on Capitol Hill by Southern Democrats and recalcitrant Republicans. Johnson had an even broader view of the nation's domestic problems than did Kennedy. He heard a "call for revolutionary new programs to attack one of the most stubbornly entrenched social ills in America."[13] Less than two months after becoming president, Johnson used his first State of the Union address to declare war on poverty. "Let this session of Congress be known as the session which did more for civil rights than the last hundred sessions combined . . . as the session which declared all-out war on human poverty and unemployment in these United States"[14]

Johnson knew there was no single battlefield on which that war would be fought. Poverty in America could be traced to the denial of civil rights, the lack of job training and education, and the inadequacy of health care. But Johnson knew the barriers to achieving success were not the result of a failure of imagination or a lack of resources. The barriers were political. The House Rules Committee stood between any bill reported from a standing committee and a floor debate. In the Senate, a filibuster or unlimited debate stood between the majority and its ability to enact legislation. Southerners controlled both processes.

Under JFK, the House Judiciary Committee had given its approval to the president's civil rights proposal, but Rules Committee chairman Howard Smith of Virginia "was still fighting the Civil War" and didn't believe in racial equality. President Johnson orchestrated a meeting with Martin Luther King and several other high-profile civil rights leaders. It was a signal to Congressman Smith and others that, although a fellow southerner, LBJ was dead serious about passing a civil rights bill prior to the November 1964 election. Photographs of black leaders sitting in the White House with the Texan president stirred southern ire as well as public support. Opinion polls demonstrated a sudden surge in backing for the law, and religious organizations clamored to show their support. JFK had previously maneuvered an increase in the size of the Rules Committee, packing it with more sympathetic members. The new members coupled with Johnson's strategic moves and growing public support forced Smith's hand. On January 30, 1964, his committee voted 11–4 to allow the legislation to proceed to a floor debate.[15]

Yet remaining, however, was the greatest political barrier. In the last decade, 120 civil rights bills had been referred to Mississippi senator James Eastland's Judiciary Committee. Only Eisenhower's 1957 civil rights bill was ever seen again. Johnson persuaded Senate majority leader Mike Mansfield to employ a seldom-used tactic and report the bill directly to the floor, bypassing Eastland's black hole.

The civil rights bill faced a filibuster and a questionable fate in a Senate with a southern power base known for filibustering civil rights proposals to their demise. The fate of the Civil Rights Act of 1964 was to be determined by whether its supporters could persuade enough members to vote for cloture, thus limiting the time for debate. That would take the vote of two-thirds of the Senate. The hurdle was extraordinarily high. "Never in history had the Senate been able to muster enough votes to cut off a filibuster on a civil rights bill."[16]

The filibuster began on March 30, 1964, and turned out to be the longest in American history. Eventually a cloture petition was filed, seeking to end the debate. Forty-one senators signed, including McGee ally Frank Moss of Utah. McGee did not. Filing the petition was only the first and perhaps the easiest step. The bill's advocates went to work lining up the two-thirds majority required to pass the debate-ending motion. A coalition of thirty-three conservative Republican and Southern Democratic senators were classified as "reasonably sure against cloture." That left no room for the loss of even one of those who had not made their positions evident. Among a list of twelve "crucial senators" was Gale McGee.[17]

Civil rights activists had reason to worry about the Wyoming senator's vote. Just a few months earlier, Isaac Moore, the Colorado and Wyoming legal counsel for the NAACP, came to Cheyenne to accuse McGee of being "one of those who consistently votes against us." He said McGee voted for NAACP causes only once in the previous year.[18] However, McGee had voted for the highly controversial public accommodations provisions of the civil rights act when it came before the Commerce Committee, telling his colleagues that private property rights should never "be permitted to precede human rights."[19]

Yet his failure to sign the cloture petition was troublesome. It reminded civil rights supporters that one of McGee's first votes as a senator was cast in 1959 against cloture reform. Back then he explained his vote. "I felt it was morally wrong to change long-standing Senate rules merely to get at integration."[20] When he failed to join Karl Mundt of South Dakota and Mike Monroney of Oklahoma, two of those "crucial senators," in a May 31 announcement in support of cloture, advocates became even more nervous. His vote was crucial, and civil rights advocates worried about how McGee would now balance the moral wrongs of Jim Crow with challenging Senate traditions.

As the Senate debated the bill, McGee's thoughts returned to his 1959 trip through Africa. He recalled being confronted in Ghana by students holding up a newspaper with a photograph of a lynched black American youth hanging from a deserted tree. "Will the American senators explain this?" they demanded. McGee told the Senate, "No longer is the question one which can be locked up in the closet of our nation. The force of history has jerked it out of that closet and cast it into the middle of the world." He believed the turning point was World War II when Americans discovered that "the blood of a colored man was as red as the blood of a white man."[21]

The long debate was finally limited when on June 10 McGee and seventy of his colleagues voted for cloture. Under the cloture rule, the debate was permitted to continue until it ended on June 19 with an emotional speech from Republican floor leader Everett Dirksen of Illinois. At the end of Dirksen's speech, he read a telegram from forty state governors calling for passage of the act.

"We, the 40 undersigned Governors of the United States of America, record our conviction that the prompt enactment of Civil Rights legislation by the Congress of the United States is in the national interest." Wyoming governor Cliff Hansen was one of the signers.[22]

The acting president *pro tempore* of the Senate then announced, "The bill having been read the third time, the question is, shall it pass?" The roll was called. All one hundred senators were present for the historic vote. McGee joined seventy-two senators voting "aye."[23] McGee was the only member of Wyoming's congressional delegation to vote for the act.[24]

Anti–civil rights constituents back home attacked him viciously. Ralph Schauss, a Casper businessman, wrote a letter to the editor of the *Riverton Ranger* saying it was "McGee who forced this police-state legislation on freedom of choice and association loving Americans."[25] McGee heard plenty from those who believed that evil hearts could not be changed by legislation. "Churches, not Congress, should address the civil rights issues, which are 'moral' matters, not subject to legislative solutions," wrote a constituent from Lander.[26]

Those views were affirmed two days later. On June 21, Michael Schwerner, Andrew Goodman, and James Chaney, three white civil rights workers, disappeared in Neshoba County, Mississippi. Sometime later their brutalized bodies were found. McGee was quick to express his horror at the level of violence and what he called the "climate of terror that exists in some parts of our nation."[27] A day short of one month after the bill passed, racial violence broke out in Washington, Des Moines, Cleveland, Brooklyn, and elsewhere.

By now, McGee was fully on board with other liberals in defending the movement and no longer counseling patience. When a constituent from Kaycee expressed a belief that civil rights demonstrators should be "arrested, tried, and hung by the neck until dead for they are certainly traitors," McGee expressed shock. He compared the actions of the demonstrators to those who "took part in the Boston Tea Party and who formed a group to defy the soldiers of King George III."[28]

A March 23, 1965, letter to the editor of the *Casper Star* accused civil rights demonstrators of "creating more ill feelings between the races." C. E. Reed wrote, "A negro can get an FHS loan and build as nice a home as I can, but it doesn't have to be next to mine for him to have that equal right." He argued that church leaders should refrain from speaking about civil rights. Reed claimed he had heard a civil rights leader say "that the red china leaders told them to band together against the whites."

The letter was placed on McGee's desk with a note from a staffer. "Do you want to answer this or ignore it completely?" McGee chose to answer and defended the religious leaders who were involved. He said the segregationists were "ungodly and unchristian." McGee challenged the assumption that the civil rights movement was led by Communists, saying, "It is led and supported by dedicated Americans who have risked their lives, and in some cases given their lives, for the cause in which they believe so deeply." McGee said he hoped their sacrifices were not in vain.[29]

Meanwhile McGee was waiting to learn who he would face in a 1964 reelection contest. The GOP convinced themselves that conservative voters in Wyoming would deny the liberal Democrat a second term. The *Wyoming Stockman-Farmer,* a popular rural newspaper, editorialized, "McGee is such a controversial figure in Wyoming that it would be naïve to think that a switch from Kennedy to Johnson is going to save the day for him."[30]

Optimistic Republicans, including Wyoming's popular U.S. representative William Henry Harrison, were standing in line hoping to get a nomination they felt confident would land them in a Senate seat in 1965.[31] McGee was determined to put on an early show of strength. In June 1963, fourteen U.S. senators, including Mike Mansfield, joined Vice President Johnson and Interior Secretary Stewart Udall in a hugely successful "Gale McGee Appreciation Dinner" filling Cheyenne's largest venue, the Frontier Pavilion.

Johnson at first declined the invitation. His regret letter to McGee opened with the salutation, "Enticement, thy name is Gale McGee."

Johnson wanted to go but didn't feel he could get away. "I feel like retreating from Washington and joining you, but this is another instance when I am unable to yield to my desires."[32] Johnson eventually yielded to his desires and flew to Wyoming for the event. He told the crowd of more than 1,250, "Gale McGee is a builder, not a bellyacher. He is a doer, not a doubter. He is a man of great faith, not a man of dark fears."[33] The success of the event and the size of the crowd were misleading.

The *Wyoming Stockman-Farmer* reported that 70 percent of its readers thought Harrison could defeat McGee. Only 16 percent felt the incumbent was doing a good job, while 43 percent assessed his performance as poor. One respondent said it was "imperative that McGee be retired if we are to remain a free nation." But another noted that McGee's friendship with influential politicians would make it very difficult to defeat him.[34] One of those was the president.

"Gale, I am cutting [the budgets of] everybody in the United States but you." President Johnson was on the other end of the phone. "That Riverton project in Wyoming costs $12,878,000. It's for livestock and irrigation. Know anything about it?" Yes, the senator knew about it. He'd been working with the folks in Riverton for months trying to make the water project politically and economically viable. "Well," Johnson said, "I can start it with $500,000. It could be one of nine or ten reclamation projects started next year. How much would it help you?"

McGee assured him, "It would help us a great deal." Johnson shot back, "I'm not talking about 'us.' I'm talking about helping you."[35] LBJ knew how to help his friend with rural voters.

This half a million dollars was but a small fraction of the total their senator, a member of the Appropriations Committee, was able to garner for his constituents. Most Wyoming communities benefited from those federal expenditures whether they were for water and reclamation projects, jobs and economic development, roads and bridges, or education. Even the harshest critics of government spending expected their senator to "bring home the bacon." But McGee was wearying of how much the expectation exceeded the gratitude. Even more he resented the flourishing antigovernment rhetoric from many of those who were not bashful about seeking his assistance in obtaining government funds. He knew the state relied on federal dollars to balance its budget and to accomplish important work. That river of resentment burst its banks early in 1964. As McGee walked into a meeting of the Cody Chamber of Commerce on January 9, he noted the large gathering included a number of public officials and others who had been very critical of the federal government and his votes. He recognized among them those who had also sought his help in receiving federal largesse for their pet projects. He was ready for a confrontation, bluntly declaring that people who condemn federal aid with one hand and ask for it with the other were hypocrites.[36]

The following day he attacked those "in Wyoming who conduct a continual tirade against the federal government, who would have you believe your enemy is in Washington." He said they had "a strange way of showing the patriotism they routinely espouse." During a Democratic Party dinner in Sheridan that week, McGee called those who "continually downgrade the American government" enemies of freedom. Recalling the assassination of Kennedy, the senator said, "We have paid a heavy price for permitting the erratic, the distorted, and the hateful among us to determine the climate of American opinion."[37] Later that week he addressed a Chamber of Commerce meeting in Rawlins, blasting those who demanded budget cuts while seeking government funds for their own projects. "What it all boils down to is the question of how willing you really are to practice what you preach."[38]

On the heels of conservative senator Barry Goldwater's formal announcement that he would run for president in 1964, McGee added fuel to the fire he had started earlier by saying the state legislature was too heavily influenced by the John Birch Society. McGee openly criticized conservative members of the state legislature, charging them with being part of a scheme "to destroy democracy as we know it." He called conservative Wyoming legislators "gullible" and said they had been too quick to adopt ideas that have been ridiculed.[39]

The 1964 Senate race was on, and though the polls and the pundits questioned the odds of his being reelected, McGee was determined not to go down without a fight. Events combined to boost his reelection odds. Two Republicans who might have been his most formidable opponents opted out of the contest in spite of all the indications that McGee was vulnerable. Republicans had been pushing Cliff Hansen, in the governorship for only two years, to run against McGee.[40] Since 1946, seven men had served as governor. Some were elected governor. Others ascended to the office when the incumbent chose to leave for the Senate. Only Milward Simpson had completed a full four-year term, and Hansen felt he was obliged to fill out a full term. In January he said no to running against McGee. Congressman William Henry Harrison also declined.[41]

The second event boosting McGee's chances came when the 1963 session of the Wyoming legislature enacted a number of right-wing proposals and infuriated organized labor by passing a right-to-work law. Few, if any, actions of the Wyoming legislature ever proved more divisive than a bill outlawing union shops. The right-to-work law was designed to diminish the strength of labor unions by making it unlawful to require a worker to join and pay union dues. Workers could choose whether to join but could not be denied the benefits of a union-negotiated contract. Predictably fewer workers would choose to belong to the union. Both supporters and opponents of the legislation knew it would result in significantly fewer union members in Wyoming and diminished support for Democratic Party candidates. In the long term, that would benefit Republicans. But in the first statewide election following the bill's controversial enactment, Democrats were the political beneficiaries.

The GOP held large majorities in both houses when the Wyoming legislature convened in January 1963: 16–11 in the Senate and 37–19 in the House. Along party lines, the Senate quickly passed the right-to-work bill. When it got to the House, debate heated considerably. Each side bought newspaper and radio ads extolling their positions. The halls of the legislature filled to overflowing with proponents and opponents, each as angry as the other. Debates in the corridors of the Wyoming Capitol were as bitter as those on the floor of the House and the Senate.

When the bill came to the floor, Speaker of the House Marlin Kurtz of Cody was fearful that threats against members favoring the bill might result in violence. At Kurtz's urging, Governor Hansen stationed "eleven police officers and a contingent of National Guard troops to [be] on hand at the Capitol when the bill was being debated." The bill passed 33–23 and was sent to the governor for his signature.[42] As he signed the bill into law, Hansen accurately predicted the right-to-work controversy would cause Republicans trouble in the 1964 election.[43] Others accurately predicted the law would substantially weaken the influence of organized labor over the coming years.[44]

McGee took an unusual step for a federal lawmaker. He interjected himself in state legislative disputes when he issued a statement opposing right-to-work, saying it would injure Wyoming's working people.[45] Following the adjournment of the 1963 legislature, McGee continued his feud with state legislators, blaming them for the loss of new job opportunities. A New York firm had told him it would not relocate to Wyoming because of the passage of the law.[46]

During that same session, a number of resolutions were introduced expressing the sense of the legislature on national issues. One reaffirmed "support for the House Committee on Un-American Activities and the Senate Internal Security Committee."[47] A second opposed any future increase in social security taxes.[48] Another called for the end to all foreign aid.[49] A resolution asked Congress to repeal the Arms Control and Disarmament Act.[50] The legislature went on record opposing any additional wilderness land designations in the state.[51] They passed another resolution asking for the establishment of a "Court of the Union" to review decisions made by the U.S. Supreme Court.[52]

The resolutions were part of what the Democrats branded the legislature's "reactionary record."[53] McGee sniffed out the influence of the John Birch Society, which supported each resolution. With his reelection at stake, McGee was willing to take a long shot, placing a bet that the voters would reject right-wing extremism. Many would have predicted Cassius Clay had better odds, although Sonny Liston was favored 8–1 to defeat the "Louisville Lip" for the World Heavyweight title in February 1964.

The McGee campaign strategy for 1964 was the same as the senator had spelled out in his August 1963 memorandum to President Kennedy. JFK had asked McGee to study the impact of groups like the John Birch Society on his and the president's chances for reelection. The president's plan was to attack them early through congressional investigations in order to marginalize the right, long before the November election. McGee suggested otherwise.

"But one word of caution, it seems to me, is in order," McGee's memo to the president warned. "It revolves around the question of timing. A wide-open investigation in the Congress of the right-wing groups now might have the effect of killing them dead before next fall." McGee thought that making the extremists the issue in 1964 was preferable to running them off the playing field too early.[54] It was clear that the relentless attacks on the right wing were paying off when McGee's colleague, Senator Milward Simpson, was forced to deny he was a member of the John Birch Society. Using language evoking memories of the victims of Joe McCarthy's attacks a decade earlier, Senator Simpson said, "I am not now nor have I ever been a member of the John Birch Society."[55]

The GOP state chairman, John Wold, said McGee should take a "loyalty oath" after the senator's criticism of right-wing influences in the state.[56] Democratic Party chairman Walter Phelan counterpunched. He called on Wold to take a sanity oath. "If Mr. Wold thinks everyone in Wyoming is supposed to agree with the right-wing record of the 37th Legislature and deny the existence of right-wing groups in Wyoming, it seems far more appropriate to ask a sanity oath of Wold than a loyalty oath of Senator McGee."[57]

Although Congressman Harrison and Governor Hansen chose not to oppose him, McGee was deemed by most observers to be vulnerable enough that two other heavyweight Republicans did decide to make the run. One was John Wold. A geologist from Casper, he had served in the Wyoming legislature. His primary election opponent was Kenny Sailors, who had made his name playing on the University of Wyoming's 1943 NCAA national championship team as the tournament's Most Valuable Player. Sailors played professional basketball from 1946 until 1951 for teams including the Boston Celtics and Denver Nuggets. Basketball historians credit him with the invention of the jump shot.[58] Sailors left the hard court of basketball for the hard knocks of Wyoming politics. He was elected to the Wyoming House of Representatives in 1954, serving two terms. In 1960, he finished a close second in a five-candidate primary for Wyoming's lone U.S. House seat. Two years later he finished a more distant second to Milward Simpson for the U.S. Senate nomination. Sailors returned in 1964 for his last shot at a Republican nomination.[59]

August was a month of omens for McGee, some bad, some good. Both parties held their national presidential nominating conventions, Wyoming hosted a visit from the First Lady, and a primary election determined that John Wold would face off against Gale McGee in November. It was also the month Lyndon Johnson signed the Gulf of Tonkin resolution.

Toss out the term "Gulf of Tonkin" at a baby-boomers' cocktail party and watch. The ensuing melee will likely be rather one-sided, but it will create an argument over how the Vietnam War started. Robert McNamara, LBJ's defense secretary, said later that the period of time from July 30 to August 7, 1964, was "the most controversial period" of the war. Until that time, few Americans gave much thought to the conflict in Southeast Asia. That changed when the president told them the North Vietnamese had attacked U.S. ships. In the days following the August 1964 incident, there was a national consensus that the North Vietnamese must pay the price. However, that consensus began to unravel not long after the ink dried on the congressional resolution authorizing President Johnson to respond militarily to the attack.

The most striking thing about the incident is its geography. Vietnam is a long thin strip of land some 2,140 miles in length with more square miles than Texas and about half the size of Alaska. It shares borders with China to the north, Laos and Cambodia to the west, and mostly saltwater to the east. The Gulf of Tonkin is in the northernmost part of Vietnam where it shares a coastline with China. The island of Hainan Dao on the east portion of the Gulf is the southernmost province of the People's Republic of China. Yet, in August 1964, only a couple of senators thought it was odd that U.S. warships were operating that far north and that close to China.

The Gulf of Tonkin was hotly debated for seven years before the release of the Pentagon Papers shed light on what had happened. These were part of a larger secret study ordered by McNamara to document the political and military decisions leading United States through the war. The Pentagon never expected the documents to be read by members of the public. Dr. Daniel Ellsberg, a onetime Defense Department analyst, changed that when he secretly sent the study to the *New York Times*.

Through the Pentagon Papers, Americans learned the CIA had prepared plans for "sabotage and psychological operations against North Vietnam" during the first month of the Johnson administration.[60] In the months leading up to the North Vietnamese attack at Tonkin, the United States orchestrated "an elaborate program of covert military operations against the state of North Vietnam" to disrupt infiltration into the South. The administration's motives included seeking a war resolution from Congress, a declaration drafted two and a half months before the confrontation in the waters of Tonkin.[61] Prior to Tonkin, as U.S. planes flown by Thai pilots strafed North Vietnamese villages, bombing targets had already been determined. A "comprehensive list of 94 targets, from bridges to industries," was prepared at a conference in Honolulu on the first two days of June. Meanwhile, U.S. bombing raids against the North expanded during the summer of 1964 leading up to Tonkin. Trained sabotage teams were airlifted and dropped along with PT boats for raids along the North Vietnamese coast. South Vietnamese naval forces under the command of Gen. William Westmoreland raided islands in the Gulf of Tonkin on July 30.[62]

With these operations under way, the USS *Maddox* headed into the Gulf on August 2, and North Vietnamese patrol boats "began their high-speed run at her." LBJ promptly ordered additional naval forces including the destroyer *C. Turner Joy* and aircraft carriers *Ticonderoga* and *Constellation* to support the *Maddox*. Two nights later, "North Vietnamese torpedo boats then attacked both the *Maddox* and the *Turner Joy* in what was the fateful clash in the Gulf."[63] In his 1995 memoir, Secretary McNamara said the attack on the *Maddox* "is indisputable." He admitted the second attack was less certain.[64]

President Johnson then carried out what analysts writing in the Pentagon Papers called "recommendations made . . . by his principal advisers earlier that summer and subsequently placed on the shelf." Bombing targets were selected from the list of ninety-four drawn up at the Honolulu Conference. That afternoon, LBJ ordered "reprisal" air strikes. It was then that the previously drafted Gulf of Tonkin resolution was conveyed to William Fulbright, chairman of the Senate Foreign Relations Committee, and his House counterpart, Thomas E. Morgan of Pennsylvania.[65]

McGee promptly announced his support for the resolution. "There has been no foot-dragging in this crisis," the Wyoming senator said. "No Communist can misinterpret what this means, namely, that we do not intend to be pushed around by the Reds."[66]

Fulbright scheduled an immediate hearing. Among committee members, only Oregon senator Wayne Morse questioned why the *Maddox* was in the Gulf of Tonkin in the first place. Morse told his colleagues the *Maddox* was there as part of "a clear act of aggression against the territory of North Vietnam, and our ships were in Tonkin Gulf standing as a cover for naval operations of South Vietnam."[67] McNamara denied any knowledge of the attacks. For the time being, however, the Foreign Relations Committee relied on McNamara's testimony.

The Senate voted on the Gulf of Tonkin resolution on August 7, 1964. Gale McGee, Frank Church, George McGovern, and ninety-five of their colleagues supported it while only Senators Ernest Gruening of Alaska and Wayne Morse of Oregon voted no.[68] The war was on and quickly becoming more and more of a reality for Americans. But the real escalation would not come until after the president was reelected.

Later in August, the McGees accompanied Lady Bird Johnson on an extensive Wyoming trip. American flags flew across Jackson Hole as the First Lady arrived to begin the historic trip on August 14, 1964. A western band played as she entered the town square in a horse-drawn carriage.[69] She stayed at the nearby Jackson Lake Lodge and hosted a large group of Wyoming female political and business leaders before rafting the Snake River. Later more than 4,000 people greeted her in Green River. A full page of photographs of the event chronicled the First Lady's stopover in the following week's *Green River Star*. After a parade through the small town, she enjoyed a buffalo barbecue complete with Native American dancers from the Wind River Indian Reservation. She then took a boat ride on the Flaming Gorge Reservoir after which she dedicated the $81 million dam on the Wyoming-Utah border.[70] Two weeks later, the Green River paper was still talking about the First Lady's trip and all the publicity it generated around the nation. "Indications have been that every section of the nation has given publicity to our area in one form or another."[71]

The day after the First Lady returned to Washington, August 18, John Wold won the Wyoming Republican Party's nomination for the Senate by a scant 1,756 votes over the inventor of basketball's jump shot. McGee handily defeated token primary opposition from Wayne Kinney, a member of the Benjamin Franklin Party who worried about the United States not being on the gold standard. Republicans worried more that there were nearly the same number of Democrats voting in their primary as there were Republicans voting in theirs, always a bad omen for the GOP. However, they were buoyed when Goldwater was nominated for president.

H. L. Mencken once said, "There is something about a national [political] convention that makes it as fascinating as a revival or a hanging."[72] That would accurately describe the 1968 conventions of the Republican and Democratic Parties.

Traditionally the party in the White House is allowed first choice of its national convention dates, most often deciding on a date closer to the fall election in order to achieve maximum exposure. The Democrats decided to meet August 24–27 in Atlantic City, New Jersey. The Republicans opted to gather July 13–16 in San Francisco.

The Republicans nominated seven men and a woman for president, but Goldwater wrapped up his party's nomination. The roll of state delegations was called alphabetically, but the matter was decided long before it got to last-place Wyoming. On the convention's final evening, Goldwater spoke after being introduced by Richard Nixon, who by then had lost both the presidency and the California governorship in back-to-back campaigns. Goldwater made it clear he planned to run as a doctrinaire conservative. "Our people have followed false prophets," he said. What resulted was a litany of attacks on big government, violence in the streets, welfare programs, and foreign policy. And then came the oft-quoted denouement: "Extremism in the defense of liberty is no vice. Moderation in the pursuit of justice is no virtue."[73]

In the exuberance of the moment, former Wyoming governor and convention delegate Nels Smith crowed, "There is no question that we can beat McGee. The state will go unanimously Republican. There's no question about it."[74]

Lyndon Johnson nearly withdrew before the 1964 Democratic National Convention. One of his biographers, Merle Miller, revealed how close he had come. White House adviser George Reedy told Miller, "The night before the convention he walked around with me on the White House grounds saying he was going to announce his withdrawal the next day.[75]

In his memoirs, Johnson acknowledged his deep desire not to run that year. "I felt a strong inclination to go back to Texas while there was still time, time to enjoy life with my wife and my daughters, to work in earnest at being a rancher on the land I loved and to slow down, to reflect, to live." Johnson prepared to announce his withdrawal. His draft statement concluded, "Therefore I shall carry forward with your help until the new president is sworn in next January and then go home as I've wanted to since the day I took this job."[76] When Lady Bird was told of her husband's decision, she sent him a note. "Beloved, to step out now would be wrong for our country, and I can see nothing but a lonely wasteland for your future. Your friends would be frozen in embarrassed silence and your enemies would be jeering."[77] Johnson changed his mind.

There was more drama around his selection of a running mate. After ruling out Robert Kennedy, Sargent Shriver, and anyone else close to the Kennedys, Johnson decided between the two Minnesota senators, Eugene McCarthy and Hubert Humphrey. A Johnson-Humphrey ticket emerged from the convention in Atlantic City.

McGee returned to Washington when the Senate reconvened. On September 2, senators gave final approval to LBJ's Medicare legislation. McGee voted for the bill while his GOP colleague, Senator Simpson, voted against it. Republican Senate nominee John Wold accused the Democrats of trying to buy votes using the public purse.[78]

Summer turned to fall. *The Carpetbaggers*, starring George Peppard and Carroll Baker was a box-office hit as outsiders streamed into Wyoming to boost the chances of one or the other of the Senate candidates. The Democratic vice presidential candidate, Hubert Humphrey, came for McGee while GOP vice presidential candidate William Miller came to campaign for Wold. Democratic South Carolina segregationist senator Strom Thurmond switched to the Republican Party and came to campaign against McGee. The two Senate colleagues stopped for a haircut, coincidentally at the same Casper barbershop at the same time, exchanged greetings, and went back to the battlefield.

Thurmond told cheering Wyoming Republicans he had become "nauseated" by the Democratic Party. He said they were leading the nation "down the road to a socialistic dictatorship."[79] Thurmond called McGee "a friend of mine" but went on to say, "He is far to the liberal side."[80] Across town that same evening at a Young Democrats gathering, George McGovern stumped for McGee. He compared McGee to the late JFK and said his Wyoming colleague "understands fully the urgency and the necessity of peace."[81]

With Goldwater winning the GOP presidential nomination, Wyoming Republicans followed him far to the right. When New York governor Nelson Rockefeller was challenging Goldwater and came to Wyoming to make his case to the 1964 state Republican convention, one delegate was quoted as saying, "Well, if we're going to invite Rockefeller out here to speak, we might just as well have McGee."[82] The conservative wing of the state GOP despised Gale McGee, and they were not bashful in showing how much.

Years after leaving the Senate, Gale and Loraine harbored stingingly bitter memories of that campaign. Loraine remembered a woman "out in Big Piney who was the wife of a very prominent political family" who, as her husband drove alongside McGee's car, "spat on me through the window." As they stood outside post offices handing out campaign brochures, people would "grab the literature, wad it up, and throw it on the ground." There were near physical confrontations when Loraine and McGee's staff felt certain the senator's physical safety was at risk. The whispering campaign coloring McGee as a "pinko" got louder as the John Birch Society made the defeat of the Wyoming senator its number one national goal.

The campaign exposed dramatic policy differences between the two parties. Referring to the war on poverty and the recently passed Medicare legislation, Wold accused McGee of "buying the election this fall."[83] Congressional action on civil rights, the Economic Opportunity Act, and health care framed the 1964 campaign into a classic contest between liberal and conservative views. Wold opposed expansion of social security to cover the medical costs of the elderly, that is,

Medicare, saying it would bankrupt the retirement system. He railed against the war on poverty, telling audiences that the Job Corps could not meet the demand for skilled labor.[84] Wold echoed the opposition of a group of Wyoming ranchers who complained that the "youths selected for the camps might be undesirables."[85]

McGee focused on Wyoming issues including irrigation projects, sugar quotas, federal dollars for roads and highways, and his votes to protect the oil depletion allowance for Wyoming's oil and gas industry. Occasionally McGee abandoned his message to blast the John Birchers who were working hard for his defeat. He tried to find the middle ground between right and left. "The Lord didn't give all the wisdom to conservatives or liberals," he often said, "and we should constantly seek the best answers from each philosophy."[86]

During the closing days of the campaign, GOP state chairman Stan Hathaway hammered McGee repeatedly for his support of liberal causes. Comparing McGee's low ratings with conservative organizations to his much higher ratings with groups like the AFL-CIO and Americans for Democratic Action, Hathaway said the senator was "type-cast as a liberal."[87]

John Wold accused McGee of taking money from a "shadowy and dangerous disarmament lobby." He was speaking of the Council for a Livable World, a national organization working to end nuclear proliferation. Wold claimed the Council was soliciting foreign donations to help McGee.[88] Wold attempted to link Chinese development of an atomic bomb with the Council and demanded McGee return the money Council members had contributed to his campaign.[89] Wold's criticism was blunted when a former national commander of the Veterans of Foreign Wars endorsed McGee. John W. Mahan said, "Your tremendous record for these Americans who fought for our country and those they left behind warrants the support of every veteran and his family for your reelection to the United States Senate."[90]

McGee touted his seniority. He predicted a Johnson victory and said it was important that Wyoming have a senator with a direct line to the White House.[91] However, a late September poll showed large numbers of Wyoming Democrats planning to cross over and vote for Republican candidates. Hathaway claimed defections were running as high as "10 to 25 percent, depending on the county."[92] He predicted

LBJ's endorsement of McGee would "bring a smashing success for John Wold as our next U.S. senator."

McGee's reelection was anything but certain. He had barely won six years ago when the John Birchers were not well organized. Now they were. They didn't have to turn many votes around to change the 1958 result. In order to win, Republicans believed McGee needed to persuade at least 6,000 Republican voters to cross over.[93] They didn't think he could get it done, and McGee's people were not sure he could either. In late September, McGee's pollsters said that at best he was running even with Wold.

The senator placed a call to Jack Valenti, one of LBJ's closest White House aides. He told Valenti that Johnson was running well ahead of Goldwater in Wyoming but that he feared independents and moderate Republicans might split their vote, supporting the president and McGee's GOP opponent. Valenti told Johnson that McGee "desperately wants you to come to Wyoming. He says it will be the difference between victory and defeat for him out there."[94] Johnson put a trip to Casper on his campaign schedule.

Nixon had come to campaign for McGee's opponent six years earlier. He came again on October 22, 1964, to help John Wold, but by that point, just as it was by the time Nixon came in 1958, the GOP was anticipating the worst. It was becoming clear Democrats around the country would win a huge victory at the polls.

McGee's frenetic campaign schedule was abruptly interrupted by a medical emergency that threatened to end his campaign and perhaps worse. In October he was rushed to a Georgetown hospital. It came little more than a year after a September 1963 scare during which McGee spent several days hospitalized. This time his staff initially said he had suffered a "case of intestinal or stomach flu." Later they acknowledged it was related to his diabetes.[95] He had been admitted in a diabetic coma following a severe insulin reaction. Knowing that people with diabetes are at greater risk for heart attacks, Dr. James Fitzgerald, McGee's personal physician, immediately considered the possibility. He diagnosed his patient as having suffered a heart attack. Fitzgerald consulted with the senator's brother, Dr. Dean McGee, then practicing medicine in Lexington, Nebraska, and they concurred on the diagnosis.

Unlike with previous hospitalizations, Loraine immediately decided that Gale's medical condition was to be kept secret among the inner circle. Only Loraine, the McGee children, Liz Strannigan, his personal secretary, and chief of staff Dick Cook knew the truth. Each was aware that his diabetes was already the subject of rumors leading to quiet discussions in Wyoming about his fitness to serve in the Senate. In truth, while his diabetes was severe, it was managed successfully over the years, enabling McGee to live longer than doctors had predicted.

He was released after about a week in the hospital at his insistence. At home, Loraine arranged a bed in the family room so that Gale need not use the stairs. He rested quietly for the next two weeks. But opening day of pheasant season was upon them. Anyone who knew Gale McGee knew he never missed a pheasant season. If he missed this one, rumors would fly as people speculated. Just as special arrangements were made so that he could take care of phone calls, respond to correspondence, and perform other Senate duties from home, arrangements were also made to avoid missing the hunting season.[96]

Advised by his doctor against walking those long uneven fields, he told Burt Huntington, the publisher of the *Lovell Chronicle* and a longtime hunting partner, that he had hurt his foot and asked him to drive his pickup truck into fields where McGee could hunt without long walks. The senator hunted pheasants on November 1, two days before the 1964 election.

McGee could afford to relax that weekend because he knew the tide had turned decisively days before he suffered the heart attack. His forced absence from the campaign trail caused no harm. Six months earlier it appeared possible, even likely, that McGee could lose his seat. By the end of September, a Senate Campaign Committee poll showed that "Republicans could spend all the money in this world" and not beat McGee.[97] In late October, pollster Palmer Hoyt cabled the president, "Here's something I think will ease your mind a lot. I have just mailed you the finals on the Wyoming poll."[98] Both Johnson and McGee were now safe in Wyoming.

The Republicans had convinced themselves that McGee, the liberal Democrat, could be beaten in conservative Wyoming. They figured 1958 was a fluke, lost only because of Drew Pearson's last-minute attack on Frank Barrett. Historically, the Republicans were better financed and better organized than Wyoming Democrats. The 1964 campaign was no exception. But McGee was easily reelected, receiving 76,485 votes to Wold's 65,185.

Some attributed McGee's 1964 success solely to the "Johnson landslide." Indeed, LBJ won by a huge margin, garnering 486 Electoral College votes compared with Goldwater's 52. Johnson won Wyoming's 3 Electoral College votes with a 57–43 percent advantage, becoming the last Democratic presidential candidate to win the state. Even so, there was more to McGee's surprising win than Johnson's coattails. Wyoming historian and political scientist John T. Hinckley analyzed the results, and he credits two factors. One was the success of the McGee campaign in registering new voters and getting them to the polls. But Hinckley said the "largest single factor, after the Johnson landslide, was organized labor and Wyoming's right-to-work law."[99] Wold admitted as much. "They hung right-to-work around my neck from the very start, and I couldn't get rid of it." Ironically, the law that eventually eliminated organized labor as the most significant political force behind the Wyoming Democratic Party received credit for McGee's reelection the year after it was enacted.

1. President Kennedy and Senator McGee arrive in Cheyenne aboard *Air Force One* on September 25, 1963. Courtesy of Robert McGee.

2. Senators George McGovern (D-SD), Gale McGee, and Frank Church (D-ID) meet with President Johnson at the White House to discuss a Vietnam policy speech Johnson would deliver at Johns Hopkins University on April 7, 1965. Gale McGee Collection, American Heritage Center, University of Wyoming.

3. 1970: Senator McGee, chairman of the Senate Post Office and Civil Service Committee, meets with President Nixon, Postmaster General Winton Blount, and Senator Hiram Fong (D-HI) in the Oval Office to discuss the postal workers' strike of 1970. Gale McGee Collection, American Heritage Center, University of Wyoming.

4. Senator McGee and President Ford attend an April 1975 reception honoring Wyoming senator Clifford Hansen. Gale McGee Collection, American Heritage Center, University of Wyoming.

5. President Jimmy Carter signs the American Convention on Human Rights at the Pan American Union Building in Washington on June 1, 1977. *From left to right*: Paraguay's ambassador to the Organization of American States, Marion Lopez Escobar; Marcelo Huergo, OAS staff member; Gale McGee, U.S. ambassador to the OAS; Juan Pablo Gomez, OAS Council chairman; and President Carter. Associated Press Images LIC-00917954.

6. Gale McGee and his father, Garton, celebrate their birthdays on St.
Patrick's Day 1961, at the White House along with Gale's mother, Frances,
and President Kennedy. Gale McGee Collection, American Heritage Center,
University of Wyoming.

7. Senators Edmund Muskie (D-ME), Gale McGee, Eugene McCarthy (D-MN), Philip Hart (D-MI), and Frank Moss (D-UT), freshmen members of the U.S. Senate Class of 1958, pose for a *Look* magazine portrait. Photo by Arnold Newman; Courtesy Getty Images.

8. On the morning following Gale McGee's November 1958 election victory, the senator-elect and Loraine smile as they display the *Rocky Mountain News* headline reminiscent of the 1948 *Chicago Tribune* headline prematurely announcing Dewey's "victory" over Harry Truman. Gale McGee Collection, American Heritage Center, University of Wyoming.

9. Senators Joe O'Mahoney (D-WY), Clinton P. Anderson (D-NM), Wayne Morse (D-OR), and McGee celebrate the Senate's vote to reject President Eisenhower's nomination of Lewis Strauss to be secretary of commerce on June 19, 1959. Courtesy of Robert McGee.

10. July 11, 1971: William Ruckelshaus (*right*), head of the Environmental Protection Agency, Senator McGee, chairman of the Appropriations Committee Subcommittee on Agriculture, Environmental, and Consumer Protection, and Nathaniel Reed (*center*), assistant secretary of the interior, during a Senate inquest into the shooting deaths of hundreds of bald and golden eagles. Gale McGee Collection, American Heritage Center, University of Wyoming.

11. McGee's Senate staff gathers to celebrate his St. Patrick's Day birthday on March 17, 1971. *From left to right:* Dick McCall, Dudley Miles, Irma Hanneman Pearson, Bob Bullock, Rosemary Urbigkit, Del Kendall, Senator McGee, Betty Cooper, Loraine McGee, Jan Stoorza, Liz Strannigan, Jim Burridge, and Dick Cook. Courtesy of Robert McGee.

12. Senator McGee and Senator Albert Gore Sr. (D-TN) meet with South Vietnam's president, Ngo Dinh Diem, in Saigon in 1959. Courtesy of Robert McGee.

13. Senator McGee joins LBJ's deputy secretary of defense, Cyrus Vance (*center*), on a fact-finding mission to Vietnam in March 1966. Gale McGee Collection, American Heritage Center, University of Wyoming.

14. As the Senate delegate to the United Nations in 1972, McGee addresses the UN General Assembly. Courtesy of Robert McGee.

15. In June 1979 a meeting of foreign ministers of the Organization of American States met to discuss a crisis in Nicaragua arising when the Sandinistas overthrew the Somoza dictatorship. *Left to right:* Secretary of State Cyrus Vance, Assistant Secretary of State for Inter-American Affairs Viron "Pete" Vaky, Ambassador Gale McGee, and Hodding Carter, assistant secretary of state for public affairs and State Department spokesman. Courtesy of Robert McGee.

16. Senator McGee was a member of a U.S. Senate delegation to China soon after Nixon normalized U.S. relations with that country. McGee met with Premier Zhou Enlai in Peking in July 1973. Courtesy U.S. Senate Historical Office.

17. Gale McGee hunts pheasants in a cornfield near Huntley, Wyoming, in 1958. The photo appeared in *Life* magazine. Photo by Carl Iwasaki/The *Life* Images Collection; courtesy Getty Images.

18. Gale and Loraine McGee were full partners in the life they shared. Here the two are shown attending a Railroad Brotherhood dinner in Rawlins, Wyoming. Courtesy of Robert McGee.

19. Liz Strannigan served as Gale McGee's personal assistant from the time he was first elected to the Senate in 1958 until his death in 1992. Courtesy of Robert McGee.

20. Christmas 1968 Christmas card shows the McGee family with the White House in the background. *From left to right*: Robert, Lori Ann, Gale, Loraine, Mary Gale, and David. Courtesy Robert McGee.

21. Gale McGee studying in his dorm room at Normal School and Teachers College at Wayne, Nebraska. The school's name later changed to Nebraska State Teachers College and is now known as Wayne State College. Courtesy Robert McGee.

22. Sammy the dog joins Professor McGee and colleague Ruhl Bartlett, professor of history at Tufts University in Massachusetts. Behind Bartlett are members of the University of Wyoming History Department and longtime McGee allies Fred Nussbaum, Al Larson, unknown man, and Bill Steckel. Courtesy Robert McGee.

11

Wars Can No Longer Be Won,
but They Can Be Lost

Lyndon Johnson came to Washington as a legislative secretary in 1930 and served in the U.S. House and Senate for a dozen years each and as vice president. He was now president. The time for celebration was limited by the extraordinary challenges he and others confronted while serving in public office during those days.

If Johnson gave serious thought to not running on the eve of his party's convention the previous August, regret at having done so must have set in not long after his inauguration. Before the cherry blossoms bloomed in the Washington spring of 1965, dark clouds began to gather. Eight U.S. Marines were killed and hundreds more were wounded in a Viet Cong mortar attack at Pleiku on February 7. Malcolm X was murdered two weeks later. Then in March came the violence at Selma and elsewhere throughout the South. As much as Johnson beseeched his fellow Americans not to "reopen old wounds and rekindle old hatreds," violence on the streets of America and in the jungles of Vietnam defined the coming years.

Charles Cooper had a ringside seat to one of the ugliest fights of the Vietnam War. It was a one-sided battle, unfolding not in the jungles of Southeast Asia but in the Oval Office. Cooper was an aide to Adm. David L. McDonald, a member of the Joint Chiefs of Staff. He had been asked to hold up a large map of Southeast Asia mounted on a piece of plywood as McDonald and the other members of the Joint Chiefs met with President Johnson.

LBJ convened the meeting to receive their recommendations for ending the war. As Cooper labored to hold the heavy plywood still, the Joint Chiefs explained their proposal to mine Haiphong Harbor, blockade the North Vietnamese coastline, and bomb Hanoi. Johnson didn't seem to understand. "So, you're going to cut them off, keep them from being reinforced, and then you're going to bomb them into the Stone Age?" Yes, that was the plan.

"You goddamn fucking assholes." Cooper was stunned as the president of the United States began streaming obscenities. "You're trying to get me to start World War III with your idiotic bullshit, your military wisdom." After taking the time to insult each man individually, the president calmed himself and asked, "Imagine that you're me; that you're the president of the United States and five incompetents came into your office to try to talk you into starting World War III. What would you do?" After a few more explosions and expletives, the president told them that they had contaminated his office, and he then unceremoniously dismissed them. "Get the hell out of here right now."[1]

Whether reading Johnson's memoirs, the Pentagon Papers, or Senator McGee's correspondence from those days, it is clear the president was forced to navigate a narrow space between those who wanted an all-out war and those who wanted an immediate peace. It was no different for the Senate's most vocal proponent of Johnson's Vietnam policies. McGee attempted to moderate those who thought the United States should use nuclear weapons and strategies that could have drawn the Chinese and the Soviets into the conflict while attempting to explain what was at stake to those who wanted the United States to walk away. How did it happen that one of the Senate's most consistent liberals became the president's point person for a war that, day by day, became increasingly unpopular among liberals and others?

There is a clear, traceable line leading back to Gale McGee's doctoral studies at the University of Chicago, his Russian studies at the Council on Foreign Relations in 1952, and his pre-Senate writings on international affairs. Once a "militant isolationist" (his own description), he evolved into a militant proponent of the theory that a balance of power among adversarial nations is the only alternative to war.

Dr. McGee scrutinized history and found that wars resulted when an imbalance of power was allowed to define the relationship between nations. It was the imbalance between Hitler's Germany and other European nations that gave the German dictator confidence that he could conquer the continent and perhaps the world. It cost millions of lives to restore the balance of power and bring peace. When he cast his eyes on the Far East, McGee feared the same if China were permitted to control the region.

Washington Post columnist Walter Lippmann lived in an elegant home near the Washington National Cathedral. Lyndon Johnson felt welcome to "drop by and bum a drink" in earlier days.[2] But now the columnist and the president didn't share many drinks. Lippmann was one of the first of the president's inner circle to turn against him for his handling of the Vietnam War. Lippmann had greatly annoyed Johnson with a column calling for negotiations while denouncing the war and raising the issue of the war's morality and the "gigantic risks" he saw inherent in Johnson's decision to escalate the fighting.[3]

On a cold February evening in 1965, the columnist hosted a small group of senators to celebrate his birthday and to engage them in a conversation about the war. They were Gale McGee, George McGovern, and Frank Church. Over dinner, McGee explained his "balance of power" ideas to dubious colleagues. Neither Church nor McGovern then supported an immediate pullout, but they told McGee the war's end should be negotiated and the sooner the better. As they talked, respectfully countering one another point by point, it occurred to each that this was a debate deserving of a wider audience.[4] "It was on that occasion," McGee recalled, "that we kind of agreed officially to transfer this conversation to the floor of the Senate."[5]

McGee and McGovern were history professors, and they knew a "teachable moment" when they saw one. The genesis of the national debate over Vietnam, which began in the spring of 1965, was orchestrated that night by these three. It catapulted McGee into his role as the chief Senate proponent of the war.

The Senate convened at noon on February 17, 1965. The chaplain's prayer paid heed to America's "inner strife and fears of outward foes." Daniel Inouye of Hawaii assumed the chair as acting Senate president *pro tempore*. A few bills were introduced, and other routine business was conducted. Senators used three-minute speeches to complain about the commercialization of George Washington's birthday, to recognize Lithuanian Independence Day, to pay tribute to the Salvation Army, and the like. A couple of senators spoke briefly about Vietnam, raising concerns about growing opposition to the war. A lengthy debate was held on legislation dealing with the Federal Reserve Board and requirements regarding maintaining gold certificates.

And then it began.[6] Senator Church initiated the debate with a discussion of how thin the United States had spread its resources in attempting to halt the international advancement of communism. Referring to the 1960 trip he and McGee had taken to Africa, Church said the U.S. policy on that continent floundered as a result of U.S. efforts to control too many of Africa's decisions, what he called "the mistake of too much intervention." He then moved to Vietnam. "The hard fact is that there are limits to what we can do in helping any government surmount a Communist uprising. If the people themselves will not support the government in power, we cannot save it." The Idaho lawmaker quoted President Kennedy. "We must face the fact that the United States is neither omnipotent nor omniscient, that we cannot always impose our will on the other 94 percent of mankind." Church called for a negotiated settlement.

McGee took his turn. He and Church had learned a great deal about Vietnam and Africa traveling to both places together. His remarks made clear they had not, however, learned the same things during those trips. He contested Church's call for negotiations and reminded his colleagues the United States never offered to negotiate European issues with the Soviets. Instead, he said, the United States drew a line in Europe and warned the Soviets "we were ready to fight if the Russians moved into those areas. There should be the same sacred line in Vietnam."

Church responded. McGee's analogy was flawed. "If we believe that a white western nation can intervene and take over this kind of war, convert it into an American war, and then settle it in any durable way, I simply disagree." McGee rebounded, raising the issue at the heart of his support for LBJ's policy. "If we, through a policy of hesitation or a policy of premature negotiation, make it possible for the Chinese to move into Southeast Asia, however surreptitiously, we jeopardize the political balance of the world."

Church answered, predicting continued U.S. military responses would only force North Vietnam to send more troops into the South where the government was too weak to deal with them. That in turn, Church argued, would require the United States to send more American combat troops and then perhaps China would one day join the battle. "We can go down that road," Church said, "with all the attendant pain, costs, and tragedy."

It was then McGovern's turn. Thanking both McGee and Church for the high level of their debate, he aligned himself with Church's call for negotiations. "Our military embrace of the South Vietnamese rulers may have actually opened the way for Communist gains in Southeast Asia and delayed the development of a responsible government." He posited the possibility of both the Soviet Union and China coming to the aid of their allies in North Vietnam.

The old debate coach was clearly enjoying the exchange, calling it "fascinating and enlightening." McGee said negotiations would signal to North Vietnam and China that the United States is a "paper tiger, tired and ready to go home." He urged colleagues to wait patiently for a more opportune time to negotiate. McGee spelled out the steps he saw leading to that opportunity. First, he said the United States should draw a firm line at the 17th parallel. "That means when 1,000 troops come over the border from the north, it requires a full division to match them." McGee reminded Church how they had flown together above the jungles witnessing North Vietnamese troops "pitter-pattering down the jungle trails, their activities quite obscured by foliage or darkness." McGee believed increased infiltration from the North should be met with increased U.S. bombing of North Vietnamese military facilities. If that didn't work, bombing should be expanded to include the destruction of the North's bridges, highways, and railroads. If necessary, bombs should be dropped on their manufacturing and industrial centers.

Church doubted the North would give up its interest in the South even with such punishing American bombs. "They have been engaged for many years in their revolution, first to throw out the French. The ambition of Hanoi is to reunite the country. Efforts to deny that will not succeed."

McGee closed with a full-throated defense of the domino theory. "The fact remains that if Vietnam goes, Cambodia goes, Thailand goes, Indonesia goes, the Philippines go. This is only the proverbial camel's nose under the tent." The debate ended, and the Senate adjourned at 7:28 p.m.

McGee's performance earned him a personal phone call "from a very high administration official thanking him for the speech."[7] It was a grateful Lyndon Johnson. Frank Church's performance, on the other hand, earned him an angry confrontation with the president, who demanded to know who the Idaho Democrat talked to before his speech. "Why, Mr. President, I had a long talk with Walter Lippmann." The president snarled, "The next time you want a dam built in Idaho, go ask Walter Lippmann."[8]

Church's speech also landed him on Project MINARET's government surveillance list. According to documents declassified in 2013, almost fifty years after Church's speech, U.S. government agencies requested surveillance of prominent Americans during the Vietnam era through a top secret domestic surveillance program called Project MINARET. The surreptitious program's targets included civil rights leader Martin Luther King Jr. and heavyweight boxing champion Muhammad Ali as well as Senator Church.[9]

The morning following the McGee-Church-McGovern debate, the *Washington Post* front-page headline read, "Viet Crisis Stirs Senate; Some Cut Party Lines."[10] On February 28, the *New York Times* devoted a full page to the debate.[11] On the left was a portrait of Senator McGovern, McGee on the right, each presented in large five and a half inch by two full column portraits. "It's a bitter war," the article began, "brothers against brothers, Democrats against Democrats, Republicans against Republicans." McGee told the *Times* that Vietnam posed a serious threat to U.S. security. Losing the war, he said, would open the door to Chinese expansionist goals. McGovern countered, "We have to recognize that we are not omnipotent." McGovern said the conflict was little more than a civil war. McGee agreed but said that fact should not "get us off the track." The real threat, he believed, was China.

McGovern said the United States should negotiate a settlement. McGee proposed giving the North Vietnamese an ultimatum saying, "We don't want your land, you are free to do anything you wish, but we want you to seal off the 17th parallel. Now, if you don't we will bomb your military fields and encampments as proof that we mean business. If that still doesn't convince you, we will bomb your bridges, your railroads, and your highways." McGovern predicted McGee's idea of sealing off the 17th parallel would require "five or six American divisions and involve enormous casualties." McGee countered. "Our real test is to get through to the other side that we mean to stay there as long as necessary to guarantee the chance for Southeast Asian governments to develop in their own way and not to have some outside influence imposed upon them."

Their debate continued on March 8 during an hourlong nationally televised program on CBS Reports entitled "Vietnam: The Hawks and the Doves." The program was one of the first times those terms were used to describe competing sides of this growing national debate. CBS newsman Charles Collingwood called the escalation of combat a "crossroads." Senator McGee, on the other hand, echoed the Johnson position. Escalation, he said, was "a necessary forerunner to any meaningful negotiations." McGovern replied, "There are problems all around the world that do not lend themselves to a military solution, and particularly a military solution imposed by foreign troops." The contrast between the two sides was immediately clear and irreconcilable. The hawks were convinced that escalation of the war was the only way to end it while the doves saw escalation as an inevitable path to a long, uncertain war.

The intellectual sophistication of their debates evidenced the fact that the two Democrats were the only members of the Senate holding doctoral degrees. This exchange led the media and others to identify McGee as the spokesman for Johnson's Vietnam policy. At the conclusion of the CBS debate, Collingwood summarized that McGee was a hawk on Vietnam and McGovern was a dove. Those terms were used for the remainder of the war to define the divide in America.[12]

President Johnson planned a major address to the nation for April 7, 1965, at Johns Hopkins University, when he would explain his Vietnam policy to Americans. Johnson was told that Senator Church planned his own speech on Vietnam the following day. The president summoned Church, McGovern, and McGee for a meeting in the Oval Office. LBJ hoped to persuade Church to tone down his planned speech. McGee and McGovern were there because Johnson knew the two had been invited to be a part of a CBS News analysis of his speech immediately after it was televised. The president read the text of his Johns Hopkins speech to the three.[13] While the speech threatened that the United States would not withdraw from the North, it also held out a carrot. The United States would provide a billion dollars to develop the Mekong River delta.[14] Just as the TVA had modernized that American river valley under the New Deal, so it was that LBJ thought he could earn North Vietnam's trust by doing the same for Vietnam.

The morning following Johnson's speech, the Senate convened at 10 a.m. Frank Church rose to speak. He was unaware that the week before the Johns Hopkins speech, U.S. Army Commander William Westmoreland had asked the president for more troops to hold the line against growing Viet Cong strength. Neither did he know that the day he, McGee, and McGovern met with Johnson, the president had already signed an order changing the Marines' mission from defense to offense and sending the additional 20,000 combat troops.[15]

Focusing on what Johnson told him and his two colleagues the night before, Church seemed reconciled to Johnson's position. "I believe most Americans will applaud President Johnson's address at Johns Hopkins University last night. I was much encouraged by it." He added, however, that he hoped the Senate would not be "a bear pit for the bellicose" but "the center for a widening debate on the premises and principles, which should underlie a sound American policy in Vietnam."[16]

The national and international exposure shattered McGee's routine. He was besieged with media calls from around the world. Invitations by the basketful came from colleges, national organizations, media outlets, and others. Americans were ready to debate the war. Gale McGee and George McGovern traveled the country, participating in campus "teach-ins." McGovern was the leading antiwar voice of the times, and he called McGee "the Senate's most articulate defender of Administration policy."[17] A constituent inquired, "How does it feel to be agreeing with all those vociferous Republicans?" McGee replied, "It is a rather unnerving experience for me to find some of my supporters in the Vietnam situation to be those who, up until now, believed I was in league with the ghost of Joe Stalin."[18]

In an April 29, 1965, speech titled "An Academic Looks at Vietnam," McGee complained about what he saw as one-sided media coverage of antiwar protests on college campuses. Unlike many who supported the war, McGee said the articulate voices coming from the administration and the Senate should be joined "from the campuses of our great educational institutions."[19] McGee told fellow senators that media coverage of protests conveyed an erroneous image that everyone was against the president's policies. Not so, said McGee, who appealed "to the currently silent segments of our campuses . . . to declare themselves now in a public way."[20]

His speech caught the president's attention. LBJ telephoned McGee to thank him for his comments and to ask him to disclose information illicitly obtained by the FBI.[21]

It was a Sunday afternoon. Mary Gale was on her way outside to play with friends. The telephone on the wall of the McGees' Maryland home rang, temporarily interrupting her plans.

"Hello?" she said.

"Sugar, is your Daddy home?"

"Yes. Who's calling, please?"

"It's Lyndon, sugar. Tell him it's Lyndon."

"Okay. Hang on." Not sure where her Daddy was and anxious to get out the door, Mary Gale hollered, "Daddy, Lyndon's on the phone." She left the phone to run outside to play while the president of the United States waited.[22]

When McGee picked up the dangling receiver, the president thanked him for his support, but what Johnson most wanted to talk about was how distressed he was with the antiwar activity in the country and particularly on college campuses. "The Communists believe we will throw in the towel because of all the pressure here at home," he told McGee. "Every facilitator that the Communist world has is being used to divide us. One of their boys in this DuBois movement, this youth organization, his mother is really one of the leaders in the Communist Party in this country.[23] Edgar Hoover is very unhappy about this."

Johnson told McGee the Communists were at the heart of organizing the antiwar activity on college campuses, adding, "Now Hoover has most of these groups infiltrated, his people go right with them and hear all these discussions." Johnson said Hoover had "a big file" on the antiwar movement. "Our well-intentioned friends don't know. I thought you ought to have the background that their principal play is to bring pressure on us to throw in the towel and that's what they are trying to get the students to do." McGee said he was deeply disturbed about what he had just been told, and he offered to help. Before ending the call, the president promised he would get some "CIA and FBI messages and ask someone to come talk to you."

FBI agent D. W. Bowers arrived late in the afternoon of May 3 at McGee's office to brief him "regarding the Communist Party activities with respect to the Vietnam situation." As the two sat in the senator's private office, McGee spoke of his conversations and debates with friends in the academic community. He acknowledged that most were opposed to the war and that he was "striving to sway their opinions wherever possible." The senator worried aloud that those who agitated against the war received more publicity than those who supported the president. McGee asked Bowers to keep him informed on the activity of the W.E.B. Du Bois Clubs, saying he was particularly interested in any evidence the Bureau had "concerning Communist activities and influences in the academic and student fields."

Bowers went away unsatisfied. He did not get the commitment he came for. McGee did not accept LBJ's invitation to publicly disclose Hoover's allegations of Communist influence among antiwar activists, and Bowers dismissed McGee as a "liberal in some of his thinking." Bowers reported to his superiors that the Wyoming senator "does not know the best way to combat the current surge of Communist activities on the campuses." Bowers's report betrayed some annoyance that McGee found it difficult to separate "honest, conscientious dissent from Communist activities."[24]

In a Senate speech three months after the LBJ phone call, McGee elevated the significance of the debate being kindled on college campuses across the country. "The outcome of the debate will undoubtedly shape the future of the entire world for years to come." Gale McGee had deep respect for dissent. As a former university professor who had once risked his job to oppose textbook censorship, Johnson's use of the FBI to infiltrate U.S. campuses conflicted with McGee's views of academic freedom. He said he supported the teach-ins on campuses even though "I have been the object of much criticism because of my position" on Vietnam.[25] Talking about campus protests, he referred directly to what he had been told by Johnson, though not in a manner LBJ had hoped. "I know full well that this debate has taken on many of the aspects of a protest movement on the campus, that in this movement there are professional revolutionaries and malcontents as well as bona fide academics and students. I realize that perhaps there are even a few persons who might think they take orders from Moscow or Beijing and are working to turn this activity to their advantage."

McGee reminded senators that he had always encouraged dissent in academia and had hoped for "a dialogue rather than a monologue." He chided some of the protesters, saying there were some among the demonstrators "whose lack of enthusiasm for bathing causes concern among more traditional members of society." But McGee also warned against "new witch hunts" led by those who were fearful of dissent. He worried aloud that stifling dissent would endanger academic freedom. His words must have disappointed the president, who thought he could persuade McGee to expose what LBJ saw as the Communist infiltration his FBI director alleged existed.

George McGovern praised McGee's speech. "Although the senator from Wyoming and I have not agreed in all instances on the issue of our involvement in Vietnam, I have never for one moment doubted his sincerity and good faith." McGovern criticized those in the academic community who had not treated McGee with respect.

Mutual respect characterized the war debates between these two and Senator Church. When Church sent him a copy of an article he had written contesting the Wyoming senator's position on negotiations, McGee responded, "While we certainly have some differences of opinion on the best course of action . . . I thought that your presentation was a most excellent, concise, and forthright exposition of your point of view and should be considered by all who would understand the many complex aspects of our involvement in Vietnam."[26]

While respectful of opposing views, McGee made no apology for his outspokenness in favor of the war. Though he was firm about his belief that a balance of power was the only alternative to larger wars, McGee said he asked himself each night, "Suppose you're wrong on Vietnam?" But McGee's nocturnal doubts seemed to disappear in the heat of daytime oratory.[27] His "daytime oratory" supported the rights of the war's critics as much as it supported the war.

The senator's constituents wrote about an array of matters though not very often about Vietnam. People in Wyoming worried about Cuban immigrants who might be Communist agents, about the Dominican Republic, an LBJ proposal to enter into negotiations with Panama for a new treaty, about the high cost of foreign aid, and the possible admission of Red China to the UN. Throughout 1965, correspondence regarding Vietnam didn't start to fill even a single file folder.

A few were genuinely interested in learning what the United States was doing in Southeast Asia. McGee wrote a detailed four-page response to Phil Miller, a constituent from Dubois, who questioned U.S. policy. McGee raised the balance of power, explaining, "Under no circumstances shall Southeast Asia be permitted to fall under the control of Mainland China." He was willing to commit the United States to a long haul in Vietnam. "Given that definition of our priorities, there can remain nothing mystifying or uncertain about our policy in Vietnam whether that includes air strikes, foot soldiers, or naval power. The point is that whatever has to be done to achieve those goals must be done."[28]

Often the focus on the war gave way to the civil rights struggle. A growing number of black community leaders had lost patience with the political system. Martin Luther King endeavored to persuade his followers that meeting white violence with peaceful nonviolence would eventually win out. He visited Watts after the destruction and called the riots "environmental and not racial. The economic deprivation, social isolation, inadequate housing, and general despair of thousands of Negroes teeming in Northern and Western ghettos are the ready seeds which give birth to tragic expressions of violence."[29]

Gale McGee agreed with King. The Wyoming senator hit back at those who criticized the president and other Democrats over their failure to stop the riots. He said the critics were the same folks who voted against the model cities funding bill, the rent supplement bill, the war on poverty program, the food stamp program, the Civil Rights Act of 1966, the rat extermination program, funds for education, and the minimum wage. "It's easy to shout 'fire,' but it's quite another thing to pitch in and help fight the flames."[30]

From his earliest days as a leader of the movement, Dr. King said the question confronting oppressed people is how their struggle against injustice is to be waged. King said there were two alternatives. "One is resort to the all too prevalent method of physical violence and corroding hatred." But King encouraged a nonviolent strategy, which he said is "based on the conviction that the universe is on the side of justice."[31] Thus martyrdom was a mark of the American civil rights movement served by the unilateral disarmament of those who accepted King's nonviolent strategies. One of the martyrs was a white minister from Casper.

March 7 was a pleasant Sunday evening in an early 1965 Boston spring. Reverend James Reeb and his wife, Marie, had recently moved there from Washington DC. Reeb was raised in Casper, Wyoming, where he and Marie wed in 1950. Reeb attended seminary, was ordained, and began a ministry in Philadelphia. At first a Presbyterian, he eventually found a home serving one of the nation's historic faith communities at All Souls Unitarian Church in Washington. But Reeb was not fully satisfied. He wanted direct contact with those he served. He found it when he was hired by the American Friends Service Committee to work in the minority communities of Boston. Then came "Bloody Sunday."

Sitting in their comfortable living room, hundreds of miles from Selma, the Reebs were among millions of Americans witnessing the horror. From their soft couches across the country, Americans saw blacks being clubbed, gassed, and run over by policemen on horseback. Whites gathered along the Edmund Pettus Bridge, including many who had been in their church pews just a few hours earlier, and they cheered as black men, women, and children screamed and tried to run away. They were felled by the fists of their tormenters, bloodied by clubs, gagged breathless by gas grenades thrown indiscriminately, and chased down by horses and dogs.

Jim Reeb was deeply affected by what he saw, though he felt not so much a witness as a complacent accomplice. The next day, Dr. King challenged white clergy to join the struggle. By 10 p.m. that evening Reeb was seated on a flight to Atlanta. By breakfast time the following day he and dozens of others from around the nation were standing with King in Selma. The next day, March 9, Reeb joined hundreds in a march to the bridge, which ended without violence when King led the marchers in prayer and then stood and departed without crossing. That night after dinner, as he and two other white clergy left Walker's Café in Selma, they heard footsteps approaching from behind. "Hey, niggers," one of the men shouted in the clergymen's direction. "Hey, you niggers." One of the men used both hands, swinging a club like a baseball bat and hitting Reeb in the head. "Here's how it feels to be a nigger down here!" the attacker screamed.[32]

As soon as Senator McGee heard the sad news, he went to the floor of the Senate. He told his colleagues of the savage attack in Selma and acknowledged Reeb's parents, Mr. and Mrs. H. D. Reeb of Casper. McGee saluted Jim Reeb's bravery.

It is indeed a sad and tragic situation when Americans must suffer such a grievous injury in defense of a right that most of us take for granted. Yet it is heartening to note that there are still many Americans who take their commitment to our ideals and to human freedom seriously enough that they are willing to risk personal danger to see that these commitments are extended to all citizens.[33]

McGee extended sympathy to Reeb's wife and children and offered a prayer for his recovery, a prayer not answered. Jim Reeb died the following day.

McGee returned to the Senate floor to eulogize Reeb. He inserted into the *Congressional Record* a eulogy given during a Casper memorial service by a classmate of Reeb's and a friend of McGee's. Frank Bowron answered a woman who asked why Reeb bothered to go in the first place. "He had no business getting involved," she said. Bowron said, "Jim Reeb was taught right here in Casper that his going to Selma was the right thing to do, the decent thing, the Christian thing." Bowron shouted, "All America is standing trial for the murder of Jim Reeb."[34]

On April 1, McGee introduced an early version of "hate-crimes" legislation, making it a federal crime to kill anyone engaged in advocating for civil rights.[35] He then joined sixty-six other senators in introducing the Voting Rights Act of 1965.[36] The legislation was debated later that spring, and Gale McGee proved to be one of the bill's strongest advocates. He had been deeply moved by Jim Reeb's death. He recounted how Reeb and others had courageously given their lives for the cause. "That these lives must be sacrificed [and] that this bill must be enacted is a sad commentary upon the state of the nation."[37] McGee warned the Senate this would not be the last time they would "have to stand up and be counted."

Thereupon the Voting Rights Act of 1965 passed the Senate, 77–19. After the bill cleared the House of Representatives, President Johnson signed it into law on August 6. He then handed one of the pens he had used to the Wyoming lawmaker who cosponsored and so eloquently defended the law, one that McGee proudly displayed in his office for the remainder of his Senate service.

The ornate room where the Senate Foreign Relations Committee conducts its business seems undersized considering the giants of American history who have spent time there and the enormity of the decisions that have been made around the large conference table at the center of the room. The walls of this room overheard U.S. senators debate the issue of neutrality before America entered the war in 1941. These walls witnessed decisions made about World War II and European reconstruction, the Cold War, Korea, Vietnam, and the Middle East.[38] This was where Senator William Borah of Idaho attempted to isolate the United States from World War II. Here Arthur Vandenberg of California declared that foreign policy stops at the water's edge. "To these rooms have come heads of foreign nations, American presidents, secretaries of state, and countless others to inform and advise the committee in fulfillment of the Senate's constitutional role in the foreign policy of the United States."[39] John F. Kennedy and Barack Obama were once members.

In this room, the Senate first discussed the resolution giving Lyndon Johnson the authority to wage war in Southeast Asia. With the growing debate, this room was where men and women, selected to sit around its conference table, considered whether the Senate should demand greater involvement in determining U.S. foreign policy.

In late March 1966, Gale McGee was appointed to the Senate Foreign Relations Committee, a prize he had coveted since first running for the Senate.[40] With his membership on the Appropriations Committee, Wyoming's senior senator now had seats on the two most powerful and influential committees in the Senate.

As majority leader, Johnson appointed McGee to the Appropriations Committee. As president, he arranged for a committee membership exchange when Russell Long of Louisiana told him he preferred McGee's Commerce Committee assignment to his own seat on the Foreign Relations Committee. Johnson and Secretary of State Dean Rusk felt McGee could balance the national debate on the war, which they worried was decidedly one-sided. Foreign Relations Committee chairman J. William Fulbright had begun to sour on the war and was not pleased to have McGee join his committee. The president had to intervene to secure Fulbright's acquiescence. It was an omen of the ill will that would become more evident between the chairman and his new committee member.[41]

At the end of March 1966, as Senator McGee prepared to travel to Vietnam, the body of one of his constituents was being prepared to return to Wyoming. Mike Beck was a popular, soft-spoken senior at Cheyenne Central High School. The year he graduated, his name and photograph graced at least nine pages of Central's 1965 yearbook, *The Pow-Wow*. He was a star on both the football and wrestling teams. Beck was also a member of the International Relations Club, whose mission was, said the editor of the *Pow-Wow*, to stimulate a belief that "good foreign relations are necessary for world peace."[42]

As classmates prepared to go to college, Mike joined the U.S. Marine Corps within days of receiving his diploma. Mike soon completed basic training at Camp Pendleton, and he was in Vietnam by August 14. Seven months later on March 28, 1966, Mike's division was dispatched to assist another Marine unit experiencing heavy Viet Cong fire near Lam Loc hamlet. The enemy was waiting to ambush the Americans, and the battle disintegrated into hand-to-hand combat. Warriors from both sides used everything they had, from grenades and bayonets to bare fists, battling until after sundown.

The Marines recovered their dead comrades' bodies at dawn. Among the dozen was Mike Beck, nineteen years old. Barely ten months out of high school, he became one of 120 from Wyoming who were killed fighting the Vietnam War.[43] He died on the day his U.S. senator began a ten-day tour of Vietnam with Deputy Secretary of State Cyrus Vance.

McGee went to Vietnam at the personal request of the president. He arrived in Saigon along with Vance, whom McGee had known from the time they shared at the Council of Foreign Relations. "The President picked Cy and me as a two-man team to fly over to Vietnam and to try to analyze, in our judgment, what the issues were coming to be."[44]

This was McGee's third trip to Vietnam. This time the war and its South Vietnamese dissenters were on full display. Vance and McGee witnessed the bombing of the Victoria Hotel in Saigon and a street demonstration involving more than 10,000 Buddhists. They were denied access to Hue because of the threatening antiwar demonstrations at the university in that South Vietnamese city. Upon his return, McGee spoke to colleagues, reporting on the restlessness among their Vietnamese allies. He said no one knows what the future holds. "While no one dare predict with certainty, the time will not wait for a suspended judgment. History is never that kind to us."[45]

McGee reported his conclusions that the recent large military buildup had put the United States "on the verge of substantial military breakthroughs." He urged colleagues not to be discouraged by the criticism here and in Vietnam. Finally, with an accuracy his colleagues would never have predicted at that moment, McGee told the Senate he didn't expect this conflict to end with a "clear-cut verdict" or a peace treaty. More likely, he thought, was a steady reduction in hostilities.[46]

In a private White House meeting with the president, McGee expressed some concerns. He advised LBJ to put pressure on the South Vietnamese government to upgrade its military units, which were at about half strength. He also recommended that U.S. forces be assigned to more combat to "break the back of some of the enemy forces." He knew the political costs of more American casualties, he told Johnson, but felt that was the best shot at shortening the war.[47]

On full display in the Senate Foreign Relations Committee meeting room was the conflict between McGee and Fulbright. The earliest and most vocal supporter of the Gulf of Tonkin authorization, Fulbright has become an outspoken war critic. From the beginning, observers watched and waited, knowing it was only a matter of time before the antipathy between Fulbright and McGee erupted. "McGee will probably try to restrain his tongue for a time, but his deeply held foreign policy views will eventually force him to clash with members such as Chairman J. William Fulbright, who opposes the administration's intervention in what he terms a Vietnamese civil war."[48]

In fact, it already had. During a late April hearing, Fulbright asked Defense Secretary Robert McNamara rhetorically whether strong nations have a tendency to become arrogant. McNamara replied, "Some have, and some have not." Fulbright responded, "Every country has believed that God was on their side when they waged war." McGee couldn't hold his tongue. Interrupting the chairman, he used language uncommonly strong for a senator. "We are not a military people. I cannot quite buy the allegation that we have heard here that great military power induces arrogance and self-righteousness. I resent that as an American."[49]

During a televised committee hearing, McGee thought Secretary of State Dean Rusk was being treated disrespectfully. "I raised with the chairman my doubts about whether this was the way to run a committee." Fulbright insultingly thanked the senator from Wyoming for his "suggestions on how to run the committee from the lowest ranking member of the committee who has been with the committee the shortest length of time."[50]

McGee did not confine his criticism of Fulbright to the committee meeting room. Speaking on the campus of Oregon State University in mid-July 1966, the senator asserted that both McNamara and Rusk deserved better treatment than was afforded by the Foreign Relations Committee. Blaming the presence of television cameras, McGee said committee members had "abused and insulted" the two men. "While McGee named no names, he was obviously referring to the intense questioning of the two cabinet members by chairman J. William Fulbright, Sen. Wayne Morse, and Sen. Eugene McCarthy."[51]

While displeasing Fulbright, McGee was making his mark at the other end of Pennsylvania Avenue. Johnson was concerned that Dean Rusk might decide not to stay on as secretary of state. LBJ adviser Walt Rostow told the president that the cabinet job "is now so exhausting" and is taking a huge toll. LBJ asked Rostow to make recommendations for the next secretary of state, and he came back with a list of possible candidates. McGee was on the list. Rostow reminded the president, "He has shown guts on Vietnam."[52]

Rostow was a Gale McGee fan. On February 17, 1968, when LBJ asked Rostow to thank McGee for his speech printed in the *Congressional Record,* he did so, saying, "May I add a personal note? I find your steadiness amidst the swirling currents of the mass media and Congress one of the finest political performances I can recall in recent years. I am sure you would take the positions you have taken for only one reason: because you believe they are right."[53]

McGee, who previously heard little about the war from his constituents, was besieged with Vietnam-related mail in 1966. Letters from home reflected the same discord over the war as was being heard in the halls of Congress. One writer was "proud to be from Wyoming and have a Senator that feels as you do about the Vietnam crisis."[54] Another was ashamed "when I read the gloating reports of how many of our boys have been killed in North Vietnam."[55] One asked simply, "Will you please use your influence to end the war in South Vietnam?" A Casper resident told his senator, "Up to now, I believed we were doing the right thing." Now, he said, the war seemed "hopeless," and he asked, "Why are we there?" McGee's response was lengthy. He cited the "marvelous and almost unbelievably powerful attack" the United States had mustered against Viet Cong forces and "massive results of the B-52 raids on the Ho Chi Minh trail": "I realize that many people are troubled by our commitments in Vietnam and by the cost in lives and dollars that it is costing, but I believe that we have no choice but to defend freedom where we can where it is threatened around the world."[56]

The Reverend Otis Jackson of St. Matthew's Cathedral in Laramie told McGee he thought the United States was the aggressor in Vietnam and destroying that nation seemed "a peculiar way to help a country."[57] To the contrary, said R. R. Bostwick of Casper. He was unhappy the United States was not making use of all of its "firepower" including nuclear weapons. Mr. Bostwick advised McGee, "We should either go in there to win, using all our firepower, or we should get out."[58]

Sydney Spiegel of Cheyenne told McGee there was no difference between the senator's views on the war and "those of the right-wingers you are purporting to oppose so fervently."[59] Spiegel, a Democratic Party activist, advised the senator "to consider me, from now on, a political enemy." McGee snapped back, his brief letter containing nothing more than an Abraham Lincoln proclamation.

> If I were to try to read, much less answer, all the attacks made on me, this shop might as well be closed for any other business. I do the very best I know how, the best I can, and I mean to keep doing so until the end. If the end brings me out alright, what is said against me won't amount to anything. If the end brings me out wrong, ten angels swearing I was right would make no difference.[60]

However, Gale McGee's skin was not so thick as he sometimes portrayed. He wouldn't say what his close aides were willing to admit. "One of the most painful experiences the Senator has undergone," wrote McGee staffer Jim Fagan to a political friend, "has been the almost hateful abandonment of him by many people he considered his close friends and intellectual allies on the sole consideration that he and those close allies do not see eye-to-eye on Vietnam."[61] It would only get worse as the Wyoming Democratic Party began its own divisive debate on the war.

In 1966, Stokely Carmichael formed the Black Panther Party, and in October it adopted its platform. "The Second Amendment to the Constitution of the United States gives a right to bear arms." The Panthers called on "all black people to arm themselves for self-defense." Fred Hampton, the influential Black Panther leader from Chicago, went further. "We're going to organize and dedicate ourselves to revolutionary political power and teach ourselves the specific needs of resisting the power structure, arm ourselves, and we're going to fight the reactionary pigs with international proletarian revolution."[62]

Martin Luther King had his hands full keeping the movement anchored in nonviolence. When King's people attempted to sing "We Shall Overcome," the Panthers sang "We Shall Overrun."[63] Militant influences on the civil rights movement were nothing new. Robert F. Williams, a movement leader in North Carolina, wrote a classic revolutionary book in 1962. In *Negroes with Guns* Williams "asserted the right of Negroes to meet the violence of the Ku Klux Klan with armed self-defense."[64]

He had done so himself in the summer of 1957 when a group of club-toting whites attacked blacks protesting a "whites only" municipal swimming pool in Monroe, North Carolina. Blacks thwarted the attack when they went home and returned armed with rifles, shotguns, and pistols. The incident persuaded Williams and others that the only way to protect themselves was to arm themselves. "When Dr. King paraphrased Gandhi and said, "Do to us what you will and we will still love you," Williams cried, "No, I say, an everlasting no to this. Two hundred years of appeal by accumulative suffering to the hearts of racists is enough, enough, enough. The American Negro is not a downtrodden Hindu."[65]

American cities were scarred by at least forty-three race riots in 1966.[66] Senator McGee was as disturbed as anyone by the violence, but he advised against "allowing this dissatisfaction to divert our attention from the basic issue and the basic problem," which he saw as the denial of human rights.[67] In a September Senate speech, McGee called on "the more militant spokesmen and leaders of the movement" to "eschew lawless activity" and de-escalate the violence. He said whites should also "ease off." He said to both black and white, "Reason, not fear, is the only way to deal with race relations in America."[68]

As 1966 came to an end, McGee was again sent to Asia, this time with Senator Frank Moss of Utah. The assignment was a review of the political and military status of the countries surrounding the Chinese rim. They spent thirty-one days covering a dozen nations, traveling more than 30,000 miles. "Whatever the rationale, there is no denying that China is uppermost in the minds of the Asian nations sharing common frontiers with China," McGee's final report emphasized. They found that despite "carping comments" about the U.S. bombing of

South Vietnam, what worried these countries most of all was China. Guessing at China's intentions preoccupied the discussions these two senators had with Asian leaders. McGee reported their biggest concern was that the United States might withdraw from Vietnam, jeopardizing the safety of the other nations in that region. But it was a double-edged sword. All of these nations "still questioned the necessity of bombing North Vietnam." They worried that U.S. bombing could bring the Chinese into the war.

Upon his return, McGee learned he had been dumped from the Foreign Relations Committee. "The chairman had succeeded in pushing me off by shriveling up the size of the committee." Even though the Democrats lost just three seats in the 1966 election, reducing their majority to 64–36, Senator Fulbright used the election results to realign committee membership. McGee was gone. "I always kinda felt that he didn't need to cut it back," McGee said later. "Nonetheless, this was his device of getting, I think, less at me but at Lyndon."[69] It may have been Fulbright's way of getting to Johnson, but the Arkansas senator with so much power was likely still stinging from a July 1966 comment McGee gave to a national magazine. *Newsweek* quoted Fulbright as complaining about "the arrogance of power. McGee retorted, calling Fulbright's criticism 'the arrogance of dissent.'"[70]

Fulbright may have felt that losing his seat on the Foreign Relations Committee would temper McGee's role in supporting the war. It did not. Answering for Johnson's war policies consumed more of the senator's time. The war was also consuming more of LBJ's time and American resources. Taxpayers were weary. A Gallup poll in late 1966 said 73 percent opposed any new taxes to pay for the war. Liberals like McGee and Johnson harbored hopes for the Great Society, believing for a time that the United States could win the war in Vietnam while fighting the domestic war on poverty. However, the nation could not fight the two wars simultaneously. The war on poverty was suspended.

In February 1967, McGee was afforded an opportunity that must have given him great personal satisfaction. He was invited by the University of Illinois to debate the war with Dr. Hans Morgenthau, his former University of Chicago professor. Twenty years earlier, McGee and Morgenthau had found much about which they could agree on foreign affairs. Vietnam changed that.

As McGee was a spokesperson for the war, Morgenthau made headlines with his opposition. Like the senator, the professor appeared frequently on campuses across the country. As the two argued, McGee said that as the principal WWII victor, the United States was bequeathed the burden of keeping the status quo. "Containment," he said, "is a substitute for war." Morgenthau countered, "Containment will only work so long as China is weak. When China is strong, it is a question of who will contain who." Morgenthau opposed U.S. bombing and criticized McGee's stance against negotiation. He said, "It makes little difference who governs Vietnam. What is important is that we disengage ourselves without a loss of standing."[71]

Later in 1967, Robert Welch, director of the John Birch Society, issued a report blaming Johnson for the deaths of American soldiers. Reading it provided McGee and others with an answer to the question of why so much of their mail contained the same charges made with identical phrasing. Postcards and letters often began with "When are we going to win this war in Vietnam—and why not?" The query was set forth verbatim in Welch's report. Other letters used Welch's lines, "Why fight 'em in Vietnam and help 'em elsewhere?" and the John Birch Society claim that the United States refused to allow "the best trained troops in the world," that is, the forces commanded by Chiang Kai-shek on Formosa, to fight the North Vietnamese.[72]

McGee issued a point-by-point response to the Bircher claims. "Under the cloud of a nuclear holocaust, which can destroy the human race, we no longer dare to measure wars as one might measure a basketball game. Wars can no longer be won, but they can be lost." He pointed out that the best use of Chiang's army was to keep the Red Chinese "pinned down" where they are, and putting Formosa's troops in Vietnam might well trigger Mao's decision to send combat troops to aid North Vietnam.[73]

In April, McGee's friend Marvin Tisthammer of Torrington wrote to urge officials "to pull out the stops" on the military and let them win the war. He was unhappy with the protesters and hoped the Justice Department "takes care of Clay the way it should," a reference to heavyweight boxing champion Cassius Clay, who refused induction into the armed forces. He noted there were a lot of Republican farmers and ranchers backing McGee, "although it is hard to get them to admit their support." Tisthammer closed by reminding McGee that the pheasants "are beginning to hatch," promising some good hunting come the fall.[74]

In May 1967, McGee's office asked the State Department to review claims made by Senate opponents of the war. They admitted having "some difficulty in coming up with any significant factual errors in reviewing recent speeches made on Vietnam."[75] It seemed the Senate adversaries, McGee, McGovern, and Church among others, were working with the same facts but reaching far different conclusions about their meaning.

The volume of McGee's mail in 1967 reflected the impossible position in which elected officials were finding themselves as a growing and contentious debate raged across the nation. The letters demonstrated the widening gulf between Americans. Some wanted peace at any cost. Others wanted victory at any cost. Some blamed LBJ. Others blamed Congress. A few thought the United States should use nuclear bombs, while many were appalled at the destruction being wrought by conventional weapons. Growing numbers saw conspiracies involving the United Nations. Gruesome photos of dead soldiers and children accompanied some letters. An issue of *Ramparts* magazine sent to the senator displayed a mock photo of a Vietnamese child crucified like Christ on its cover.[76] A few writers blamed the Democrats for starting the war, others for losing it, and still others for not ending it. Letters came from some who had taken part in protests and others from those who demanded the protesters be tried for treason.

In April, one of Dr. McGee's professors from the University of Chicago wrote. Dr. J. Fred Rippy, now seventy-five years old, retired, and caring for his frail wife in North Carolina, took time to note he followed his former student's work on Vietnam. Without judgment pro or con, Rippy said he had "noticed you support LBJ on the Vietnam issue. I read all your Senate speeches on this subject." McGee thanked Rippy for his letter, confiding, "Vietnam has been an exceedingly difficult question for a former academic. I say that because so many of my so-called friends in the profession have been exceptionally abusive in the 'advice' they have passed along to me on our policy there."[77]

On June 4, 1967, McGee was invited to give the commencement address at American University in Washington. It was his son David's graduating class. McGee urged the graduates not to simply focus on the brutality of the war. That, he said, missed the point. If Japan had been stopped in Manchuria, McGee asserted, the war might have been averted in 1931. U.S. policy preventing any one European nation from dominating Europe had been successful. "To understand Viet Nam is to understand that the issue is not Viet Nam. It is rather a chance for stability in all of Eastern Asia."[78] Later that month Senators McGee and McGovern faced off at a New York convention. McGovern argued Ho Chi Minh represented no threat to U.S. security. McGee countered, "It is a lawless world, sometimes made up of good guys and sometimes bullies. The only substitute for war is a balance of power."[79]

Sharing stages with liberals like McGovern and Frank Church underscored what many observers, particularly antiwar activists, thought to be an anomaly. They wanted to know how a liberal like McGee could possibly support the war? McGee answered, "We will not attain liberal goals for ourselves or the rest of the world if we abandon Vietnam to communism."[80] It was classic New Deal philosophy applied to the rest of the world.

It was unavoidable that the war would eventually divide Wyoming Democrats as it was dividing the nation. A June 1967 meeting of the state Democratic Party in Cheyenne exposed the growing chasm. Party chairman John J. Rooney joined Senator McGee in supporting President Johnson's policies. Rooney, a former FBI agent, warned his fellow Democrats that there were Communists "where you least expect them." Rooney urged Wyoming's Democrats to stand with LBJ and McGee. After all, Rooney said, their government leaders knew more about the war than they did, and their decisions should not be questioned.

One woman in the audience, Linda Miller of Dubois, openly challenged Rooney. "Are we not Americans first and party members second?" She was advised, "We as patriotic Americans must rally around the flag."[81]

Attending that meeting also was Mariko Miller, the daughter of a Japanese diplomat who played a role in trying to avoid a Japanese-U.S. war in the days ahead of December 7, 1941. After Pearl Harbor, she returned with her parents to Japan where they spent the war years. In 1953 Mariko married a Tennessee lawyer named Mayne Miller, and the couple moved to Wyoming where she became a Democratic Party activist.[82] Mariko became an increasingly loud antiwar voice. The heated discussions between these two intellectuals, McGee and Mariko, provided Wyoming Democrats as clear a picture of the war's competing arguments as any debate in which the senator had engaged. Their debates also highlighted the fact that McGee and a growing number of his own party faithful were starting to travel in different directions.

President Johnson's staff followed McGee's work closely and reminded him to watch each time the senator appeared on *Meet the Press* or other network television programs, which was not infrequent.[83] But McGee was becoming frustrated. He had walked the plank for Johnson, and all he had received in return was the rejection of being cast off the Foreign Relations Committee. In the fall of 1967, McGee told Dean Rusk he planned to leave the Senate altogether if he was not able to regain his seat on the committee. The following month McGee's name came up in a conversation Rusk had with LBJ. Rusk relayed McGee's plans to LBJ during a Saturday morning phone call on December 9. "If he doesn't get back on the Foreign Relations Committee, he's seriously thinking of leaving the Senate."[84]

Rusk raised the possibility of appointing McGee to replace Arthur Goldberg as UN ambassador. Johnson replied, "I would take him in one minute." The president hung up and immediately phoned McGee.[85]

"I called you for two reasons," Johnson said, opening the conversation. "I just wanted to tell you how very proud I am of you and all you've done in this critical period for your country and how courageous, how exacting it's been." The president then said he called to ask McGee to accept his appointment as ambassador to the United Nations. "Oh, my," responded McGee, uncharacteristically staggered. "I . . . well . . . that would be the most honorable sort of thing. I would just feel so incapable, you know."

"No. No, you're not incapable of anything," Johnson interrupted. The president launched into a monologue about his frustrations with some of the appointees sent previously to the UN. "People go up there and think they're secretary of state, and just think they don't need to check anything here and it causes us problems . . . badly . . . and then they go out to a cocktail party and tell everybody they talk to, well, Rusk is a son of a bitch."

Johnson dangled another possibility, telling McGee that anyone who took the UN job "ought to be qualified to be secretary of state." He then charged at McGee with characteristic Johnson flattery. "I'm thinking of what's best for the country," he said, "and I don't know of a human that I think is as knowledgeable in this general field, that is not New York oriented, that is as articulate, and that I think makes as good an impression on TV, and I've watched them all, and I think you have a little of the mold of Wilson and a Lincoln combination. I think you have a little of the George Marshall and Sam Houston. I think you look a little bit frontier and pioneer and a fellow that's pulled himself up by his bootstraps, and I think you have enough sophistication and articulation that you're my type of man."

But Lyndon Johnson wanted to make certain McGee understood who was not his "type of man." He continued, "I don't want one of these Adlai Stevensons. I liked him but to me I always kind of felt like he had to squat to pee."

As McGee nodded audibly, Johnson went on with his pitch telling McGee what challenges he would face at the UN. "Now you've got the greatest problems in the Middle East, and that's the most interesting thing." The president called Vietnam "just chicken feed compared to what the Russians are doing over there."

Although McGee didn't ask, Johnson knew there had already been speculation that he might not seek another term. He told McGee not to worry about finding another job "if I didn't run, if I died." He assured McGee he could become president of any university in America. McGee was stunned and said he needed some time to think. LBJ said yes, "but not very long." Johnson told the senator to "talk to your wife. We can talk about it maybe in the morning, maybe tonight."

12

Reaping the Whirlwind

The year 1968 was wracked by chaos and crisis, turbulence and tragedy, bookended by two rather optimistic events. On New Year's Day
it seemed most of Wyoming was in New Orleans. Gale, Loraine, and
their son Robert were among the thousands of Wyoming fans traveling
to watch their football team, one of the university's best ever, playing
in the Sugar Bowl. The Cowboys lost to Louisiana State University,
20–13. Still it was a welcome respite from politics and the daily news.

Nearly twelve months later, just a few days before one of the most
turbulent years in American history ended, Frank Borman, James
Lovell, and William Anders left here for "eight days in space" (it was
actually six days from launch on December 21 through reentry on
the 27th). The United States finally made up for *Sputnik*. As Apollo
8 became the first manned space ship to orbit the moon, astronauts
read the creation myth from the Hebrew Bible's book of Genesis
and sent back photographs of the earth. It all seemed so serene and
peaceful. "Ah, you may leave here, for eight days in space, but when
you return, it's the same old place."[1]

Philosopher William Dean studies the spiritual culture of nations,
which he finds has more to do with the nation's belief in itself than
with religious beliefs.[2] A spiritual culture provides a national vision
enabling people to interpret events shaping their place in the world.
"The nation is informed," Dr. Dean observes, "by the spiritual culture's sense of the whole as the nation makes decisions that determine
the country's course in the world." The spiritual culture reflects the
dominant ideals and values of a country. The years after World War

II had been easier, and dominant national values were recognizable until John F. Kennedy's assassination. The civil rights movement and the nation's unending struggle over racial identity coupled with the war in Vietnam increasingly left the United States without a dominant spiritual culture. In 1968, the nation reaped the whirlwind.

A January 1968 public opinion poll informed voters what they already knew. Public confidence in Congress was at a five-year low. While today's members of Congress would covet such numbers, members of the 90th Congress were distressed to learn that while 41 percent of the public thought they were doing a good job, 59 percent disagreed.[3] Many voters were angry about the war in Southeast Asia, but not all for the same reason. Some were furious the United States could not or would not win the war. Others demonstrated their unhappiness on the streets, demanding their government end the war and bring the troops home. Growing numbers of Americans began to view the failures in Vietnam as the result of an incompetent government, their own.

A little more than three weeks into the New Year it got even worse. North Korea perpetrated an international crisis by hijacking an American ship. On January 23, North Korean warships supported by MIG fighter jets forced the USS *Pueblo* to allow itself to be boarded. The ship was captured, and one crewman was killed. The others were badly beaten and taken as "prisoners of war." Their ordeal was front-page news throughout 1968. For many voters, it was the last straw.

Three days after the ship's capture, Gale McGee addressed the *Pueblo* crisis in a speech thought by no less an astute observer than Senator Robert Byrd to be one of the classic speeches in the history of the Senate.[4] McGee said that while several analysts had ascribed a variety of motives for the North Korean seizure of the ship, the most likely "may lie in the contrast between the two Koreas."[5] McGee called economic and political developments in South Korea since the end of the war fifteen years earlier "a miracle." He spoke of the infusion of democracy through free elections, the development of an industrialized economy, and South Korea's participation "in the international community." McGee praised the South Koreans for committing troops to the fight in Vietnam.

He found the contrast with the North to be stark. "North Korea has not entered into a period of prosperity since the end of the war. As a result, we have noted in North Korea a rather steadily mounted drive . . . to disrupt, to discombobulate, to tear apart the fabric of stability and orderly change, which are characteristic of the South." The senator continued, "Having said that, Mr. President, we should strive then to fit this incident into its proper context as we seek to arrive at justice and equity, and the acquittal of the national honor in an affair that was clearly a breach of international law and procedures in international waters." McGee asked Americans to temper their anger with rationality.

Twice, as Senator McGee's allotted time expired, Senator Byrd asked for unanimous consent that he be allowed to continue. "Mr. President," McGee continued. "I would like to say that the more powerful our Nation becomes, the more limited become our options for actions in isolated instances or in related crises; that the limitations of great power are sometimes frustrating." Byrd asked his Wyoming colleague to yield for a question. "Would the distinguished Senator from Wyoming also agree that, while the saber may ultimately have to be used, rattling the saber at this point makes more difficult the President's . . . efforts to achieve the release of the 83 men and their ship?"[6] McGee replied, "A loud saber rattling would risk whatever chance there may be, if there is a chance, to get those men freed."

As McGee completed his speech, Byrd was effusive in his praise. "I do not know of anyone in this body who is more knowledgeable on the subject of the war in Vietnam or other difficulties in the Far East, to wit, Korea, than is the distinguished senator from Wyoming. His was a speech advocating not cowardice but restraint, not hasty and impulsive action but careful, reasoned action."

Constituents writing to the senator were not impressed with America's restraint. His mail reflected a national frustration born of the failure to win the war in Vietnam, now manifest in the unwillingness of the U.S. government to use harsh military action against North Korea. Roy Norman of Sheridan told McGee that the North Vietnamese harbor at Haiphong should be bombed in retaliation for the *Pueblo*. "Feel these two areas are related. Take firm action. Don't make me ashamed to be an American."[7] McGee responded by attempting to persuade constituents that the harsh military action they encouraged would lead to the deaths of all American captives. Cheyenne constituent Arthur W. Kirchner admitted, "After reading your comments on this situation, I feel I understand the situation better."[8]

The war in Vietnam did not go away as the United States addressed the crisis with North Korea. The Tet Offensive started a few days after the capture of the *Pueblo*. By the time the crisis ended with the release of the crew on December 23, troop levels in Vietnam had reached 540,000, and the death toll for U.S. troops topped 31,000 with more than half that number killed in 1968 alone. A Gallup poll showed for the first time that a majority of Americans thought the war was a mistake.[9]

As the war worsened, LBJ's search for a UN ambassador continued. McGee's response to Johnson's December 1967 push to appoint him UN ambassador is not recorded in either the president's files or those of the senator with the exception of a brief comment Johnson made to George Ball four months later as he continued his recruitment efforts to identify an ambassador. Johnson asked Ball to accept the appointment, but Ball declined. He and the president went on to review other possibilities. Johnson read a list prepared by Dean Rusk. John McCloy and Nicholas Katzenbach were among those mentioned. And then McGee's name was offered. "Now," said Johnson, "Gale would take it and would be interested if I urged him to take it, and certainly would if I ran again, he told me that sometime ago."[10] However, it had now been a month since Johnson told the nation:

> With America's sons in the fields far away, with America's future under challenge right here at home, with our hopes and the world's hopes for peace in the balance every day, I do not believe that I should devote an hour or a day of my time to any personal partisan causes or to any duties other than the awesome duties of this office—the Presidency of your country. Accordingly, I shall not seek, and I will not accept, the nomination of my party for another term as your President.[11]

Johnson's March 31, 1968, withdrawal stunned Senator McGee. Two days before the announcement, he had issued a statement strongly supporting Johnson's renomination. "He deserves the support of the American people. He has mine."[12] Afterward, he admitted surprise. "I had to listen to the replay again to still believe it," McGee said.[13]

McGee wasn't interested in leaving the Senate for an appointment that would expire less than a year later if Johnson decided not to seek a second full term. However, neither was he satisfied with his role in the Senate as 1968 rolled around. Following Johnson's announcement, he and Lady Bird invited the McGees to late-night White House visits more often. At times they cruised the Potomac River on the presidential yacht. They talked about their time together in the Senate and the decisions of the last five years. "Oh, a lot of it was kind of rehashing all the things that had gone on before. Reconstructing them, second guessing again, and reminiscing a good bit."[14]

On one such occasion, "the President did talk seriously about what my future might be." LBJ made one last try at luring McGee away from the Senate. He asked him to come to Austin to serve as the director of his new presidential library. Gale and Loraine seriously discussed the possibility over the next several days. Ultimately they concurred that leaving the Senate for academia at that time would feel too much like retreating from the real world. So McGee told the president he felt he could do more in the Senate.[15]

McGee may have been surprised by LBJ's shocking announcement that he would not run for a second term, but it seemed to leave much of the country precariously dangling between hope and despair. It's not as though many didn't welcome Johnson's withdrawal. Especially in the antiwar community, the decision created great expectations.

The first electoral test of LBJ's war policies came in the New Hampshire primary contest on March 12, 1968. Just as in the Tet Offensive six weeks earlier, when enemy troops lost the battle but achieved a major public perception victory, so it was for Eugene McCarthy in New Hampshire. The president defeated McCarthy by a margin so slim that much of the nation believed it proved Johnson too unpopular to win reelection. Before Johnson could withdraw, Robert Kennedy entered the race.

Now Johnson was out. Americans opposed to the war could begin looking to the possibility of electing a peace candidate like McCarthy or Kennedy. Perhaps the long war could end and the troops could be brought home. But the president's March 31 speech was followed so quickly by the April 4 assassination of Martin Luther King that hope found neither the time nor the place to take root. McGee joined many of his colleagues and thousands of others traveling to Atlanta for Dr. King's memorial service, marching alongside Wilt Chamberlain to the burial site. He mourned along with many of his constituents. However, not all were pleased with their senator's demonstration of grief. Their letters signaled a sea change in attitudes, a shift toward bitterness and incivility. A Casper resident wrote a week after King's death that she "knew" King was "a high paid Communist" and that King was "even below Kennedy."[16] Another constituent complained bitterly to McGee because he had taken time to go to Atlanta to honor King.[17] The violence that followed King's murder unleashed a torrent of angry letters from Wyoming. McGee responded to each, explaining his views that the real problem was poverty, prejudice, and the lack of opportunity. He told them that what he called "attained influence or the luck of birth" had, for many, created "self-righteousness," a "stain of pride and unawareness [that] can very well lead us to apartheid, if not a civil crisis of unrelenting dimensions."[18]

McGee eulogized the slain civil rights icon. "Our land has been visited once again by the senseless violence of an assassin." He said he hoped King's "gospel of peace and nonviolence" would prevail.[19] It did not.

Although a great deal of emphasis was placed on the race-related violence that followed Dr. King's assassination, the support for nonviolence among African Americans had begun to wane before Memphis. Some white Americans believed the real problem was a "weak" government, unwilling or unable to resolve the matter. Clyde Lewis of Cheyenne wrote McGee, blaming "a weak-kneed Attorney General" for the civil rights riots.[20] When constituents complained that the government was not doing enough to stop the riots and punish the rioters, McGee agreed the law should be enforced, but encouraged constituents to see the broader picture. "While enforcing our present laws we must also be aware of conditions which give rise to lawlessness and must improve these conditions to every extent possible."[21]

Then came the assassination of Robert Kennedy. The déjà vu sensation already imprinted on the national psyche moved much of the nation over the last remaining ledge, from despair to hopelessness. Hours after Kennedy's death, McGee went to the Senate floor to express outrage. It had only been a couple of months since the two Senate colleagues locked horns on the war. The New York senator had called for a halt in the bombing of North Vietnam, and the Wyoming lawmaker had called RFK's proposal "totally irresponsible."[22] On June 6, McGee began his memorial to the second slain Kennedy brother by listing the names of recent assassin victims. Some were popular, beloved figures, others were not, but the list was long: John F. Kennedy, Martin Luther King, George Lincoln Rockwell, Malcolm X, Medgar Evers, and now Robert F. Kennedy. All were dead at the hands of assassins in the last five years. McGee thought the killings reflected "the evil virus of extremism injected into our body politic." He faulted both the left and the right. "The one describes the president as a 'traitor' or a 'comsymp' (Communist sympathizer), and the other denounces the president as a 'murderer.' On one side, the poisonous vernacular of extremism demands 'Impeach Earl Warren,' and on the other, it spits out, 'Hell no, we won't go.' One brand of extremism can call a Martin Luther King 'nigger,' while another cries back, 'Burn, baby, burn.'" McGee said the death of "this remarkable young leader" would portend increasing anger across the nation, and he called on politicians to "learn to disagree without being disagreeable and quit demanding that candidates hit hard, low, and often in order to excite their audiences."[23] Gale and Loraine rode the special train from Washington to New York to attend Robert Kennedy's funeral.

It quickly became clear Johnson's presidency would be followed by either Hubert Humphrey or Richard Nixon. Activists felt there was no alternative but to abandon electoral politics for civil or uncivil disobedience. They set their sights on the Republican and Democratic National Conventions scheduled later that summer.

With the war in Southeast Asia and the domestic political battles as an ever-present backdrop, the work of the Senate went on as usual. McGee fought the plans of the Union Pacific Railroad to discontinue passenger service through Wyoming.[24] He continued funneling millions into the state for everything from schools and outdoor recreation to water and highway projects.[25] He worked to create a refuge for wild horses in the Pryor Mountains, arguing that the horses "represent a fast diminishing remnant of our past, which should be preserved."[26] During the spring, McGee was kept busy delivering high school commencement addresses across the state ahead of the 1968 Democratic National Convention in Chicago.

He sounded an early warning about plans of left-wing groups to disrupt the Democrats' convention set for late August. "Violence has become alarmingly common among those who plan to converge on the Democratic Convention in Chicago next month."[27]

The GOP National Convention met first, opening August 4 in Miami Beach. Wyoming's Republican governor, Stan Hathaway, a Nixon supporter, advised delegates of a pre-convention poll showing Rockefeller was the most popular candidate in Wyoming from both parties. Even so, Hathaway told reporters, "I know of no one who favors Rockefeller."[28] All twelve Wyoming delegates voted for the nominee, Richard Nixon. Activists reserved most of their antiwar zeal for Hubert Humphrey and the Democratic National Convention, but the Republicans did not escape without violent protests. The National Guard was called in, liquor stores closed, and an 8 p.m. curfew imposed to quell the violence that accompanied the final days of the GOP convention.[29] The Democrats were next.

Jack Anderson predicted the weekend before the Democratic Party convention opened that delegates were in for a great deal of chaos. "Chicago is threatened with an invasion of Black Panthers, pacifists, hippies, and yippies who plan to disrupt the Democratic Convention with everything from peaceful protests to violent upheaval."[30]

Fourteen-year-old Mary Gale McGee watched as hundreds of those "Black Panthers, pacifists, hippies, and yippies" mixed with armed soldiers outside the hotel on a hot August night in Chicago. With her father's help, she got a job working in Humphrey's headquarters during the convention. She was paid a dollar an hour to answer phones, make copies, and run errands.

She had a front row seat to the street protests, and so she saw one protester, "a flower child," walk up to one of the uniformed National Guardsmen and place a flower in the barrel of his M16 rifle. In one of the few light moments that evening, the Guardsman gently removed the flower, stuck it in his pocket, and smiled at the woman. But much of what Gale and Loraine's young daughter saw that week was alarming. "I remember the thousands of protesters and National Guardsmen standing in lines, their uniforms and guns making quite a frightening impression on me," she said years later. "Wasn't this scene only supposed to happen in wars?"[31] Her parents were alarmed. Mary Gale might be in the middle of the rioting. They went looking for her and found her alone, left by the adults to tend Humphrey's office.

Inside the convention hall delegates and party officials were fighting their own battles. Robert S. Vance of Alabama, chairman of the convention's Credentials Committee, imposed a loyalty oath. Vance feared the antiwar delegates would support a third party candidacy. He demanded that in order to be seated, each delegate would be required to pledge his or her allegiance to the Party's ultimate nominee. Eight members of Wyoming's delegation, including Nora Mix of Cody, the vice chair of the Wyoming Democratic Party, supported Eugene McCarthy. They all refused to sign Vance's oath, and eventually Vance backed down.[32]

Aside from determining whom to nominate for president, Vietnam was the most divisive issue delegates faced. On August 20, McGee testified before the Platform Committee urging them to avoid putting specifics in the platform "about coalition governments, bombing halts, and the other paraphernalia" of what he called "political hucksterism." The committee agreed. Eventually the Platform Committee rejected all proposals from party doves in favor of endorsing Johnson's policies across the board.[33] Before nominating Humphrey for president and Senator Edmund Muskie for vice president, the convention adopted the platform. Delegates defeated a "minority report" offered by war critics that recommended an unconditional end to all bombing. Led by McGee, nineteen Wyoming delegates opposed the antiwar statement. The others went back to Wyoming determined to find an antiwar candidate to oppose McGee in 1970.

The director of mental health services for the Wyoming Department of Health blamed the Vietnam War for a surge in suicides among the state's young people. Dr. Arthur Davidson said, "I believe a lot of these youths have no goals in life. Many are discouraged with the situation in Vietnam."[34] In truth, as the war continued and more Americans died, the draft became a greater source of anxiety for young men and their families.

As draft calls increased, McGee received numerous requests for assistance from those wishing to avoid being sent to Southeast Asia. Some were students hoping to remain in college for graduate work (graduate school deferments were ended in February 1967), many were needed on the ranch or farm, some felt their health was not good enough to allow them to serve, several thought the draft was a form of slavery denying basic human rights, and at least one was unhappy that conscientious objectors could get deferments.

McGee steadfastly refused to interfere with draft board decisions. He received a request from Teno Roncalio to help a Rock Springs family who owned a small laundry. The father was "crippled" by polio, and the mother had "crippling arthritis." They had but one son, and he was needed to run the family business. McGee declined, citing his policy.[35]

An especially emotional letter came from Arden Coad, a father in Dubois and a close friend of the senator. He had only one son, and he had just received his induction notice. Coad advised his son to make other choices, go to jail or to Canada, but to refuse to serve. His son chose to accept induction. "Frankly, under the circumstances I wish he would have done one of the two. But you can't change with a few angry words what you have taught for 18 to 20 years." Mr. Coad ended indicting the war by bluntly asking for the senator's help. "We are asking you to keep our only son out of Vietnam."[36]

When Coad had not received a response nearly three weeks later, he wrote a second time. McGee then acknowledged he was late in responding because he had needed more time to think about what to say to his friend. The senator's response was nearly two and a half pages long. McGee knew how hard it was for Mr. Coad to write his letter. He asked Coad to understand how equally difficult it was for McGee to respond. McGee defended the war but would not impugn "the motives, integrity, or patriotism of those who disagree." He implied antiwar constituents were the smaller group. "With the magnitude of our effort in Vietnam I do not understand how it could be continued without the backing and support of the vast majority of our people." McGee wrote, "You must realize there are two legitimate sides to this question and that those of us who generally support our policies in Vietnam do so only after considerable soul searching and that our views are also based on a deep and abiding personal conviction." Finally McGee told his friend, "I cannot comply with your request that your son be assigned to a duty which would insure he would not be sent to Vietnam."[37]

The exchange between Senator McGee and this constituent symbolized more than a difference of opinion on the Vietnam War. While the senator continued to analyze American involvement in an academic manner based on sound foreign policy and his deep understanding of international affairs, many of his constituents had, by then, adopted an emotional response to the ongoing war. For McGee, it remained a question of the "balance of power" and the domino theory. For Arden Coad and others, the war had become more about the carnage, the human costs, and their own children.

Despite that divide, similar correspondence received from friends like Bob and Cordelia Peck were a source of pain for McGee. Cordelia sent a Christmas card in 1968 with a handwritten message: "We know that your responsibilities are awesome; may you be able to find some peace, some sense of Christmas, of joy, during this holiday season. We are much distracted and dismayed by the war, as well as some of the domestic problems. But mostly the war. It is the source of too much bitterness, ugliness, violence. It should be concluded. No consequence of withdrawal could be worse than the consequence of continuation. This is our Christmas wish. Sorry. I had to say it."[38]

Gale McGee had not reached his conclusions on Vietnam lightly, and he was not going to abandon them even though it meant disappointing and even losing longtime friends. The senator was convinced that each side of the debate offered an honest assessment and deserved to be heard. Speaking to the annual American Legion convention in Cheyenne that June, McGee asked Legionnaires to "embrace a new patriotism, the patriotism of patience and perseverance."[39] He said, "Just as you resent a bearded, draft-card burner who shouts, 'Hell no, we won't go,' you should resent a retired general of the Air Force who maintains that the only way to insure a lasting peace is to bomb the enemy into total oblivion."

McGee admitted, "The United States is not committed to a total military victory over the enemy in Vietnam."[40] The United States was there only to allow the South Vietnamese to determine their own destiny. That was not the sort of war strategy that most Americans understood. The idea that thousands of American soldiers were dying in a war in which we didn't intend to conquer the enemy gave rise to more distrust and conspiracy theories.

The divide was also quickened by a growing sense that the U.S. government didn't want to win, was incompetent, or both. As it became clear the United States was not going to win the war in a traditional sense, many concluded the war was ill-conceived from the start and should never have been fought while other Americans turned on their own government. It was the fault of the politicians, they charged, for not committing to a victory. The vice tightened further around politicians supporting the war. Attacks came from the left and the right.

William J. Lederer wrote a book titled *Our Own Worst Enemy*. Lederer was well known then as the coauthor of *The Ugly American*, and readers trusted his views of the events in Southeast Asia. After reading his 1968 book, they trusted their own government less. Lederer described how the United States spent millions hiring translators who could not translate. He detailed corruption in the hiring of Vietnamese workers in the military PX system that allowed for theft and black marketing of goods, including the sale of American weaponry to the enemy. He claimed that every South Vietnamese government had been put in power by the Americans and found corrupt by the Vietnamese people. Lederer told of how U.S. military officers contrived the body counts so it would appear the war was being won. He reported that most of the bombs dropped from U.S. planes fell on unoccupied real estate because pilots found flying over urban areas to be too dangerous. In a nutshell, Lederer alleged the U.S. government was losing the war because of its incompetence and willingness to accept South Vietnamese corruption.

Lederer concluded, "We cannot carp and flail and start looking for someone else to blame for America's shameful and unnecessary failures. The people who have botched things are your neighbors, your friends, your relatives, your countrymen. They are ourselves."[41] Many didn't think they or their neighbors, friends, relatives, and countrymen were at all to blame. It was, they felt, their government.

Senator McGee's constituents wrote to him, suggesting Lederer had explained why the war had not been won. It had been, they concluded, not because of the strength of the enemy but because of the complicity of their own government. "When my wife and I read it we were almost speechless," wrote James P. Berry from Big Horn, "and the more I think about it, the madder I become. I have thought for some time there must be a reason for our unsuccessful attempts to win over there. This seems to be the cause of our failure."[42]

As always, Gale McGee got hit from both sides. Democratic Party stalwart and Cheyenne businessman Attilio Bedont wrote, "The so-called credibility gap is reduced to its true meaning, lies and more lies as a basic instrument of government." Bedont said Americans are being subjected to daily "brainwashing." He promised to do "everything in my power to discredit your position and insure your defeat the next time out."[43]

Although the weight of the mail received by Senator McGee shifted decidedly against the war by 1968, he also received letters and petitions in support of continuing the fight. Nonetheless, there were longtime friends and supporters beginning to reevaluate not only the war but also their feelings about McGee. It wasn't only the numbers of friends' letters opposing the war but the emotionality with which opinions were expressed. A longtime supporter, Gertrude Olsen of Pinedale, wrote in March. "You are not going to like what I have to say because it is emotional." And it was. "Why oh why must you become a stooge for the military and all the worst in man? I'm heartsick and ashamed for you and for Wyoming and it is time you knew this. Gale! Gale! How can you go this way?"[44] McGee responded, expressing his disappointment that she and others were unable "to concede that those who support our policies do so as a result of deep concern, in good faith, and out of personal conviction."[45]

It was not as though Gale McGee did not have moments of second-guessing himself. Around this time, he told a historian, "I'm still not sure I was right. But as you re-sort these things and you try to fit the pieces back together again and again and again, I still come out essentially with the same position. But it's a worrisome and it's a troubling one, especially in the middle of the night, when you can't hear anything but your own conscience. It really bothers me, but I still think it's close to the mark."[46]

McGee's frustration had not lessened since he told Dean Rusk that he might not run again in 1970 unless the conflict with Foreign Relations Committee chairman Bill Fulbright was resolved and he was allowed to return. It didn't help when, in the spring of 1968, the White House told McGee to "lay off" when he defended LBJ and the war with a charge that Fulbright was "doing more harm than the Republicans."[47] McGee was further annoyed when he was mentioned as a possible keynote speaker for the 1968 Democratic National Convention and then later told he would not be selected because his voice would not "qualify as the voice of unity because of the emotions separating Democrats on Vietnam."[48]

It seemed that all he had earned for his stalwart support of the administration over the last few difficult years was doors slammed in his face. The Wyoming senator set out to challenge Fulbright and other Vietnam critics by writing a book. Less than two years earlier, Fulbright had published *The Arrogance of Power*. McGee's book, published in the fall of 1968, was *The Responsibilities of World Power*. Lyndon Johnson promptly ordered the purchase of 1,000 copies of the McGee book.[49]

Fulbright, who had sponsored the Gulf of Tonkin resolution before becoming an opponent of the war, argued that the U.S. Senate no longer fulfilled its responsibilities in foreign affairs. He said senators "have only ourselves to blame," and he regretted his committee had not held serious hearings before approving Johnson's resolution.[50] Fulbright acknowledged that the military solution, which had seemed so promising, had turned into a disaster. He therefore urged an immediate withdrawal.

McGee's book was less political and more academic. He reiterated a belief that balancing power among competing nations is the only means of preventing wars. McGee, the historian, provided a succinct survey of the Vietnamese people from their origins two thousand years earlier in the Yellow River valley of China. His book took readers from the early history of Vietnam to the early nineteenth-century French colonial period and the 1940 Japanese conquest. McGee described the Communist government emerging under Ho Chi Minh, the postwar reestablishment of French control, and its demise at the 1954 battle of Dien Bien Phu. "At this same time," McGee explained, "there was growing concern both in the United States and Great Britain that the implications of the conflict in Indochina extended far beyond the borders of that particular region." He added that the war was the culmination of forces unleashed by "the defeat of Germany and the collapse of Japan, which were to engulf the United States in a new series of crises and responsibilities."[51]

According to McGee, our role in Vietnam grew from what the senator called a "postulate that no one nation ought ever to be in a position to dominate the Far East."[52] In that context lived the threats imposed by Red China giving meaning to a view that Southeast Asia had become vital to American security. The analysis led foreign policy thinkers, including President Eisenhower, to compare what was at stake to a row of dominoes. "You have a row of dominoes set up, you knock over the first one, and what will happen to the last one is the certainty that it will go over quickly."[53]

McGee's analysis concluded that the United States had no alternative but to "stay the course." He said, "We were and are right in believing that the United States cannot afford a world in which aggressors are permitted to impose their will by force on their victim."[54]

The book addressed what was called "the credibility gap." The phrase was a then-popular description of a growing sense that the administration had not been honest about the war with the American people. McGee answered those critics: "The role of the government may often appear to be contradictory or complex. There is no substantive evidence, however, that the government is deliberately deceptive; nor is it involved in a conscious conspiracy to keep the public in the dark." McGee then added words that would later sound naïve in a post-Watergate world. He said, "The government does not lie."[55]

Until recently, historians and political scientists thought the Watergate scandal began in 1972 with the burglary of the office of the Democratic National Committee in the Watergate Complex of Washington DC. Tim Weiner, who won a Pulitzer Prize for his reporting on government secrecy, has given reason to revise that date back to 1968. "For those who lived under Nixon," Watergate "is worse than you may recall. For those too young to recall, it is worse than you can imagine."[56]

With the benefit of new scholarship and more than 2,600 hours of taped conversations emanating from Nixon's Oval Office during his presidency, Evan Thomas believes that, as a candidate in 1968, "Nixon was trying to sabotage the [Vietnam] peace process before it even began."[57] As the general election neared and Nixon's poll lead over Humphrey narrowed, the Republican nominee learned that Johnson's negotiations with North Vietnam were about to produce a breakthrough. As Nixon feared all along, it seemed that just before election day, the United States and its enemy might sit down to talk peace, a move that would greatly aid Humphrey. Nixon determined he would do everything possible to thwart the peace process.

After months of delicate discussions with America's South Vietnamese allies, it appeared LBJ had an agreement that would meet the demands of the North for starting talks. Johnson ordered a pre-election halt to the bombing. Suddenly the South Vietnamese were dragging their feet, and because of phone taps and undercover work, Johnson knew why. South Vietnam's president, Nguyen Van Thieu, preferred the anticommunist hardliner Nixon to Humphrey. When Nixon sent a secret intermediary to Saigon to tell the South Vietnamese to "hold on," it was all the reason they needed to announce a boycott of the Paris Peace Conference. Johnson and his advisers made a decision that disclosing Nixon's conduct would be so shocking that it would do serious harm to the nation, and so voters never knew.

The Watergate scandal began during the first month of Nixon's first term when he told White House chief of staff Bob Haldeman he wanted all files on the bombing halt. A year before the break-in at the Watergate, Nixon ordered a break-in at the Brookings Institute after an aide assured him the bombing halt files were there complete with the narrative of his efforts to keep South Vietnam away from the 1968 peace talks.[58]

Nixon won the presidency by a scant seven-tenths of 1 percent of the popular vote. What followed was a scandal-ridden administration that included an illegal war in Cambodia, more than 20,000 additional U.S. war dead, revelations of political break-ins, dirty tricks, abuse of the IRS and the CIA, and the only presidential resignation in U.S. history.

Watching the evolution of Senator Gale McGee's thinking about Nixon as the scandal grew proved to be a metaphor for the transition experienced by the nation as it moved from barely electing him president in 1968 to awarding him one of the greatest landslides in U.S. history in 1972 to demanding his resignation less than two years later. But then McGee and his fellow countrymen could be excused. "Americans lacked a fair warning in 1968, thanks to Johnson's decision to keep CIA, NSA, and FBI reports on the Chennault Affair classified."[59]

13

It's Nice to Have Dick Nixon
to Kick Around Again

As the New Year got under way in 1969, Nixon named his cabinet, McGee fought grazing fee increases and won his long crusade for an August congressional recess, Joe Namath "guaranteed" the world his New York Jets would win their Super Bowl against the Baltimore Colts, and the Wyoming Supreme Court ruled that women could tend bar.

In January, McGee was named chairman of the Senate Post Office and Civil Service Committee. To his delight, he also regained his seat on the Foreign Relations Committee. Ironically, it was a seat vacated for McGee by the 1968 antiwar candidate Eugene McCarthy. McCarthy had wearied of politics but not so much that he didn't take the opportunity to get a bit of revenge.

McCarthy was still feeling the sting of Bobby Kennedy's late entry into the 1968 presidential race, a door opened by McCarthy's near win over the incumbent in New Hampshire's primary. Ted Kennedy sought membership on the Foreign Relations Committee to better position himself to oppose Nixon on Vietnam. However, Senate protocol guaranteed the first opening to McGee because he was a former member. Kennedy hatched a plan to expand membership. McCarthy the dove blocked Kennedy's plan and then resigned his seat in favor of Gale McGee the hawk. Syndicated columnist Joseph Alsop explained, "McCarthy hated the Kennedys. He gave up his seat on the Foreign Relations Committee in order to beat Teddy. That was the real explanation of why he gave up his seat."[1] The antiwar folks were appalled, but McGee's interest in remaining in the Senate was rekindled.

Soon after rejoining Fulbright's committee, McGee called on Americans to "lend their support wholeheartedly to President Nixon" in the "hope his administration has great success."[2] Within four months of taking office, Nixon "ruled out attempting to impose a purely military solution on the battlefield."[3] Nixon's plan, which he called "Vietnamization" of the war, meant bringing American troops home and replacing them on the battlefield with South Vietnamese soldiers while bombing the North into submission. With the South secure, he could force the North to negotiate peace. The new president believed that "by assuring South Vietnam's security, he would not be the first American president to lose a war."[4]

When McGee wrote, "The government does not lie," he could not have comprehended Nixon and the people who surrounded him. Unaware of either Nixon's treachery in the '68 campaign or his plans for an illegal war in Cambodia, McGee was true to his own beliefs. He would not allow a change in the party occupying the White House to alter his views on Vietnam. If American involvement in Southeast Asia was critical before November, McGee believed it remained so now.

While the Wyoming senator continued to support the war, he also continued to support the rights of those who protested it. In an address to the American Association of School Administrators, McGee urged schools to look differently at student activists. "These people are serious in intent and deed. Like it or not, they speak to and for a large part of the students and young adults in America."[5] McGee urged Americans not to overreact to campus disorders. Even so, he was alarmed by the size and vehemence of the antiwar movement on Vietnam Moratorium Day, October 15, 1969.

Several senators endorsed and some even planned to participate in Moratorium Day. Informed of the magnitude of what was coming, McGee tried to worry colleagues with what he believed to be the implications of the impending massive demonstrations. "By endorsing such a movement, they may be helping to uncork the bottle which will let loose a genie which may never be recaptured. That genie may be the national impulse toward a new isolationism. It could even be a precedent for barricade-street style politics in America."[6]

Hundreds of thousands gathered in more than a dozen American cities on October 15 to demand an end to the war. In Boston 100,000 heard George McGovern rail against Vietnam. Across the Atlantic, a young Rhodes scholar named Bill Clinton organized a march in Oxford. A month later, half a million people came to the Washington Mall to protest the war. John Lennon joined them and sang, "Give Peace a Chance." McGee said those who participated in the moratorium exhibited a "high degree of irresponsibility."[7]

The antiwar protests began to move from the streets and campuses in the United States to the foxholes of Vietnam. By late 1969, some troops in the war zone openly criticized the war, and others refused to follow orders to join the fight. "I am sorry, sir, but my men refuse to fight. We cannot move out." It was the voice of an Army captain reporting over a crackling radio to the battalion commander.[8] An Army corporal wrote McGee in September, suggesting that the senator might change his mind about the war "if you were here and saw the horrible things happening to American boys."[9]

On New Year's Day 1970, the Wyoming press corps named John Wold "Man of the Year." Wold beat out Governor Stan Hathaway and Senator Gale McGee for the honor. The state's editors and broadcasters said Wold's victory over William Henry Harrison in the 1968 GOP primary for the U.S. House and his win over Democrat Velma Linford in that November's general election "boosted Wold back into political prominence" after his 1964 loss to McGee.[10] Wold began planning a November rematch against McGee.

McGee was aware that his position on the war was a cause of growing concern among fellow Wyoming Democrats. He invited George McGovern to speak for him on January 15, 1970, on the Laramie campus. If there was a hotbed of antiwar sentiment in Wyoming, it was Laramie. McGovern acknowledged the differences between the two over the war, saying they were honest differences. The South Dakotan talked less about the war and more about McGee's work on environmental matters. "I don't know of any one of my colleagues in the U.S. Senate that I trust more on this issue than Gale McGee."[11]

The environment had begun to take on more weight as a matter of concern among Americans. In the early 1960s, the environmental concerns of McGee's constituents revolved mostly around road construction, insect control, and grazing permits in national forests. The senator was called upon to intervene in occasional disputes between landowners and the Forest Service.[12] McGee's official papers reveal no constituent concern about the Wilderness Act of 1964, which he supported and which was signed by President Johnson in September of that year. The act was based on a congressional determination of the need to "assure that an increasing population, accompanied by expanding settlement and growing mechanization, does not occupy and modify all areas within the United States and its possessions."[13] There were few hints of the cultural and economic conflicts the act eventually stirred up between environmentalists and ranching, timbering, and mining interests. Later the Wilderness Act became the source of hard-fought battles between commercial users and those seeking to protect the land from development. Little of that conflict was apparent in 1964 when more than 2 million acres of forest were set aside as Wyoming wilderness.[14]

In the late 1960s environmental issues were becoming much more contentious. On January 1, 1970, President Nixon signed the National Environmental Protection Act. By then membership in environmental organizations such as the Sierra Club, the Izaak Walton League, the Wilderness Society, the National Wildlife Federation, and the Audubon Society had soared. Plans were under way for an event that would force environmental issues to the top of the nation's agenda, Earth Day 1970.[15]

Gale McGee's interest in environmental issues had also begun to flourish when, once again, the war in Vietnam sucked the air out of American politics. But first McGee and Nixon teamed up to end what the senator thought was the greatest domestic crisis in forty years.

In March, thousands of postal workers, unhappy with the 4.1 percent raise given them by a Congress that raised its own salary by 41 percent, began a work stoppage in New York City. In spite of a warning from the new chairman of the Senate Post Office and Civil Service Committee, the strike quickly spread across the country as nearly 30 percent of all postal workers were on the picket line. McGee cautioned postal workers that a strike would not accomplish their goals of a greater wage hike.[16] The employees ignored his warning and walked off the job. "Letters, bills and checks to pay those bills, birthday cards, passports, legal documents, and even draft notices piled up in mail sacks on post office floors across the nation."[17]

McGee had been chairman for less than a year and was still becoming familiar with the job and its duties. The committee was one of the Senate's earliest standing committees, created in 1816. Among its responsibilities was to make certain the U.S. mail was delivered. But suddenly it wasn't.

McGee declared the strike "the most serious domestic crisis in forty years."[18] Wyoming Republicans, sensing this could become a major issue in the coming Senate race, blamed McGee.[19] McGee blamed the president, who he said had blocked a pay raise in order to trade it for Nixon's plans to reform the postal service. He called that "cruelly unfair."[20] Nixon called up National Guard units to deliver the mail.[21] Within a few days, the troops were sent home as postal workers returned to their jobs and the White House opened settlement talks with union officials. Soon the two sides came to an agreement: Nixon got his postal reform, and the workers received a 14 percent wage hike. McGee's proposal for creation of a separate commission to establish postal rates was approved as a part of the compromise.[22] He was pleased, saying, "The agreement proves the feasibility of free and unfettered collective bargaining at the federal level."[23] U.S. Postmaster General Winton Blount credited McGee for the resolution of the disagreement, saying the senator had provided the president with "wise counsel."[24]

The postal strike of 1970 had one historically important but unintended consequence. Nixon was proud of the role he played in ending the strike but concerned there was no adequate record of what happened in the Oval Office. He wanted historians to have the information they needed to tell the story accurately. After the strike was settled, Nixon lamented, "God damn it, we did pretty well. We brought everyone together. And we met there in the Oval Office, and it took us a couple of weeks, but by golly we settled the strike. I wish we had recorded exactly what went on."[25]

Alexander Butterfield, the assistant to Nixon's chief of staff, Bob Haldeman, was assigned the responsibility for installing a voice-activated taping system in the Oval Office.[26] From then on, Butterfield's taping system "recorded exactly what went on."

As pleased as McGee was to be back on the Foreign Relations Committee, he felt increasingly lonely. Nearly all the committee's Democrats who had voted for the Gulf of Tonkin resolution had turned against the war. At times he found himself the only member of the committee from either party supporting the president.[27] Nixon was about to make McGee even lonelier.

On the first day of May 1970, the *Wyoming Eagle*'s front-page headline announced, "U.S. Troops in Cambodia—WAR EXPANDED." Although he had been secretly bombing Cambodia since March 1969, Nixon had just made public his decision to invade Cambodia. A couple of weeks earlier, he was been urged to invade Vietnam's neighbor by the commander of U.S. forces in the Pacific, Adm. John McCain, whose son was then a prisoner of war in North Vietnam. McCain told Nixon the United States "should send every weapon it could find" to stop a Communist takeover of Phnom Penh.[28] Nixon looked out the window of the Oval Office and muttered to no one in particular, "Damned Johnson, if he'd just done the right thing, we wouldn't be in this mess now."[29]

On April 30, 1970, Nixon informed the nation, "This is the decision I have made. In cooperation with the armed forces of South Vietnam, attacks are being launched this week to clean out major enemy sanctuaries on the Cambodian-Vietnam border."[30] The next day McGee reassured his constituents, saying only history would show whether Nixon was right. He urged Americans to withhold judgment.[31] They didn't.

On May 4, National Guard troops called to quell an anti-Cambodian invasion demonstration at Ohio's Kent State University opened fire on students. Four died. That brought the demonstrations home to Wyoming. The Wyoming New Democratic Coalition, a group of activists largely cemented by their antiwar views, voted to censure Nixon over his invasion of Cambodia.[32] Wyoming's Young Democrats called for Nixon's impeachment, and for the first time Governor Hathaway faced antiwar protesters during "Governor's Day" at the university when he conducted his annual review of the Reserve Officer Training Corps (ROTC) units on campus.[33]

On May 6, violence was narrowly averted on the UW campus when armed highway patrolmen confronted five hundred antiwar demonstrators. Students erected an American flag along with a black flag reading, "Kent State." The governor ordered that the flag be removed. But the students refused and formed a ring around the flagpole. "Some 30 state highway patrolmen wearing helmets and carrying billy clubs marched onto the campus and made a second, outer ring around the pole. They were flanked by students who jeered, laughed, and baited them." Security lowered the American flag to half-staff after an agreement was reached that allowed the students to raise their "Kent State" flag.[34]

The former UW professor attempted to calm students by proposing a different outlet. McGee called on young people to "put your work where your rhetoric is." He said they should focus their time on registering voters and getting them to the polls.[35] But the students wanted to talk about the war. A contingent persuaded the university student council to conduct a campus election on war-related resolutions, one of which condemned the Kent State killings as "senseless murders." It passed, but a second resolution condemning Nixon for invading Cambodia narrowly failed, 1,082–973.[36]

A spillover into an already divided Wyoming Democratic Party was inevitable. The Cheyenne newspaper reported, "There were signs Monday that a split could be widening within the Wyoming Democratic Party over the Vietnam War as State Senator Mike Svilar said he could not support Senator Gale McGee in November."[37] Three relatively well-known Democrats met to talk about who might challenge McGee in the coming primary. They were Svilar, mountaineer Paul Petzoldt, and Pinedale lawyer John Mackey. Eventually the latter two gave ground to Svilar. McGee welcomed the debate that a primary contest would engender, saying that a primary would signal a healthy Democratic Party. "A political party is dead if it doesn't have any stirring differences in the ranks."[38]

As the primary contest evolved, McGee talked about Wyoming issues, not the war. "McGee Gains State Funds OK," "McGee Asks Senate Approve Postal Bill," or "McGee Glad of Nixon Support of Wool Quota." Svilar struggled to gain traction, and as he did, his attacks on McGee became more visceral. First he said he could not support McGee even if the senator won the nomination. Besides, the challenger asserted, McGee "might feel more at home on the other ticket."[39] Svilar then sharpened his attack. "I watched Gale McGee change his position on gun control, on the oil depletion allowance, on grazing fees, and on peace." Svilar said Wyoming boys were fighting the war in Southeast Asia to fulfill McGee's belief in the "balance of power, whatever that is."[40]

In the end, the Svilar campaign was a hopeless single-issue effort to unseat a popular incumbent. The *Laramie Daily Boomerang* described Svilar's quixotic challenge as having "given rise to one of the strangest alliances in the history of Wyoming politics." The report noted that as a state senator, Svilar opposed many proposals favored by the Wyoming New Democratic Coalition, which now supported Svilar's candidacy. Included were Svilar's votes against welfare program funding, increased mineral taxes, and mined land reclamation standards. The article claimed the war alone had relegated the Svilar coalition to "the status of a one-issue faction."[41] The editor of the *Casper Star-Tribune* predicted an easy McGee victory. "Wyomingites are still not Don Quixotes or even Sancho Panzas."[42]

Democratic voters had little interest in tilting at windmills alongside the antiwar movement. Most supported the war and awarded Senator McGee 32,661 votes to Svilar's 8,378. On the other side of the ballot, Republican voters nominated John Wold again, setting up a 1970 rematch of the 1964 contest.

The primary produced warning signals for McGee's chances for a third term. In his first and second campaigns of 1958 and 1964, the numbers of voters from each party taking part in the primary were substantially the same. The 1970 margin gave the Republicans a margin of 5,881 votes, significantly greater than they had in 1966.[43] That fall's general election produced a GOP senator, U.S. House member, and governor. McGee's campaign turned to a voter registration campaign in an attempt to level the playing field.

McGee looked at the troubling numbers and remembered the days he had spent with his Republican mother back in Norfolk, Nebraska, walking the precincts, making sure everyone was registered and that everyone voted. Beginning early that summer, McGee operatives busily recruited volunteers to knock on every door in the state. Using volumes of county clerk reports indicating who was and was not registered, the volunteers visited the homes of all unregistered voters.

"Do you lean toward Democrats, Republicans, or independents," each was asked. Lists were then compiled of all who indicated a preference for Democrats or independents. Door knocking and telephone volunteers used those lists to relentlessly contact residents until they registered. Thousands did.

Early one morning, Gale and Loraine walked from their house to their car parked out front of their Maryland home. Loraine noticed a car sitting across the street that didn't belong in the neighborhood. She had seen it parked there on other occasions. As they opened their car doors, a friendly neighbor lady got their attention. "There has been a fellow out there," she said, "taking pictures of your house and your car when you leave and pretty soon, he goes away."[44] Loraine began to notice the same car followed her when she drove the Chrysler they leased. It was obviously disconcerting, though they believed it had something to do with the campaign. McGee called J. Edgar Hoover's office and asked that the FBI look into the matter. The Bureau discovered the fellow following the McGees was an employee of Wackenhut Corporation.[45]

George Wackenhut was well known as a hard-right businessman. He accumulated dossiers on thousands of Americans he believed to be Communists or simply left-leaning. According to *Age of Surveillance*, a 1980 book by Frank Donner, Wackenhut maintained files on antiwar and civil rights protesters, and he proudly claimed to have files on more than 2.5 million "suspected dissidents."[46] Now it appeared that Wackenhut was working for someone associated with the Wold campaign. But what were they looking for? McGee surmised it had something to do with the Chrysler. He leased the car, as did others, from a company that gave discounts to senators. Photos of the car began to appear in Wyoming newspapers.[47] He sought advice from Mississippi senator John Stennis, chairman of the Ethics Committee. Stennis told him to avoid the controversy by purchasing the car. The McGees did, and the matter went away.

In the midst of the 1970 campaign, the Council for a Livable World, the liberal organization that supported McGee in 1958 and 1964, threatened him. If he didn't "change his spots" on Vietnam, they promised to work for his defeat. George McGovern, a leading antiwar figure, was president of the Council. He and McGee were also close friends. McGee told McGovern of the threat, and McGovern threatened to resign from the Council if they didn't shut down their anti-McGee talk.[48] Nixon, perhaps out of gratitude for McGee's support on the war, never came to Wyoming to campaign against the incumbent. But his vice president and his daughter Tricia did. Ms. Nixon campaigned for Wold in the week before Election Day.[49] In August, Spiro T. Agnew scheduled a ten-day campaign trip to support GOP Senate candidates, including a September 10 Casper speech for John Wold. Agnew was hamstrung by McGee's record of supporting the Nixon administration's war policies. So the vice president simply attacked McGee as a "liberal" for the senator's votes on domestic matters.[50]

As the 1970 Senate race entered its final weeks, reports appeared in the media quoting a Fair Campaign Practice Committee official warning "television viewers to watch out for a flood of 'sophisticated smear.'" The article specifically cited ads linking two Republican and six Democratic Senate candidates "to crime and violence." One of the Democrats targeted was Gale McGee.[51] He considered the last-minute attacks to be so unfair that after the election, he called on his colleagues to institute a fair campaign code of ethics and to bar from Senate membership anyone violating the standards.[52]

Those tactics had little impact on the final results. By the time the November general election rolled around, Wold was "banking on the state's Republican majorities, doubts about McGee's position on gun control, and a plea for a shift in congressional thinking to assist the Nixon administration to carry him through."[53] McGee was counting on the new voters his team had registered that fall.

McGee was reelected, defeating Wold 67,027 to 53,279. The McGee campaign had succeeded by more than doubling the Democrat's November vote total over that which he had received in the August primary. McGee's victory bucked the national trend that year. Although the Democrats lost two Senate seats to the Republicans nationwide, McGee widened the margin of victory in 1970 over his total against the same opponent six years earlier.

As he and his fellow Democrats celebrated, it could have occurred to no one that this would be the last time in at least two generations that a Wyoming Democrat would win a seat in the U.S. Senate.

"It's a crying shame," Wendell Beaver of the National Wildlife Federation wrote tongue in cheek about Wyoming in January 1970. He sarcastically decried the lack of bumper-to-bumper traffic, lines to wait in, and social problems to solve. "All they have is the matchless splendor of the Big Horns or the mountains of the Wind or the Gros Ventres or the Medicine Bow or the blue-green sage flats of endless vistas."[54]

That is what had brought McGee to Wyoming nearly a quarter of a century earlier. McGee was not simply an academic environmentalist. Though he had not spent a lot of time or political capital on conservation issues before 1970, he had fished countless miles of trout streams, hunted pheasants across rows of cornfields, and hiked the state's forests and mountains. McGee harbored an innate respect for conservationist values. As he started a third Senate term, Americans were becoming more environmentally conscious. So was Wyoming's senior senator, as environmental challenges moved to the forefront in his state.

Bruce Hamilton, the deputy national executive director of the Sierra Club, wrote an obituary for Tom Bell, one of Wyoming's most esteemed voices on environmental matters, when Bell died August 30, 2016. Hamilton explained the issues that McGee and Wyoming faced in the early 1970s.

> Near Pinedale, the Atomic Energy Commission wanted to use nuclear bombs to frack tight shale beds to release natural gas. Along the Green River in southwestern Wyoming, there was a proposal to divert water across the Continental Divide to feed giant coal-fired power plants. Another plan called for tapping groundwater and mixing it into a coal slurry that would be shipped to Arkansas. National forests were being cut at a rate that greatly exceeded sustained yield in order to supply local timber mills that were sized for forest liquidation. Next to Yellowstone National Park, geothermal energy developers wanted to develop power plants that would not only pollute the park but also potentially dry up the world-famous geysers. There were even plans to lease and drill for oil in designated wilderness.[55]

Gale McGee was "the man in the arena" for all of these fights, but there were three especially highly charged controversies that marked him as one of the Senate's great conservationists: the practice of clearcutting in the national forests, shooting eagles from helicopters, and the plan to detonate a nuclear bomb under some of the most beautiful land and most fragile geologic structures in Wyoming.

The fight to end clearcutting began in 1969 with a hike through the Bridger National Forest. McGee saw large swaths of barren land dotted with stumps and rotting slash, the residue of timbering operations. All of the trees were cut down, and nothing grew in their stead. McGee began asking questions about the efficacy of the practice he learned was called "clearcutting." Some told him it was an acceptable "silvicultural technique."[56] Clearcutting, they said, helped forests remain healthy over time. What he saw didn't appear to him to be healthy forests.

In 1971, he turned to Mike Leon for advice. Leon was a brilliant thinker and writer, McGee's friend, and staff adviser on conservation matters. Mike told the senator clearcutting was "a subsidy" to the timber industry. The process allowed logging companies to increase the total board feet of timber produced, significantly increasing sales from the same leased area. "Clearcutting is essentially a subsidy," Leon told the senator. "The process is a shortcut, saving time, requiring minimum personnel, and concentrating energy in an efficient if nonetheless devastating way."[57]

Conservation activists were excited when McGee took an interest in an issue that had long troubled them. In April 1971 Keith Becker, the executive director of the Wyoming Outdoor Council, urged McGee to seek a moratorium on clearcutting. Becker told the senator that Forest Service policies allowing for "mining our present forests at the expense of our children were harmful just as surely were the 'Timber Baron Policies' on our public lands at the turn of the century."[58]

That summer Gale McGee spent a day in Montana's Bitterroot National Forest. Guy "Brandy" Brandborg, the forest supervisor, wanted him to see a "large clearcut with bulldozed terraces gouged into the mountainside." McGee was deeply disturbed by what he witnessed, calling the scene "a crime against the land and the public interest." A photo taken of McGee and Brandborg with the clearcut in the background appeared that fall in the *New York Times,* and the public began to share McGee's interest in the subject.[59]

And then came the Finis Mitchell photographs. Finis was a mountaineer, conservationist, retired railroader, former Wyoming legislator, and a fine photographer who had climbed 280 of the 300 mountain peaks of the Wind River Range. There he and his wife stocked 314 virgin ponds and lakes with more than 2.5 million trout they packed in using milk cans. Congress gave thanks by naming the 12,482-foot Mitchell Peak after him. Few were considered more knowledgeable about Wyoming mountains than Finis. In 1972, he took graphic photos of the damage loggers had done in the forests and sent them to Senator McGee.

The photos show moonscape-like vistas across wide swaths of Wyoming forests. Acres of stumps and slash replaced thriving trees. The wasteland was bordered in the distance by the green of the trees whose turn to be cut down was coming. Oftentimes, young and old trees alike were harvested, milled on the spot and shipped out to lumber yards across the West. Seldom was the surviving mess cleaned up, and the areas were not reseeded.[60]

Mitchell typed notes on the back of the photos. One explains that the image is an example of "what was left 15 years ago." He said the Forest Service planned to replant but never did, largely because "in lots of Wyoming only glacial grindings of granite into crystal sands don't grow trees."[61]

People from across the country sent him photos taken in their nearby forests, all depicting the same moonscapes. McGee and his staff made visits to see the impact of clearcutting in West Virginia, Montana, Idaho, Oregon, and Washington. The Wyoming lawmaker relied on the visual evidence but also went looking for scientists who understood the impact of the practice. He identified a number of scientific studies showing how clearcutting depleted soil-based nutrients, rendering it much more difficult to restore seedlings to the lands where a prior generation of trees had been removed.[62]

McGee was appalled by what he saw, calling it "the rape of the land, with some large forest areas completely gone for my generation and the next."[63] He declared war on the clearcutters after an executive order proposed by the President's Council on Environmental Quality, which would have regulated clearcutting, was derailed by the timber industry. The executive order, had it been signed by Nixon, would have prohibited all clearcutting in areas of scenic beauty where soil erosion was a risk and where regeneration of trees was deemed unlikely.[64]

When the president did a turn-about and announced he had changed his mind and would not sign the executive order, many saw collusion between the timber industry and the Department of Agriculture. McGee announced his Senate Appropriations Committee Subcommittee on Agriculture, Environment, and Consumer Protection would investigate the decision. Simultaneously he introduced legislation similar to that which he had sponsored a year earlier placing a two-year moratorium on the practice pending further studies of the impact on forested land.[65] McGee decried the environmental impact of clearcutting, saying the forests "have been depleted to the point it would shame Paul Bunyan."[66]

Realizing the economic impact on local timbering companies could be devastating, the Wyoming senator agreed to a proposal made by Mike Leon for a financial subsidy. During the moratorium, the industry would receive payments for planting rather than harvesting trees. "As I understand it, there are some five million acres that have yet to be reforested. If we could activate your suggestion," he told Leon, "then perhaps the moratorium could become a model of how to effectuate a shift in our priority system so that we are putting back rather than taking out."[67] McGee had strong allies in the environmental community such as the Sierra Club, the Wilderness Society, and Friends of the Earth. But he was about to meet the timber lobby.

In December 1971, the head of a prominent national conservation organization called the White House to speak with Nixon adviser Charles Colson. He wanted to discuss plans to permit the timber industry to log some 187 million acres of woodlands. Colson was unavailable, the operator said. "How can I help you?" When the caller explained what prompted the call, he was told, "You'll have to talk to Ralph Hodges. He's handling all timber matters for us. I will give you his phone number."[68]

Hodges was the vice president and general manager of the National Forest Products Association, the most powerful timber lobbyist in the country. When McGee questioned Agriculture Secretary Earl Butz about the demise of the proposed executive order, Butz admitted the information he used to justify recommending that the president refuse to sign came from Hodges and the timber lobby. He did not ask for any information from the environmental community because his primary interest in the nation's forests was to harvest timber.

Following hearings in March 1972, the Senate Interior Committee turned down McGee's request for a moratorium, choosing instead to recommend guidelines for clearcutting to Butz's Agriculture Department.[69] The timber lobby won a battle but not the war. The political effort stimulated new scientific research on clearcutting. The industry argued the practice was justified because the trees would not reproduce in their own shade. In other words, leaving some of the trees uncut, they claimed, did not promote additional tree growth. Conservationists believed otherwise. Meanwhile, private and government researchers jointly determined that the conservationists were correct.

The editor of a respected industry journal, *American Forests*, reported, "Jerry F. Franklin of the Forest Service and Dean S. Debell of Crown Zellerbach Corporation agree. In fact, they come straight out and say there is no ecological necessity to clearcut most forest types."[70] He said the studies proved the timber industry was inclined "to eat their own young" and that the study Senator McGee had proposed would prove beneficial to the foresters and the public.

Mike Leon congratulated his boss, expressing "admiration and respect for your willingness to hang tight on this issue when you had no certainty vindication would come so early or from such unimpeachable sources."[71] McGee's next environmental battle offered even less certainty of vindication.

James Michener called Van Irvine "an authentic westerner, one who has been involved in most of the situations cattlemen face."[72] Irvine grew up hating eagles. As a youngster in the 1930s, he would rope Golden Eagles when he found them in vulnerable positions where they could not quickly take flight such as in the bottom of a deep ravine. Back then, Irvine would drag them to higher ground and release them. By the time he was in his mid-twenties, he was shooting the birds "whenever possible."[73]

Irvine called the eagle killings a "habit" he had learned from his father-in-law, Herman Werner. They were classic Wyoming ranchers who saw the birds as a threat to their livestock and therefore their livelihood. The two purchased the Diamond Ring Ranch in 1963. Their first run-in with Senator McGee came when they decided to fence some of the land without obtaining the required federal permits. McGee initiated a Senate investigation.

A few years later, Irvine was invited to buy the Bolton Ranch between Saratoga and Rawlins along the North Platte River. He wasn't much interested. "Too barren. Too remote. Serious lack of fences and other improvements. Too many eagles and coyotes I suspected." But his father-in-law was "enthralled" with the ranch and bought it. After receiving the deed, Irvine and Werner flew over the ranch, "and we saw coyotes in packs and eagles by the score."[74]

Werner built some fencing and put several thousand lambs on the land. Irvine never learned to like the ranch. However, Werner did. His son-in-law said Werner "kept bringing in sheep and feeding the coyotes."[75] According to Irvine, his top ranch hand came in one day and told him they had only one lamb left. "Herman, like any red-blooded American entrepreneur, tried to do something about it. He purchased a helicopter, hired a pilot and a gunner, secured a pick-up load of ammunition, and went to work."[76]

It wasn't long before hikers stumbled upon a grisly find. On the first day of May 1971, a couple of high school students were on a bird-watching excursion in Jackson Canyon some ten miles south of Casper. The area was prime eagle habitat, and they wanted to see the magnificent birds. The boys discovered seven dead golden and bald eagles. The following day the students led a party from the Murie Audubon Society to the site. Along the way they found six more carcasses. A week later, Wyoming state representative John F. Turner, a respected expert on eagles, reported there were twenty-five eagle carcasses piled in a ditch near Rawlins. Each had been shot. [77]

There wasn't much of a mystery about who did this. Herman Werner was proud of his accomplishment. During a Natrona County Woolgrowers dinner the previous November he had displayed a photograph "of a pile of dead eagles 6 or 8 feet high and 10 or 12 feet in diameter." Van Irvine said, "The shit hit the fan a few days later."[78] The photo vanished, and sometime later a man showed up unannounced at the offices of the Department of the Interior in Washington. "I'm the man you're looking for," he said. It was James Vogan, the pilot of the helicopter used in the shootings.[79]

McGee initiated a Senate investigation, and hearings were held in June and December 1971 before the Subcommittee on Agriculture, Environmental, and Consumer Protection of the Appropriations Committee. McGee was the subcommittee chairman. In June, Vogan, seated before a table stacked high with the carcasses of dead eagles, invoked his constitutional privilege against self-incrimination.[80] Upon receiving a grant of immunity, Vogan testified, admitting he flew the helicopter while others, to use Vogel's term, "sluiced" the birds from the aircraft. The term refers to the unsportsmanlike practice of shooting a sitting bird. He acknowledged he had witnessed the shooting deaths of more than five hundred eagles and knew of others. He claimed he had personally never shot a bird from a helicopter. "This does not say that I have not taken a shot at an eagle from the ground, because I have. I missed."[81]

Testimony before the McGee committee further disclosed that 222 coyotes, 6 elk, 5 bobcats, a bear, and several deer and antelope were also killed in the operations.[82] Vogan told the committee of Herman Werner's involvement. Werner, he said, paid $25 per eagle and $50 for a coyote, fox, or bobcat. Later Vogan told the press that at least 770 eagles had been shot. John Turner worried this slaughter "could push the eagle to the horizon of oblivion."[83]

Other birds had been poisoned. Placed in the carcasses of antelope, thallium sulphate caused the deaths of eagles feeding on the dead animals. A witness at the December hearing said he knew of sheep men who would "drive across grazing areas tossing it out left and right."[84] Natrona County attorney John Burk said carcasses of seven antelope found on the Diamond Ring ranch were loaded with enough thallium sulfates to kill all of the animals in the state.[85]

Eventually four men, including Van Irvine, were charged with a total of 114 state game violations stemming from poisoning the eagles. Irvine pleaded nolo contendere (no contest) to the twenty-nine charges filed against him on the condition that the charges against the other three men be dismissed. He was fined the minimum amount on all charges, $675 plus $4 court costs.[86]

The accusations against Werner were more serious. Federal crimes were implicated. Even so, without the McGee hearings, charges might never have been filed. Testimony during those proceedings angered many around the nation. President Nixon's interior secretary, Rogers C. B. Morton, said the destruction of the eagles was a "national outrage."[87] Nonetheless, according to a report published later at audubonmagazine.org, the U.S. attorney in Wyoming "balked" at prosecuting Werner. Richard V. Thomas figured no Wyoming jury would ever convict him.[88] Nathaniel Reed, the newly confirmed assistant secretary of the interior for fish and wildlife and parks under Nixon, appealed to the U.S. attorney general, Elliott Richardson. Werner was charged, but he would never be convicted.

Werner's trial was set to begin on October 29, 1973. He died on August 8, after the truck he was driving inexplicably veered into the path of an oncoming truck outside of Rawlins.[89]

Having locked horns with Wyoming's formidable timber and ranching interests, Senator McGee was now invited to take on the U.S. Atomic Energy Commission and a powerful international energy company headquartered in Texas. The El Paso Natural Gas Company planned to detonate a series of five nuclear explosions underground in Sublette County. The atomic bomb dropped on Hiroshima had the explosive force of 15 kilotons. That is 15,000 tons of trinitrotoluene, or TNT. The bomb dropped on Nagasaki weighed in at 21 kilotons. The "bombs" El Paso Natural Gas planned to detonate under Sublette County had a combined total of 500,000 tons of TNT.[90] What's more, the idea had the imprimatur of the U.S. Atomic Energy Commission under a program touting the peaceful use of nuclear technology, what the agency called "Project Plowshare" after the prophet Isaiah's promise that "they will beat their swords into plowshares."

It was an atomic form of "fracking," a controversial process whereby chemicals are inserted in tight geologic formations to fracture the rock in order to free deep pools of oil or natural gas. The so-called Wagon Wheel project planned to use not chemicals but nuclear explosives. Supporters said it would create underground chimneys, freeing deep reserves of natural gas from ancient rock formations that were not otherwise particularly permeable. Opponents said it would unleash destructive earthquakes and do severe environmental damage to the entire Yellowstone geologic region.

On March 20, 1972, more than five hundred Sublette County residents gathered at the Pinedale High School to learn more about the swirling rumors.[91] Wyoming's elected officials began to take notice. Initially Governor Hathaway told a Pinedale constituent that the possible exposure to radiation was significantly less than a common X-ray and that the benefits of the blast "outweigh its probable environmental costs."[92] However, within days of the Pinedale gathering, the governor joined Senator Cliff Hansen in calling on the Atomic Energy Commission to hold hearings at Pinedale.[93] Teno Roncalio, Wyoming's lone member of the U.S. House of Representatives, jumped in immediately to support those who wanted the project derailed. The state's senior senator was more cautious.

McGee had been corresponding with Sublette County residents, telling them that the matter would not be decided by the numbers of opponents but by "which side of the issue can present the most sustained and rational argument." He challenged the project's opponents to do their homework, to develop a fact-based argument, and not to rely on emotion. He warned one Project Wagon Wheel opponent, longtime friend Sally Mackey, that while the nuclear test itself could be disastrous, "The real disaster in this case would have been the hurried and ill-conceived strategies that sought to stop the test."[94] He made clear to Ms. Mackey that for the time being he remained uncommitted.

Sublette County activists formed the Wagon Wheel Information Committee, which became an effective grassroots force for disseminating information and raising questions and doubts about the project. The committee amassed hundreds of pages of scientific research documenting their concerns. They methodically put that information into the hands of decision makers, policy makers, and opinion makers. Petitions were circulated statewide, and forums were held to expose citizens' objections. A string of news releases were employed to educate and motivate the public. Political parties took up the issue, and some candidates began voicing opposition. Wagon Wheel was fast becoming a major statewide political issue.

McGee was no longer uncommitted. The people of Sublette County had done precisely what he asked of them. They gave him what he had requested in his letter to Sally Mackey, "the most sustained and rational argument." Project Wagon Wheel acquired an enemy where it needed one the least, on the powerful Senate Appropriations Committee. McGee wrote another letter to Mackey. "I applaud your efforts to be heard and promise my every effort on your behalf in this project."[95]

On August 8, McGee notified Dr. James R. Schlesinger that his office had studied the project thoroughly. He said the Environmental Impact Assessment was lacking and that "it is evident that many of the assurances claimed by the Environmental Statement's analysis of Project Wagon Wheel are without basis."[96] McGee advised the AEC chairman that he could not "in good conscience support the project, either as a matter of merit or as a consideration for federal appropriations." He further demanded the release of a report he knew the AEC had buried in its files. It was a study of collateral damage that the five underground nuclear explosions could be expected to cause. The report was released at the senator's request. It disclosed that two Sublette County dams could be rendered "unstable" by the explosions and discussed "the possible collapse of some lake shorelines" and damage to bridges if the detonations were permitted."[97]

In early 1973, former Washington governor Dixie Lee Ray was named chairman of the Atomic Energy Commission. McGee appealed to her to stop the project. Using the citizens' poll, McGee reminded the new chairman that her predecessor had committed the AEC to pull the plug on Wagon Wheel if "overwhelming local opposition could be demonstrated."[98] McGee demanded to know, "What value, if any, does the Commission place on the stable and sensible way of life of citizens in one of the most sparsely populated counties in one of the most sparsely populated states of the union?"

McGee's position on the Senate Appropriations Committee afforded the opportunity to demand a Government Accounting Office cost-benefit analysis.[99] This report was the final nail in Wagon Wheel's coffin. The GAO found too many uncertainties to proceed with the detonations. "What is clear in this report," McGee said, "is that more research and careful consideration is required before any decision can be reached as to either the feasibility or desirability of using any particular stimulation technology for the recovery of natural gas in this region."[100]

With Congressman Roncalio and McGee continuously fighting the project on several fronts and the Wagon Wheel Information Committee's strong grassroots organization, Project Wagon Wheel, died an agonizingly slow death. In May 1974, McGee persuaded the members of the Public Works Subcommittee of the Senate Appropriations Committee to "forbid the future use of [federal] funds for underground blasts to stimulate oil and gas recovery."[101] The idea of detonating a series of nuclear bombs beneath Sublette County was forgotten.

As McGee worked on these environmental issues, he was also required to tend to the foreign policy matters on his desk. The war in Vietnam continued to occupy his time on the Foreign Relations Committee, and in the fall of 1972 the president appointed him to be a member of the U.S. delegation at the United Nations. During each session of the General Assembly, the president selected a senator to serve with the U.S. delegation. Appointed by Nixon, McGee served during the 27th General Assembly alongside George H. W. Bush, then the ambassador to the UN, the job Lyndon Johnson had worked so vehemently to persuade McGee to take five years earlier.

Gale McGee had visited more countries than any other UN delegate. Of the 132 member nations, McGee could boast of having been to 91. He had also traveled to five of the non-member nations, Taiwan, West and East Germany, South Vietnam, and South Korea.[102] During his three-month 1972 assignment to the UN, he was afforded a unique opportunity to get to know the ambassadors as well as the current heads of state from dozens of countries.

Nixon asked McGee to work on four matters that he deemed urgent: the Palestinian refugee crisis, the question of apartheid in South Africa, the peacekeeping powers of the UN, and the reduction in dues paid by the United States to the international body. Toward the end of McGee's tenure, Ambassador Bush was tapped by Nixon to become chairman of the Republican National Committee. Bush agreed but told the president he wanted to stay on at the United Nations until the vote on U.S. dues reduction. "This is critical. Gale McGee is handling this for us."[103] The *New York Times* agreed this was "a crucial vote" for U.S. interests.[104] McGee succeeded in gathering a majority of the General Assembly to support the dues reduction despite heavy opposition from the Soviet Union whose ambassador attempted to persuade developing nations that the United States was simply trying to shift the burden of funding the UN to them.[105]

Upon his return to the Senate, McGee took it upon himself to educate constituents about what he worried was an "erosion of support for the UN." "Get US out of the UN" billboards dotted Wyoming highways. McGee explained such slogans "do nothing to enhance our prestige or our image as an international leader." He acknowledged that many of his constituents were still outraged over a UN vote to admit the People's Republic of China and expel Taiwan. However, McGee explained, "The organization was never intended to be a 'playground' of the United States." He concluded by calling the UN "a crucial hope for the future of mankind."[106]

The war in Vietnam ended when Nixon announced, "We have finally achieved peace with honor." It was January 27, 1973, when the formal peace agreement was signed in Paris. "With a view toward ending the war and restoring peace in Vietnam," the treaty's preamble read, the United States, North Vietnam, and South Vietnam at long last ended the war.[107] The agreement, however, did not end the fighting between North and South Vietnam, nor did it end the U.S. bombing of Cambodia, although Congress had voted to put a stop to it by August 15. By now, McGee had quietly broken with the president, having tired of defending his war in Cambodia.

It was early January 1973 before the peace agreement was reached and after a Democratic Party Senate caucus voted to end funding for the war. The White House asked McGee to speak out against his party's position. He agreed, but he was not happy about it. By now the Pentagon Papers had been made public, and McGee was aware of the deceptions surrounding the Gulf of Tonkin resolution. He had read the once secret internal memoranda from people he trusted, like George Ball, who were long ago advising LBJ that the war was never winnable. His disheartenment can be heard in words spoken as though through clenched teeth, evidencing a sense that McGee no longer trusted Nixon.

"Most of us have been torn very badly, shocked very deeply, by the events that have transpired in Southeast Asia, particularly since Election Day, November last," McGee told his colleagues. "The resumption of the bombing, the consequences of that bombing, the discouragement and further delay in arriving at a settlement—all have combined to have a shattering effect on most of us." However, McGee argued that partisan resolutions would not shorten the war. "The best chance at this moment is that somehow we luck out in Paris." He closed with words that could not have pleased the White House. "For better or worse, the president of the United States, under the Constitution, is the officer in charge as the war winds down."[108]

But McGee was in no mood to please the White House. He was embarrassed to be the lone Democrat defending the extension of the war. As he walked off the floor, Dick McCall, his foreign affairs adviser, met him. McCall still remembered McGee's words more than forty years later: "Never again."[109] Gale McGee had made his final Senate speech defending Nixon's conduct of the war. By month's end, Nixon announced the war was over, although it didn't actually end until April 1975 when the last Americans left and the South fell to the North.

Gale McGee celebrated the Fourth of July 1973 in Peking. He was a member of the second congressional delegation to visit China since Nixon had thawed Sino-American relations with his historic trip in February 1972. It was the first official celebration of U.S. Independence Day in Peking since 1949, and it took place in the recently built American Liaison Office.[110]

Before flying to China, the delegation was hosted at the newly opened Peking mission in Washington. The following day, the delegation stopped over in San Clemente, Nixon's "Western White House." The president asked to meet with the congressmen before their trip. He briefed them on the improved status of American relations with China and shared his ideas for how to continue improving them.

The delegation landed in Shanghai on July 2. The congressmen visited schools, medical facilities, industrial plants, communes, and historic sites in six major Chinese cities: Peking, Sian, Nanking, Suchou, Wuhsi, and Shanghai. The United States was still dropping bombs on

Cambodia. The delegation expected the subject to be raised when they met with Zhou Enlai, and McGee knew that as spokesmen for the United States in China, they would have to defend their country's policies.

David K. E. Bruce was the first U.S. emissary appointed to serve in China once diplomatic relationships were established following the Nixon visit. Ambassador Bruce remembers this was "the worst" congressional delegation he ever hosted. Bruce's assessment had nothing to do with Gale McGee. It was Senator Warren Magnuson, head of the delegation, who earned Bruce's undiplomatic wrath. Magnuson arrived unhappy that Chinese officials of insufficient rank met the delegation at the airport. Magnuson then summoned a foreign service officer to "fetch a forbidden box of Havana cigars from the Cuban embassy." Worst of all, thought Bruce, "Magnuson stepped over the line by discussing the American bombing of Cambodia with Zhou."[111] Magnuson "raised hell" about the U.S. bombing, and an argument about U.S. bombing erupted among the congressional delegation members in the presence of the Chinese leader. According to Tom Korologos, a White House official accompanying the delegation, McGee was the statesman. He conciliated and calmed the tensions among the delegation members.[112]

During their briefing at San Clemente, Nixon told the delegation, "Zhou is one of the most sophisticated people ever, but he is 74. A remarkable man. Listen to him. He is a giant in the world."[113] Nearly two decades later, Gale McGee spoke admiringly of the Chinese premier. The Wyoming lawmaker had met hundreds of international leaders ranging from Khrushchev to Golda Meir, Franco, Tito, Nasser, and Indira Gandhi. He called Zhou "the most impressive world figure I have ever met."[114] McGee recalled his meeting with Zhou in a 1990 oral history interview with longtime personal secretary Liz Strannigan. Zhou discussed his predecessor's "great plans for the expansion of the Chinese empire into Southeast Asia."[115]

In the course of a rather long conversation with Zhou Enlai, it naturally wandered to, "What about Mao?" Of course, the point was made rather strongly by Zhou that Mao had gone berserk, and that if we—"if you people, the United States, had not been there in Southeast Asia for the reasons that you were there, my predecessor Mao would have had it under his control. Your being there made the difference." But he, likewise, was very strong on the point that Mao would have stolen all of Southeast Asia if the U.S. hadn't been present.[116]

Zhou's comments were an affirmation of the domino theory, which had been at the heart of Kennedy's, Johnson's, and Gale McGee's central arguments for the Vietnam War, the domino theory. In their 1973 conversation, the Chinese leader vindicated McGee and others who argued throughout the war that if Vietnam fell, so it would be for the entire region. "It's one of those 'what-ifs' in history. Much as we fouled a lot of things up in that part of the world because of Vietnam, one of the accidental things that happened was that we may have made a long-range difference in the way things are now because of our presence there."[117]

Following their return, the senator received heavy criticism because his wife, Loraine, had accompanied him. "Who Paid for China Trip?" blared a July 17 *Casper Star-Tribune* headline. A few days later, the same newspaper answered its own question. "Government Footed Bill for Mrs. McGee's Trip." Because this trip was undertaken at the specific request of the president, the U.S. Air Force had paid the costs.[118] When asked about the matter, McGee's office withheld the real purpose of Mrs. McGee's accompaniment. Loraine always accompanied Gale. Whether back to Wyoming or to China, she was ever-present. She was the reason McGee's diabetes was well enough managed that he outlived the doctors' first prognosis. She traveled with him acting as a nurse to protect him from diabetic episodes. She monitored his blood sugar, made certain the right foods and drinks were readily available, and knew how to detect early signals of an oncoming diabetic coma even when they came while he slept.

Later when McGee served as ambassador to the Organization of American States, the State Department questioned the expenses related to Loraine's travel. An official told him it would be cheaper to simply have a trained nurse available at each stop along the route.

McGee explained why that was impractical. "No use," he objected. "They have to sleep beside me to detect perspiration, which is a warning of a diabetic coma."[119]

Malcolm Wallop's name was first mentioned in February 1974 in connection with the possibility that he might seek statewide office. The Sheridan County state senator was owner of the Polo Ranch and an heir to British royalty.[120] The following day, a popular front-page cartoon in the *Casper Star Tribune* called "The Old Grouch" commented, "I'd run for Governor but I'm afraid I'd be Walloped."

Wallop surprised most observers when he finished second by 814 votes following a recount in that year's divisive GOP primary. Wallop was encouraged by the result and looking for another opportunity.

If one had been looking closely, they would have noticed the opening of a rift between McGee and some of his constituents. It started with his change in dress. Since becoming a senator, his wardrobe had consisted mostly of dark suits and nondescript ties. His conservative attire blended in with what was worn regularly by his Senate colleagues. Suddenly it was replaced. In August 1972, political advocate Ralph Nader's "Congress Project" profiled members of Congress. Of Gale McGee, Nader wrote, "The next surprise is the Senator himself. The rugged looking man is stylish, wearing longish hair brushing the collar of his red polka-dot shirt."[121] McGee had reverted to an earlier time when he had been much more stylish and edgy.

It did not go without notice when McGee began routinely donning loud sports coats of many colors, some checkered or plaid, others striped, paired with flashy ties atop wide-collared pastel shirts. McGee was considered "the most fastidious" of the senators when it came to his hair. He wore a "shock of dark curly hair" longer than the others. "He doesn't care what people say," said Mr. Vagelis, his Senate barber. "That's why he is doing his own thing. I like him."[122] In Washington, his colleagues ribbed him about the length of his hair and the rainbow-imaged colors of his clothing. Back home, some constituents growled.

Late in 1973, an issue arose that no one could have predicted would cause grief for McGee. He received a letter from the Iriberry Brothers, ranchers near Buffalo. They were concerned about regulations proposed by the U.S. Department of Labor dealing with requirements for housing sheepherders. They said the new regulations placed onerous demands on ranchers to upgrade housing for the herders including the provision of indoor toilets and showers. They said it would be impossible for them to "install indoor toilets and showers in sheep wagons for reasons obvious to anyone knowledgeable about the sheep business."[123]

Other letters followed. The senator urged the Department of Labor to exempt sheep ranchers from the new regulations. The Department assured McGee and his constituents that variations could be granted in instances where the herders were "camping on the range, away from base camps."[124] McGee thought that would put the issue to rest. But this sort of thing was just waiting for a creative political consultant to turn it into one of the most effective political television ads in history.

The senator downplayed his involvement in foreign relations matters to avoid criticism that he was giving too little attention to Wyoming issues. Even so, Nader's "Congress Project" profile hinted at the growing perception that McGee was becoming aloof from the folks back home. McGee was described as "an internationalist," a war hawk, a civil rights advocate, a labor spokesman, and a guardian of local interests such as oil and gas. Nader said McGee had "established himself as more of a national figure than a senator representing local interests."[125] The report called the Wyoming senator "a latecomer to strong support of the right to bear arms." Worse, McGee admitted to Nader's people that he "voted against the wishes of his constituents on foreign policy." The Nader document went on to quote an unnamed McGee staff member as saying he always advised the senator to steer clear of foreign policy issues while in Wyoming. "They don't give a damn about foreign policy."

The source of alienation among Wyoming voters extended beyond anyone's perception of Gale McGee. The nation was in the midst of cultural disorientation. A 1973 poll revealed that in the eight-year interval between JFK's election and Richard Nixon's, "the number of Americans who felt alienated from their government more than doubled from 33 to 70 percent." During that period, voter participation was cut nearly in half.[126]

It's Nice to Have Dick Nixon to Kick Around Again   249

The Wyoming senator thought the problem had more to do with barriers to voting than voter alienation. As the chairman of the Post Office and Civil Service Committee, McGee held great influence over legislation affecting federal employees. He thought too many of them avoided political activity by using the Hatch Act as an excuse. The law put limits on the extent to which government employees can engage in politics. McGee concluded the law had transformed public employees "into politically gutless wonders and deprived the nation of the brains and muscles of its most educated voters."[127]

Calling U.S. voter turnout "dismal," McGee blamed an antiquated voter registration system. He said that before states began adopting complicated registration requirements, 80 percent of eligible voters took part in nearly fraud-free elections. "By 1924, after registration laws, only 48 percent of voting age Americans voted."[128] A Yankelovich poll following the 1972 presidential election concluded that voter registration laws were the reason that 26 million voters stayed away from voting booths that year alone.[129] McGee began work on a legislative package aimed at increasing participation in U.S. elections.

The Nixon administration opposed an earlier McGee bill. The March 1972 vote fell only five senators short with eight of the members absent.[130] McGee repackaged his bill and tossed it into the hopper in February 1973. The bill created a voter registration office within the Census Bureau. Before each national election, voter registration applications were to be sent to all eligible voters preaddressed to return to local election officials.[131] Nixon was still opposed as were most Senate Republicans and a handful of Southern Democrats. McGee's bill was strongly backed by civil rights groups such as the Leadership Conference on Civil Rights, the AFL-CIO, the National Farmers Union, and the United Steelworkers of America. The GOP looked at the lineup of supporters and saw it as an effort to increase the numbers of registered Democrats.

The opposition argued the bill would spawn voter fraud. Not so, said McGee. He cited a University of North Dakota study which showed that North Dakota elections conducted with no voter registration requirements produced no fraudulent voting. McGee called "disenfranchisement by archaic registration procedures" the "biggest fraud of all."[132]

When McGee's bill arrived on the Senate floor, it was met by a filibuster. David Minton, a McGee staffer who served as staff director of the Post Office and Civil Service Committee, looked perturbed as one senator followed another to McGee's desk asking and receiving his approval for amendments to the bill. One of the chief opponents was GOP leader Robert Taft Jr. of Ohio. When he showed McGee his proposed amendment, the Wyoming senator nodded his approval. "Jesus Christ, Senator," Minton blurted out, "not that one." McGee, Minton said, "gazed down at me with this look of incredulous pity." He told his young staffer, "You've been here all these years and you really don't know the first thing about how this place works."[133]

Gale McGee knew "how this place works" and what it would take to break the filibuster. On May 9, 1973, the bill finally received a roll call vote. Loaded with amendments McGee hoped would be deleted either in the House or a conference committee, it passed the Senate 57–37, not a sufficient margin to overcome a threatened Nixon veto.[134] The bill later failed in the House by a scant 7 votes.

Voter registration reform was eventually enacted. On May 20, 1993, little more than a year after Gale McGee's death, President Bill Clinton signed the National Voter Registration Act on the South Lawn of the White House. Loraine and their son Robert, Robert's wife, Mary Lou, and their sons Kirk and Scott attended the ceremony where Vice President Al Gore singled out McGee's efforts. "Gale McGee introduced the first motor voter bill a long, long time ago when he was in the Senate," said Gore. "It should have passed then."[135]

The new law expanded voting rights and made registration much less burdensome. Except in those states seeking an exemption, eligible voters can now register when applying for or renewing a driver's license. Although the percentage of eligible Wyoming voters who were registered dropped from 62 percent in 1978 to 50 percent in 2012 and turnout fell from 42.2 percent in 1978 to 25 percent in 2012, Wyoming asked for and received an exemption.[136]

In the spring of 1972, the manager of Walt Disney's ranch invited the McGees to stay at the company lodge near Dubois for a few days' rest. There they learned a bordering fifteen-acre ranch was for sale. The acreage stretched from the top of a large hill through aspen, pine, and spruce trees to Six Mile Creek at the western edge. Gale and Loraine quickly made arrangements to purchase the property.

The McGees scheduled as much time as possible at the ranch during congressional recesses and trips to the state. The senator was able to relax and unwind at the ranch more so than anywhere else. They aptly named it the Lazy G. It was a modest place consisting of a two-bedroom log structure built in the mid-1960s. The McGees eventually added a master bedroom and bath onto the house. There was also a one-room rundown cabin built in the late 1940s or early 1950s. A small fish pond bordered the north edge near a small weathered horse barn. Jack Cunningham, a local bank and train robber, had built it at the turn of the century.

Gale had three horses, one of which had been given to him by Cliff Hansen. He loved to ride through the mountains with his daughters. He fished nearby creeks, sawed logs for rails to repair his fence, and drove through the valley in the evenings hoping to spot a moose or an elk. Often he and Loraine just sat on the narrow front porch at the end of the day sipping Wild Turkey, the "official" drink of the Lazy G.

One afternoon Gale invited longtime friend Ruhl Bartlett, the eminent professor at Tufts University, to go fishing. Like most fishing buddies, they split up, hiking off in separate directions as soon as they got out of McGee's old Suburban. McGee was fishing along a narrow canyon when he heard rustling branches. He looked up and saw a cow moose charging him. All he could do was race the moose to a nearby pine tree. McGee climbed the tree and held on. The moose stopped, looked up at him, and slowly collapsed in the soft grass to take an inconvenient six-hour nap. McGee tried to rouse the animal to no avail. He had to wait it out. In the meantime, Bartlett couldn't find him. Loraine was frantic because it was well past Gale's dinner time, and she was worried about an insulin reaction. At long last the moose awakened, looked up at the treed senator, sniffed, and walked away.[137]

The cabin at the Lazy G had what was called "a cabin phone," which meant Gale could call out but nobody could call him. It was a "party line," meaning the same phone line was shared by two or three of his neighbors who could pick up their receiver and listen in on your calls. The Nixon White House complained about how difficult it was to reach McGee, so Gale worked out an arrangement with the owner of the Rustic Pine Tavern in nearby Dubois. Jim Miller was a good friend and the Dubois realtor from whom the McGees has purchased the ranch. Miller did most of his real estate business out of the Rustic Pine. Since Jim could most often be found, he and Gale agreed to an arrangement to accommodate the president. When the bartender answered a phone call from Nixon's office, he would holler out across the bar so other patrons would hear, "Hey, Jim, it's the White House." Jim would get in his old pickup truck and drive the sixteen miles out to the Lazy G and tell the senator he needed to call Washington. McGee would then place the call on his cabin phone's party line, giving little heed to which of the neighbors might be listening. The system would not have passed today's security regimen, but in 1972 it worked well.

Beginning shortly after Nixon's historic 1972 landslide over George McGovern and his second inauguration in January 1973, Watergate was the backdrop for virtually everything Senator McGee and his colleagues did during the president's abbreviated second term. It dominated the news as it consumed public attention. Wyoming's senior senator was rather circumspect in the public statements he offered on the growing scandal. Despite their partisan differences, Nixon and McGee got along well and were in frequent contact. Loraine and Gale were guests at Tricia Nixon's White House wedding to Edward Cox and were frequently included in state dinners hosted by the Nixons.

More than his personal relationship with Nixon, McGee harbored a deep respect for the office of the president. From the beginning of Watergate, McGee was uncomfortably aware that he could end up being one of a hundred jurors to decide the president's guilt or innocence. As the U.S. House prepared to consider articles of impeachment, he refused to join the firebrands calling for the president's head. "Men come and go," the senator told constituents. "The question is far bigger than Democrats or Republicans or Independents. It is a question that really holds very much of the resilient qualities capable of emanating from our system of government, and we have to evaluate it as Americans first and as partisans last, if at all."[138] The Casper newspaper's front-page cartoon "The Old Grouch" said, "It's sure nice to have Dick Nixon to kick around again."[139] But McGee steadfastly avoided taking partisan advantage of Nixon's growing troubles. He said the scandal resulted in most Americans wishing "a plague on both your houses."[140]

On May 18, 1973, the Senate Select Committee to Investigate Watergate convened. Sam Ervin of South Carolina gaveled the committee to order, television cameras whirred, and testimony began. From the start, the public was enthralled as they heard sworn statements linking the president of the United States to crimes far more serious than the June 1972 break-in at the Watergate offices of the Democratic National Committee.

As Americans began reaching conclusions about Nixon's future, McGee said they "should tone down their rhetoric." The onetime history professor hearkened back to the impeachment attempt against Andrew Johnson following Abraham Lincoln's assassination. McGee said the episode was "about the most disgraceful affair in American history" and that the United States risked the same with Nixon unless the country relaxed and awaited all the evidence.[141]

Privately the Wyoming lawmaker expressed dismay about what he was hearing. Daughter Lori Ann asked whether he thought it was "politics as usual." No, he answered, there had always been political pranks. But those things were "a far cry from the recent tactics of robbery, wiretapping, release of contrived and untrue letters."[142]

In late 1973, McGee went so far as to call for the resignation of any senator calling for Nixon's impeachment. He felt senators, who might be called upon to be Nixon jurors, should remain uncommitted for now.[143] But the day-to-day television coverage of the Ervin committee didn't quell the cry from around the nation for Nixon's demise. Clint Eastwood's classic movie *Hang 'em High* was playing in Wyoming theaters as John Dean began telling his story to a onetime student of Professor Gale McGee.

After James Neal secured a guilty verdict against the union leader, Jimmy Hoffa called Neal "the most vicious prosecutor who ever lived."[144] Neal was the lead Watergate prosecutor, a Tennessean whom legendary UW coach Bowden Wyatt recruited to come to Laramie. Neal was a star running back on the school's undefeated 1950 Gator Bowl football team. Within a few months of Neal's first meeting with Dean, he persuaded the former White House counsel to enter into a plea agreement leading to guilty verdicts in the cases Neal brought against Haldeman and Ehrlichman.

For the moment, the bulk of letters McGee received from Wyoming carried views opposed to how the president was being treated. The "Old Time Barracks" vfw members in Riverton petitioned McGee to oppose impeachment, as did hundreds of others. A. H. Trautwein, president of the Wyoming Bancorporation, spoke for many Wyoming people. "The Watergate investigation has become totally partisan and vindictive in nature."[145] They were not privy to what Dean was telling Neal behind closed doors and likely not prepared for what was about to happen.

On July 16, 1973, Alexander Butterfield was asked whether he was aware of the existence of recording devices in the White House. He was. He had installed them in the Oval Office in 1970 at the president's request. It appeared that every conversation since then was on a tape somewhere, including those most at issue in the investigation. Watergate shifted immediately to congressional and court fights to obtain the tapes.

The fight over the White House tapes led directly to one of the most dramatic weekends in the Watergate controversy. The "Saturday Night Massacre" began when Nixon ordered Attorney General Elliott Richardson to fire Special Prosecutor Archibald Cox. Richardson refused. Nixon fired Richardson and demanded that Deputy Attorney General William Ruckelshaus fire Cox. He also refused and was fired. Finally the president found someone to carry out his wishes. In a move that likely cost him a seat on the U.S. Supreme Court years later, U.S. Solicitor General Robert H. Bork dismissed the special prosecutor.

The weight of the mail the senator received from Wyoming abruptly shifted.[146] McGee acknowledged he had never received so much mail on a single subject. Opinions were running heavily in favor of the president's impeachment or resignation, "156 for, 26 against" since the Saturday Night Massacre.[147] McGee's supporters were ready for some "red meat," but he wasn't ready to toss it out. He called Nixon's actions "a serious exercise in poor judgment, which has deeply shocked us all." Still the senator urged caution.[148] Nonetheless, the odds makers saw no other outcome now than the impeachment of the president. Three days later, hoping to stem the impeachment talk, Nixon announced he would give the tapes to John J. Sirica, the chief U.S. District Court judge for the District of Columbia.

A few weeks after the firing of Cox, Richardson, and Ruckelshaus, McGee spoke to a large convention of corporate leaders in Washington about the scandal underlying Watergate: illegal campaign contributions. "The blame," he said, "does not lie alone with the Haldemans, the Ehrlichmans, or the Mitchells who coerced illegal corporate contributions for the campaign to reelect the president. The blame also rests with those corporations which thought they could buy a president."[149]

Senator McGee's view of the scandal began evolving when Nixon made a startling announcement. After his long battle to avoid giving the tapes to the court, he said earlier that two key tapes, which he promised Judge Sirica, didn't actually exist.[150] Now Nixon said he had found there was also a gap of eighteen and a half minutes in the tapes. White House chief of staff Alexander Haig said it was the result of an unidentifiable "sinister force."[151] Nixon blamed it on his secretary, Rose Mary Woods, claiming it was an accident. In a Chicago speech, McGee called that "the most incomprehensible straining of credulity that one could imagine." He said, "Anyone with any brains could have made up a better story."[152]

The following spring, the Nixon White House issued 1,308 pages of Watergate tape transcripts.[153] Nixon hoped the transcripts would dissuade the courts and the Congress from demanding the actual tapes. But most were no longer willing to accept the president's assertions at face value. The transcripts "proved" Nixon had not been told of the plan to pay hush money to the Watergate burglars.[154] The tapes proved otherwise. The written transcripts were loathsome. With their release, the term "Expletive Deleted" entered the English lexicon. Used to avoid some of the president's harshest curse words, it shocked many to know he talked like that. The Reverend Billy Graham, a Nixon spiritual confidant, told a friend the words he read made him "want to throw up."[155]

No other member of the Senate displayed greater respect for the office of president than Gale McGee. Through the long, bitter debate over Vietnam, it was his guiding principle as it was now for Watergate. Nonetheless, the transcripts convinced McGee that the time for patience was over. McGee waited to speak out until the Wyoming Democratic State Convention in May 1974. "Indeed, this revelation," McGee said, referring to the written transcripts, "is too much for the public to stomach." Stopping just short of calling for the president's resignation, the senator quoted a *Chicago Tribune* editorial that concluded, "He must go." The Wyoming lawmaker said he hoped Nixon would now "address himself to the judgment of history."[156] The first signal McGee offered that he had begun to see impeachment as inevitable came with his May 1974 newsletter to constituents. A full page was titled "Senator Answers Frequently Asked Questions on the Impeachment Process."[157]

The battle continued at an increased pitch and with much higher stakes. The final showdown took place during a historic session of the U.S. Supreme Court. Justice William Rehnquist recused himself, and the eight remaining justices heard oral arguments lasting three hours and three minutes in the matter of *United States v. Nixon*. Leon Jaworski, the special prosecutor who had replaced Archibald Cox, began grimly. "This case goes to the heart of our basic constitutional system. In our view, this form of government is in serious jeopardy."[158]

On July 24, 1974, as the U.S. House Judiciary Committee began considering articles of impeachment, the Supreme Court handed down its decision.[159] It was unanimous. Richard Nixon was ordered to release all of the White House tapes relevant to Watergate. James Neal, the former Cowboy football star who was the government's top trial lawyer in its case against Haldeman and Ehrlichman, put it aptly when he spoke of those tapes in his closing argument months later. "Can you compare the White House, perhaps when Jefferson was drafting his Second Inaugural or Lincoln writing 'with malice toward none,' with the tapes you've heard in this courtroom?"[160]

The words on the Nixon tapes hit Gale McGee harder than most. The senator who had written in 1968, "The government does not lie," felt betrayed by his own trust in the system. However, he was not nearly so naïve as he was made to sound if those five words are taken out of context. His book offered an explanation apropos to Nixon's fate. McGee explained that the government was constantly "under the scrutiny of the press as it is, and much as it must remain ever at the mercy of searching inquiries from Members of Congress, it couldn't get away with it if it so designed."[161] That is precisely what had "done in" the Nixon presidency.

McGee reconsidered his decision not to call on the president to resign. "The president has now confessed," said the saddened senator.[162] By the end of July, the Judiciary Committee voted to recommend three articles of impeachment to the full House. On August 8, 1974, the man who once told his advisers, "You don't strike at the king unless you kill him," resigned the presidency.[163]

14

Wyoming's Way of Life Is at Stake

Gerald Ford took office as the first appointed vice president of the United States when Spiro Agnew was forced to resign because of criminal conduct. Ten months later, on August 1, 1974, he answered a phone call from Richard Nixon's chief of staff, Alexander Haig. "Mr. Vice President, it's urgent that I see you as soon as possible."[1]

Nixon was resigning. Ford became the first unelected president because of the criminal conduct of the elected president. If one had not lived through those days, it would be difficult to estimate the trauma the nation experienced and how the scandal impacted the government in such a short period of time. The Watergate scandal consumed every waking minute of the Nixon administration for months, leaving a great deal of pressing work for the new president. The economy was teetering from the impact of inflation. There were major international problems in the Middle East and American-Soviet relationships. In order to focus on those matters, Ford first had to deal with cleaning up the Nixon problem.

On September 8, a month after Nixon's resignation, Ford announced he had granted "a free and absolute pardon unto Richard Nixon for all offenses against the United States of America which he, Richard Nixon, has committed or may have committed or taken part in during the period from January 20, 1969, through August 9, 1974."[2]

Ford later explained his decision to the House Judiciary Committee, which had voted to impeach Nixon. After discussing the challenges the nation faced following Nixon's departure, Ford said, "We would needlessly be diverted from meeting those challenges if we, as

259

a people, were to remain sharply divided over whether to indict, bring to trial, and punish a former president who is already condemned to suffer long and deeply in the shame and disgrace brought upon the office that he held."[3]

Senator McGee's cautionary path led him slowly to the conclusion that Nixon should resign. However, his feelings about Nixon's pardon were surprisingly firm. McGee told constituents that Ford's decision was "troublesome and far-reaching." He said the decision negatively impacted the ability of the nation to restore confidence after the long Watergate ordeal.[4] McGee called the consequences "most ominous."[5]

His constituents agreed. When George O. Pearson of Sheridan wrote to tell his longtime friend that Ford had acted courageously, McGee wrote back. "You might be interested to know that in all the mail I have received on this matter from Wyoming (and it's been considerable), yours is the first letter in favor of this pardon."[6]

The 1970s not only witnessed the Watergate scandal but also brought a number of embarrassing revelations about the Central Intelligence Agency. A Select Committee on Intelligence Activities was authorized to conduct a wide-ranging inquiry, and McGee's friend Frank Church was named chairman. The Select Committee determined the CIA had plotted along with organized crime to murder Fidel Castro. The agency had also been involved in plots to kill Patrice Lumumba and the Diem brothers in Vietnam. By the fall of 1975, the committee's investigation was winding down, and Church filed its final reports. While McGee was willing to acknowledge the CIA had made some serious mistakes, he worried about the report's impact on national security, saying that "if we don't get that back together we are going to be left naked before the world."[7] The process embarrassed the CIA and other players in the country's intelligence gathering community. It also cost Director William Colby his job. Colby's firing was a part of what the press called the "Halloween Massacre," Ford's late October reorganization of his cabinet, which had implications for Wyoming.

Dick Cheney replaced Donald Rumsfeld as White House chief of staff. Before Rumsfeld relinquished his duties to Cheney, Ford asked him to identify a replacement for Colby as CIA director. Rumsfeld assembled a list of fourteen possible nominees, including Gale McGee.

Rumsfeld told the president that the Wyoming senator was a sixty-year-old former professor with a PhD who had lectured extensively on foreign affairs, was a member of the Council on Foreign Relations, and was a onetime member of the U.S. delegation to the UN. Rumsfeld identified McGee's attributes for the job, telling Ford he was a "respected leader within the foreign relations community; [a] knowledgeable defender of strong intelligence community; [with] excellent rapport with Congress; respected for his independence."[8]

Rumsfeld solicited input from administration officials, ranking potential appointees in the "aggregate of the number of times an individual favored one of the possible candidates." McGee's name was third on the shortlist submitted to Ford.[9] However, the president chose someone whose name didn't appear on Rumsfeld's list. Ford's preference was Washington powerhouse attorney Edward Bennett Williams. When he turned the job down, George H. W. Bush, the chairman of the Republican National Committee, was nominated.[10]

McGee was likely unaware he had come so close to being asked to take the job. But he had known Bush from the days they shared at the United Nations, greatly respected him, and thought he was highly qualified to head the agency. When Senate Democrats, like Ted Kennedy of Massachusetts, Philip Hart of Michigan, Alan Cranston of California, Frank Church of Idaho, and Warren Magnuson of Washington State opposed the Bush nomination, McGee defended him. While Bush opponents complained about the GOP national chairman taking over the CIA, McGee lauded Bush for having taken his party's chairmanship during the toughest days of Watergate and filling the role "in a very statesmanlike manner." He encouraged his colleagues to confirm Bush based on his skills as an "administrator with a sense of public responsibility." The Senate then voted 64–27 to confirm Bush.[11]

Wyoming Republicans expected Ford to nominate former governor Stan Hathaway to serve as U.S. Federal Court judge for the District of Wyoming. Cliff Hansen, Wyoming's Republican U.S. senator, had formally recommended Hathaway for the judgeship in a January 15, 1975, letter to the president.[12] But Ford had other ideas.

On April 4, Ford formally announced Hathaway's nomination to be the next secretary of the interior.[13] The nomination was generally popular in Wyoming but not universally so. The views of Wyoming pioneer Alice Shoemaker of the CM Ranch near Dubois represented the thinking of many conservationists. They credited the governor with protecting industry from environmental regulation. "I am confident that if there is any way to prevent this appointment," Shoemaker wrote in a letter to McGee, "You will know what to do and will do it."[14] To the contrary, McGee felt it was his duty to help ensure the success of the nomination of Wyoming's former governor. They were members of different political parties, but McGee knew the significance of having a Wyoming appointee lead the department that most impacts the state's interests. With Democrats controlling the Senate majority and thus the outcome of Hathaway's nomination, the burden fell on the shoulders of Wyoming's senior senator to round up the necessary votes. It was not going to be easy, but McGee knew much of the Senate would look to colleagues in the West for guidance.

The first sign of trouble came shortly after Ford's announcement. On April 8, Frank Church stopped just short of coming out against Hathaway. Church said that while he was pleased that the president had looked to the West for a nominee, he was troubled that Ford "has picked a man whose nomination has caused deep concern among conservationists throughout the nation."[15] The words of one of the most influential westerners on the Interior Committee were a strong signal that the nomination was sailing into stormy waters.

The White House issued a point-by-point rebuttal to the charges against Hathaway. It had been Hathaway who proposed Wyoming's Air Quality Act. Hathaway's Outdoor Advertising Act had reduced the number of billboards dotting the state roads and highways. It was Hathaway who requested the moratorium on the hunting of grizzly bears. He drafted the Mined Land Reclamation Act and imposed severance taxes on mineral development. It was Hathaway's idea to create the Wyoming Permanent Mineral Trust Fund to set aside mineral tax dollars for future generations. He created the Department of Environmental Quality to administer his Environmental Quality Act. Hathaway had supported the Wyoming Stream Preservation Feasibility Study and the enactment of the Environmental Pesticide Control Act of 1973.[16]

The environmental lobby was relentless. The day after the White House released its defense of Hathaway's record, the Environmental Defense Fund issued a full response. It charged that the White House analysis "discloses a pattern of misleading statements, exaggeration, and selective omissions." The analysis reviewed the record the White House developed and concluded, "Of the few pieces of legislation which are environmentally sound, Governor Hathaway typically attempted to weaken the bills while they were in the legislature."[17]

During his April 20 confirmation hearing, Hathaway's critics accused him of myriad "offenses." They said he supported unfettered coal development, failed to act decisively against a proposal to use Wyoming water to move coal out of the state through a coal slurry pipeline, supported clearcutting over McGee's objections, advocated for loose restrictions on air and water quality, and requested "blanket permits to hunt down golden eagles."[18]

Bart Koehler of the Wyoming Outdoor Council complained that Hathaway had an "antagonistic attitude toward the [wilderness] concepts and a shallow understanding of the law." Charles Callison of the National Audubon Society said the former Wyoming governor exhibited a "non-comprehension" of the purpose and the needs of national parks. Brock Evans of the Sierra Club told the Interior Committee that Hathaway had an "overwhelming commitment to industrial development of public resources and a very small commitment to environmental protection."[19]

Through it all, Gale McGee was one of Hathaway's staunchest defenders. He accompanied him on visits to nearly all of the Senate Democrats, saying to each, "This is the most popular politician in Wyoming. If you don't confirm him, he will go back home and run against me for the Senate," McGee said jocularly. "And he will beat me."[20]

McGee testified before the Senate Interior Committee as it considered the Hathaway nomination. "Few nominees ever come before the Senate as well informed or as well prepared for their intended responsibilities as Governor Hathaway."[21] Many of the committee members had yet to be persuaded. In early May, Colorado senator Gary Hart announced he would vote no.[22] With Hart's opposition and the uncertainty over which way Frank Church might vote, McGee spent his time tenaciously lobbying the remaining Senate Democrats.

The Senate took up the nomination on June 11, 1975, and Vice President Nelson Rockefeller presided in case his vote was needed to break a tie. Following a bitter debate pitting Democrats against one another, Stan Hathaway's nomination was approved by a vote of 60–36.[23] He was sworn in on June 14 and served as secretary of the interior for forty-two days.

Soon after taking office, Hathaway was found to be suffering from depression. His doctor ordered him hospitalized, and on July 25 Hathaway submitted his resignation. McGee announced the decision to his Senate colleagues the following day. "It is most unfortunate that the vicissitudes inherent in the human condition we all share have been visited upon this able and dedicated public servant at the acme of his public life as he was setting about a new position of service to the entire nation."[24]

Stan Hathaway returned to Wyoming and formed one of the state's premier law firms, Hathaway, Speight, and Kunz. He served on the board of directors of a number of large corporations and remained one of the most beloved and respected personalities in Wyoming until his death in 2006.

The battle over the Hathaway nomination was indicative of a larger war being fought between environmentalists and the minerals industry in the context of the mid-1970s energy crisis. In 1974, the U.S. Bureau of Mines estimated that of the 434 billion tons of coal lying beneath the nation's surface, 297 billion could be retrieved only by deep mining techniques. That left a sizeable 137 billion tons that could be harvested through strip mining.[25] A large portion of those billions of tons lay at or just below the surface of federally owned lands in Wyoming. Between 1970 and 1975, Wyoming coal production more than tripled from 7 million to more than 23 million tons.[26]

It wasn't only coal but also uranium and trona bringing heavy investments of outside money. New power plants were built, and more were planned. Historian Phil Roberts recalled those days. Few Wyoming communities "were prepared for the onslaught of miners, construction workers, and employees for support companies that descended on Wyoming in a brief period of time."[27] Finding a place to live was nearly impossible. Many people lived in trailers, which soon accounted for one-fifth of all available housing in the midst of the boom. Workers slept in campers, their cars, pickup trucks, tents, and, if their company provided them, the barracks of man camps. Schools overflowed, classes were held in modular units, and class sizes were far too large. Some teachers quit for higher wage jobs in the mines, and many high school students dropped out for the same reason. Resources of social service agencies were dangerously stretched. Domestic violence and child abuse were epidemic. Law enforcement was unable to keep pace with rising crime rates, which included a heavy dose of drug crimes and prostitution. City services could not meet the demands for sewer, water, and electricity, streets and roads.

Thoughtful community leaders felt helpless in the face of what they believed to be the ravaging of their rural parts of the country so that populous areas could have the energy. They knew they did not have the votes to protect themselves from purely political decisions about their future. A National Academy of Sciences report "unwittingly touched off a bombshell. Certain sites," it said, "must be given up as impossible to reclaim or even rehabilitate, and for those 'hopeless areas' it coined the term 'National Sacrifice Area.'"[28]

Overwhelmed mayors and county commissioners turned to their congressional delegation. The Surface Mining and Reclamation Act of 1974 and the Federal Coal Leasing Amendments Act of 1976 were proposed to level the playing field between rural and urban America's needs. McGee saw the legislation as "preventive medicine against the illnesses caused" by the impact of strip mining.[29] President Nixon had called for legislation to regulate abuses of surface and underground mining in order to protect the environment in his State of the Union message in February 1973.[30] A bill passed the Senate but failed in the House. The matter remained on the congressional agenda after Gerald Ford became president. Ford didn't share Nixon's concerns, and in December 1974 he vetoed the first Surface Mining and Reclamation Act passed by Congress.[31]

The president felt the bill would seriously damage the coal industry, reducing production by as much as 141 million tons. He committed his administration to working with Congress to find an acceptable compromise.[32] In February 1975, McGee signaled his willingness to find common ground with the White House. He reminded his colleagues what was at stake. "As we once again begin the arduous task of developing a federal strip mine bill, let us not forget that strip mining cannot be put on an island unto itself. Without controls, its effects on people and communities are frightening."[33] Bob Wallick, who ranched near Big Horn, told McGee what was at stake, nothing less than a way of life. Wallick colorfully explained that, like the time when foreigners "traded beads to Indians for this land," the large mining companies "are now trading 'beads' to the people of Wyoming for their land, water, other natural resources, and way of life."[34]

The senator charged that President Ford "failed to envision the societal dangers of mining in launching a reckless course toward rapid coal development."[35] As the 1975 debate proceeded, McGee became more and more upset about the president's views and his veto: "To allow surface mining without the protections of this bill would be a reckless course. To again fail to realize the enactment of a surface mining law would be a mistake with which we would all have to live. I am not willing to call upon my state to make the supreme sacrifice."[36]

All efforts to compromise failed when Ford vetoed a subsequent offering, the Surface Mining Control and Reclamation Act of 1975. The following year, after both Ford and McGee were defeated in the 1976 election, Congress passed and President Carter signed a much tougher strip mining reclamation act, which Carter called "one of the most significant environmental statutes in recent years."[37]

For many years afterward, Wyoming people remembered McGee, Cliff Hansen, and Teno Roncalio, the three members of the state's congressional delegation, for their bipartisan efforts to enact the Federal Land Policy and Management Act (FLIPMA). Congress and the White House spent years studying the questions swirling about the management of federal lands. In the early 1960s, the Public Land Law Review Commission was created, and its report *One Third of the Nation's Land* was released in 1970. Its recommendations were contained in the 1976 Federal Land Policy and Management Act.

As a member of the House Committee on Interior and Insular Affairs, Teno Roncalio saw the momentum behind the bill as an opportunity to address his state's need for money to meet the costs of mineral development. His amendment to FLIPMA provided a significant increase in the state's share of royalties derived from mining federally owned lands. For decades, entities producing minerals on federal lands paid a royalty ranging from 5 to 12.5 percent. The state received 37.5 percent of the total royalty, and the remainder went to Washington. FLIPMA proposed an increase in the states' share to 50 percent. That would substantially increase the flow of federal mineral royalties into state coffers to help pay the enormous costs of increased mineral production on the state and its impacted communities.

With Roncalio taking the lead in the House, Democrat McGee and Republican Hansen teamed up in the Senate. The three recognized this as a once-in-a-lifetime opportunity for Wyoming. It seemed that nearly everyone thought the act would be the answer to the serious problems facing mineral-producing states—everyone that is except the president. The day before the nation celebrated its Bicentennial in 1976, President Ford crushed the hopes of many in Wyoming by vetoing the bill. Although FLIPMA had passed the House 344–51 and the Senate by 84–12, the president was willing to risk an override. Ford's veto message claimed that while he supported increasing federal mineral royalty payments, the bill was "littered with many other provisions" he believed would inhibit coal production and create barriers to energy independence.[38]

The Senate debated whether to override the veto on August 3, 1976. Wyoming's two senators led the charge. Cliff Hansen said Ford's veto "was based on factual errors." Wyoming was willing to do its part to provide badly needed coal to the rest of the country, Hansen assured his colleagues, but that would require the safeguards in the legislation that the president had vetoed. McGee reminded the Senate that Ford had also vetoed efforts to provide environmental protection against strip mining, evidencing the administration's "calloused disregard for the problems which face the Western states as national pressures for energy development increase."[39]

The lengthy debate notwithstanding, the vote to override Ford's veto was not close. Seventy-six senators voted to enact the bill notwithstanding the president's objections. Only seventeen voted to sustain the veto. In fiscal year 2015, federal mineral royalties added $689.3 million to Wyoming's revenue stream.[40]

Earlier in 1976, Secretary of State Henry Kissinger accepted Senator McGee's invitation to come to Wyoming. On February 4, Kissinger spoke to a crowd of more than 7,000 at the historic University of Wyoming Fieldhouse. He delighted the large crowd, telling them he had heard there were two kinds of people in Wyoming, "ranchers who did a little rustling and rustlers who did a little ranching." Kissinger then got serious, recounting the nation's difficult last fifteen years. "We have passed through a decade and more of tragedy. We have been witness to assassination; we have suffered through a tragic war that shattered our domestic unity; and we have endured our greatest Constitutional crisis since the Civil War." That wintery day in Laramie, Kissinger said the United States had "come through these difficult times with our institutions as strong as ever."[41] Following three decades of additional experience and reflection, he saw it differently. In his 2014 book, *World Order,* Kissinger defined the turning point in American history. "Roughly coincident with the assassination of President John F. Kennedy, the national consensus began to break down."[42]

That "national consensus" had a decidedly liberal bent, having given America the New Deal and more recently the Civil Rights Act of 1964, the Voting Rights Act of 1965, Medicare, Medicaid, the War on Poverty, the Environmental Protection Agency, the Wilderness Act, the Clean Air and Water Acts, and countless other pieces of social and economic reform laws. Gale McGee had been elected at the zenith of the twentieth century's liberal movement. Much of his eighteen years in the U.S. Senate were a victory lap for liberals coming out of the New Deal and riding high through the New Frontier and the Great Society, though in retrospect, the latter began to look more like the movement's death rattle. Historian James Piereson writes, "It now seems clear that Kennedy's assassination had the effect of draining much of that political energy out of the liberal movement." He suggests, "Under the leadership of Franklin Delano Roosevelt, liberalism redefined and re-energized itself, much to the benefit of the nation."[43]

But the national consensus built in the liberal era was now challenged and not only by the Kennedy murder with the attendant doubts in the minds of the public about the Warren Commission findings and multiple conspiracy theories about who actually killed the president. There had also been the Vietnam War, Watergate, *Roe v. Wade*, a sexual revolution, and the domestic racial and political violence of the 1960s and 1970s. Even those who had benefited from the agenda flowing out of the nation's liberal consensus began to see government as too big, too intrusive, and too threatening.

The coming election would measure the strength of those who defended government against those who attacked it. Gale McGee was on one side, while Jimmy Carter and Malcolm Wallop were on the other.

15

Time for a Change

Gale McGee returned often to the University of Wyoming, a place of solace and comforting memories. In the spring of 1976, the senator was on campus to speak to a gathering of professors. He was reminded of those days almost three decades earlier when, as a young professor, he was a part of a faculty committee boldly standing against the efforts of the UW board of trustees to censor textbooks. "At the time of the inquiry I was the only member of that committee without tenure," McGee reminisced, poignantly adding a reference to his upcoming battle for reelection. "As I look around the room today, I see I am still the only one without tenure."[1]

As political minds began turning to the 1976 Senate race, it seemed tenure would be no more necessary to McGee's Senate career then than it was to his professorial career in 1947. The *Washington Star* assessed the 1976 Senate contests around the nation a year before those campaigns got under way. "They are older now, these solid citizens of the U.S. Senate. The hair is showing tattletale gray, jaw lines have gone to jowls, and reading glasses peek out from breast pockets. They are short on charisma but long on clout."[2]

The newspaper discussed the political futures of Gale McGee and seven of his 1975 colleagues who were the last remaining among the fifteen Democrats elected in the Class of 1958. The newspaper believed McGee had "few political problems back home." The reporter recounted how the 1958 results gave the Democrats a 64–34 Senate margin and said the GOP had never recovered. The margin going into the 1976 contest was 62–38. "In 15 of the 32 seats, incumbents are considered overwhelming or fairly strong candidates." Among those on that promising list was Gale McGee.[3]

Even so, national Republican operatives made it clear that McGee was a prime target. When McGee's colleague Cliff Hansen spoke about the joint bipartisan efforts of the state's congressional delegation to pass laws benefiting the state, some Wyoming Republican officials took the GOP senator to the proverbial woodshed for what was called "his 'gee, Gale and I work so well together' stance."[4] Despite those early projections of a McGee reelection, GOP strategists sensed vulnerability.

However, a year ahead of the election there didn't appear to be any interest among Republicans in challenging the three-term incumbent. Asking who might be the "likely Republican candidate," the *Powell Tribune* said the GOP needed a new star. "Election year 1976 isn't far away and that star doesn't appear on the rise."[5] The editor of the *Newcastle Newsletter* agreed. In his February 12, 1976, column, Jim Parrish wrote, "Wyoming Republicans are hard put this year to find 'shining stars' to oppose Senator Gale McGee." Later that month the *Riverton Ranger* opined that it appeared as though McGee would have a "free ride."

Early in 1976, the Republican National Committee dispatched a staff member to Wyoming to identify a McGee opponent. Malcolm Wallop caught his attention even though Wallop had "antagonized Republican rank and filers by a delayed and back handed" endorsement of Dick Jones, the gubernatorial candidate to whom he had narrowly lost the 1974 nomination. There was also unhappiness in the ranks for Wallop's "studied disinterest" in helping with Stan Hathaway's difficult battle for confirmation as interior secretary.[6] Yet a month after it suggested McGee might get "a free ride" in 1976, the *Riverton Ranger* touted a possible Wallop candidacy, acknowledging some Republicans remained unhappy over how he had treated Jones and Hathaway but admitting "some Republicans aren't great McGee fans either."[7] It was understood that bygones could be bygones if it appeared McGee could be beaten.

What political campaign spectators have come to take for granted today was something new, even foreign, to Wyoming voters in 1976. Prior to that year political campaigns were largely put together by a group of the candidate's friends working on a shoestring budget. McGee's 1958 campaign, operated from the back room of a Cheyenne gas station, was more common than not. The age of high-priced out-of-state political consultants armed with extensive polling data and using media strategists formerly available only to those selling cereal or automobiles arrived in the state with gusto that year.

So new was the strategy that the McGee campaign didn't hire a consultant. He never had before and wouldn't start now. When solicited by an advertising agency, McGee's administrative assistant Dick Cook demurred. "I have never hired an agency as such in the past three campaigns. I do 90 percent of the work myself." Cook said he routinely hired someone to produce film for TV spots. "I then do all the editing and further production work."[8] Malcolm Wallop, on the other hand, hired a well-known and highly successful political consultant. Robert Goodman had managed winning campaigns for Senator Robert Taft Jr. of Ohio and Governor Winthrop Rockefeller in Arkansas.[9]

The *Washington Post* said Wallop was a rancher with a PhD in English who "looks as though he'd be more at ease in a library than a saddle." That image needed a makeover. "We dig up Wallop, he doesn't know where he is going. He was behind 72–18. He was nowhere. I invented him."[10] That's how Goodman later described his role in the 1976 Wyoming Senate race.

In the spring, Goodman and his staff spent "weeks in Wyoming filming, doing preliminary analysis, and consulting with core campaign staff." They added a major national polling firm to the team and began incorporating extensive opinion research into the plan. A large campaign staff was assembled and a budget of $292,650 was developed, exceeding amounts previously spent in any Wyoming political race.[11] Goodman promised contributors, "Never before in the history of Wyoming has a campaign of this intensity and organization been undertaken."[12]

Those who got to know Malcolm Wallop in his 1974 campaign for governor could be excused if they didn't recognize the Malcolm Wallop who campaigned for the Senate two years later. "Producer Robert Goodman's 1976 campaign film for Wallop caught the grandeur and independence of the west, put a cowboy hat on the Republican candidate, and to the beat of sweeping music, had him leading a horse caravan to Washington—the Wallop Senate Drive."[13] The early commercials touting Wallop's campaign were exciting. They didn't attack McGee. They didn't say what Wallop stood for or against. Nor did it tell the voters why he was qualified for the job. That wasn't their purpose.

Goodman rounded up seventy-five horses and put riders on them. Wallop the rancher knew that horses and helicopters were a bad mix because the noise scars the horses and risks a stampede. Goodman the political consultant didn't know that. Goodman hauled his cameras aboard a helicopter and began filming from above. "Then out of the west came Mr. Wallop at the head of an immense charge of horsemen, dust flying in all directions, and Mr. Goodman's big band playing its heart out with music especially written by Mr. Goodman himself." The theme was "Come Join the Wallop Senate Drive." When the stirring ad first ran on Wyoming's TV stations, Wallop wasn't particularly optimistic about catching McGee in the polls. "Our opponent, Sen. Gale McGee, was immaculate. We couldn't find anyone who wanted to go against him," Wallop said in hindsight. "But in four weeks we turned it around. More and more I am overwhelmed by the power of TV advertising."[14]

The imagery of Goodman's production was purposeful. In her book *Becoming Western: Stories of Culture and Identity in the Cowboy State,* writer Liza Nicholas discusses the "powerful resonance of symbols in the west. Goodman's ads were a reminder of the west of writer Owen Wister and painter Frederic Remington. In their west, cowboys symbolized strength and independent self-sufficiency." Nicholas recounts the cultural influences on Wister and Remington. Coming of age in the latter half of the nineteenth century, these two artists witnessed the 1886 Haymarket Riot, the Pullman Strike of 1894, and the "unrepentant working classes, and recently arrived immigrants." Remington and Wister feared America was "on the verge of a cultural Armageddon." Thus, with Wyoming, "they could imagine and create the sort of cultural icon needed to thwart the power of the problematic 'un-American' working classes and their bothersome politics, especially populism."[15] Robert Goodman saw things in much the same way as he crafted the Wallop Senate Drive.

The upheaval experienced in the United States in the 1960s and 1970s was not unlike that of Wister and Remington's times. Like them, many Wyomingites saw their state as "the eternal keeper of the cultural symbols of the 'true' West."[16] The Wallop Senate Drive employed the right symbolism, a cowboy hat on the candidate's head and visions of horses amidst flying dust. It captured the sentiment of those who longed for a return to an earlier time.

For his part, Gale McGee sounded and looked like a senator, not a Wyoming cowboy. Historian T. A. Larson dubbed him "the most gifted public speaker and debater the state ever had."[17] He was an intellectual who had published a scholarly book. He sat comfortably in seats of power and could easily speak with any of the world's leaders. McGee was more at home standing at the podium of the United Nations than at a branding on some Wyoming ranch. But by 1976, the bottom had dropped out of the political market for such a person.

Wyoming people wanted to look at their politicians and see themselves. With his deep, resonating voice, McGee didn't sound like many of his constituents. There were no reported sightings of McGee in a pair of faded Levis and scuffed cowboy boots. No one ever saw him with a cowboy hat atop his bushy, well-groomed hair. His dress was always "senatorial," although in recent years he had worn flashy sport coats and ties. His appearance set him apart from most of the folks he met on the streets of Pinedale or Pine Bluffs or elsewhere across the Cowboy State. It wasn't who any pollster told him he should be. It was simply who he was.

Until 1976, Wyoming people tolerated and many even appreciated the differences. They had been drawn to McGee's senatorial demeanor. It's what filled his classes during his days as a popular history professor at the University of Wyoming. It contributed mightily to his 1958 election and two subsequent reelection victories. Until now it seemed Wyoming people thought a senator ought to look and sound like a senator. But as the voters turned against Washington, they also turned against the symbols of Washington.

Wallop knew how much things had changed since McGee was last reelected. He knew because Goodman's pollsters told him about the changes in attitudes among Wyoming voters. The Wallop Senate Drive planned from the beginning to attack McGee's support of government regulation, the federal budget deficit, the 1975 congressional pay raise, and his support of unions, especially the Postal Workers Union. Goodman's pollsters advised the challenger's campaign that voters were no longer impressed by an incumbent's seniority.[18]

McGee chose to use neither pollsters nor professional consultants. His campaign bus was without headlights as it hurtled down an unmapped dark highway in the wrong lane.

When constituents asked him to do what he could to eliminate the Environmental Protection Agency (EPA) and the Occupational Safety and Health Administration (OSHA), McGee exhibited little sympathy for their arguments. He defended the government, writing lengthy responses designed to educate the constituent on the purpose of each agency and why it needed to continue functioning. "While I have no particular love for the EPA," McGee wrote, "I do believe this nation's effort to clean up its air and water is among the most important and praiseworthy accomplishments of the last 20 years."[19] Likewise he defended the even more disliked OSHA, reminding those who asked that it be eliminated that the agency was created with the support of President Nixon. McGee acknowledged isolated problems that he felt were being addressed and predicted the complaints would lessen if the "states took more initiative to protect workers."[20]

Still his mailbox filled to overflowing with letters seeking the demise of both federal agencies. Some complained about the EPA's efforts to remove lead from gasoline. Others expressed a general sense that they should not be "pushed around" by federal agencies. Jason Long of Casper told McGee the EPA was "one more nail in the coffin of our freedom."[21]

McGee's chairmanship of the Senate Post Office and Civil Services Committee made him an easy target. Stories reporting the problems of the Postal Service were a mainstay of most Wyoming newspapers throughout the 1976 election cycle. When news stories reported slow or lost mail or whenever the price of a postage stamp increased, his adversaries blamed him. A year ahead of the 1976 campaign, McGee's committee was accused of "tacking an amendment on another amendment in a secret session of the obscure Post Office and Civil Service Committee." The amendment provided a cost-of-living increase in the salaries of members of Congress and other high-ranking government officials.[22] In September 1975, a columnist for the *Washington Star* wrote a story about the day the new law passed under the headline "A Day You'll Live to Regret." Letters to the editors of Wyoming newspapers began flowing profusely, expressing constituent unhappiness with the pay raise.

To make matters worse for McGee, President Ford rejected a proposal for an 8.6 percent raise, recommending a 5 percent increase instead. That forced a widely publicized showdown in the Senate. McGee defended the higher number, which was rejected by a 53–39 Senate vote. The *Casper Star Tribune* said, "The political corpse was laid at the feet of Senator Gale McGee." They accurately foretold that the issue would haunt the senator in his reelection effort.[23]

His opponent's campaign knew how deep voter resentments ran about their government. People told Wallop pollsters that they saw government as too big and intrusive. They felt overwhelmed by what they believed to be a relentless onslaught of government regulation. They didn't believe Washington cared about or understood their lives and how or whether they made a living. Wallop's pollsters told him about those sentiments just as Jimmy Carter's pollsters had told him. Thus Wallop's campaign theme was not much different from the theme of the Democratic Party's 1976 presidential candidate. In his speech accepting the nomination, Carter said, "It is time for the people to run the government, and not the other way around."[24] Wallop's message sounded much the same. "If the choice comes down to myself and Sen. McGee," Wallop told one newspaper, "it will be a question of less or more control."[25] He told another, "The federal government has taken on an insensitivity, a monumental inefficiency, and a sense of remoteness."[26] McGee defended the federal government when Wallop said the nation needed smaller government and less regulation.

If McGee could feel the shifting tides, he chose not to shift with them. The three-term senator never lost his inclination to teach as he endeavored to instill a broader view of current events in the minds of his constituents. "There is a sense of despair at the uncertainty we find in the hearts of the American people," he admitted. But he asked listeners to consider whether Americans had become too focused "on taking things apart, in finding something wrong" instead of doing the hard work of "putting things back together again."[27]

The Republican strategists carefully cast their candidate as "local." Wallop's campaign made perfectly clear who the antithesis to 'local' was—it was the political establishment that didn't understand Wyoming. Wallop sought to make sure the voters had reason to fear such people. He raised gun control as an example, suggesting the government could come to take away their guns. "If the government is the holder of our guns, who is the master and who is the slave?" he asked.[28]

In response, McGee urged voters to ask what he said was a simple question. "With a Democratic Congress, do you protect Wyoming best with two Republican senators?"[29] The Democrat's campaign relied on his conviction that voters would return to a long-standing view that what mattered in Washington was power through seniority. McGee boasted, "With my seniority and key committee assignments Wyoming doesn't have to take a backseat to anyone in the U.S. Senate."[30] He cited the override of Ford's veto of the bill increasing Wyoming's share of mineral royalties and the confirmation of Stan Hathaway as interior secretary as examples of his clout in the Congress.[31]

Wallop's strategy was to discount the significance of his opponent's committee assignments. He blamed McGee's membership on the Senate Appropriations Committee for OSHA, saying McGee and his committee colleagues had increased funding for OSHA by $4 million above the House recommendation.[32] Wallop called seniority "a poor excuse for an issue." He said, "Seniority doesn't represent an understanding of the needs and problems the state faces."[33] Wallop accused McGee of using his "clout" to push the unpopular congressional pay raise through Congress in five days. But, he charged, McGee had proved unsuccessful otherwise. "How powerful is a man who can only manage to get 22 of his 487 legislative proposals enacted into law between 1971 and 1975?" He said McGee was paid $44,000 a year, made another $20,000 "moonlighting," and was "absent from work 22 percent of the time."[34]

Nonetheless, McGee continued his message. "The only way Wyoming can be protected is if we maintain our clout."[35] But Wallop remained on message, and Robert Goodman's TV campaign was the talk of the state, creating laughs of the kind the one being targeted doesn't want to hear. Goodman's most effective television production conjured up the resentments of Wyoming ranchers about OSHA regulations imposing health standards for their sheepherders. One regulation required ranchers to provide portable toilets at intervals throughout the pasture. Liza Nicholas's book described the Goodman ad. "A cowboy buckles his chaps and saddles his horse. 'Everywhere you look these days,' the narrator says, 'the federal government is telling you what to think, telling you how you ought to do things, setting up rules you can't follow.' The cowboy straps a portable toilet on his horse and rides off with the words, 'I think the federal government has gone too far.'"[36]

On the first Saturday in October, the Wyoming Cowboys football team defeated nationally ranked Arizona State University, 13–10. It was an "upset omen" just as UW's 1958 victory over powerhouse Oregon State had been. In September reporters covering the national campaign downgraded McGee's chances for reelection from "a sure thing" to "favored but not entirely secure."[37] By early October, the pundits who long thought McGee's reelection was probable began to take a second look. Many were no longer so sure McGee would prevail. "In Wyoming, Sen. Gale McGee is facing stiffer than expected competition from Republican state senator Malcolm Wallop."[38] The darkening clouds must have brought memories of his 1958 campaign against incumbent senator Frank Barrett, when McGee ran as the youthful, aggressive candidate against an opponent many felt had grown out of touch.

As the last days of the campaign came and went, newspaper headlines variously called the race tough, bruising, and vicious. McGee started telling supporters that his chances of reelection were "iffy."[39] Candidates and their campaigns made charges and countercharges. Partisans from both sides wrote dozens of letters to the editor, many containing undisciplined and even false claims. There was now "blood in the water." Outsiders rushed in. During the final week of the campaign, a group calling itself the Ad-Hoc Committee to REJECT McGee suddenly appeared, claiming members from all parts of the state. Their large newspaper ads said McGee was not a native of Wyoming and had once been a Republican. It said McGee was a member of the Council on Foreign Relations, an organization they claimed had been lobbying for "One World Government." The ads accused McGee of supporting legislation aiding the enemy during the Vietnam War.

McGee, they said, could not be trusted on gun control and had supported Communists.[40]

This committee ran ads paid for by unidentified "citizens from all around the country." The ad blamed McGee for "wild" government spending and called him "one of the worst friends taxpayers have in Washington." The group acknowledged, "We don't know anything about McGee's opponent. But he could hardly be worse than McGee."[41]

Wyoming Republicans circled the wagons around the Wallop Senate Drive. Forgotten was the bitterness over Wallop's reluctance to endorse Dick Jones, the GOP 1974 gubernatorial nominee. Jones appeared on behalf of the Republican Senate candidate in mid-October. Forgotten were McGee's yeoman efforts to make sure Stan Hathaway was confirmed a year earlier. "Too many politicians let their office become more important than the people they represent," Hathaway said as he endorsed Wallop in the days before the election.[42]

Perhaps most hurtful was how easily Wyoming conservationists forgot McGee's stout environmental record. *High Country News*, an environmentalist newspaper, said, "Wallop, a state senator, had a strong environmental voting record in Wyoming, and ran an unsuccessful bid for governor two years ago on an environmental quality platform."[43] A *New York Times* editorial said Wallop was "an environmentalist who rightly worries that his state may be strip-mined and polluted in the rush for energy." The editor added a cautionary note ignored by Wyoming environmentalists. "But after a losing campaign for governor two years ago, he has tried to move closer to the severe conservatism of most Wyoming Republicans, an ideological shift of gears that is always hard to bring off successfully."[44]

The *Times* concluded, "Mr. McGee deserves reelection." Many Wyoming environmentalists didn't agree. Some remained unhappy with the senator over his support of Governor Hathaway's Interior Department appointment. But there were deeper causes. Though their views of Wallop as a conservationist would change once he went to the Senate, most of the conservation community came from historically Republican families with decidedly conservative opinions on most other matters. An opportunity to elect a Republican to the Senate was no small thing. McGee's work to stop clearcutting and the Wagon Wheel Project as well as his courage in confronting the powerful ranchers who had shot eagles from helicopters meant little now. Wallop was "the conservationists' choice" in 1976.[45]

Also forgotten was the fact that Gale McGee brought more federal dollars into his state than any member of Congress in history. Those millions upon millions funded public works, post offices and other federal buildings, health and educational programs, water projects, roads and bridges, recreation areas, and much more.[46] His influence resulted directly in the employment of thousands of Wyoming people.

McGee proudly pointed to projects funded in all of the state's twenty-three counties through his eighteen years on the Senate Appropriations Committee. His staff created a multipage document detailing the funding and other benefits that flowed into every corner of Wyoming directly from the Senator's growing seniority. Stories were told of how McGee was able to use his "clout" to keep federal offices open in small communities when federal bureaucrats decided they weren't necessary.

Nearly every school district in the state had received significant funding. There was not a community college in Wyoming that hadn't been given large grants through McGee's influence. A water treatment plant in Sweetwater County received a nearly $500,000 check, a senior citizen housing project in Wheatland was funded, money was obtained to remodel the Soldiers and Sailors Home in Buffalo, millions went to the University of Wyoming for buildings and research, and federal money obtained by the incumbent funded modern water service to forty-six families in the small town of Worland. The McGee campaign told the story of how much it had meant to Wyoming to have one of its senators with his hands on the levers of the power that moved federal money.

But Wallop's pollsters knew that argument, which had proved so successful in previous campaigns, had lost its "clout." Wyoming people were now more fearful of big government than they were grateful. Most claimed they were ready to sacrifice the flow of federal appropriations for a conservative candidate who promised to reduce the size of the government and slash its budget. When McGee touted the amount of federal dollars he procured for Wyoming, Wallop's campaign charged that McGee was bribing the voters with federal funds.[47]

It was the night before voters went to the polls when one of the most fascinating exchanges of the campaign occurred between McGee and a reporter. It was Democratic Party tradition to hold a campaign's final rally at Hudson, a small town midway between Lander and Riverton in Fremont County. Six hundred Democrats and Independents and a few Republicans packed the gymnasium of the Hudson school that November evening. McGee was exhausted as he neared the end of the long trial. He was speaking softly, hoarsely, and candidly to Bill Sniffin of the *Wyoming State Journal.* Following the election, Sniffin wrote about the conversation. "'We were wrong about Vietnam,' Gale McGee told me in the last days of this year's campaign. 'I was one of the biggest backers of our involvement there and, in hindsight, it wasn't wise that we were there."[48]

The senator had confidentially expressed similar doubts to his wife and daughters over the years but had never been so candid with a reporter. Perhaps they were nothing more than the less-than-thought-out words of a fatigued candidate nearing the end of an exhausting campaign. Maybe they were words of regret, a reflection McGee needed to get off his chest. Following the Hudson rally, Gale and Loraine drove across the state on the same road they had so often taken together in the last eighteen years. They headed home to Laramie to await the voters' verdict.

Former Wyoming congressman William Henry Harrison once cagily observed, "If one remains in public office long enough, eventually he or she will be defeated."[49] And so it was. After three terms, eighteen years, Gale McGee lost. On November 2 he received 70,558 votes, whereas Malcolm Wallop received 84,810. Most painful next to the defeat itself was that McGee lost in Albany County, his home and a liberal university community where there may well have been some lingering resentment about McGee's role during Vietnam.

The first person to telephone McGee to express his dismay at the results was Richard Nixon. The former president somehow tracked McGee to the Laramie motel in which he spent the night. Nixon wanted to let the fallen senator know how much he had appreciated their friendship and McGee's counsel.[50] A few days later, McGee received a note from Wallop: "I have been meaning to write to you to express my respect and admiration for you and Loraine. Your words on Tuesday night were so admirably generous and courteous that all Wyoming stood a little taller. May your path, wherever it leads, be as satisfying and as rewarding as the road you just turned off. It was well traveled."[51]

Malcolm Wallop likened his win to "Alice in Wonderland."[52] Others didn't see it as much of a surprise. For the next few weeks, the hottest ticket in town was shared among those who wanted to dissect McGee's loss. The *Rocky Mountain News* offered a poignant one-line analysis based on Goodman's effective anti-OSHA TV ad. "The Wyoming cowboy's inalienable right to relieve himself behind a bush is safe for another six years."[53]

"The message in McGee's defeat?" asked the editor of the *Riverton Ranger,* who then answered his own question. "Less federal regulation and smaller government."[54] A week later, the same editor expounded on his previous answer. "The many trickles of discontent—the Postal Service, OSHA, taxes, inflation, federal pay raise, government interference in private lives—came together in a river of dissatisfaction beyond McGee's power to turn it aside."[55]

James Flinchum of the *Wyoming State Tribune,* one of Senator McGee's longtime detractors, wrote, "Malcolm Wallop effectively employed the issue of big government." Flinchum reacted to McGee's campaign. "We believe the public is beginning to understand that the more boodle a congressman or senator brings back to his state or district from Washington in the long run means just more government spending out of his constituents' own pocketbooks."[56]

The *Casper Star-Tribune* appeared to have taken a "man-on-the street" poll.

As for the Democratic Senator's loss to Republican Malcolm Wallop, recriminations, soul searching, speculation, and sad but not surprising personal charges can be heard daily. They range from incumbency: too long on the job, a poorly organized and executed campaign, the Postal System, pay raises, failure of county organizations to get to work for McGee because they believed his competition was a pushover, lethargy on the part of Democrats attributed to a full lunch bucket, backlash from Watergate, a distrust of all long-term Washington figures.

Add to this claims that McGee ran an imperious, almost arrogant campaign, as did his aides, that he didn't even believe it necessary to conduct a poll to determine his strengths and weaknesses, his age, Wallop was simply the better man, the attacks from the ultra-right, and that McGee was too pro-labor or not pro-labor enough."[57]

Another pundit simply said, "The voters were unimpressed by a campaign that implied that 'being there' was the greatest accomplishment of an 18-year career."[58]

Writer Liza Nicholas echoed some of historian James Piereson's views about the enormity of the change in America's political culture since Gale McGee was first elected in 1958. Back then, Piereson wrote, "Liberalism was without doubt the single most creative and vital force in American politics."[59] Piereson said of those days when Gale McGee began his Senate career, "Liberalism owned the future." Like Kissinger, Piereson feels the JFK assassination spelled the beginning of the end for the nation's liberal consensus. By 1976, it no longer held power. Nicholas noted the rising distrust of government. "Wallop's campaign also reflected the national rise of conservative populism, which began in the 1960s with the New Right's response to public impatience with the antiwar movement and governmental solutions to social problems."[60]

The commentator Gale McGee most valued was his wife. Loraine was asked in 1979 whether she had been devastated. She replied, "Not devastated. I guess because when you get into this, you know that someday the ball is apt to bounce the other way. But as with anything, you learn that life goes on and there is a life after the Senate."[61]

The senator called it "a considerable shock." McGee admitted he had not seen it coming and that he expected to win reelection right up to the moment when CBS anchor Walter Cronkite said he hadn't.[62] To his credit, McGee never exhibited a moment's bitterness. In a letter to a friend who asked why he thought he had lost, McGee said, "In 1976 there was one basic defeating mind-set. It was created by the Democratic presidential candidate, Jimmy Carter; namely, running against Washington. I was so strongly identified with Washington under both Republicans and Democrats that I made no bones in my campaign about defending the importance of a strong national government under the constitutional processes." He acknowledged that his position "obviously wasn't the majority view."[63]

"We had our differences," McGee said of Wallop, "but our exchanges, when we appeared together, were always low key and rational." He remembered the campaign as "a gentlemanly election. Much mutual respect type of election," he said, adding a final note. "It was just time for a change."[64]

16

A Third Career

It was March 17, 1977, Gale McGee's sixty-second birthday. It was also, of course, St. Patrick's Day. McGee celebrated with his colleagues in the Senate Foreign Relations Committee conference room. Alabama senator John Sparkman convened the hearing, held for the purpose of considering one of President Jimmy Carter's appointments. This morning McGee was seated where he had never before been seated, at the witness table, dressed in a celebratory green suit with matching tie.

McGee first met the new president when Carter was the governor of Georgia. Carter arranged to have the 1974 Organization of American States (OAS) General Assembly meet in Atlanta. The senator and Loraine flew to the conference with Henry Kissinger, who was to give the keynote address. The occasion was memorable. McGee upstaged Kissinger's speech when he suddenly collapsed and was rushed to a hospital by ambulance suffering from a diabetic episode.

In December 1976, outgoing CIA director George Bush personally recommended to Carter that McGee be appointed to succeed him at the CIA. Bush told McGee that it was "by far the most fascinating job in the government and something in which you might be interested."[1] McGee expressed an interest in one of Bush's old jobs, but not that one. McGee was more interested in taking the position once offered him by Lyndon Johnson, ambassador to the United Nations. In the end, Carter appointed Adm. Stansfield Turner to head the CIA and named his old Georgia friend Andrew Young ambassador to the UN. Gale McGee was named "Permanent Representative of the United States of America to the Organization of American States, with the rank of Ambassador."

Accordingly, Senator Sparkman gaveled the March 17 hearing to order to consider McGee's nomination. Glancing at McGee's green sport coat, he told his colleagues, "I want to say that today is St. Patrick's Day. I told Gale McGee I would have to get some greenery. He said I should not bother about it, that he would have plenty of it here, and he certainly does. But I didn't know he meant he was going to be wearing it."[2]

The chairman joked about the momentary absence of Republican members. "I would certainly like to have a full house when we go after Gale." The nominee was asked a few questions giving hint to the thorny issues that would occupy his time as OAS ambassador. Sparkman wanted to know about McGee's attitude about the Carter administration's push for human rights in Latin America and his position on normalizing relations with Cuba. He also warned that much of his mail was against the negotiations for a treaty ending U.S. sovereignty over the Panama Canal. Sparkman advised his old friend, "It is not going to be an easy matter when the time comes to consider that treaty."[3]

Sparkman told his committee that their former colleague "will go to that job as well prepared as any representative we have ever had in that place." Michigan Republican Robert Griffin said he had offered the new president "only one bit of advice. I said that you ought to find a good place to use Senator Gale McGee."[4] Dean Rusk told him, "You need Gale McGee."[5] Within a couple of weeks after the election, McGee received a phone call from the president-elect. Carter anticipated a bruising fight over the Panama Canal treaties and didn't want a career foreign services officer but rather a Senate insider. Having successful tenures as a university professor and a senator, McGee embarked on a third career.

The Organization of American States was created in 1948. Growing out of Cold War competition between the United States and the Soviet Union for the loyalty of Third World nations, the OAS was established with the goal of implementing provisions of the UN charter that envisioned "regional organizations should play a part in the peaceful settlement of disputes," a role subordinated to the UN's Security Council.[6]

It was hoped the OAS would bridge economic and political relationships between North, Central, and South America. It had not, however, fully succeeded in reducing the suspicions and resentments many of those nations harbored about the United States. As McGee told the Senate, "Our size has always been one of the problems, because our size is approximately equivalent to all of the rest of them population-wise, and Gross National Product-wise. That is the problem."[7] McGee recognized there had been a history of the United States taking other nations in the Americas for granted. He and Carter said they were committed to changing that.

As he prepared to begin his new job, McGee met with Frank Ortiz over lunch in the Senate Dining Room. Ortiz was an operative in Dr. Kissinger's office. He advised McGee to beware of the Argentinian OAS ambassador, Alejandro Orfila. "Never tell him anything in confidence that you don't want in the *New York Times*." The ambassador from Panama couldn't be trusted either, said Ortiz. "He is a schemer and a manipulator and just generally a bad, bad guy." The ambassador from Peru was "a troublemaker." Ortiz then asked if McGee would be offended if he told him something personal. Ortiz explained that his duties included keeping the ambassador safe, and he reminded McGee of the constant threat from Latin American guerrillas. Eyeing McGee's stylish sport coat, Ortiz said, "Don't you wear that outfit across the border!" He worried that McGee would become a target for the guerrillas. "You dress well and very colorfully. Continue to wear those up here because it will enliven the community, but don't wear them across any border."[8]

As soon as rumors spread that Gale McGee would be the new OAS ambassador, observers connected his appointment and Carter's intention of gaining approval of the Panama Canal treaties. The editor of the *Miami Herald* acknowledged that one reason McGee was an ex-senator was his support for the treaties. Nonetheless, it was widely recognized that McGee had been selected for his expertise on Latin America, an asset in the coming debate.

One of the most popular history books written on the building of the Panama Canal was historian David McCullough's *Path between the Seas.* McCullough's painstaking study of the project discloses the enormity of the U.S. commitment of money, manpower, and other resources to the project and the significant political challenges that had to be overcome to make a success of the path between the Atlantic and Pacific Oceans. McCullough called it "the largest, most costly single effort ever before mounted anywhere on earth."[9] His book leaves readers with a sense of the ownership many Americans harbored when it was proposed that the United States should set aside its claims in favor of Panamanian nationalism.

In his presidential memoir, Jimmy Carter candidly discussed the difficulty in arriving at his decision to push for a treaty "phasing out our absolute control of the Canal, as well as the acknowledgment of Panamanian sovereignty." Once Carter made the decision to proceed, his administration proposed two treaties. One provided the mechanism for managing the Canal through the end of the century, after which Panama would be given complete control. The second gave the United States the right to defend the Canal Zone from external threats. As the Panama Canal treaties were submitted to the Senate for ratification, a poll showed that "78 percent of the American people did not want to 'give up' the Canal, and only 8 percent found the idea acceptable."[10]

Gale McGee may have been new to the OAS, but not to the growing debate over the future of the Panama Canal. During the Nixon administration he had accompanied Secretary of State Henry Kissinger to the Canal Zone to sign the accord under which the two nations agreed to negotiate a new treaty. As Americans were just beginning to pay attention to the issue, Senators McGee and Harry F. Byrd of Virginia squared off in a *U.S. News and World Report* debate in 1975.[11]

Byrd argued that the Canal was too economically, politically, and militarily important to the United States for us to relinquish control to the unpredictable Panamanians. Unlike Byrd, McGee voiced concern that the United States could not defend its position in the Canal without an agreement. He believed that under the protection of a modern Navy, the Canal's importance for national defense had been significantly reduced. McGee called the Canal "out-of-date," arguing that there was a need to build a new water route between the Pacific and Atlantic Oceans. In April 1976, as he was opening his campaign for a fourth Senate term, the issue first arose in Wyoming. McGee was combative. "Some candidates insist on perpetrating myths of the past and distortions of what our true interests might be in the Canal today and how those interests might be protected."[12]

Carter trusted McGee was well prepared to enter the debate. As the administration assembled a strategy aimed at ratification of the treaties, it pulled together what the *Washington Post* identified as a "stable of speakers." Their report said, "One of the thoroughbreds in that stable . . . is Ambassador Gale McGee."[13] During an April 1977 White House strategy session led by Carter's chief of staff, Hamilton Jordan, Secretary of State Cyrus Vance suggested McGee be given the assignment to tour the country debating the treaty question with "all comers."[14]

McGee's first major Canal-related debate took place on November 29, 1977, at the Mayflower Hotel in Washington. McGee debated Kansas senator Robert Dole, who introduced McGee to his wife, Elizabeth, who said, "Just tell Senator McGee what I just told you." Dole acquiesced. "She just told me, 'Robert dear, when are you going to wake up? You follow Gale McGee and you'll stay out of trouble."[15] McGee also debated Senator Strom Thurmond (R-SC) in Columbia, South Carolina, and retired Rear Adm. William C. Mott in Little Rock.

In the course of his work promoting the treaties, McGee made more than 150 speeches in twenty-two states "from the Deep South to the Far West." In a speech to the Denver Bar Association, McGee targeted the "truth squad" created by California governor Ronald Reagan to counter speeches like the ones the ambassador gave. McGee accused Reagan of providing "misinformation" and said it was obvious the truth squad had not "read a history book for 100 years."[16]

Speaking in Omaha, McGee cautioned that failure to ratify the treaties would trigger unrest. He said the United States should be prepared to dispatch at least 100,000 troops to quell the riotous response to defeating the treaties. "It would be a serious mistake if we permitted Panama to become a trouble spot and if we got bogged down in another jungle," a reference to the American experience in Southeast Asia.[17] McGee told a Moline, Illinois, audience that if the Canal treaties are not ratified, "our problems in the hemisphere will be magnified." He said that substance, not public opinion alone, should decide the issue. "Opinion should be based on substance, not fancy. Ignorant public opinion is fraught with the most danger of all."[18] In Provo McGee said the treaties "will keep the Canal open, lessen the chance of a military takeover, emphasize neutrality, and contribute to the advancement of commerce."[19]

Evident in McGee's arguments for the treaties was his goal to improve the image of the United States as a dependable, honest partner in the Americas. At Colorado State University, McGee said the Canal was no longer a strategic priority. He said the opposition was generated by a nostalgic feeling of a "proud past."[20] That proud past included the United States bullying its neighbors, a posture McGee said we should have outgrown. "The United States is big enough and strong enough to deal in a fair manner with Panama."[21] In Laramie, the ambassador was even more direct. "We have a collection of neighbors who are very nervous about our presence. They remember the Marines and the gunboats off their shores and the 'banana republics.' It is very important that we understand the background of their reflexes."[22]

As McGee and others toiled in the vineyard, an April 15, 1978, public opinion poll showed the fruits of their endeavors. The treaties had reached a 50 percent approval rating among American voters. McGee also learned he had been correct in worrying that failure to approve the treaties would result in a military confrontation. In Panama, Gen. Omar Torrijos issued orders to his National Guard to "blow up the Canal" if the treaties were rejected by the U.S. Senate.[23] On April 18, the Senate ratified the treaties with only one vote more than the two-thirds that the Constitution requires, 68–32.

The president took a few minutes to write a personal note to his OAS ambassador. "I want to express my deep appreciation for your successful efforts in supporting the Panama Canal treaties. Without your personal help, approval of the treaties would not have been possible."[24]

Gathering votes for Jimmy Carter's signature achievement had not greatly stressed the ambassador. He rather enjoyed his new job and his post-Senate life. A month before the final Senate vote, McGee spoke to a senior reporter for the *Salt Lake Tribune*, who observed, "Gale McGee is the picture of the proverbial man who's 'happy in his work.'"

As an ambassador, McGee staunchly defended the United Nations. The anti-UN sentiment was never far from the surface. As a senator, he fought an "oftentimes uphill and lonely battle to maintain our participation in the United Nations."[25] McGee said the accomplishments of the international body extended beyond peacekeeping to halting the spread of diseases like smallpox and malaria, increasing literacy, helping colonial nations transition to independence, curbing the arms race, enhancing food supplies, and addressing nutritional needs among hungry populations. Most important politically, he thought, was the manner in which the UN provided smaller nations with a venue for airing their grievances against larger powers. It was this platform which gave some countries an opportunity to criticize the United States, often leading some Americans to question the value of the UN. McGee urged Americans to recognize that the UN was "more relevant to our needs today than it has ever been in the past."

The president and his inner circle were an occasional source of frustration. McGee told a Worcester, Massachusetts, audience at Assumption College that the Carter administration had "arrived in Washington under the conviction that the world started to turn the day they arrived."[26] He found his new job "a little disconcerting at first in getting used to it, in the sense that I was directly on the firing line rather than pontificating as a senator."[27] Occasional annoyances aside, McGee derived a great deal of fulfillment from his duties. As he told the *Salt Lake Tribune*, this was his "bag."

He led U.S. delegations to a series of OAS General Assemblies, the first of which was held in Grenada and featured a spirited debate over a resolution approving of President Carter's emphasis on improving human rights. Latin American nations were passionately divided over the issue. Some, like Chile, argued that Carter's human rights initiative interfered with their need to fight terrorism. "Terrorism and human rights are intimately related," said Chilean ambassador Sergio Diez. "This is not a child's game." McGee retorted, "Terrorism is indeed the scourge of our age, but we also know that human rights suffer when a state under attack lashes out blindly, injuring the innocent and guilty alike." McGee called terrorism "a crime against the state" and said that human rights violations were crimes "committed by the state against the individual."[28] The General Assembly passed the U.S. resolution after an acrimonious debate.

McGee played a leading role in guiding U.S. policy through the last years of Anastasio Somoza's dictatorship in Nicaragua. McGee blamed most Central American problems on the Nicaraguan dictator, including "the guerillas, casualties, human suffering, and breakdown of governments."[29] He encouraged the administration to back off its support of Somoza, who was eventually sent into exile to Paraguay where he was assassinated in 1980.

Latin American guerrillas never took a shot at the flashily dressed McGee as Frank Ortiz worried they might. However, his OAS responsibilities took him into the path of danger. It was a trip to La Paz, Bolivia, on October 20, 1979. Loraine and several OAS staff members accompanied the ambassador to attend the General Assembly. Two were former members of his Senate staff, Liz Strannigan and Betty Cooper. They flew together with Secretary of State Cyrus Vance on the luxurious aircraft known as *Air Force One* when the president is aboard. Upon arrival, they noticed a contingent of U.S. Marines stationed around the plane, all standing "at-ease," rifles resting at their sides.

The first few days were filled with sightseeing and important meetings with Latin American heads of state and others. The McGees awakened early one morning to find tanks and troops on the streets nine floors below the room in which they were staying in the La Paz Sheraton. It was the opening salvo of what came to be called "the cocaine coup" because it had been financed by the drug cartel out of its unhappiness with the current government's enforcement of drug laws.

With Marines posted at each end of his hallway to prevent secret documents from being captured, the ambassador attempted to call Washington, but the phones were down. Alejandro Orfila, who now served as secretary general to OAS, told McGee he could arrange for him and his wife to leave Bolivia immediately aboard Orfila's personal plane. But there was not enough room on the plane for his staffers. While other ambassadors jumped at the chance to leave, McGee refused the offer, advising Orfila, "We came together. We will leave together."

Alexander Watson, the deputy chief of the La Paz mission, recalled the tense situation they faced. On the streets were tanks and soldiers.

Checkpoints were "manned by illiterate 16, 17, 18-year-old soldiers from the countryside who were scared to death and whose AK-47s trembled in their hands as they put their guns up to our ears."[30]

As Liz Strannigan worked to arrange passport clearance to leave the country, there was gunfire in the downtown area not far from the hotel. "Bolivian troops opened fire on protesting crowds in the streets of La Paz."[31] Late that afternoon Strannigan was able to make arrangements for the McGees as well as staff members to fly out of the country on a plane that would have been formally designated Air Force Two had the vice president been aboard.

They made their way slowly up the steep road to the airport aptly named El Alto, which sits atop a mountain 1,500 feet above La Paz. As when they landed a few days earlier, the Marine contingent surrounded the aircraft, not "at-ease" this time but with guns raised to an "at-ready" stance. Fully loaded, the plane started down the runway, necessarily one of the longest in the world to accommodate large airplanes trying to take off at the altitude. After rumbling down most of the runway's 13,000 feet, the plane finally lifted off. After a brief stop in Lima, Peru, the group left for Washington.

Near the end of his time as OAS ambassador McGee reflected on the changes he had witnessed in U.S.–Latin American relationships. He lauded President Carter for his attention to the Southern Hemisphere. "This new emphasis of concern has begun to take off the sharp edges of our relations with our neighbors to the South."[32]

Likewise, President Carter learned to respect McGee greatly. After leaving the White House, Carter gave a speech on Middle East affairs at the International Club in Washington. Upon finishing, he saw McGee in the audience. "He came toward me with a broad smile," McGee recalled. "Gale McGee, how great to see you," said the former president. "You were one of the strongest strings in my bow. If only I could have had a couple more like you, things might have turned out differently."[33]

Ronald Reagan defeated Jimmy Carter in November 1980. On May 27, 1981, McGee received a letter from the new president accepting the ambassador's resignation. Reagan said McGee had "represented the interests of the United States with dedication and skill, adding even further distinction to your outstanding career."[34]

After his ambassadorship, McGee joined an international public relations firm. Hill and Knowlton boasted members over the years to have included Douglas MacArthur and a onetime chairman of the Joint Chiefs of Staff, Adm. Thomas Moorer.[35] McGee was named to the firm's international advisory board. That same month, McGee and his former Senate colleague from Utah opened a firm called Moss McGee Associates, specializing in developing business contacts in Latin America.[36] But Gale McGee's career as a public servant was not over.

After the fall of Saigon in April 1975, the Communists rounded up those believed to have collaborated with the United States during the war. More than a million were sent to "reeducation" camps. To avoid their fate, thousands of refugees boarded "decrepit, leaky, overcrowded" boats to make their way to the shores of other nations.[37] As the tide of refugees willing to risk their lives on the open seas to escape Vietnam increased, American public opinion clamored for the U.S. government to find a solution.

In September 1985, Reagan's secretary of state, George P. Schultz, pressed Gale McGee back into public service as a member of the Indochina Refugee Panel. The panel was tasked with reviewing U.S policy toward Indochinese refugees.[38] In the wake of the 1975 collapse of the South Vietnamese government, more than 1.6 million Indochinese people had fled their homes, creating a massive refugee crisis.[39] "Between 1970 and 1980, a decade in which the total U.S. population increased by only 11 percent, the Asian American population soared by 141 percent." President Reagan was intent on finding solutions and asked the panel to make recommendations.

In November 1985, the panel spent two weeks investigating the problem in Hong Kong, Malaysia, Indonesia, Singapore, Vietnam, and Thailand. The trip concluded with a meeting in Geneva, Switzerland, with the deputy UN high commissioner for refugees. They learned that in addition to those 1.6 million refugees already settled in the United States, another 180,000 remained unsettled, living in refugee camps.[40] They found that the "primary cause of the refugee flows" were the oppressive political and economic policies of the Socialist Republic of Vietnam, which included not only the denial of basic human rights to its own citizens but also military actions threatening Cambodia and Laos.[41]

McGee and the others concluded that the "great majority of the Southeast Asians admitted as refugees since South Vietnam fell in 1975 now have been in the United States for more than five years, the minimum residence requirement for citizenship applicants." They urged that steps be taken to encourage these residents to seek citizenship.[42] Their report was issued in April 1986. It recommended the creation of a pathway to citizenship for those already in the United States. The report acknowledged there were as many as 15,000 "Amerasians," children fathered by U.S. servicemen during the war, who were seeking admission. Approximately 3,500 had already arrived, and McGee's panel sought the expedited admission of the others. During this trip, they learned about the plight of Amerasian children. Loraine commented on how much one of the children resembled her grandson Kirk. Vietnam's foreign minister, Hoang Bich Son, told the panel his nation wanted these children removed from his nation "as soon as possible." He said they should not be considered refugees since "they were in part a U.S. responsibility."[43]

At the time McGee and the other panel members visited Vietnam, there were an estimated 7,000 former South Vietnamese military and civilian officials imprisoned in the reeducation camps as a result of their "close association with U.S. policies and programs." South Vietnam's government was willing to let them depart for the United States so long as it received assurances these expatriates would not foment revolution against their former country. The Indochinese Refugee Panel recommended that the United States take action to secure their release as soon as possible, including reexamination of laws that might "restrict activity to overthrow a foreign government."[44]

McGee had a friend well connected to the Senate's debate on immigration. Wyoming's senator Alan K. Simpson was the chairman of the Judiciary Committee's Immigration Subcommittee. Simpson and Romano Mazzoli, a House Democrat from Kentucky, were in the early stages of developing a major immigration reform bill. McGee worked with Simpson to include some of the panel's key recommendations.

Although Gale McGee continued to be a sought-after speaker, that was the finale for his lifetime of public service. He and Loraine spent more and more time at their beloved Lazy G ranch in the Dunoir near Dubois. It had long been a haven for the two of them and was even more so in these years. Each fall, as they shut down for the long, cold Wyoming winter, Gale had a routine. He busily nailed protective boards over the windows, drained the water pipes, and exterminated any remaining insects in the attic. As he ignited the "bug bomb" that September morning in 1991, the can exploded near his face. The rush of insecticide triggered a violent coughing fit. Frightened by its intensity, Loraine quickly called the Poison Control Center. She followed their directions, but the coughing didn't subside. Loraine quickly completed shutting up the house, and they drove to the Jackson Airport to catch a plane for home in Maryland.

By the time they reached their home, the coughing had lessened, but now Gale seemed disoriented. She drove him to nearby Sibley Hospital where he was diagnosed with an aneurism in the brain stem. The doctor believed the problem had been lurking for some time but was ignited by the severity of Gale's coughing. He was transferred to George Washington University Hospital, which was better equipped to treat brain trauma. Nonetheless, his cognitive abilities quickly began to decline, complicated by the challenges of his diabetes.

McGee remained at George Washington Hospital for the next three months. When the doctors determined they could do nothing more to improve his condition, he was moved to the Carriage Hill nursing home in Bethesda, Maryland. His appearance was normal, but he was clearly unable to track a conversation or to communicate much at all. Loraine hung photographs of family and friends, hoping to trigger memories, but he continued to decline. Family members visited often. Alan Simpson, someone who had been a great adversary but greater friend, also came by occasionally. The two former senators who had served a collective thirty-six years sat quietly. Alan reminisced about those years while Gale appeared to listen intently. The two had known one another since Simpson was a high school student in Cody and the McGees came to his home to visit Simpson's parents. Alan had been one of the many students competing to get a slot in Dr. McGee's history classes because, Simpson later said, "We were all inspired by this man."

Gone were the "bright twinkling eyes and that toss of his head, the big grin, the tilt of the mouth, and the sound of his laughter." Now unable to speak but with an occasional weak utterance, the voice Simpson described as "marvelous and mellifluous" had been taken. But Simpson sat with Gale for a long time, holding his hand and doing most of the talking, reminiscing about shared friendships, lives, and experiences. "I'm glad I did that," said Simpson. "I did it for myself."[45]

Liz Strannigan and Jim Burridge stopped by often, as did other one-time Senate staff members. At times he seemed to recognize them. At other times he did not. One afternoon during Gale's last spring, his son Robert visited. He thought his father seemed unusually alert, and so he began telling him about the ongoing 1992 presidential primary battles. "I told him about Bush and Buchanan, and then about Clinton, Harkin, Kerry, and Tsongas, and all the rough things they were saying about each other." Robert then said, "Dad, the Democrats are in real disarray." Suddenly his father's eyes looked very much engaged in the conversation. "He began to speak, and with a look on his face that showed something between a twinkle in his eye and perhaps a final attempt to convey some wisdom to me, he said haltingly, 'The . . . word . . . disarray was invented . . . for the . . . the Democrats.'"[46]

Gale William McGee died on April 9, 1992.

Loraine chose not to have a large funeral service but invited close friends to a memorial. Lady Bird Johnson came to pay her respects, and the following day Gale's immediate family including brothers Max and Dean gathered at Gawler's Funeral Chapel. Alan Simpson came, as did former Senate colleagues Ted Moss and Mike Mansfield. Secretary of Defense Dick Cheney was there to pay his respects. Senate chaplain Richard Halverson officiated.

During the memorial service, Simpson concluded his dramatic eulogy by saying,

And now he has gone from us. We have all loosed our grip upon him, but will retain his memory in our hearts. God has come now to take him back. We all knew on one unknown day that final event would take place. Now we give him up to you. We commend him to your loving hands. Thank you for him. May God rest his soul.

Loraine passed away on March 21, 2006, and was laid to rest next to her husband at the historic Oak Hills Cemetery near Rock Creek in Georgetown. Gale McGee's tombstone reads simply, "Professor, U.S. Senator, Ambassador."

Epilogue

This book's title, "The Man in the Arena," is intended to convey something central to Gale McGee's legacy. To be in the arena, as Theodore Roosevelt wrote in his 1910 "Citizenship in a Republic" speech, is to be one of those "whose face is marred by dust and sweat and blood, who strives valiantly." To be a man in the arena is to be at the center of controversy. As a professor, a U.S. senator, and an ambassador, McGee didn't just stumble into that arena. He sought it out.

How are we to gauge his legacy? One way is to imagine what McGee might think about his beloved Senate if he had the opportunity to visit today, more than four decades after he left it. In 1903 Senator Henry Cabot Lodge said, "Administrations come and go, Houses assemble and disperse, Senators change, but the Senate is always there in the Capitol, and always organized, with an existence unbroken since 1789."[1] True, but McGee might be understandably confused by some of the changes and appalled by others.

The technology alone would baffle him. His correspondence files are filled with onion-skin carbon copies of letters. Constituents often sent the senator an original of a document with a request that he return it to them because it was their only copy. If the senator or a constituent thought the matter was urgent, the message was conveyed by telegram. Not a lot had changed since Samuel Morse successfully tested his telegraph machine before skeptical members of Congress in 1844. "This wonderful contrivance has annihilated both time and space," commented a reporter who witnessed the test.[2]

If Gale walked into his old Senate office today, he would see fewer books lining the walls and personal computers atop every desk, each employing more calculative power than the computers used to put a man on the moon in 1969. The secretarial pool is gone, replaced by experts on social media. The use of the U.S. mail system to communicate has been all but replaced with the Internet, Facebook, Twitter, and other forms of virtual instant messaging. Each senator now has a home page on the World Wide Web, as does each Senate committee. The man with whom a president could communicate only by calling a bar in nearby Dubois to relay messages would have difficulty being available at all times to all people by cell phone. During McGee's tenure, trips home were limited. The press was more laid back, less intrusive. Certainly he might find the scrutiny under which senators now find themselves to be stifling.

More troubling than the severe technological changes would be the hyperpartisan approaches of the men and women who sit now where he once sat. Richard Nixon described McGee accurately when he wrote, "While we belonged to different parties, I treasured his friendship and his wise counsel and support on foreign policy. He was a courageous statesman who always put his country above partisan politics."[3]

As appalling as he might find the inability of the two parties to work together, he would also acknowledge that he saw it coming. Senator McGee had been one of the original warriors fighting the extremes of the early John Birch Society. He was relatively successful, but he could never have anticipated the day when extremists would have entire television networks at their command. If he came back for a visit, he would likely condemn both the left and the right for taking American politics to its current low level of discourse.

A senator with an exceptional ability to engage in serious debate, McGee would find it impossible to have a dialogue in the postfactual world in which we find ourselves today. Facts mattered as much or more than opinion when he and antiwar senators like George McGovern and Frank Church debated. They arrived at different opinions honestly. More significantly, at the end of a debate, they held one another in high esteem, respecting the right of the other to disagree.

Gale McGee would be saddened by the personal animosity that characterizes much of the conversation in today's public arena.

He would find most disconcerting the extent to which partisanship poisons debates over national security and foreign policy. It is unlikely that many in Wyoming had any idea of how intricately their U.S. senator was involved in these and most of the defining issues of the times. He intentionally played down his role because it generated criticism back home among those who claimed he gave too much attention to foreign affairs and not enough to state matters. Yet McGee remained in the arena for nearly every major foreign policy from the late 1950s through the mid-1970s. Presidents Kennedy, Johnson, and Nixon relied heavily on him for counsel and support. He was involved not only in Vietnam and Southeast Asia policy but also in U.S. initiatives in Africa and Latin America. He was at the center of the creation of the Peace Corps and the salvaging of America's foreign assistance programs such as USAID. McGee was one of the few helpful voices when major incidents like the North Korean capture of the USS *Pueblo* happened. His voice provided steady advice regardless of the president's political party.

In Gale McGee's time, politics stopped at the water's edge, meaning that U.S. foreign policy was too important to be tainted by partisanship. As controversial and divisive as was the Vietnam War, politicians generally adhered to the unwritten rules. Imagine McGee's reaction upon learning that nearly half of the Senate's members signed a letter to the head of an adversarial foreign power urging him not to negotiate a nuclear treaty with the sitting president.[4]

If McGee returned to the Senate for a glimpse, a major subject with the senators he met from the twenty-first century would be campaign funds. Former senator Tom Daschle estimated a senator must successfully solicit political contributions amounting to an average of $10,000 each and every day of their six-year term to be competitive.[5] McGee would have been required to solicit $13 each day of his last term to accumulate the $281,450 he raised in the 1976 campaign. In another era, he did his Senate job while raising sufficient campaign funding without there ever being even a hint of scandal in his personal or professional life.

As disconcerting as anything a visiting Gale McGee might find today is the sustained contempt for government. He was a public official who believed in the ability of the government to do good for its people. He saw it happen. Coming of age in the wake of the Depression, he saw the successes of the New Deal. As a liberal U.S. senator, he was a part of the golden age of legislative accomplishment. McGee and his colleagues were legislators in the best sense of the word. They crafted landmark bills like the Civil Rights Act of 1964 and the Voting Rights Act of 1965. They acted decisively to save the environment through measures like the Wilderness Act, the Clean Air and Water Acts, and the National Environmental Protection Act, while enacting Medicare and Medicaid.

He and his colleagues on both sides of the aisle believed the voters sent them to Washington to legislate. During the 86th Congress, McGee's first, senators introduced 4,149 bills and passed 1,680. During McGee's nine Congresses or three terms, the Senate averaged 4,233 bills introduced per congressional session. They passed nearly 1,400 of them per session. During McGee's final two years, the Senate passed 1,038 of the 4,115 bills that were introduced, or 25 percent. In the years since the members of the Class of 1958 departed, the Senate has never introduced the average number of bills of McGee's eighteen years in the Senate.[6] Truthfully, if Gale McGee were to return for a visit, he would encounter a sizeable number of senators who believe their job is not to legislate but to slow or stop the wheels of government from turning.

McGee and his colleagues did their jobs well, conducting the public's business during some of the most turbulent times in U.S. history. Today many Americans wish for a more civil dialogue in the public square. They long for respectful and honest debates over difficult issues. They say they are tired of negative campaigns and television and radio news shows where the hosts and guests talk past one another in echo chambers. Many have disdain for the corrupting influence money has on our system of governance. They have tired of the hyperpartisanship and gridlock, and they are worried about the growing intolerance of others. Most people would welcome an end to the extremism on both sides of the political gulf. We could learn a lot about how to realize those changes by looking at the life and times of Senator Gale McGee.

McGee was a college professor at Nebraska Wesleyan, where he taught tolerance for Japanese Americans during World War II, and at the University of Wyoming, where his history classes inspired thousands of young people. He was a U.S. senator who taught that the most divisive issues can be discussed honestly and with respect and an ambassador who believed America was strongest when it was serving the hopes of smaller, less advantaged nations.

Perhaps Gale McGee's greatest legacy is leaving us with an idea of what we once were, what politicians once were, and how to get there once again.

Notes

PROLOGUE

1. "JFK Tribute to Senator McGee," http://www.jfklibrary.org/Asset
-Viewer/Archives/JFKWHA-204–007.aspx, accessed March 6, 2015.
2. Handwritten letter from Richard Nixon to Loraine McGee, April 17,
1992, from the collection of Robert McGee.
3. Byrd, *Senate, 1789–1989: Addresses on the United States Senate*, ix.
4. Byrd, *Senate, 1789–1989*, 650.
5. White, *Citadel*, 82.
6. Sinclair, *Transformation of the Senate*, 34–35.
7. Byrd, *Senate, 1789–1989*, 654.
8. Douth, *Leaders in Profile: The United States Senate*, 423.
9. Theodore Roosevelt, "Man in the Arena," excerpt from the speech
"Citizenship in a Republic," delivered at the Sorbonne in Paris on
April 23, 1910, http://www.theodore-roosevelt.com/trsorbonnespeech
.html, accessed February 25, 2015.
10. Piereson, *Camelot and the Cultural Revolution*, 1.
11. Kissinger, *World Order*, 296.
12. Kissinger, *World Order*, 285.
13. Morgenthau to Acheson, March 30, 1963, box 2, "Acheson," Dr. Hans
Morgenthau Papers, Manuscript Division, Library of Congress.
14. *Congressional Record*, July 9, 1962, 12946.
15. Larson, *History of Wyoming*, 2nd ed., 573. O'Mahoney taught people to
pronounce his name with a rhyme: "You take the 'bahh' of the lamb,
the fruit of the bee, put them together, O'mahh'honey."

1. FROM THE "SONS OF THE MIST"

1. For more information on recorded weather, see http://www
.eyewitnesstohistory.com/charlesI.htm, accessed January 17, 2015.

2. Collard, "Oliver Cromwell and Charles I Execution Sites," http://www.traveldarkly.com/oliver-cromwell-charles-i-london-execution-sites/, accessed November 20, 2015.

3. Lysaght, *Irish Families, Their Names, Arms, and Origins*, 157.

4. McGee's great-grandfather and his son-in-law, Paul, and Paul's father also share his St. Patrick's Day birthday.

5. John F. Kennedy to Garton McGee, March 16, 1963, Personal Correspondence, box 955, Gale W. McGee Papers, AHC.

6. Sheldon Stern, recorded interview with McGee, November 16, 1982, 25, John F. Kennedy Library Oral History Program (hereafter cited as Stern interview), http://archive1.jfklibrary.org/JFKOH/McGee,%20Gale%20William/JFKOH-GWM-01/JFKOH-GWM-01-TR.pdf, accessed March 10, 2015.

7. Charles T. Morrissey interview with Gale W. McGee, "Modern Congress in American History," June 8 and 11 and September 17, 1979, Interviews: Oral History, box 958, McGee Papers (hereafter cited as Morrissey interview).

8. Kennedy, *Profiles in Courage*, 211.

9. Morrissey interview, 29.

10. McGee, "Script undertaken February 10, 1969: rewrite March 14, 1990," McGee Memoirs—UW or Wyoming, box 955, McGee Papers.

11. For more information on the impact of the Dust Bowl on Nebraska, see http://www.nebraskalegislature.gov/pdf/bluebook/44–45pdf, accessed March 16, 2015.

12. McGee script.

13. Teacher's contract dated September 16, 1936, "Teaching certificates, contracts 1936–7–8–9," box 943, McGee Papers.

14. "Members of Religious Sect Made to Kiss Flag in Wyoming," *Corpus Christi Times,* June 19, 1940, 1.

15. Okihiro, *Storied Lives,* 38–48.

16. "Nine New, One Returning Japanese Meet Requirements, Enter for Work Here, More Expected Soon," *Wesleyan,* February 5, 1943, 1.

17. "Nine New, One Returning Japanese Meet Requirement," 41.

18. For more information on the experiences of Japanese Americans at Nebraska Wesleyan, see www.livinghistoryfarm.org/farminginthe40s/movies/tada_life_14.html, accessed January 3, 2015.

19. Betty Cooper to Dr. William Moore, February 11, 1998, document provided to author by Ms. Cooper.

20. Morrissey interview, 31–32.

21. For more information on Charles Lindbergh, see http://www .charleslindbergh.com/americanfirst/speech3.asp, accessed on December 31, 2014.

22. Morrissey interview, 31.

23. McGee to Nebraska Selective Service Board, undated, "McGee Memoirs: UW or Wyoming," box 943, McGee Papers.

24. Maj. Dwight Williams to McGee, May 22, 1942, "McGee Memoirs: UW or Wyoming," box 943, McGee Papers.

25. Notes on conferences with H. V. Gaskill, January 17, 1944, "McGee Memoirs: UW or Wyoming," box 943, McGee Papers.

26. Letter to Lancaster Selective Service Board, "McGee Memoirs: UW or Wyoming," January 22, 1944, box 943, McGee Papers.

27. Morrissey interview, 32.

28. Rippy, *Bygones I Cannot Help Recalling*, 2, 76, 80, 114, 139, 167.

29. Scholarly writings of McGee, box 938, McGee Papers.

30. "A Survey of Foreign Efforts to Align with the United States, 1789–1919," box 938, McGee Papers, 58.

31. Rippy, *Bygones I Cannot Help Recalling*, 114.

32. "Founding Fathers and Entangling Alliances," final bound copy, box 939, McGee Papers, iii.

33. "Founding Fathers and Entangling Alliances," 248.

34. Morgenthau and Thompson, *Politics among Nations*, 6.

35. Stuart Kennedy, interview of McGee, December 9, 1988, Association for Diplomatic Studies and Training, Foreign Affairs Oral History Project, http://www.adst.org/OH%20TOCs/McGee,%20Gale.toc.pdf, accessed December 1, 2014 (hereafter cited as Association for Diplomatic Studies and Training, Kennedy interview).

36. Larson, September 4, 1979, box 18, folder 16, T. A. Larson Papers, AHC.

37. "Random Notes: Off-the-Cuff Reflections," memorandum, "McGee and Personalities," box 955, McGee Papers, 2.

38. McGee to the editor, *Denver Post*, May 25, 1951.

39. Morrissey interview, 20.

2. NOTHING TO LOSE BUT A LITTLE SELF-RESPECT

1. Larson's notes on 3 × 5 inch cards, box 18, folder 16, Larson Papers.

2. F. L. Nussbaum to McGee, April 6, 1946, box 18, folder 16, Larson Papers.

3. Warren Rovetch to McGee, January 16, 1959, box 5, folder 1, McGee Papers.

4. Note, box 955, "Diabetes," McGee Papers.

5. Mason, *Laramie: Gem City of the Plains*, 95–99.

6. Gressley, *Voltaire and the Cowboy*, 7.

7. "Bill Nye and the *Boomerang*," in *"Wyoming Tales and Trails,"* http://www
.wyomingtalesandtrails.com/laramietpris2.html, accessed on January 8, 2015.

8. Hardy, *Wyoming University*, 146.

9. McGee to Humphrey, August 11, 1947, "Contract, Tenure, etc.," box 943,
McGee Papers.

10. Minutes, University of Wyoming Trustees meeting, October 24–25, 1947,
http://www.uwyo.edu/trustees/board-meeting-archives/1940–1949
-minutes/1947-board-of-trustees-meetings.html, accessed January 13, 2015.

11. Schlesinger, *Vital Center*, 205.

12. "Sad Story from Wyoming," December 30, 1947, reprint of *St. Louis Post
Dispatch* editorial in *Laramie Republican Boomerang*, 4.

13. *Common Sense*, January 19, 1948. *Common Sense* was a short-lived publication
by University of Wyoming students. Its purpose was to oppose the book
investigation. The student publisher was Walter G. Urbigkit, who later
became a state legislator and a justice on the Wyoming Supreme Court.

14. Hardy, *Wyoming University*, 154.

15. "Textbook Controversy at the University of Wyoming, 1947–1948," summary of Constitution Day lecture by UW history professor Phil Roberts, September 18, 2006, http://uwacadweb.uwyo.edu/RobertsHistory
/uw_text book_controversy_1947.htm, accessed January 15, 2015 (site
discontinued).

16. "Rough Draft: Textbook Controversy," box 943, Textbook Investigation,
McGee Papers.

17. Handwritten notes, McGee Personal Miscellaneous Office, 1981–82, box
954, and "Random Notes: Off-the-Cuff Recollections," McGee Memoirs,
box 955, McGee Papers.

18. Alan K. Simpson, "Eulogy for Gale W. McGee," April 11, 1992, Eulogies,
box 958, McGee Papers.

19. Interview with McGee, box 2, folder 30, Hardy Papers, AHC.

20. "UW Faculty Committee Maintains Book Probe Hearing Still Needed,"
Laramie Republican Boomerang, January 21, 1948, 1.

21. Ralph Conwell to McGee, January 26, 1948, "Textbook Investigation,"
box 943, McGee Papers.

22. Elizabeth Strannigan to Senator and Mrs. McGee, undated, box 562,
folder 1, McGee Papers.

23. "An Open Letter to Gale McGee," *Laramie Republican Boomerang*, April
14, 1950, 4.

24. Information cited in this section relevant to McGee's consideration to running for the U.S. House in 1950, unless otherwise noted, is found in GWM Personal Politics: Pre-Senate, box 944, McGee Papers.
25. G. D. Humphrey to Richard H. Plock, October 5, 1950, box 213, folder 35, University of Wyoming's President's Office Records, AHC.
26. By July, McGee had announced he would not run, eliminating any urgency to adopt a policy.
27. O'Mahoney was first appointed to the Senate in 1933 when Senator John Kendrick died while in office. He was elected to a full term in 1934 and reelected in 1940 and 1946. He was defeated in 1952 by Frank Barrett and elected a final time in 1954 following the suicide of Senator Lester Hunt.
28. Scrapbook, William Henry Harrison Papers, box 15, AHC.
29. Larson, *History of Wyoming*, 1st ed., 515.
30. Joe Frantz, interview with McGee, Joe Frantz Oral History, box 956, McGee Papers.

3. THE GOOD NEWS FROM FOGGY BOTTOM

1. U.S. Department of State, "NSC-68, 1950," Office of the Historian, http://history.state.gov/milestones/1945–1952/NSC68, accessed January 21, 2015.
2. U.S. Senate Historical Office, "Joseph R. McCarthy: A Featured Biography," http://www.Senate.gov/artandhistory/history/common/generic/Featured_Bio_McCarthy.htm, accessed January 21, 2015.
3. "Senator McCarthy Attacks 'Commie-crats' in Government," *Riverton Review*, October 16, 1952, 1.
4. 1951 WYO, University of Wyoming yearbook, 31.
5. "Responsibilities of World Power" became the title of a book McGee wrote eighteen years later.
6. McGee, "A Debate Resumed," *American Scholar* 19, no. 2 (Spring 1950): 204–5.
7. McGee, memorandum, "Institute of International Affairs of the University of Wyoming," box 201, folder 4, UW President's Office Papers, AHC.
8. McGee's notes, Speech Outlines: All Subjects, box 955, McGee Papers.
9. McGee's notes, Odds and Ends: Memoirs, box 955, McGee Papers.
10. Talking points "Nuclear Weapons and Foreign Policy" (Henry A. Kissinger) and "Decline of America" (Hans J. Morgenthau), Institute brochure 1958, box 942, McGee Papers.
11. "A China Policy for the U.S.," *South Atlantic Quarterly*, Publications, box 29, McGee Papers.
12. Council on Foreign Relations, "CFR History," http://www.cfr.org/about/history/cfr/, accessed on January 27, 2015.

13. McGee, "Prospects for a More Tolerable Co-existence with Soviet Union," February 18, 1953, McGee Papers for CFR, box 941, McGee Papers.
14. Notes and letters from McGee's time at the Council of Foreign Relations, notes from meetings, 1953, box 940, McGee Papers.
15. McGee, "American Hunger for Sudden Performance," an undated 21-page article. Notation in red letters at top of first page says, "Not for Publication." Date can be estimated given the article's reference to what he called two recent events, one of which was Stalin's death, which occurred on March 5, 1953, GWM: Miscellaneous, box 942, McGee Papers.
16. McGee, "American Hunger for Sudden Performance," box 942, McGee Papers.
17. McGee, "A China Policy for the United States."
18. McGee, "A China Policy for the United States."
19. McGee, "Early Cold Wars," *Current History: The Monthly Magazine of World Affairs,* June 1950, 343–53; Gale McGee Publications, box 29, McGee Papers.
20. Letters confirming dates and letters thanking McGee for speaking, box 943, Associated Clubs, McGee Papers.
21. McGee, "Good News from Foggy Bottom," GWM Personal, box 944, McGee Papers.
22. George Nimmo to McGee, March 20, 1955, "Includes 1955–8," box 943, McGee Papers.
23. McGee to Dr. G. D. Humphrey, May 3, 1955, "Leave of Absence for JCO'M 1955," box 943, McGee Papers.

4. BEHIND THE IRON CURTAIN

1. Memorandum, May 25, 1956, FBI file on Senator Gale W. McGee, released pursuant to the Freedom of Information Act, August 25, 2010, box not yet assigned, McGee Papers.
2. Unless otherwise attributed, the quotes in this chapter are found in columns Gale and Loraine sent to Wyoming newspapers describing the trip. "Gale McGee," box 211, O'Mahoney Papers, AHC.
3. Diary of Loraine McGee, personal collection of Robert McGee.
4. Handwritten notes, Seminar Russia 1956–7, box 940, McGee Papers.
5. Whenever Gale spoke to a Wyoming church about the Russian trip, this hymn was sung.
6. Solokhov, *And Quiet Flows the Don,* 496.
7. Sullivan, *Stalin's Daughter,* 141.
8. "What a Job to Buy Soap in Moscow," *Rocky Mountain News,* September 13, 1956, 49.

5. DRUNKARDS CAN'T DO THAT

1. Dickson, *Sputnik*, 1.
2. "Threshold of Space," *Kemmerer Gazette*, January 23, 1958, 8.
3. "Dems Charge Humiliation," *Wyoming Eagle*, December 7, 1957, 25.
4. "Cheyenne Boy Sees Sputnik Early Sunday," *Wyoming Eagle*, February 11, 1958, 3.
5. Transcript of September 17, 1959, meeting between the Senate Foreign Relations Committee and Nikita Khrushchev, box 5, folder 3, McGee Papers.
6. May 4, 1956, memo to Hoover, FBI file on Gale McGee, box not yet assigned, McGee Papers.
7. "Encourage Dennis the Menace: McGee Advises," *Wyoming Eagle*, October 5, 1957, 4.
8. Editorial, *Laramie Daily Boomerang*, July 17, 1957, 4.
9. McGee to Dr. Frederick Ingvoldstad, October 3, 1956, "Round the World," box 943, McGee Papers.
10. Simpson to McGee, November 9, 1956, Personal Correspondence 1956–58, box 943, McGee Papers.
11. No records were kept of the number of high school commencement addresses McGee gave during his lifetime, but thousands of Wyoming students heard one when they graduated. Two generations of the Petera family are examples. Carol and Pete graduated from Sundance High School in 1952. During the author's September 18, 2015, telephone interview with Carol, eighty-one, she recalled being inspired by Dr. McGee's address titled "The Hammers of Today Will Drive the Spikes of Tomorrow." Her son Michael graduated from Jackson High School two decades later. Senator McGee, Carol said, gave his commencement address as well.
12. "Religion Most Powerful Anti-Red Force," *Sheridan Press*, September 27, 1957, 4.
13. Author's telephone interview with former senator Alan Simpson, May 1, 2015.
14. McGee to Mike Mansfield, January 9, 1958, Personal Correspondence 1956–58, box 943, McGee Papers.

6. NOT EVEN A DARK HORSE BUT A HOPELESS ONE

1. Handwritten notes, announcement, box 921, McGee Papers.
2. News reports, Personal: Miscellaneous Press, Photos, etc. Pre '58, box 920, McGee Papers.
3. Editorial, *Powell Tribune*, June 6, 1958. The editor was a young journalist named Dick Cook. He became McGee's press secretary in 1959 and later his chief of staff.
4. Survey conducted April 7–14, 1958, Campaign re Barrett: Voting Record, box 920, McGee Papers.

5. Strannigan oral history interviews of Gale W. McGee, "Interviews with Gale McGee/Oral History," no. 7, 4, box 958, McGee Papers.

6. Memorandum, May 28, 1958, from Elmo Roper and Associates, Campaign re Barrett: Voting Record, box 920, McGee Papers.

7. Ursel Wambolt to "Dear Fellow Democrat," July 12, 1958, Armstrong: 1958," box 921, McGee Papers.

8. "Clean Politics," *Laramie Boomerang*, August 22, 1958, 4.

9. "Armstrong Blasts McGee But Gets No Reply from Rival," *Lander Journal*, August 19, 1958, 1.

10. "Walks from Glenrock to Cast Ballot," *Casper Tribune Herald*, August 19, 1958, 2.

11. "Dems Lead GOP in Wyoming," *Rock Springs Rocket Miner*, September 4, 1958, 1, reported "Wyoming has gone Democratic in a primary for the first time since 1938." It added that 38,704 Democrats had voted in the August primary compared with 38,486 Republicans.

12. Roncalio to McGee, May 27, 1957, Fellowship: Correspondence 1957, box 934, McGee Papers.

13. Bert Hanna, "The Egghead in Wyoming's Senate Race," *Denver Post*, undated clipping, 1958 Campaign, box 921, McGee Papers.

14. "Dr. Gale McGee Should Also Resign," *Lusk Herald*, January 16, 1958, 9.

15. *Lusk Herald*, January 16, 1958, 4.

16. Hansen to members of the Board of Trustees, March 8, 1958, box 227, folder 11, Milward Simpson Papers, AHC.

17. Resolution, Politics, box 241, University of Wyoming President's Office Records, AHC.

18. Reed to Governor Simpson, August 7, 1958, box 227, folder 11, Milward Simpson Papers.

19. W. E. Kuhn, June 13, 1958, box 227, folder 11, Milward Simpson Papers.

20. Schrecker, *No Ivory Tower*, 105.

21. Letters, Conwell and McGee, brochure, box 942, McGee Papers.

22. Reed to Simpson, July 21, 1958, box 227, folder 11, Milward Simpson Papers.

23. McGee to Clements, December 10, 1957, Democrats: Senatorial Campaign Committee, box 921, McGee Papers.

24. *Campaigner*, published by McGee for Senate Club, September 18, 1958, Campaign: Communications Press, box 920, McGee Papers.

25. William Howard Moore to "Outstanding Former Faculty Awards Committee," February 9, 1998, provided to author by Betty Cooper.

26. McGee notes, McGee Personal and Memoirs, box 955, McGee Papers.

27. Association for Diplomatic Studies and Training, Kennedy interview, 27.

28. "Out in the Open," editorial, *Powell Tribune,* September 26, 1958, Campaign News Clippings: 1958, box 921, McGee Papers.

29. "Mrs. Roosevelt Asks Voters to Defeat Barrett," *Rocky Mountain News,* June 26, 1958, 23.

30. Undated newspaper clipping, "Election Campaign 1958," box 922, McGee Papers.

31. "Jim's Jottings," *Lusk Herald,* April 10, 1958, 9.

32. Campaign address, box 5, folder 1, McGee Papers.

33. "Candidate Injures Shaking Hand," *Wyoming Eagle,* October 18, 1958, 3.

34. "McGee Challenges Barrett to Debate Political Issues," *Casper Tribune-Herald,* September 16, 1958, 2.

35. Larson, *History of Wyoming,* 2nd ed., 547.

36. Morrissey interview, 69.

37. "McGee Accuses Opponent of Complacency about Defense," *Wyoming Eagle,* October 16, 4.

38. Photo and caption, *Wyoming Eagle,* September 5, 1958, 4.

39. Author's interview with Jack Speight, former Wyoming Republican Party chairman, August 4, 2015.

40. Darlene Elliott to McGee, October 22, 1958, Campaign re: Barrett, box 920, McGee Papers.

41. Conwell, "Does Doc McGee Doctor His Economics Dangerously?" *Lusk Herald,* October 16, 1958, 9.

42. Newspaper ad paid for by "Faculty Friends of Gale McGee," box 18, folder 16, T. A. Larson Papers, AHC.

43. Conwell, *Lusk Herald,* October 23, 1958, 15.

44. Newspaper ad, *Wyoming Eagle,* November 1, 1958, 22.

45. Larson, "An Open Letter to the People of Wyoming," October 27, 1958, Campaign: Communications Press Releases, box 922, McGee Papers.

46. McGee personal notes, "Tic Points: Memoirs: JFK," and McGee's "Random Notes, 1962–1969," page 40, personal collection of Elizabeth Strannigan.

47. *Rock Springs Rocket Miner,* September 30, 1958, 2.

48. "Ike to Name Strauss," *Laramie Daily Boomerang,* October 25, 1958, 1.

49. "Key Senate Races" *TIME,* November 3, 1958, http://content.time.com/time/magazine/article/0,9171,810557,00.html, accessed August 4, 2015, site now requires subscription.

50. Frantz interview, 6.

51. Washington Merry-Go-Round, *Laramie Daily Boomerang,* October 30, 1958, 4.

52. "2 Republicans Deny Pearson Tax Charge," United Press International, November 4, 1958.

53. Anderson to Pearson, memo, October 22, 1958, Pearson Papers, LBJ Library.

54. Bress to Pearson, October 22, 1959, Pearson Papers. LBJ Library.

55. Pearson to Barrett, October 20, 1959, Pearson Papers. LBJ Library.

56. "Frank Barrett Dies Memorial Day, Last Rites Saturday Morning at 10:00 in High School Auditorium," obituary, *Lusk Herald*, May 31, 1962, http://www.niobraracountylibrary.org/obituaries/?id=371, accessed December 20, 2015.

57. Al Toffler, "A Freshman's Washington Merry-Go-Round," *Pageant Magazine*, June 1959, 14.

58. Stern interview, 6.

59. Matthews, *U.S. Senators and Their World*, 68.

7. A NAME TO BE RECKONED WITH

1. Byrd, *Senate of the Roman Empire*, 5.

2. Gale W. McGee, "After Panama: Some Lessons and Opportunities in the Aftermath of the Canal Treaties Debate," 2.

3. Matthews, *U.S. Senators and Their World*, 44.

4. Risen, *Bill of the Century*, 193.

5. Morrissey interview, 48, 49.

6. Morrissey interview, 47.

7. David McGee, "A Family Affair," 43.

8. Morrissey interview, 53.

9. Mrs. J. J. Hickey to the editor, "For the Record," *Reporter*, April 6, 1967, 5.

10. White to the editor, *Reporter*, March 17, 1967.

11. Morrissey interview, 53.

12. *Congressional Record*, March 7, 1961, 3369.

13. Pearson, Washington Merry-Go-Round, *Rock Springs Daily Rocket*, August 29, 1959, 4. Pearson also reported that Barrett had encountered McGee aide James Fagan on a Casper street shortly after the election. "Without a word, Barrett walked up to him and smacked him on the nose."

14. Elizabeth Strannigan, McGee's secretary, by author, Rock Springs, Wyoming, March

15. Morrissey interview, 10.

16. Unofficial staff list, Eulogies, box 958, McGee Papers.

17. Matthews, *U.S. Senators and Their World*, 84, 85.

18. Mary Lippincott Swartz to McGee, Defense: Air Force, box 2, McGee Papers.

19. John Querard to McGee, Defense: Army, box 2, McGee Papers.

20. Glen Hagen to McGee, NASA, box 8, McGee Papers.

21. Joseph Payne to McGee, box 558, folder 8, McGee Papers.

22. In the beginning, senators were paid six dollars per day. They received a raise to eight dollars in 1855. The following year the salary was raised to $3,000 per year. From McGee's freshman year, Senate salaries were $22,500 until 1964, when raised to $30,000. While McGee was a member, salaries were raised again in 1969 to $42,500 and in 1975 to $44,600. As of 2015, salaries for nonleadership members are $174,000 annually.

23. Pearson, Washington Merry-Go-Round, *Wyoming Eagle,* January 16, 1959, 6.

24. Alvin Toffler, "A Freshman's Washington Merry-Go-Round," *Pageant,* May 1959, 13.

25. Undated memo headed "The Honorable Dale McGhee [*sic*]," FBI file on Gale McGee, box not yet assigned, McGee Papers. An agent's response to Hoover dated July 2, 1964, identifies the source as Frank A. Capell and questions his reliability. Capell, who died in 1980, was a right-wing, anticommunist author and essayist. He was the publisher of the newsletter *Herald of Freedom* in Zarephath, New Jersey. Later he wrote a book claiming Henry Kissinger was a Soviet agent.

26. Toffler, "A Freshman's Washington Merry-Go-Round," 20.

27. Morrissey interview, 15.

28. Larson, *History of Wyoming,* 2nd ed., 573.

29. McGee to Allott and from Smathers to McGee, May 29, 1962, Correspondence, box 588, McGee Papers.

30. "Art of Politics" NEA (National Education Association) *Journal,* February 1963, 36.

31. Zelizer, *Fierce Urgency of Now,* 20.

32. Mrs. Franklin Roosevelt to Gale McGee, October 14, 1958, Miscellaneous 1958–1960, box 924, McGee Papers.

33. U.S. Senate Historical Office, "Cloture Rule," March 18, 1917, http://www.Senate.gov/artandhistory/history/minute/Cloture_Rule.htm, accessed February 10, 2015.

34. Ray Robinson to McGee, January 13, 1959, box 9, folder 7, McGee Papers.

35. McGee to Robinson, January 14, 1959, box 9, folder 7, McGee Papers.

36. McGee to Claire and Mike Leon, January 20, 1959, box 559, folder 6, McGee Papers.

37. Panel's questions for McGee, "College News Conference," May 3, 1959, box 9, folder 9, McGee Papers.

38. Newsletter, "Senator Gale McGee's Senate Summary," March 1959, box 557, folder 11, McGee Papers.

39. White, *Citadel,* 59.

40. Baker, U.S. Senate historian, *Traditions of the United States Senate*, 9.

41. Senate, "Maiden Speeches, 1878–1920," https://www.senate.gov /artandhistory/history/minute/Maiden_Speeches.htm, accessed May 5, 2015.

42. *Congressional Record: Senate*, February 19, 1959, 2741.

43. *Congressional Record: Senate*, February 19, 1959, 2746.

44. Edward R. Murrow to McGee, March 23, 1962, personal collection of Robert McGee.

45. Thonsenn, *Representative American Speeches, 1964–1965*, 73–88.

46. Honan, "Art of Oratory in the Senate of the United States," 161, 165.

47. "How Colleagues Rate Them" *Talamac Magazine*, October 1960, 15–17, box 18, folder 16, Larson Papers, AHC.

48. White, January 20, 1959, column, box 9, folder 6, McGee Papers.

49. Letter to Hoover, April 25, 1959, FBI file on Senator Gale McGee, box not yet assigned, McGee Papers.

50. "Report of the Committee on Interstate and Foreign Commerce on the Nomination of Lewis L. Strauss of New York to Be Secretary of Commerce," June 4, 1959, 4.

51. "Report of the Committee on Interstate and Foreign Commerce on the Nomination of Lewis L. Strauss of New York to Be Secretary of Commerce," June 4, 1959, 606.

52. Lyon, *Eisenhower: Portrait of the Hero*, 605.

53. Anderson, *Outsider in the Senate*, 187.

54. Wildavsky, *Dixon-Yates: A Study in Power Politics*, 31–32.

55. Senator O'Mahoney to James Demmler, chairman of the Securities and Exchange Commission, December 17, 1954, Strauss, Lewis: Nomination for Secretary of Commerce, box 307, O'Mahoney Papers.

56. "Statement of Senator Joseph C. O'Mahoney," May 18, 1959, Strauss, Lewis: Nomination for Secretary of Commerce, box 307, O'Mahoney Papers, AHC.

57. "Statement of Senator Joseph C. O'Mahoney (D) Wyoming, on Senate Floor," May 19, 1954, Strauss, Lewis: Nomination for Secretary of Commerce, box 307, O'Mahoney Papers.

58. Author's interview with James Burridge, former member of Gale McGee's Senate staff who was present during the questioning of Strauss, November 11, 2014.

59. Strannigan interviews, November 5, 1989, 4; "Interviews with Gale McGee/Oral History," box 958, McGee Papers.

60. Gale McGee to constituents seeking information on the Strauss nomination, Strauss, Lewis: Nomination for Secretary of Commerce, box 307, O'Mahoney Papers.

61. Newsletter, "Senator Gale McGee's Senate Summary," May 1959, box 557, folder 11, McGee Papers.

62. Newsletter, "Senator Gale McGee's Senate Summary," May 1959.

63. Abell, *Drew Pearson Diaries, 1949–1959*, 519.

64. Strannigan interview, November 5, 1989, #3, 2; "Interviews with Gale McGee/Oral History," box 958, McGee Papers.

65. McGee's notes, Lewis Strauss Hearings, box 955, McGee Papers.

66. Baker, "A Slap at the 'Hidden-Hand Presidency,'" 12.

67. "Strauss Affair," TIME, June 15, 1959, http://content.time.com/time /magazine/article/0,9171,892639,00.html, accessed July 10, 2015.

68. *Congressional Record,* June 9, 1959, 10267.

69. Baker, "A Slap at the 'Hidden-Hand Presidency,'" 1.

70. McGee's notes, Lewis Strauss Hearings, box 955, McGee Papers.

71. "Joseph C. O'Mahoney, 78, Dies; Wyoming Senator for 25 Years," *New York Times*, December 12, 1962, 36.

72. American Enterprise Institute, "Conversation with the Honorable Gale McGee," October 30, 1978, 4–5, Interviews: Oral History, box 958, McGee Papers.

73. Library of Congress to McGee, October 30, 1959, box 557, folder 8, McGee Papers.

8. GIVE ME FOUR MORE VOTES

1. Blog: "06880: Where Westport Meets the World, http://06880danwoog .com/tag/john-f-kennedy/, accessed February 14, 2015.

2. Eventually McCraken's complaints were answered, at least for some of the Wyoming delegates. Most were moved to the Blair House, a newly remodeled hotel on Wilshire Boulevard; letter from McCraken to delegates, May 23, 1960, box 9, folder 6, J. J. Hickey Papers, AHC.

3. Strannigan interview, no. 7, 7; "Interviews with Gale McGee/Oral History," box 958, McGee Papers.

4. Strannigan interview, no. 3, 1; "Interviews with Gale McGee/Oral History," box 958, McGee Papers.

5. Morrissey interview, no. 2, 5.

6. Morrissey interview, no. 3, 2.

7. Dallek, *An Unfinished Life*, 178.

8. Johnson, *A White House Diary*, 59, 507, 569.

9. Johnson conversation with Gale McGee on December 9, 1967, Lyndon B. Johnson Presidential Recordings, tape: WH6712.01, Conversation: 12504, December 9, 1967, https://millercenter.org/the-presidency

/secret-white-house-tapes/conversation-gale-mcgee-december-9–1967, accessed August 2, 2015.

10. Strannigan interview, no. 3, October 28, 1989, 2; "Interviews with Gale McGee/Oral History," box 958, McGee Papers.

11. Transcript of telephone conversation between McGee and Johnson, May 12, 1966, WH6712.01, Miller Center, University of Virginia, https:// millercenter.org/the-presidency/secret-white-house-tapes/conversation -gale-mcgee- and-office-conversation-may-12–1966, accessed August 2, 2015.

12. Miller, *Lyndon*, 179.

13. Johnson conversation with McGee, December 9, 1967.

14. Strannigan interview, no. 3, November 5, 1989, 13; "Interviews with Gale McGee/Oral History," box 958, McGee Papers.

15. Text of JFK's January 2, 1960, announcement, John F. Kennedy Presidential Library, http://www.JFKlibrary.org/Research/Research-Aids/Ready -Reference/JFK-Fast-Facts/Announcement-of-Candidacy.aspx, accessed February 18, 2015.

16. Wallace to Senator Kennedy, August 6, 1959, box 0975, JFK Papers, JFK Library.

17. Roncalio to Kennedy, July 21, 1959, box 0975, JFK Papers, JFK Library.

18. Edward M. Kennedy to Robert Kennedy and Robert Wallace, memo, November 16, 1959, box 0975, JFK Papers, JFK Library.

19. Stern interview, 3.

20. Roncalio to McGee, November 6, 1959, box 0975, JFK Papers, JFK Library.

21. Roncalio to Edward Kennedy, January 20, 1960, box 0975, JFK Papers, JFK Library.

22. Roncalio to "Jack, or Ted, or Teddy" (likely meant "Bobby"), April 23, 1960, box 0975, JFK Papers, JFK Library.

23. "A Man Who Takes His Time," *TIME*, April 25, 1960, http://content.time.com /time/magazine/article/0,9171,826270,00.html, accessed August 7, 2015.

24. "Larry L. King, Playwright of 'Best Little Whorehouse in Texas,' Dies at 83," obituary, *Washington Post*, December 21, 2012, http://www.nytimes .com/2012/12/22/arts/larry-l-king-texan-author- and-playwright-dies-at -83.html, accessed August 4, 2015.

25. "A Man Who Takes His Time," *TIME*, April 25, 1960.

26. Larry L. King, "My Hero LBJ," *Harper's Magazine*, October 1966, 51–61.

27. Courtney Sheldon, "A Capital Interview with Senator McGee," *Christian Science Monitor*, May 25, 1960, 22.

28. Stern interview, 8.

29. Official Report of the Proceedings of the Democratic National Convention 1960, 22, 29.

30. Official Report DNC 1960, 110.

31. W. H. Lawrence, "Kennedy Nominated on the First Ballot; Overwhelms Johnson by 806 Votes to 409; Wyoming's Vote Puts Bostonian over Top before Acclamation," *Los Angeles Times*, July 14, 1960, 1.

32. Official Report DNC 1960, roll call of states begins at page 159.

33. King, "My Hero LBJ," 60.

34. Official report records that State Democratic Party chairman Teno Roncalio announced Wyoming's vote. Official Report DNC 1960, 167. However, the news film from that night shows national committeeman Tracy McCraken making the announcement. https://www.youtube.com/watch?v=EvPkS-YSFdw.

35. King, "My Hero LBJ," 60.

36. Morrissey interview, 13.

37. LBJ to McGee, July 28, 1960, Senate Papers, box 373, White House Central File, Lyndon B. Johnson Presidential Library.

38. McCraken to Senator Jackson, August 24, 1960, "Gale McGee Campaign," box 563, McGee Papers.

39. McCraken to JFK, August 31, 1960, box 562, folder 1, McGee Papers.

40. McCraken to McGee, September 1, 1960, box 562, folder 1, McGee Papers.

41. McCraken to Kennedy, telegram, August 31, 1960, and a September 17 letter from Kenneth P. O'Donnell confirm JFK would come to Wyoming on September 23, 1960, box 562, folder 8, McGee Papers.

42. Remarks of Senator John F. Kennedy at Cheyenne, Wyoming, September 23, 1960, JFK Library, http://www.JFKlibrary.org/Research/Research-Aids/JFK-Speeches/Cheyenne-wy_19600923.aspx, accessed February 20, 2015.

43. Press release from Senator McGee's office, Press, box 28, folder 5, McGee Papers.

44. Strannigan interviews, November 11, 1989, 8; "Interviews with Gale McGee/Oral History," box 958, McGee Papers.

45. Department of Defense memo re: schedule, box 562, folder 1, McGee Papers.

46. For an in-depth discussion of this history, see Adam Hochschild, *King Leopold's Ghost*.

47. Undated briefing paper to McGee from David M. Burns, Department of Defense, acting public affairs officer, box 562, folder 1, McGee Papers.

48. Daniel Yergin and Joseph Stanislaw, *Commanding Heights*, http://www.pbs.org/wgbh/commandingheights/shared/minitext/prof_kwamenkrumah.html, accessed February 24, 2015.

49. Strannigan interviews, no. 6, 6; "Interviews with Gale McGee/Oral History," box 958, McGee Papers.

50. Stern interview, 20.

51. McCraken to Hickey, December 23, 1960, box 11, folder 9, Hickey Papers, AHC.

52. Karpan, "A Political History of Jack R. Gage," *Annals of Wyoming*, 199.

9. SEARCHING SOULS, MINDS, AND SPIRITS

1. News reports, Personal: Miscellaneous Press, Photos, etc. pre '58, box 920, McGee Papers.

2. BACM Research, "Pentagon Papers: The Complete Report Un-redacted," on a CD, vol. 1, "Viet Nam and the U.S. (1945–1950), United States–Viet Nam Relations 1940–1967, Final Report, Viet Nam Task Force, Office of the Secretary of Defense," B 34–36.

3. Lacouture, *Ho Chi Minh: A Political Biography*, 20, 24.

4. "McGee on Mend in Hospital after Diabetes Attack" *Wyoming Eagle*, January 21, 1961, 3.

5. "January 20, 1961: Poet Robert Frost at President John F. Kennedy's Inauguration," https://www.youtube.com/watch?v=XInL2u0DP88.

6. Strannigan interviews, November 11, 1989, 4; "Interviews with Gale McGee/Oral History," box 958, McGee Papers.

7. Dick Cook to Wyoming sportscaster Larry Birleffi, June 20, 1961, box 576, folder 2, McGee Papers.

8. Blumenthal and Morone, *The Heart of Power: Health and Politics in the Oval Office*, 139.

9. Strannigan interviews, November 11, 1989, 4; "Interviews with Gale McGee/Oral History," box 958, McGee Papers.

10. Lederer and Burdick, *Ugly American*.

11. James Gibney, "The Ugly American," a review of *Edward Lansdale's Cold War* by Jonathan Nashel, *New York Times*, January 15, 2006, http://www.nytimes.com/2006/01/15/books/review/the-ugly-american.html, accessed January 7, 2016.

12. "U.S. Perceptions of the Insurgency, 1954–1960," section IV-B-1, BACM Pentagon Papers, 48, 67.

13. Zimmer, *Vietnam War Debate*, 25.

14. Saigon hearings before the Senate Subcommittee on State Department Organization and Public Affairs of the Committee on Foreign Relations, December 7–8, 1959, U.S. Government Printing Office.

15. Author's email interview with Robert McGee, February 4, 2015.

16. "Vietnam: A Living Example for Implementing the American Spirit," a speech by Senator Gale McGee to the U.S. Senate, February 9, 1960, reprinted in *Vital Speeches of the Day* 26, no. 14 (May 1, 1960): 440–43.

17. Fulbright to McGee, February 10, 1960, box 29, folder 10, McGee Papers.

18. Durbrow to McGee, February 27, 1960, box 29, folder 10, McGee Papers.

19. O'Daniel to McGee, May 10, 1960, and McGee to O'Daniel, May 18, 1960, box 29, folder 10, McGee Papers.

20. "U.S. Needs 'New Face,' Senator Says," *Irving (Texas) Daily News*, October 31, 1960, box 28, folder 5, McGee Papers.

21. Speech titled "A Sense of Urgency" to the March 25–28, 1960, Convention of the American Association of School Administrators in Philadelphia, box 579, folder 10, McGee Papers.

22. "Peace Corps Analysis by Wyoming Senator," *Hoya* 42, no. 21 (April 20, 1961): 1.

23. Administration's Proposal, "Peace Corp: Presentation of FY 1962 Program to the United States Congress, June 1, 1961," box 41, folder 6, McGee Papers.

24. Scott Stossel, "Sargent Shriver and the Birth of the Peace Corps," *Peace Corps Online Magazine*, http://peacecorpsonline.org/messages/messages/2629/2024714.html, accessed March 17, 2015.

25. Statement of the Honorable Robert Sargent Shriver Jr., Director of the Peace Corps, box 41, folder 6, McGee Papers.

26. *Congressional Record*, March 4, 1963.

27. Speech, "A Sense of Urgency," 302, box 70, folder 5, McGee Papers.

28. Sorensen, *Kennedy*, 533.

29. "Study Mission to South America November–December 1961," 3, 7, Report of Senators Gale W. McGee, Frank Moss, Claire Engle, and Stephen Young, February 13, 1962, U.S. Government Printing Office.

30. Author's interview with John Sanbrailo, executive director of the Pan-American Development Foundation, April 16, 2015, Washington DC.

31. Personnel Administration and Operations of U.S. Agency for International Development, report of Senator Gale McGee to the Committee on Appropriations, November 29, 1963, U.S. Government Printing Office, 3 (hereafter cited as McGee, USAID Report).

32. McGee, USAID Report, 11.

33. McGee, USAID Report, 43–44.

34. Mulloy, *World of the John Birch Society*, 7, 8; also see Grove, *Inside the John Birch Society*.

35. Mulloy, *World of the John Birch Society*, 49.

36. David Jansen, "Rightists Strong: A Senator Warns," *New York Times*, May 15, 1966, 22.

37. Drew Pearson, "GOP Seeks John Birch Alliance," *Washington Post*, July 1, 1961, D13.

38. Battaglio, *David Susskind: A Televised Life*, 43, 119.

39. Strannigan interviews, no. 3, November 5, 1989, 7; "Interviews with Gale McGee/Oral History," box 958, McGee Papers.

40. *Congressional Record*, April 12, 1961, 5607.

41. Grove, *Inside the John Birch Society*, 121.

42. "Publicity Makes Birch Society 'Pull in Horns,'" *Rock Springs Daily Rocket*, April 8, 1961, 2.

43. McGee to Kennedy, memo, August 16, 1963, Kennedy Papers, Presidential Papers, President's Office Files, Subjects. Right-wing Movement, Digital Identifier: JFKPOF-106–013, http://www.jfklibrary.org/Asset-Viewer /Archives/JFKPOF-106–013.aspx, 3.

44. "Cody's Birchers Smile, Right-to-Worker Avers," *Wyoming Eagle*, May 2, 1963, 4.

45. Martin Morse Wooster, "Too Good to Be True," *Wall Street Journal*, April 1, 2005, 3.

46. Wooster, "Too Good to Be True," 3–4.

47. McGee to Kennedy, August 16, 1963, 4.

48. *FOX Nation 5th Anniversary Classics Flashback: Paul Harvey, 1965: "If I Were the Devil (Warning for a Nation),"* http://nation.foxnews.com/paul-harvey /2012/03/21/1965-if-i-were-devil-warning-nation-paul-harvey, accessed March 19, 2015.

49. Morrissey interview, 37.

50. "Conspiracy USA," *Look*, January 26, 1965, 21.

51. Morrissey interview, 38.

52. Morrissey interview, 43, 59.

53. Strannigan interview, November 5, 1989, 10; "Interviews with Gale McGee/Oral History," box 958, McGee Papers.

54. Strannigan interview, November 5, 1989, 10, 44; "Interviews with Gale McGee/Oral History," box 958, McGee Papers.

55. McGee to Kennedy, August 16, 1963, 1.

56. Sorensen, *Kennedy*, 470.

57. Strober, *Let Us Begin Anew*, 278, 286.

58. Ibach and Moore, "The Emerging Civil Rights Movement," http://www
.uwyo.edu/robertshistory/civil_rights_movement.htm, accessed March
16, 2015.

59. "No One Shows Up for Civil Rights Hearing in Cody," *Rock Springs Daily
Rocket,* March 18, 1961, 2.

60. "NAACP Asks Cooperation in Ending Discrimination," *Wyoming Eagle,*
August 8, 1961, 3.

61. Charles Diggs to Milward Simpson, October 10, 1957, and Simpson's
October 30 reply, Civil Rights, box 161, Milward Simpson Papers, AHC.

62. Guenther, "List of Good Negroes," 26, 4, 12.

63. Guenther, "List of Good Negroes," 24, 27.

64. Guenther, "List of Good Negroes," 27–29.

65. Ibach and Moore, "Emerging Civil Rights Movement," 170.

66. Larson, *History of Wyoming,* 1st ed., 524.

67. King to McGee, "Civil Rights," box 1, McGee Papers.

68. All letters described are found in Civil Rights, box 1, McGee Papers.

69. *Brown vs. Board of Education of Topeka,* 347 U.S. 483, 74 S. Ct. 686, 98 L.
Ed. 873 (1954).

70. Senate file 19, Senate Journal of the Thirty-Third Legislature, State of
Wyoming 1955, 440.

71. Committee on Commerce, "Civil Rights: Public Accommodations," 905, 910.

72. President John F. Kennedy, Annual Message to the Congress on the
State of the Union, January 11, 1962, http://www.presidency.ucsb.edu
/ws/index.php?pid=8045, accessed on April 24, 2015.

73. News release, May 6, 1960, box 20, folder 2, McGee Papers.

74. *Congressional Record,* July 9, 1962, 12943.

75. *Congressional Record,* July 9, 1962, 12947.

76. Blumenthal and Morone, *Heart of Power,* 155–56.

77. Stern interview, 30.

78. Blumenthal and Morone, *Heart of Power,* 156–59.

79. Arturo Gonzalez to McGee, September 15, 1962, box 56, folder 6, McGee
Papers.

80. Ashby and Gramer, *Fighting the Odds,* 154.

81. *Scottsbluff Star-Herald,* undated clipping, box 56, folder 6, McGee Papers.

82. Ashby and Gramer, *Fighting the Odds,* 154.

83. *Congressional Record,* August 14, 1961, 15233.

84. Franz interview, 23.

85. Tom Wilson (McGee's press staff) to United Press International, telegram, October 23, 1962, box 588, folder 1, McGee Papers.

86. "1,000 Could Be Affected in Cheyenne," *Wyoming Eagle,* July 10, 1963, 1.

87. Statement of Senator Magnuson, August 26, 1963, *Congressional Record,* 15890.

88. "President Kennedy Averts Rail Strike, *Wyoming Eagle,* July 11, 1963, 1.

89. *Congressional Record,* August 26, 1963, 15954.

90. This and other observations made herein by McGee are contained in a series of letters he and Loraine sent their children while on this journey. Letters are in the private collection of Robert McGee.

91. Committee on Foreign Relations, "Study Mission to Southeast Asia," 6, 14.

92. Committee on Foreign Relations, "Study Mission to Southeast Asia," 10.

93. Committee on Foreign Relations, "Study Mission to Southeast Asia," 11.

94. BACM Pentagon Papers, "U.S. Perceptions of the Insurgency 1954–1960," Section IV-B-1, 48.

95. BACM Pentagon Papers, "U.S. Perceptions of the Insurgency 1954–1960," IV-A-5, A-30.

96. Gale McGee, "United States: Bastion of Freedom," July 19, 1963, Gale W. McGee Bibliography File, U.S. Senate Historical Office, 16.

97. Talbot, *Brothers,* 214, 215.

98. Dallek, *An Unfinished Life,* 668.

99. Sheehan, Kenworthy, Butterfield, and Smith, *Pentagon Papers,* 86.

100. McGee, *Responsibilities of World Power,* 223.

101. Miscellaneous Quotes, box 962, McGee Papers.

102. McGee, *Responsibilities of World Power,* 230–34.

103. McGee, *Responsibilities of World Power,* 232.

104. Franz interview, 15.

105. October 31, 1963 JFK Press Conference, http://www.jfklibrary.org /Research/Research-Aids/Ready-Reference/Press-Conferences/News -Conference-63.aspx, accessed April 20, 2015.

106. Sheehan, Kenworthy, Butterfield, and Smith, *Pentagon Papers,* 216–19.

107. U.S. Department of State, telegram to the embassy in Vietnam, November 27, 1963, 8:40 p.m., August–December 1963, document 332, http://history.state.gov/historicaldocuments/frus1961–63v04/d332, accessed April 20, 2015.

108. U.S. Department of State, telegram to the embassy in Vietnam.

109. McGee, *Responsibilities of World Power,* 234.

110. BACM Pentagon Papers, C45–46.

111. "Links Scientific Progress, Resource Development," *Laramie Daily Boomerang,* September 26, 1963, 1.

112. Philip White, "JFK Visits Wyoming," *Casper Star-Tribune,* September 25, 2013, http://trib.com/news/state- and-regional/govt- and-politics

/years-ago- today-inspiring-jfk-drew-crowds-on-wyoming- tour/article
_591d01c3-f024–5ddc-8ef9-bc52afd05a5a.html, accessed April 21, 2015.

113. Papers of John F. Kennedy, President's Office Files, Speech Files, Address at
the University of Wyoming, Laramie, Wyoming, 25 September 1963, Digital
Identifier JFKPOF-046–052, JFK Library, https://www.jfklibrary.org/Asset
-Viewer/Archives/JFKPOF-046–052.aspx, accessed April 27, 2015.

10. A MAN OF GREAT FAITH, NOT DARK FEARS

1. Strannigan interviews, no. 3, October 28, 1989, 9; "Interviews with Gale
McGee/Oral History," box 958, McGee Papers.

2. Author's email interview with Robert McGee, September 11, 2015.

3. Strannigan interviews, November 11, 1989, 3; "Interviews with Gale
McGee/Oral History," box 958, McGee Papers.

4. "CNN Poll: Who Killed Kennedy?" November 22, 2013, http://
politicalticker.blogs.cnn.com/2013/11/22/cnn-poll-who-killed
-kennedy/, accessed July 12, 2015.

5. "Yellowstone Volcano: Is the Beast Building to a Violent Tantrum?"
National Geographic News, http://news.nationalgeographic.com/news
/2001/08/0828_wireyellowstone.html, accessed May 24, 2015.

6. Strannigan interviews, November 11, 1989, 5; Interviews with Gale
McGee/Oral History," box 958, McGee Papers.

7. Franz interview, 46.

8. Strannigan interview, no. 9, February 24, 1990, 8; "Interviews with Gale
McGee/Oral History," box 958, McGee Papers.

9. Franz interview, 38.

10. Sheehan, Kenworthy, Butterfield, and Smith, *Pentagon Papers*, document
#21, 134.

11. Zelizer, *Fierce Urgency of Now*, 63.

12. Dallek, *Lyndon B. Johnson and His Times*, 188.

13. LBJ, *Vantage Point*, 70.

14. Johnson, "Annual Message to Congress on the State of the Union," January 8, 1964, http://www.presidency.ucsb.edu/ws/?pid=26787, accessed
July 17, 2015.

15. Zelizer, *Fierce Urgency of Now*, 86, 92–95.

16. U.S. Senate Historical Office, "June 10, 1964: Civil Rights Filibuster
Ended," http://www.Senate.gov/artandhistory/history/minute/Civil
_Rights_Filibuster_Ended.htm, accessed June 16, 2015.

17. Civil Rights Documentation Project, Dirksen Congressional Center,
http://civilrightsactof1964.org/1964_february.htm#sthash.mkyHUsSV
.dpuf, accessed July 18, 2015.

18. "McGee Is Accused of Voting Consistently against Negroes," *Wyoming Eagle*, August 14, 1963, 5.

19. *Congressional Record*, April 13, 1964, 7792.

20. *Senator Gale McGee's Senate Summary*, newsletter, March 1959, box 557, folder 11, McGee Papers.

21. *Congressional Record*, April 13, 1964, 7796.

22. *Congressional Record*, June 19, 1964, 14510.

23. *Congressional Record*, June 19, 1964, 14511.

24. McGee to George Lev, March 12, 1965, box 96, folder 5, McGee Papers.

25. "Letters to the Editor," *Riverton Ranger*, September 10, 1964, 8.

26. M. E. Edwards of Lander to McGee, April 7, 1964, box 96, folder 5, McGee Papers.

27. McGee to Charlotte Lipton, November 6, 1964, box 77, folder 5, McGee Papers.

28. McGee to Mrs. Garvin Taylor, March 15, 1965, box 96, folder 5, McGee Papers.

29. Reed's and McGee's letters are found in box 96, folder 5, McGee Papers.

30. "Harrison Favorite against McGee," *Wyoming Stockman-Farmer*, January 1964, 28; also see "GOP Eager to Tackle McGee, Wold Declares," *Wyoming Eagle*, January 1, 1964.

31. Rep. Harrison was the great-great-grandson of the ninth president of the United States and the grandson of the twenty-third president.

32. LBJ to McGee, June 14, 1963, Vice Presidential Papers, "1963 Congressional File-Mc," box 271, LBJ Library.

33. "Remarks of Vice President Lyndon B. Johnson Testimonial Dinner for Senator Gale McGee," Vice Presidential Papers, "1963 Congressional File-Mc," box 271, LBJ Library, 2.

34. "November Poll Shows Harrison Leading McGee," *Casper Tribune*, January 7, 1964, 2.

35. Recording of December 20, 1963, telephone conversation between President Johnson and McGee, http://web2.millercenter.org/lbj /audiovisual/whrecordings/telephone/conversations/1963/lbj_k6312 _11_18_19_mcgee.mp3, accessed June 21, 2015.

36. "McGee Blasts Cody for Aid Hypocrisy," *Wyoming Eagle*, January 10, 1964, 1.

37. "McGee Indicts Detractors of American Government," *Wyoming Eagle*, January 11, 1964, 4.

38. "McGee Urges Wyoming Businessmen: Be Honest," *Wyoming Eagle*, January 15, 1964, 4.

39. "McGee Charges State Legislators Voted to 'Destroy Our Democracy,'" *Wyoming Eagle*, January 14, 1964, 4.

40. "Hansen Says He'll Stay as Governor," *Casper Star-Tribune*, January 26, 1964, 1.

41. "Harrison Won't Try for Senate," *Casper Tribune*, January 30, 1964, 1.

42. Digest of Senate Journal, 1963, 45–46; also see "Right to Work Signed," *Wyoming Eagle*, February 9, 1963, 4.

43. "Hansen: 'Misunderstandings," *Wyoming Eagle*, May 14, 1963, 4.

44. Larson, *History of Wyoming*, 2nd ed., 544.

45. "Work Right Head Cuts McGee," *Wyoming Eagle*, January 26, 1963, 31.

46. "McGee Says Identity of Firm is Confidential," *Wyoming Eagle*, April 20, 1963, 1.

47. Digest of Senate Journal, 1963, 171.

48. Larson, *History of Wyoming*, 2nd ed., 557.

49. Digest of House Journal, 1963, 505.

50. Digest of House Journal, 1963, 506–7.

51. Digest of House Journal, 1963, 501.

52. "Super Court' Measure Approved," *Wyoming Eagle*, February 13, 1963, 4.

53. Larson, *History of Wyoming*, 2nd ed., 558.

54. "Memorandum for the President," McGee to Kennedy, August 16, 1963, Kennedy Papers, Presidential Papers, Presim dent's Office Files, Subjects. Rightwing Movement, Digital Identifier: JFKPOF-106–013, http://www.jfklibrary.org/Asset-Viewer/Archives/JFKPOF-106–013.aspx, 3.

55. "Simpson Asserts He's No Bircher," *Wyoming Eagle*, August 13, 1963, 4.

56. "Wold Speaks Out against Sen. McGee," *Wyoming Eagle*, August 2, 1963, 24.

57. "Phelan Says GOP Chairman Should Take 'Sanity Oath," *Wyoming Eagle*, August 3, 1963.

58. Christgau, *Origins of the Jump Shot*, 204.

59. John Waggener, Kenny Sailors Oral History Interview, American Heritage Center, University of Wyoming, http://digitalcollections.uwyo.edu:8180/luna/servlet/detail/uwydbuwy~91~91~1894719~258359:Oral-History-Interview-with-Kenny-S?trs=1&qvq=q%3ASailors5192010.mp3%3Bsort%3ARID%2CDescription%2CTitle%2CDate_Original%3Blc%3Auwydbuwy%7E91%7E91&mi=0&cic=uwydbuwy%7E91%7E91&sort=RID%2CDescription%2CTitle%2CDate_Original, accessed June 30, 2015.

60. Sheehan, Kenworthy, Butterfield, and Smith, *Pentagon Papers*, 246; also McNamara, *In Retrospect*, 129.

61. Sheehan, Kenworthy, Butterfield, and Smith, *Pentagon Papers*, 244; language for the resolution was initially drafted on May 25, 1964, Document #66, 245, 294.

62. Sheehan, Kenworthy, Butterfield, and Smith, *Pentagon Papers*, 245, 259, 267.

63. Sheehan, Kenworthy, Butterfield, and Smith, *Pentagon Papers*, 267–68.

64. McNamara, *In Retrospect*, 128.

65. Sheehan, Kenworthy, Butterfield, and Smith, *Pentagon Papers*, 267, 272.

66. "McGee Lauds Johnson for Quick Action," *Wyoming Eagle*, August 7, 1964, 3.

67. Druckman, *Wayne Morse*, 409.

68. "Tonkin Gulf Resolution," Senate Roll Call, August 7, 1964, *Congressional Record*, 18470–18471.

69. "Mrs. Lyndon Johnson Greeted Here by Cheering Throngs," *Jackson Hole Guide*, August 20, 1964, 1.

70. "Thousands Here to Greet, See First Lady," *Green River Star*, August 20, 1964, 1.

71. "Report Wide Publicity from Lady Bird's Visit," *Green River Star*, August 27, 1964, 1.

72. White, *Making of the President 1964*, 201.

73. White, *Making of the President 1964*, 228.

74. Wyoming to Go GOP in '64 as Never Before: Smith," *Wyoming Eagle*, July 17, 1964, 18.

75. Miller, *Lyndon*, 390.

76. LBJ, *Vantage Point*, 93.

77. Miller, *Lyndon*, 391.

78. "Wold Charges Democrats Buying Votes," *Wyoming Eagle*, September 3, 1964, 4.

79. "Thurmond Says U.S. Is Headed for Dictatorship," *Casper Star Tribune*, October 4, 1964, 2.

80. "Move toward Socialism," *Riverton Ranger*, October 2, 1964, 1, 5.

81. "McGovern Gives Plug for McGee," *Casper Tribune*, October 4, 1964, 2.

82. Morrissey interview, 42.

83. "Wold Charges Democrats Buying Votes," *Wyoming Eagle*, September 3, 1964, 4.

84. "Candidates Intensify Campaigning," *Wyoming Eagle*, September 15, 1964, 4.

85. "Anti-Anti-Poverty War Action Led by Albany," *Wyoming Eagle*, August 26, 1964, 4.

86. "Mix Liberal, Conservative, McGee Urges," *Wyoming Eagle*, September 18, 1964, 18.

87. "McGee Still Liberal, Says GOP Leader," *Casper Tribune*, September 28, 1964, 20.

88. "Wold Says McGee Funds Come from Out of State," *Casper Tribune*, September 8, 1964, 2.

89. "Senatorial Candidates Push Campaigns in Council Conflict," *Sunday Rock Springs Miner*, October 18, 1964, 2.

90. "Stars, Candidates Highlight Wind-up Democratic Rally," *Rock Springs Daily Rocket*, October 24, 1964, 1, 4.

91. "Senator McGee Links Bid to 'Power," *Casper Tribune*, October 4, 1964, 1.

92. "Canvas Shows Heavy Defection from Dems," *Casper Tribune*, September 25, 1964, 2.

93. Robert Peck, "Two Different Dreams about McGee," *Riverton Ranger*, October 29, 1964, 10.

94. Valenti to LBJ, memo, September 24, 1964, box 11, Aides Files: Manatos, Presidential Papers, LBJ Library.

95. "McGee Gets Insulin-Sugar Tests, Checkup," *Wyoming Eagle*, September 14, 1963, 4.

96. Facts surrounding McGee's heart attack were obtained in an email interview with Robert McGee, February 26, 2015.

97. Mike Manatos to Larry O'Brien, memo, September 22, 1964, box 11, Aides Files: Manatos, Presidential Papers, LBJ Library.

98. Telephone notes, October 23, 1964, Transcripts of Lyndon Johnson's telephone conversations, box 6, Presidential Papers, LBJ Library.

99. John T. Hinckley, "1964 Election in Wyoming," 523–26.

11. WARS CAN NO LONGER BE WON, BUT THEY CAN BE LOST

1. Appy, *Patriots*, 121–23.

2. Telephone call, LBJ to Lippmann, December 1, 1963, http://web2 .millercenter.org/lbj/audiovisual/whrecordings/telephone/conversations /1963/lbj_k6312_01_15_lippmann.mp3, accessed July 20, 2015.

3. Lovegall, *Choosing War*, 351.

4. Logevall, *Choosing War*, 349.

5. Franz interview, 38.

6. *Congressional Record*, February 17, 1965, 2869. The entire debate can be found between pages 2869 and 2990.

7. Lovegall, *Choosing War*, 350.

8. Chalmers Roberts, "Mr. Church Goes to Washington," *Washington Post Book World*, November 25, 1985; also, Schmitz and Fousekis, *Frank Church, the Senate, and the Emergence of Dissent on the Vietnam War*, 573.

9. "National Security Archive Discovers Vietnam Era Surveillance Targets," http://gwtoday.gwu.edu/national-security-archive -gw-discovers-vietnam-era-surveillance-targets; accessed July 19, 2015; also see "American Cryptology during the Cold War 1945–

1989," http://nsarchive.gwu.edu/NSAEBB/NSAEBB426/docs/2
.Americanpercent20Cryptologypercent20During percent20thepercent
20Coldpercent20Warpercent201945–1989percent20Bookpercent20
IV percent20Cryptologicpercent20Rebirthpercent201981–1989–1999
.pdf, accessed July 19, 2015.

10. "Viet Crisis Stirs Senate; Some Cut Party Lines," *Washington Post*, February 18, 1965, 1.

11. John W. Finney, "Vietnam: A Debate over U.S. Role," *New York Times*, February 28, 1965, E3.

12. William Small, "Congress, Television, and War Protests," www
.americanheritage.com/category/article-keywords/vietnam-wars,
accessed July 20, 2015.

13. Schmitz and Fousekis, *Frank Church, the Senate, and the Emergence of Dissent on the Vietnam War*, 575.

14. *Public Papers of the Presidents: Lyndon B. Johnson*, April 7, 1965, part 1, 394–99.

15. Sheehan, Kenworthy, Butterfield, and Smith, *Pentagon Papers*, 409–11.

16. Sheehan, Kenworthy, Butterfield, and Smith, *Pentagon Papers*, 7494–95.

17. McGovern, *A Time of War, a Time of Peace*, xii.

18. McGee to Mrs. Emily Ridgway, March 16, 1965, responding to a letter from Ridgway dated March 10, 1965, box 576, folder 9, McGee Papers.

19. Gale McGee, "An Academic Looks at Vietnam," April 29, 1965, box 262, McGee Papers.

20. *Congressional Record*, April 29, 1965, 8976.

21. LBJ to McGee, phone call, April 29, 1965, citation no. 7384 Speaker: tape: WH6504.07, http://web2.millercenter.org/lbj/audiovisual
/whrecordings/telephone/conversations/1965/lbj_wh6504_07_7384
.mp3, accessed July 23, 2015.

22. Author's email interview with McGee children, January 31, 2015.

23. Refers to the W.E.B Du Bois Clubs made up of antiwar "leftists." A discussion of their role is found in "An Examination of the Vietnam Antiwar Movement at Wisconsin State University–La Crosse, 1965–1973," by Benjamin Weihrauch, http://murphylibrary.uwlax.edu/digital/jur
/2002/weihrauch.pdf, accessed July 20, 2015.

24. Memorandum: Re: Senator Gale W. McGee," from D. W. Bowers to Deloach, May 4, 1965, FBI file on Senator Gale W. McGee, being processed for inclusion in McGee Papers.

25. McGee, "Academic Freedom," *Congressional Record*, 18304–8.

26. McGee to Church, March 14, 1966, Series 2.2, box 30, folder 12, Frank Church Papers, Boise State University.

27. "He's a Sucker for the Balance of Power," *Washington Post*, May 8, 1966, E4.

28. McGee to Phil Miller, June 29, 1965, box 110, folder 1, McGee Papers.

29. Martin Luther King and the Global Freedom Struggle, "Watts Rebellion," http://kingencyclopedia.stanford.edu/encyclopedia/encyclopedia/enc_watts_rebellion_los_angeles_1965/, accessed July 23, 2015.

30. "Easy to Shout Fire," *Wyoming Eagle*, September 20, 1967, box 142, folder 7.

31. Marble and Mullings, eds., *Let Nobody Turn Us Around*, excerpts from "Nonviolence and Racial Justice," by Martin Luther King, 401–3.

32. Marble and Mullings, *Let Nobody Turn Us Around*, 169–70.

33. *Congressional Record*, March 10, 1965, 4632.

34. *Congressional Record*, March 22, 1965, 5515–16.

35. *Congressional Record*, March 22, 1965, 7834.

36. *Congressional Record*, March 18, 1965, 5411.

37. *Congressional Record*, May 26, 1965, 11746.

38. *Congressional Record*, May 26, 1965, 11746.

39. Senators John Sparkman and Clifford Case, "History of the Senate Foreign Relations Committee Room," preface, "Senate Foreign Relations Committee," U.S. Senate Historical Office.

40. "Senator McGee Assigned to Foreign Relations Committee," *Wyoming Eagle*, March 26, 1966, 1.

41. McGee lost the Foreign Relations Committee seat after the 1966 elections when GOP gains required a realignment of seats between the two parties. He was reappointed to the Committee in January 1969, when ironically, Minnesota senator Eugene McCarthy, an influential Vietnam War opponent, offered to vacate the seat in favor of McGee. Strannigan interviews, no. 2, September 16, 1989, 7, 9; Interviews with Gale McGee/Oral History, box 958, McGee Papers; Franz interview, 3.

42. *Pow-Wow 1965*, Cheyenne Central High School Yearbook, 29.

43. "Operation Indiana, March 28, 1966, 1st Battalion, 7th Marine Regiment, http://www.virtualwall.org/units/opindiana.htm and "Operation Indiana," http://www.marzone.com/7thMarines/Hst0106.htm, accessed July 30, 2015.

44. Franz interview, 6.

45. *Congressional Record*, April 28, 1966, 9371.

46. *Congressional Record*, April 28, 1966, 9374.

47. Franz interview, 9.

48. "He's a Sucker for the Balance of Power," *Washington Post*, May 8, 1966, E4.

49. "Power Akin to Freedom," TIME, April 29, 1966.

50. Franz interview, 42.

51. "Arrogance of Dissent," *Newsweek*, July 18, 1966, 27.

52. President's special assistant Walt Rostow to President Johnson, memo, May 10, 1966, Office of the President, LBJ Library.

53. Rostow to McGee, February 17, 1968, "Walt Rostow, Secret: Eyes Only," box 262, White House Central Files, LBJ Library.

54. Herman Vaughn to McGee, February 28, 1966, box 134, folder 7, McGee papers.

55. Elizabeth Marsh Jensen to McGee, June 13, 1966, box 135, folder 7, McGee Papers.

56. Letters to and from McGee and C. W. Culbertson, April 12, 1966, and April 20, 1966, box 136, folder 1, McGee Papers.

57. Rev. Otis Jackson to McGee, February 15, 1966, box 136, folder 1, McGee Papers.

58. R. R. Bostwick to McGee, February 3, 1966, box 136, folder 1, McGee Papers.

59. Sydney Spiegel to McGee, April 9, 1966, box 136, folder 1, McGee Papers.

60. McGee to Spiegel, April 18, 1966, box 146, folder 1, McGee Papers.

61. Jim Fagan to Marian M. Nilson, February 1, 1966, "Aides Files: Manatos," box 11, LBJ Presidential Papers, LBJ Library.

62. Marble and Mullings, *Let Nobody Turn Us Around*, 470, 479.

63. Burrough, *Days of Rage*, 39.

64. Williams, *Negroes with Guns*, 39.

65. Williams, *Negroes with Guns*, 32.

66. Manchester, *Glory and the Dream*, 1305.

67. McGee to Frank Calkins, August 17, 1966, box 116, folder 3, McGee Papers.

68. *Congressional Record*, September 29, 1966, 24361.

69. Strannigan interviews, number 2, September 16, 1989, 8; Interviews with Gale McGee/Oral History, box 958, McGee Papers.

70. "Arrogance of Dissent," *Newsweek*, July 18, 1966.

71. "Morgenthau: Communism Not Main Foreign Policy Problem," *Daily Illini*, February 22, 1967, 1.

72. Robert Welch, "Truth about Vietnam," *American Opinion*, 1967, box 164, folder 2, McGee Papers.

73. "GWM Response to Welch 'Truth about Vietnam,'" box 164, folder 2, McGee Papers.

74. Marvin Tishtamer to McGee, April 30, 1967, box 164, folder 2, McGee Papers.

75. William L. Simmons to Dick Cook, McGee's administrative assistant, May 5, 1967, box 164, folder 2, McGee Papers.

76. "Children of Vietnam," reprint, *Ramparts Extra,* January 1967.

77. J. Fred Rippy to McGee, April 2, 1967, and McGee's response, April 11, 1967, box 164, folder 4, McGee Papers.

78. "McGee, Gale W., Bibliography File," U.S. Senate Historical Office.

79. United Press International story, "Subject McGovern and McGee," June 21, 1967, box 164, folder 6, McGee Papers.

80. "Wyoming's McGee Is One Liberal Who Supports the War, *Denver Post,* January 30, 1967.

81. Miller to McGee, June 4, 1967, box 164, folder 6, McGee Papers.

82. *Bridge to the Sun,* "Mariko," http://bridgetothesun.org/?page_id=15, accessed July 12, 2015.

83. "Memorandum for the President" re: Sunday TV discussion shows, February 25, 1967, box 262, White House Central File, LBJ Papers, LBJ Library.

84. Transcript of telephone conversation between President Johnson and Secy Dean Rusk, December 9, 1967, 10:12 AM, File: "July–December 1967" Document no. 12503, box 6, LBJ Library.

85. Telephone conversation between President Johnson and Senator Gale McGee, December 9, 1967, 11:00 AM, File: "July–December 1967" Document No. 12504–12505, box 6, LBJ Library, a recording of the conversation may be accessed at WH6712.01, Presidential Recording Program, Miller Center, University of Virginia.

12. REAPING THE WHIRLWIND

1. P. F. Sloan, "Eve of Destruction," a popular 1960s protest song.

2. Dean, *American Spiritual Culture,* 21.

3. "Confidence in Congress at Low Ebb," *Washington Post,* January 22, 1968.

4. Byrd, *Senate, 1789–1993,* Vol. 3, *Classic Speeches, 1830–1993.*

5. *Congressional Record,* January 26, 1968, s468.

6. *Congressional Record,* January 26, 1968, s469.

7. Roy Norman to McGee, telegram, January 30, 1968, box 174, folder 1, McGee Papers.

8. Arthur W. Kirchner to McGee, February 9, 1968, box 174, folder 1, McGee Papers.

9. "Vietnam War Statistics," http://www.shmoop.com/vietnam-war /statistics.html, accessed August 20, 2015.

10. Transcript of telephone conversation between President Johnson and George Ball, April 25, 1968, 10:12, document no. 12927, box 9, LBJ Library.

11. Cox, "Johnson, Lyndon Baines (1908–1973)," Encyclopedia of the Great Plains.

12. "McGee Sees Support for Johnson," *Wyoming Eagle,* March 29, 1968, 39.

13. Cox, "Johnson, Lyndon Baines (1908–1973)."

14. Frantz interview, tape 2, 16.

15. Frantz interview, tape 2, 16–17.

16. Rightmire to McGee, April 11, 1968, box 170, folder 9, McGee Papers.

17. Lee to McGee, April 12, 1968, box 170, folder 9, McGee Papers.

18. McGee to numerous constituents, April 1968, box 170, folder 9, McGee Papers.

19. *Congressional Record,* April 5, 1968, 9140.

20. Lewis to McGee, August 7, 1968, box 170, folder 8, McGee Papers.

21. McGee to Lewis, August 2, 1968, box 170, folder 8, McGee Papers.

22. United Press International wire story, January 22, 1968, box 262, White House Central File, LBJ Library.

23. *Congressional Record,* June 6, 1968, 16157.

24. "Hearings Asked on Passenger Train Halt," *Rock Springs Daily Rocket-Miner,* January 17, 1968, 1.

25. "Wyoming Will Receive Land, Water Funds," *Rock Springs Daily Rocket-Miner,* January 23, 1968, 5.

26. "McGee Supports Wild Horse Refuge," *Casper Star Tribune,* April 5, 1968, 2.

27. *Congressional Record,* July 17, 1968, 21689.

28. "GOP Poll Shows Rocky Favored," *Wyoming Eagle,* August 6, 1968, 5.

29. "Miami Violence Believed Fading," *Wyoming Eagle,* August 10, 1968, 36.

30. "Police Reports on Dem Convention Alarming," *Wyoming Eagle,* August 24, 1968, 3.

31. Email interview with author, January 31, 2015.

32. "Committeewoman Resents Being Asked to Sign Loyalty Oath," *Wyoming Eagle,* August 13, 1968, 4.

33. "McGee: Don't Hobble Next President on Asia Policy," *Wyoming Eagle,* August 21, 1968, 3.

34. "Viet War Depression, Moral Goal Lack Blamed in Suicides," *Rock Springs Daily Rocket Miner,* January 28, 1968, 2.

35. McGee to Teno Roncalio, March 19, 1968, box 186, folder 2, McGee Papers.

36. Coad to McGee, February 6, 1968, box 186, folder 2, McGee Papers.

37. McGee to Coad, March 6, 1968, box 186, folder 2, McGee Papers.

38. Cordelia Peck to McGee, Christmas card, box 189, folder 3, McGee Papers.

39. News release, June 21, 1968, box 188, folder 8, McGee Papers.

40. McGee to Merritt H. Hopkins, June 20, 1968, box 188, folder 8, McGee Papers.

41. Lederer, *Our Own Worst Enemy,* 232.

42. James P. Berry to McGee, May 22, 1968, box 188, folder 8, McGee Papers.

43. Attilio Bedont to McGee, March 11, 1968, box 189, folder 1, McGee Papers.

44. Gertrude Olsen to McGee, February 26, 1968, box 189, folder 2, McGee Papers.

45. McGee to Olsen, March 6, 1968, box 189, folder 2, McGee Papers.

46. Franz interview, 48.

47. Joseph Califano to LBJ, memo, March 8, 1968, White House Central File, box 262, LBJ Library.

48. Franz interview, 21–22.

49. LBJ to Douglas Carter, memo, September 9, 1968, White House Central File, box 262, LBJ Library.

50. Fulbright, *Arrogance of World Power*, 51.

51. McGee, *Responsibilities of World Power*, 31–32.

52. McGee, *Responsibilities of World Power*, 33.

53. McGee, *Responsibilities of World Power*, 49, citing "The President's News Conference of April 7, 1954, *Public Papers of the Presidents: Dwight D. Eisenhower*, 1954, 383.

54. McGee, *Responsibilities of World Power*, 234–35.

55. McGee, *Responsibilities of World Power*, 130.

56. Weiner, *One Man against the World*, 4.

57. Thomas, *Being Nixon*, 247.

58. Farrell, *Richard Nixon*, 342–43; Weiner, *One Man against the World*, 1–3.

59. Hughes, *Chasing Shadows*, 62.

13. IT'S NICE TO HAVE DICK NIXON TO KICK AROUND AGAIN

1. Greene, Joseph W. Alsop Oral History Interview, 37.

2. "McGee Asks Americans to Support Nixon," *Wyoming Eagle*, January 21, 1969, 4.

3. "Address: Vietnam Peace Initiatives by Richard M. Nixon," May 14, 1969, 3, box 198, folder 1, McGee Papers.

4. Karnow, *Vietnam: A History*, 593–594.

5. McGee, Address to the American Association of School Administrators, August 21, 1969, 3, box 202, folder 1, McGee Papers.

6. *Congressional Record*, October 14, 1969, 29825.

7. *Congressional Record*, October 20, 1969, 30544.

8. "Won't Go; Weary GIs Reply to Battle Order," *Denver Post*, August 25, 1969, 1.

9. Cormack to McGee, September 29, 1969, box 213, folder 2, McGee Papers.

10. "Wold Named 'Man of the Year,'" *Wyoming Eagle*, January 1, 1970, 2.

11. "McGovern: 'McGee's Role a Big One,'" *Wyoming Eagle*, January 17, 1970, 5.

12. Various letters, box 75, folder 7, McGee Papers.

13. "1964 Wilderness Act," http://www.foresthistory.org/ASPNET/policy /Wilderness/1964_Wilderness.aspx accessed September 25, 2015.

14. Included in the 1964 Act were the Bridger, North Absaroka, Teton, and Washakie Wilderness Areas, http://www.wilderness.net/index.cfm?fuse= NWPS&sec=stateView&state=WY, accessed September 18, 2015.

15. Sale, *Green Revolution*, 8, 23.

16. "McGee Warns against Strike," *Wyoming Eagle*, March 17, 1970, 4.

17. "1970 Postal Strike," Smithsonian's National Postal Museum Blog, postalmuseumblog.si.edu/2010/03/the-1970-postal-strike.html, accessed October 28, 2015.

18. "McGee: Strike a Crisis," *Wyoming Eagle*, March 21, 1970, 1.

19. "Gossman Blames McGee in Strike," *Wyoming Eagle*, March 24, 1970, 4.

20. "McGee: Pay Link to PO Plan Unfair," *Wyoming Eagle*, March 24, 1970, 3.

21. "Nixon Proclaims U.S. Emergency," *Wyoming Eagle*, March 24, 1970, 1.

22. "Senators Break Postal Deadlock," *Washington Post*, May 14, 1970, A31.

23. "McGee Terms Postal Pact 'Reasonable,'" *Wyoming Eagle*, April 3, 1970, 4.

24. "Postmaster Says Thanks to McGee," *Wyoming Eagle*, April 7, 1970, 4.

25. "Postmaster Says Thanks to McGee," *Wyoming Eagle*, April 7, 1970, 82.

26. Woodward, *Last of the President's Men*, 77.

27. "McGee Supporting Nixon, Often Has Lonely Role," *Casper Star-Tribune*, May 21, 1970, 1.

28. Weiner, *One Man against the World*," 84.

29. Haldeman, *Haldeman Diaries*, 153.

30. "President Nixon's Speech on Cambodia April 30, 1970," http://sites .temple.edu/immerman/president-nixons-speech-on-cambodia-april -30–1970/, accessed September 21, 2015.

31. "McGee Hold Judgment on Move into Cambodia," *Wyoming Eagle*, May 2, 1970, 3.

32. "Dem Coalition Censures Cambodian Move," *Wyoming Eagle*, May 5, 1970, 4.

33. "Gov. May Face Antiwar Protests," *Wyoming Eagle*, May 6, 1970, 4.

34. "Violence Is Averted in Flag Dispute at U of W," *Wyoming Eagle*, May 7, 1970, 1.

35. "McGee Calls on Young People to Help Get Voters to the Polls," *Wyoming Eagle*, May 9, 1970, 1.

36. "UW Cambodia Resolution Fails," *Wyoming Eagle*, May 9, 1970, 4.

37. "Svilar Says He Favors Primary Opposition to Senator McGee," *Wyoming Eagle*, May 12, 1970, 3.

38. "McGee Feels Challenge Is Good for Party," *Wyoming Eagle,* June 10, 1970, 4.

39. "Svilar Says Even If He Loses He Can't Support McGee on Viet War," *Wyoming Eagle,* June 23, 1970, 1.

40. "Svilar Questions U.S. Priorities," *Laramie Daily Boomerang,* July 1, 1970, 1, 15.

41. "Svilar Vote Will Display State's War Sentiment," *Laramie Daily Boomerang,* August 5, 1970, 6.

42. "Tuesday Crucial for Wyoming," *Casper Star-Tribune,* August 16, 1970, 6.

43. "Canvass Changes No Winners," *Rock Springs Rocket Miner,* September 3, 1970, 1.

44. Morrissey interview, 55.

45. FBI memorandum, Mr. Bishop to M. A. Jones, August 12, 1970, McGee's FBI file, not yet assigned a box, McGee Papers.

46. Donner, *Age of Surveillance,* 425.

47. "McGee Links Car Photos, Private Eye," *Washington Post,* September 10, 1970, B10.

48. Notes, Robert F. Kennedy, box 956, McGee Papers.

49. "Mrs. Stuart's Game," *Washington Post,* October 28, 1972, B2.

50. "Agnew to Hit Trail in Wyoming: GOP Seeks to Unseat Incumbent Gale McGee," *Baltimore Sun,* August 31, 1970, A7.

51. "Political Smears Warming Up," *Washington Post,* October 23, 1970, *Congressional Record,* December 18, 1970, 42486.

52. Jack Anderson, "Mudslinging Boomeranged in 1970," Washington Merry-Go-Round, *Washington Post,* January 29, 1971, D15.

53. "Senate Contest Sparks State," *Rock Springs Rocket-Miner,* November 3, 1970, 1.

54. "Shed a Tear for Poor Old Wyoming," *Jackson Hole Guide,* January 29, 1970, 5.

55. Hamilton, "Five Parting Words on Tom Bell."

56. McGee to David Deike of Laramie, March 13, 1972, box 286, folder 4, McGee Papers.

57. Mike Leon to McGee, April 2, 1971, box 254, folder 1, McGee Papers.

58. Becker to McGee, March 31, 1971, box 254, folder 1, McGee Papers.

59. Swanson, *Bitterroot & Mr. Brandborg,* 1–2.

60. Notes on back of photograph marked "Finis Mitchell Photo," box 286, folder 1, McGee Papers.

61. Notes on back of photograph marked "Finis Mitchell Photo."

62. McGee to Senator Frank Church, June 9, 1971, Series 2.3 Interior, box 2, folder 3, Church Papers, Boise State University.

63. "The U.S. Forest Service: Smokey's Strip Miners," *Washington Monthly*, December 1971, 18.

64. "Clearcutting: Pressure on Congress for Decision," *Congressional Quarterly*, March 4, 1972, 492.

65. "Wyoming Senator to Probe Clearcutting Order Demise," *Salt Lake Tribune*, February 4, 1972, 2B.

66. United Press International news release, April 5, 1971, box 254, folder 1, McGee Papers.

67. McGee to Leon, April 8, 1971, box 254, folder 1, McGee Papers.

68. "Butz: I Led Fight against Timber Curbs," *Des Moines Register*, March 7, 1972, 1.

69. "Federal Land Clearcutting Halt Rejected by Senators," *Spokesman-Review*, Spokane WA, March 26, 1972, 16.

70. "Growing Concern about Forest Management," *American Forests*, March 1974, 49.

71. Leon to McGee, April 7, 1974, box 345, folder 9, McGee Papers.

72. Van Irvine, *Anybody Can Be Slow*, book jacket.

73. Van Irvine to L. J. Hunter, August 20, 1992, 1, copy provided to the author by Hunter.

74. Van Irvine to Hunter, 6.

75. Irvine, *Anybody Can Be Slow*, 298.

76. Van Irvine to Hunter, 7.

77. Holzinger, "Eagle Killings," 1.

78. Van Irvine to Hunter, 7.

79. Dennis Drabelle, *Unfair Game*," undated, http://archive.audubonmagazine.org/archives/archives0801.html, *accessed September 18, 2015*, no longer accessible.

80. "Predator Control and Related Problems," Senate Hearings before the Committee on Appropriations, 92nd Cong., 1st sess., June 1971, Government Printing Office, 146.

81. "Sluicing the Eagles," *TIME*, August 16, 1971, 153.

82. Holzinger, "Eagle Killings."

83. "Sheepmen vs. Eagles: Slaughter in the Sky," *LIFE*, August 20, 1971, 35.

84. "Predator Control and Related Problems," Senate Hearings, 4.

85. Holzinger, "Eagle Killings."

86. Holzinger, "Eagle Killings."

87. "Sluicing the Eagles."

88. Drabelle, *Unfair Game*.

89. Irvine, *Anybody Can Be Slow*, 301.

90. "Dangers of Wagon Wheel," *Casper Star Tribune*, May 10, 1972, 10.

91. "500 Discuss Wagon Wheel," *Jackson Hole Guide,* March 23, 1972, 1.

92. Hathaway to Mrs. Vincent Birr, March 21, 1972, box 2, folder 6, Wagon Wheel Information Committee Records, American Heritage Center, University of Wyoming.

93. "Hearing at Pinedale Urged on AEC Project," *Wyoming State Tribune,* March 29, 1972, 22.

94. McGee to Sally Mackey, April 19, 1972, box 6, folder 8, Wagon Wheel Information Committee Records, AHC.

95. McGee to Mackey, September 14, 1972, Wagon Wheel Information Committee Records, box 6, folder 8, AHC.

96. McGee to James Schlesinger, August 8, 1972, box 3, folder 5, AHC.

97. "AEC Estimates Damage from Wagon Wheel," *Casper Star-Tribune,* September 22, 1972.

98. McGee to Ray, February 20, 1973, box 316, folder 6, McGee Papers.

99. Floyd Bousman to McGee, April 25, 1974, box 346, folder 10, McGee Papers.

100. McGee to the *Pinedale Roundup,* April 2, 1974, box 4, folder 48, Wagon Wheel Information Committee Records, AHC. For an interesting look at the use of fracking stimulation technology to produce millions of cubic feet of natural gas decades after Wagon Wheel's demise, see Ann Noble, "The Jonah Field and Pinedale Anticline: A Success Story," http://www.wyohistory.org/essays/jonah-field-and-pinedale-anticline -natural-gas-success-story, accessed September 29, 2015.

101. "McGee Wins Backing on Plowshare-Blast Ban," *Denver Post,* May 31, 1974.

102. Newspaper clipping from unidentified, undated paper, Personal Collection of Elizabeth Strannigan, Scrapbook, July 1972–February 1973, hereafter cited as Strannigan Scrapbooks.

103. Nixon Tapes, Conversation December 11, 1972, http://player.mashpedia .com/player.php?q=CDbil-EbSCU, accessed September 22, 2015.

104. "Crucial UN Vote," *New York Times,* November 30, 1972, Strannigan Scrapbooks.

105. "U.S.-Soviets Clash over UN Finances," *Washington Post,* November 17, 1972, A20.

106. "The United States and the United Nations: An Urgent Need for a Greater U.S. Commitment," Strannigan Scrapbook, July 1972–February 1973.

107. "Agreement on Ending the War and Restoring Peace in Vietnam," Office of the White House Press Secretary, January 24, 1973. Embargoes for release until January 27, 1973, Strannigan Scrapbook.

108. *Congressional Record,* January 3, 1973, 81.

109. Author's interview with Richard McCall, April 14, 2015.

110. "China: Report of a Special Congressional Delegation," U.S. Government Printing Office (July 1973), 13.
111. Lankford, *Last American Aristocrat*, 380.
112. Author's interview with Tom Korologos, October 16, 2014.
113. Memorandum of Conversation: President Nixon and Congressional Delegation, June 30, 1973, National Security Adviser's Memoranda of Conversations Collection, Gerald R. Ford Presidential Library, https://www.fordlibrarymuseum.gov/library/document/0314/1552590.pdf, accessed September 15, 2015.
114. "Senator's Wife Relates Her Views of China Visit," *Casper Star-Tribune*, August 4, 1973, 13.
115. Strannigan interview #8, January 20, 1990, 17; Interviews with Gale McGee/Oral History, box 958, McGee Papers.
116. Strannigan interview #9, February 24, 1990, 9; Interviews with Gale McGee/Oral History, box 958, McGee Papers.
117. Strannigan interview #8, January 20, 1990, 17; Interviews with Gale McGee/Oral History, box 958, McGee Papers.
118. "Government Footed Bill for Mrs. McGee's Trip," *Casper Star-Tribune*, August 3, 1973, 2.
119. Notes, Diabetes, box 955, McGee Papers.
120. "Wallop Ponders Governor's Race," *Casper Star Tribune*, February 27, 1974, 1.
121. "Congress Project: Citizens Look at Congress," August 1972, McGee biographical file, U.S. Senate Historical Office; Glazer, *Citizens Look at Congress.* vol. 9.
122. "Beautification of U.S. Senator," *Sunday Bulletin*, September 14, 1975, 8.
123. Iriberry Brothers to McGee, November 28, 1973, box 366, folder 3, McGee Papers.
124. U.S. Department of Labor to McGee, December 21, 1973, box 366, folder 3, McGee Papers.
125. "McGee Called Internationalist," *Laramie Daily Boomerang*, October 22, 1972, 2.
126. "Senator McGee on Registration and the Causes of Voter Alienation," guest editorial by McGee, *Washington Post*, February 11, 1973, D7.
127. "Uninvolved Called 'Chicken-spined,'" *Washington Post*, August 29, 1972, B9.
128. "McGee Assails Registration Voting System," *Rocky Mountain News*, February 4, 1973, 12.
129. Rosenstone, "Effect of Registration Laws on Voter Turnout," fn. 23.

130. "Drive Reopened for Mail Voter Registration," *Washington Post*, February 11, 1973.

131. McGee to Senator Church containing "Outline of Voter Registration Bill," March 7, 1972, Series 1.1 Legislation, box 28, folder 4, Senator Frank Church Papers, Boise State University.

132. McGee to Church containing "Outline of Voter Registration Bill," March 7, 1972.

133. David Minton to Robert McGee, July 30, 1992, from private collection of Robert McGee.

134. "McGee's Voter Registration by Mail Wins Senate OK," *Rocky Mountain News*, May 10, 1973, 30.

135. Transcript of Motor Voter Bill Signing Ceremony, White House South Lawn, May 20, 1993, News Transcripts, Inc., 1, from private collection of Robert McGee.

136. "Wyoming Voter Registration and Voter Turnout Statistics," Election Division, Wyoming Secretary of State, http://soswy.state.wy.us /Elections/Docs/VoterProfile.pdf, accessed September 20, 2015.

137. All information in this section relative to the Lazy G was obtained in the author's email interview with Robert McGee, January 14, 2016.

138. Gale McGee's "Senate Summary," October, 1973, 1, Gale McGee Newsletters, box 588, McGee Papers.

139. "Old Grouch," cartoon referred to Nixon statement when he lost the 1962 California gubernatorial contest. He told the press, "You won't have Dick Nixon to kick around anymore."

140. "Senator Requests Party Wide Effort," *Casper Star Tribune*, February 16, 1974, 13.

141. "McGee Calls for End of Impeachment Talk," *Casper Star Tribune*, May 19, 1973, 3.

142. McGee to Lori McGee, May 18, 1973, box 324, folder 1, McGee Papers.

143. "McGee Denounces Senators Talking of Impeachment," *Wyoming Eagle*, November 3, 1973, 16.

144. "Cover-up Prosecutor," TIME, October 21, 1974, box 352, folder 9, McGee Papers.

145. A. H. Trautwein to McGee, October 26, 1973, and other letters, "Impeachment of President: Against," box 322, folder 7, McGee papers.

146. "Impeachment of the President: For," box 323, folders 2 and 3, McGee Papers.

147. McGee to Charles Bell, November 2, 1973, box 323, folder 2, McGee Papers.

148. "Wyoming Senators Say Impeachment Talk Early," *Laramie Daily Boomerang*, October 24, 1973, 1.

149. "McGee Urges Corporations to Help Restore Confidence," *Laramie Daily Boomerang*, October 26, 1973, 9.

150. "Two Key Watergate Tapes Never Actually Existed," *Wyoming Eagle*, November 1, 1973, 1.

151. "Haig Says 'Sinister Force' May Have Erased Tapes," *Laramie Daily Boomerang*, December 7, 1973, 1.

152. "Tape Erasure Story," *Atlanta Constitution*, December 2, 1973, 5A.

153. "President Issues 1,308-Page Watergate Tape Transcripts," *Rock Springs Daily Rocket-Miner*, May 1, 1974, 1.

154. "Transcripts Indicate Nixon Wasn't Told about Hush Money," *Rock Springs Daily Rocket-Miner*, May 3, 1974, 2.

155. Thomas, *Being Nixon*, 671.

156. "McGee Asks Nixon to Reexamine," *Casper Star Tribune*, May 12, 1974, 1.

157. "Gale McGee's Senate Summary," May 1974, Gale McGee Newsletters, box 588, McGee Papers.

158. "Eight Justices Hear Historic Arguments," *Casper Star Tribune*, July 9, 1974, 1.

159. *United States v. Nixon*, 418 U.S. 683 (1974).

160. Mary McGrory, "Watergate as Theater: Neal's Final Scene," *Congressional Record*, January 15, 1975, 463.

161. McGee, *Responsibilities of World Power*, 130.

162. "McGee May Reconsider Nixon Support," undated newspaper clipping of an Associated Press story, Strannigan Scrapbook 1974–75.

163. Nixon Tapes, no. 949-7, July 12, 1973, Nixon Presidential Library, https://www.nixonlibrary.gov/forresearchers/find/tapes/tape949/tape949.php, accessed September 30, 2015.

14. WYOMING'S WAY OF LIFE IS AT STAKE

1. Ford, *A Time to Heal*, 1.

2. "Proclamation 4311, Granting Pardon to Richard Nixon, September 8, 1974, Public Papers of the Presidents Gerald R. Ford, U.S. Government Printing Office (1975), 103.

3. "Appearance by the President before the Subcommittee on Criminal Justice, House Judiciary Committee," October 17, 1974, digitized from box 3, White House Press Releases, Gerald R. Ford Presidential Library, https://www.fordlibrarymuseum.gov/library/document/0248/whpr19741017–023.pdf, accessed September 26, 2015.

4. "Pardon Gets State Reaction," *Sheridan Press*, September 10, 1974, 1.

5. McGee to Vincent J. Siren, September 23, 1974, box 352, folder 8, McGee Papers.

6. McGee to Pearson, September 23, 1974, box 352, folder 8, McGee Papers.

7. "McGee Criticizes the Tearing Apart of CIA," *Rock Springs Rocket Miner*, March 27, 1976, 1.

8. Memorandum for the president, July 10, 1975, Intelligence: Appointment of CIA Director, box 5, Gerald R. Ford Presidential Library.

9. Memorandum for the president, July 10, 1975.

10. Ford, *A Time to Heal*, 325.

11. *Congressional Record*, January 27, 1976, 1170, 1173.

12. "Stan Nominated for Judge's Spot," *Casper Star-Tribune*, January 16, 1975, 1.

13. News release from the White House, April 4, 1975, Series 3.3 Executive Branch, box 132, folder 7, Church Papers.

14. Shoemaker to McGee, March 28, 1975, box 391, McGee Papers.

15. News release from Frank Church, April 8, 1975, Series 3.3 Executive Branch, box 132, folder 7, Church Papers.

16. Patrick E. O'Donnell, special assistant to the president, to Church, April 14, 1975, with attached document titled "The Hathaway Administration and the Environment, 1967–1974," Series 3.3 Executive Branch, box 132, folder 7, Church Papers.

17. "Analysis of 'Hathaway Administration and the Environment 1976–1974': Prepared by the Environmental Defense Fund, April 21, 1975, Series 3.3 Executive Branch," box 132, folder 7, Church Papers.

18. Brief prepared by the Office of U.S. Senator Gary Hart (D-CO), and distributed to members of the Senate, May 2, 1975, Series 3.3 Executive Branch, box 132, folder 7, Church Papers; all other allegations contained in "The Need for a Great Conservator as Secretary of the Interior," testimony of Anthony Wayne Smith, president of the National Park and Conservation Commission, Series 3.3 Executive Branch, box 132, folder 7, Church Papers.

19. "Memorandum" from Senator Henry M. Jackson, Chairman, Senate Committee on Interior and Insular Affairs, "to identify the principal concerns expressed by witnesses respecting Governor Hathaway's nomination," May 2, 1975, Series 3.3 Executive Branch, box 132, folder 7, Church Papers.

20. Author's interview with former Hathaway aide Jack Speight, August 4, 2015.

21. Statement of Senator Gale W. McGee on Nomination of Stanley K. Hathaway, April 21, 1975, box 391, folder 4, McGee Papers.

22. Gary Hart, news release, May 2, 1975, Series 3.3 Executive Branch, box 132, folder 7, Church Papers.

23. "Hathaway Clears Senate," *Casper Star-Tribune*, June 12, 1975, 1.

24. "Resignation of Secretary Hathaway," *Congressional Record*, July 26, 1975, 25095.

25. "Strip-Mining Regulation Test Set in House," *Washington Post*, December 9, 1974.

26. Wyoming Data Handbook published by Wyoming Department of Economic Planning and Development (1971), 100, and Wyoming Data Handbook published by Wyoming Department of Administration and Fiscal Control (1977), 20.

27. Phil Roberts, "Boom and Bust in Wyoming," http://www.uwyo.edu/ahc /energyboom/boom-bust.htm, accessed November 3, 2015.

28. Helena Huntington Smith, "The Wringing of the West," *Washington Post*, February 17, 1975, *Congressional Record*, February 18, 1975, 3345.

29. *Congressional Record*, February 18, 1975, 3345.

30. *Congressional Quarterly Almanac*, 1973, 615.

31. "Memorandum Withholding Approval of Surface Mining Control and Reclamation Legislation, December 30, 1974, Public Papers of the Presidents: Administration of Gerald R. Ford, U.S. Government Printing Office (1975), 780.

32. Memorandum withholding approval of surface mining control and reclamation legislation, December 30, 1974, 781.

33. *Congressional Record*, February 18, 1975, 3345.

34. Robert L. Wallick to McGee, February 5, 1975, box 390, folder 5, McGee Papers.

35. *Congressional Record*, February 18, 1975, 3345.

36. *Congressional Record*, March 11, 1975, 6135.

37. "The State of the Union, Annual Message to Congress," January 19, 1978, Public Papers of the Presidents: Administration of Jimmy Carter, U.S. Government Printing Office (1979), 115.

38. "Veto of Federal Coal Leasing Amendments Bill," July 3, 1976, Public Papers of the Presidents: Gerald R. Ford, U.S. Government Printing Office (1979), 1958.

39. *Congressional Record*, August 3, 1976, 25203, 25205.

40. "Wyoming State Government Revenue Forecast," Consensus Revenue Estimating Group, October 2015, 15, http://eadiv.state.wy.us/creg /GreenCREG_Oct15.pdf, accessed January 14, 2016.

41. Henry Kissinger, "America's Destiny: The Global Context," University of Wyoming, February 4, 1976, *Department of State Bulletin* 74, no. 1914, March 1, 1976, 249.

42. Kissinger, *World Order*, 296.

43. Piereson, *Camelot and the Cultural Revolution*, xv.

15. TIME FOR A CHANGE

1. Author's email interview with Philip White, June 15, 2015.

2. "Class of '58 Survivors among Senators Up in '76," *Washington Star*, July 30, 1975, A-3.

3. "Democrats Expected to Keep Senate Control in '76," *Washington Post*, November 16, 1975, A2.

4. "Wyoming Intelligencer," *Casper Star Tribune*, January 29, 1976, 5.

5. "Is There a Republican Likely?" *Powell Tribune*, October 30, 1975, 4.

6. Wyoming Intelligencer, *Casper Star Tribune*, February 6, 1976, 4.

7. "Field Clears for Wallop," *Riverton Ranger*, March 23, 1976, 4.

8. Dick Cook to Image, Inc., July 25, 1975, Campaign 1975 and assorted info, box 923, McGee Papers.

9. "Wallop Senate Drive," campaign outline, Campaign Literature, box 175, Wallop Papers, AHC.

10. "Political Consultants: The New Kingmakers," *Washington Post*, June 5, 1982, A6.

11. "Wallop Senate Drive," campaign outline, Campaign Literature, box 175, Wallop Papers.

12. "Wallop Senate Drive Finance Committee Presentation," Campaign Literature, box 175, Wallop Papers.

13. "Wallop Senate Drive Finance Committee Presentation."

14. "To Raise a Politician to the Heights, Make Ads with Helicopters, Music," *Wall Street Journal*, September 24, 1979, 1.

15. Nicholas, *Becoming Western*, 114–15, 3–4.

16. Nicholas, *Becoming Western*, 114–15.

17. Larson, *History of Wyoming*, 2nd ed., 573.

18. "Wallop Senate Drive Finance Committee Presentation."

19. McGee to Nancy Siggins, April 19, 1976, box 408, folder 1, McGee Papers.

20. McGee to Tom Phipps, April 27, 1976, box 408, folder 1, McGee Papers.

21. Jason Long to McGee, July 19, 1976, box 408, folder 1, McGee Papers.

22. "Group Warns Congress Pay Raise Could Be '76 Campaign Issue," *Chicago Tribune*, August 31, 1975, 5.

23. "McGee Gets Setback," *Casper Star Tribune*, September 19, 1975, 8.

24. Jimmy Carter's acceptance speech, Madison Square Garden, New York City, July 15, 1976, http://www.4president.org/speeches /carter1976acceptance.htm, accessed October 10, 2015.

25. "Wallop: Cut Federal Regulations," *Rawlins Daily Times*, September 4, 1976, 1.

26. "Wallop Slams Bureaucracies," *Riverton Ranger*, April 27, 1976, 1.

27. "McGee Criticizes the Tearing Apart of CIA," *Rock Springs Rocket Miner*, March 27, 1976, 1.

28. "Wallop: Cut Federal Regulations," *Rawlins Daily Times*, September 4, 1976, 1.

29. "McGee Stresses Seniority," *Riverton Ranger*, September 22, 1976, 2.

30. "McGee Runs for Fourth Term," *Riverton Ranger*, September 9, 1976, 11A.

31. "McGee Says Newcomer Will Lose State Cause," *Laramie Daily Boomerang*, September 11, 1976, 4.

32. "Wallop Says McGee Is 'Desperate,'" *Casper Star-Tribune*, October 2, 1976, 15.

33. "Wallop: We Need Leadership That Understands Wyoming," *Riverton Ranger*, September 23, 1976, 1.

34. "Wallop Hits McGee's Legislative Record," *Sheridan Press*, September 25, 1976, 1.

35. "McGee Campaigns on Clout," *Jackson Hole News*, October 6, 1976, 18.

36. Nicholas, *Becoming Western*, 127.

37. "Don't Count on Presidential Coattails in 33 U.S. Senate Races," *Washington Star*, September 19, 1976, A-5.

38. "GOP May Pick Up Senate Seats," *Laramie Daily Boomerang*, October 5, 1976, 10.

39. McGee to Rosenthal, October 9, 1976, McGee 1976, Part 1, box 924, McGee Papers.

40. "Gale William McGee Fact Sheet," *Sundance Times*, October 28, 1976, 4.

41. "Gale McGee: The Bureaucrat's Best Friend," *Jackson Hole Guide*, October 28, 1976, 28.

42. "Hathaway Touts Wallop," *Rock Springs Daily Rocket-Miner*, October 21, 1976, 8-A.

43. "Wallop, Roncalio Favored by State Conservationists," *High Country News*, November 19, 1976, 4.

44. "Senate Races—II," *New York Times*, October 21, 1976, A10.

45. "Wallop, Roncalio Favored by State Conservationists."

46. Larson, *History of Wyoming*, 2nd ed., 573.

47. "Dem 'Shocked' by Anti-McGee Ads," *Rawlins Daily Times*, October 27, 1976, 12.

48. "What I'll Remember about the Campaign of 1976," *Wyoming State Journal,* November 4, 1976, 6.

49. "Morning After," *Wyoming State Tribune,* November 3, 1976, 4.

50. Author's interview with Robert McGee, January 19, 2016.

51. Wallop to McGee, November 19, 1976, Related Correspondence, box 923, McGee Papers.

52. "Wallop: Win Like Alice in Wonderland," *Laramie Boomerang,* November 4, 1976, 1.

53. "Portable Potty Ad Proves Potent in Wallop Victory," *Rocky Mountain News,* November 7, 1976, 5.

54. "Editorially Speaking Checks and Balances," *Riverton Ranger,* November 3, 1976, 4.

55. "Editorially Speaking Why McGee Lost," *Riverton Ranger,* November 9, 1976, 4.

56. "A Message from the Voters," *Wyoming State Tribune,* November 4, 1976, 4.

57. "God-speed Sen. McGee," *Casper Star-Tribune,* November 14, 1976, 4.

58. "Wyoming Politics and Government," *Wyoming News,* December 1, 1976, 8.

59. Piereson, *Camelot and the Cultural Revolution,* 1.

60. Nicholas, *Becoming Western,* 130.

61. Morrissey interview, 73.

62. Morrissey interview, 102.

63. McGee to Ray Hill, December 13, 1982, Wyoming Politics, box 954, McGee Papers.

64. Strannigan interviews, interview number 9, February 24, 1990, 11; Interviews with Gale McGee/Oral History, box 958, McGee Papers.

16. A THIRD CAREER

1. "Nominations Submitted to the Senate," March 14, 1977, Public Papers of the Presidents: Administration of Jimmy Carter, U.S. Government Printing Office, 1977, 465.

2. U.S. Senate Committee on Foreign Relations, Hearing, Nomination of Gale W. McGee to Be Permanent Representative to the Organization of American States, March 17, 1977, 2.

3. Nomination of Gale W. McGee, March 17, 1977, 16.

4. Nomination of Gale W. McGee, March 17, 1977, 4, 26.

5. Association for Diplomatic Studies and Training, Kennedy interview, 20.

6. Herz, *Organization of American States,* 11.

7. Nomination of Gale W. McGee, 13.

8. "Conversation with Frank Ortiz," notes from January 14, 1977, personal collection of Elizabeth Strannigan.

9. McCullough, *Path between the Seas*, 11.

10. Carter, *Keeping Faith*, 155, 159.

11. "Should the U.S. Give Up the Panama Canal?" *U.S. News and World Report*, 1978, 37.

12. *Congressional Record*, April 8, 1976, 5217.

13. "State Department Is 'Selling' Canal Treaties," *Washington Post*, February 2, 1978, A1.

14. "Ambassadorial Beginning," McGee Memoir Notes, personal collection of Elizabeth Strannigan.

15. Association for Diplomatic Studies and Training, Kennedy interview, 22.

16. "McGee Lashes Out at Reagan," *Riverton Ranger*, February 7, 1978, 10.

17. "Ex-Sen. McGee Calls Treaties Crucial," *Omaha World Herald*, February 11, 1978, personal collection of Elizabeth Strannigan.

18. "Canal Treaties Critical to World Image: McGee," *Sunday Dispatch*, April 16, 1978, 8.

19. "Canal Zone Never U.S. Holding, McGee Says," *Daily Universe*, Brigham Young University, March 24, 1978, personal collection of Elizabeth Strannigan.

20. "McGee Tells CSU Group Why He Favors Canal Pact," *Ft. Collins Coloradoan*, March 2, 1978, personal collection of Elizabeth Strannigan.

21. "Wyoming's McGee Has Canal on His Mind," *Branding Iron*, February 9, 1978, box 966, McGee Papers.

22. "Ambassador McGee Describes OAS Role," *Laramie Boomerang*, September 5, 1979, 1.

23. Carter, *Keeping Faith*, 176, 178.

24. Handwritten note from President Carter, May 1, 1978, personal collection of Robert McGee.

25. Speech by McGee before the Tampa Bay World Affairs Council, October 20, 1978, personal collection of Robert McGee.

26. "OAS Ambassador Lectures," *Le Provocateur*, May 4, 1979, 1.

27. Association for Diplomatic Studies and Training, Kennedy interview, 15.

28. Unclassified cable, subject "OASGA Media Reaction," box 918, folder: "OAS General Assembly, Grenada, June 14–24, 1977, McGee Papers.

29. "Ambassador in Cheyenne Says Somoza Must Go," *Wyoming Eagle*, June 24, 1979, 1.

30. "It Was Something out of a B Movie," Moments in U.S. Diplomatic History, Association for Diplomatic Studies and Training, http://adst.org/2013/06/it-was-something-out-of-a-b-movie-the-1980-coup-in-bolivia/, accessed November 6, 2015.

31. "Bolivian Democracy, Backed by U.S., Collapses in Coup," *Washington Post*, November 2, 1979, 1.

32. "Students Crowd Theater to Hear Ambassador McGee," *College of the Sequoias*, May 9, 1980, personal collection of Elizabeth Strannigan.

33. "Misc Tidbits," McGee Memoir Notes, 5, personal collection of Elizabeth Strannigan.

34. Reagan to McGee, May 27, 1981, personal collection of Robert McGee.

35. "Former Senator Gale McGee Takes Washington Post," *Wyoming Eagle*, December 5, 1981, 1.

36. "Gale McGee Opens Consulting Firm," *Casper Star Tribune*, December 15, 1981.

37. Thompson, *Refugee Workers in the Indochina Exodus*, 15–153.

38. "Indochinese Refugee Panel," U.S. Department of State press release, September 30, 1985, box 963, McGee Papers.

39. Department of State Briefing Book, table 2, box 963, McGee Papers.

40. "Briefing: A Refugee Mission," *New York Times*, November 3, 1985, box 963, McGee Papers; also see http://www.nytimes.com/1985/11/03/us/briefing-a-fefugees-mission.html, accessed November 18, 2015.

41. "Report of the Indochinese Refugee Panel," U.S. Department of State Publication 9476, April 1986, 8, box 963, McGee Papers.

42. Don Irwin, "Panel Urges Revision of Immigration Policy for Southeast Asians," *Los Angeles Times*, April 19, 1986.

43. Report of the Indochinese Refugee Panel, 21.

44. Report of the Indochinese Refugee Panel, 22.

45. Alan K. Simpson, "Eulogy for Gale W. McGee," Washington DC, April 11, 1992, Eulogies, box 958, McGee Papers.

46. Remarks by Robert M. McGee, American Heritage Center, University of Wyoming, October 9, 1992, 10, personal collection of Robert McGee.

EPILOGUE

1. U.S. Senate Historical Office, http://www.senate.gov/index.htm, accessed January 15, 2016.

2. "Technology and the Senate," U.S. Senate Historical Office, http://www.senate.gov/general/Features/TechnologyandtheSenate.htm, accessed January 15, 2016.

3. Nixon to Loraine McGee, April 17, 1992, from the personal collection of Robert McGee.

4. http://www.cnn.com/2015/03/10/politics/republican-senators-who-support-iran-letter/index.html, accessed November 22, 2016.

5. Shane Goldmacher, "Former Senate Leader Says Senators Spent Two-Thirds of Time Asking for Money," *National Journal*, http://www.nationaljournal.com/congress/2014/01/16/former-senate-leader-says-senators-spent-two-thirds-time-asking-money, accessed January 16, 2016.

6. "Vital Statistics on Congress, Senate Workload 80th to 113th Congresses, 1947–2013, Brookings Institute, 4, http://www.brookings.edu/~/media/Research/Files/Reports/2013/07/vital-statistics-congress-mann- ornstein/Vital-Statistics-Chapter-6—Legislative-Productivity-in-Congress- and -Workload_UPDATE.pdf?la=en, accessed January 14, 2016.

Bibliography

MANUSCRIPTS AND ARCHIVES

Albertson Library, Boise State University

Church, Frank, Papers. Special Collections and Archives, MS56. Collection includes correspondence, memoranda, speeches, articles, press releases, reports, studies, legislation, case files, campaign files, scrapbooks, photos, films, audiotapes, and other papers, relating chiefly to Church's career as a U.S. Senator from Idaho, 1956–1980.

American Heritage Center (AHC), University of Wyoming

Hardy, Deborah, Papers. Collection no. 400039. The collection includes research material used to publish her book on the history of the University of Wyoming, *Wyoming University: The First 100 Years, 1886–1986.* University of Wyoming, 1986.

Harrison, William Henry, Papers. Collection no. 1681, 1983-11-01. Collection includes his congressional files representing his years in the U.S. House of Representatives from 1951 to 1969.

Hickey, J. J., Papers. Acc. no. 9868. Collection includes materials related to Hickey's term as governor of Wyoming and U.S. senator.

Larson, T. A., Papers. Collection no. 400029. Collection includes materials from his tenure as a professor at the University of Wyoming as well as his service in the Wyoming State House of Representatives from 19676–1984.

McGee, Gale W., Papers. Collection no. 09800, Collection includes materials covering his life and careers as a professor, U.S. senator, and ambassador.

O'Mahoney, Joseph C., Papers. Collection no. 00275. Collection includes files from his years as a U.S. Senator from Wyoming.

Simpson, Milward, Papers. Collection no. 26. The collection includes
files from his careers as a lawyer, governor, and U.S. senator from
Wyoming.

University of Wyoming President's Office Records, Collection no.
510000. The collection includes correspondence, reports, memos,
minutes of meetings and other items pertaining to the administration
of the University of Wyoming.

Wallop, Malcolm, Papers. Accession no. 8011. Collection includes materials from Wallop's eighteen years in the U.S. Senate and his Senate
campaigns.

Association for Diplomatic Studies and Training

Foreign Affairs Oral History Project. Stuart Kennedy, interview of Gale
W. McGee, December 9, 1988, http://www.adst.org/OH%20TOCs
/McGee,%20Gale.toc.pdf

John F. Kennedy Presidential Library, Boston

Kennedy, John F., Papers. Collection includes personal and official
papers covering his service in Congress and as president. Also includes
papers chronicling JFK's interactions with Senator Gale W. McGee.

Greene, Roberta W. Joseph W. Alsop Oral History Interview—RFK #2,
6/22/1971, June 22, 1971, http://archive1.jfklibrary.org/RFKOH
/Alsop,%20Joseph%20W/RFKOH-JWA-02/RFKOH-JWA-02-TR.pdf,
accessed September 24, 2015.

Stern, Sheldon. Interview with Gale McGee, November 16, 1982, 25, John
F. Kennedy Library Oral History Program, http://archive1.jfklibrary
.org/JFKOH/McGee,%20Gale%20William/JFKOH-GWM-01/JFKOH
-GWM-01-TR.pdf

Lyndon Baines Johnson Presidential Library, University of Texas

Johnson, Lyndon Baines, Presidential Papers. Includes papers and other
documents evidencing LBJ's relationship with Senator Gale W. McGee.
The papers of Drew Pearson are also a part of the LBJ Presidential
Library collection.

Miller Center, University of Virginia

LBJ Oral Histories, phone conversations with McGee.

Richard M. Nixon, Oral Histories, White House tape recordings.

Wyoming State Archives

Barrett, Frank A., Papers. Collection no. H97–33. Wyoming State Archives
Office, Cheyenne. Collection includes mostly newspaper clippings covering Barrett's political campaigns.

Digest of House Journal of the Wyoming State Legislature, 37th State Legislature, 1963.

Digest of Senate Journal of the Wyoming State Legislature, 37th State Legislature, 1963.

PUBLISHED WORKS

Anderson, Clinton, with Milton Viorst. *Outsider in the Senate.* New York: World, 1970.

Appy, Christian G. *Patriots: The Vietnam War Remembered from All Sides.* New York: Viking, 2003.

Ashby, LeRoy, and Rod Gramer. *Fighting the Odds: The Life of Senator Frank Church.* Pullman: Washington State University Press, 1994.

BACM Research. "Pentagon Papers: The Complete Report Unredacted," available through http://www.paperlessarchives.com on a CD.

Baker, Richard A. *Conservation Politics: The Senate Career of Clinton P. Anderson.* Albuquerque: University of New Mexico Press, 1985.

———. "A Slap at the 'Hidden-Hand Presidency': The Senate and the Lewis Strauss Affair." *Congress and the Presidency* 14, no. 1 (Spring 1987).

———. *Traditions of the United States Senate.* Washington DC: Senate Office of Printing and Document Services, 2007.

Baker, Richard A., and Neil MacNeil. *The American Senate.* New York: Oxford University Press, 2013.

Battaglio, Stephan. *David Susskind: A Televised Life.* New York: St. Martin's Press, 2110.

Blumenthal, David, and James A. Morone. *The Heart of Power: Health and Politics in the Oval Office.* Berkeley: University of California Press, 2009.

Burrough, Bryan. *Days of Rage: America's Radical Underground, the FBI, and the Forgotten Age of Revolutionary Violence.* New York: Penguin, 2015.

Brookings Institution. "Vital Statistics on Congress, Senate Workload 80th to 113th Congresses 1947–2013." http://www.brookings.edu/~/media/Research/Files/Reports/2013/07/vital-statistics-congress-mann - ornstein/Vital-Statistics-Chapter-6—Legislative-Productivity-in-Congress - and-Workload_UPDATE.pdf?la=en, accessed January 14, 2016.

Byrd, Robert C. *The Senate, 1789–1989: Addresses on the United States Senate.* Washington: Government Printing Office, 1988.

———. *The Senate of the Roman Empire.* Honolulu: University Press of the Pacific, 2001.

———, comp. *Senate, 1789–1993.* Vol. 3: *Classic Speeches, 1830–1993.* Bicentennial ed. Washington DC: Senate Historical Office, 1994.

Caro, Robert A. *Master of the Senate: The Years of Lyndon Johnson.* New York: Vintage, 2003.

Carter, Jimmy. *Keeping Faith: Memoirs of a President.* Toronto: Bantam Books, 1982.

Christgau, John. *The Origins of the Jump Shot: Eight Men Who Shook the World of Basketball.* Lincoln: University of Nebraska Press, 1999.

Collard, Sophie. "Oliver Cromwell and Charles I Execution Sites." www .traveldarkly.com/oliver-cromwell-charles-i-london-execution-sites/ accessed November 20, 2015.

Council on Foreign Relations. "CFR History" http://www.cfr.org/about /history/cfr/.

Cox, Patrick L. "Johnson, Lyndon Baines (1908–1973)." *Encyclopedia of the Great Plains,* ed. David J. Wishart. Lincoln: University of Nebraska, Lincoln Center for Digital Research in the Humanities. http://www.lbjlib .utexas.edu/Johnson/archives.hom/speeches.hom/680331.asp, accessed July 30, 2015.

Dallek, Robert. *Lyndon B. Johnson and His Times.* New York: Oxford University Press, 1998.

———. *An Unfinished Life: John F. Kennedy, 1917–1963.* Boston: Little, Brown, 2003.

D'Antonio, Michael. *A Ball, a Dog, and a Monkey.* New York: Simon and Schuster, 2007.

Dean, William. *The American Spiritual Culture: And the Invention of Jazz, Football, and the Movies.* New York: Continuum, 2002.

Dickson, Paul. *Sputnik: The Shock of the Century.* New York: Walker, 2001.

Donner, Frank. *Age of Surveillance.* New York: Alfred A. Knopf, 1980.

Druckman, Mason. *Wayne Morse: A Political Biography.* Portland: Oregon Historical Society Press, 1997.

Farrell, John A. *Richard Nixon: The Life.* New York: Doubleday, 2017.

Ford, Gerald R. *A Time to Heal.* New York: Harper and Row, 1979.

Fulbright, J. William. *The Arrogance of Power.* New York: Random House, 1966.

Glazer, Sarah. *Citizens Look at Congress.* Washington: Grossman, 1972.

Gressley, Gene M., ed. *Voltaire and the Cowboy: The Letters of Thurman Arnold.* Boulder: Colorado Associated University Press, 1977.

Grove, Gene. *Inside the John Birch Society.* Greenwich CT: Gold Medal Books, 1961.

Guenther, Todd. "The List of Good Negroes: African American Lynchings in the Equality State." *Annals of Wyoming* 81, no. 2 (Spring 2009): 26.

Haldeman, H. R. *The Haldeman Diaries: Inside the Nixon White House.* New York: G. P. Putnam's Sons, 1994.

Hamilton, Bruce. "Five Parting Words on Tom Bell: Visionary, Advocate, Mentor, Fighter, Friend." The Bull's Eye, https://thebullseye.media/tom-bell-visionary-advocate-mentor-fighter-friend/, Accessed September 4, 2016.

Helms, Richard. *A Look over My Shoulder: A Life in the Central Intelligence Agency*. New York: Ballantine, 2003.

Herz, Monica. *The Organization of American States*. New York: Routledge, 2011.

Hinckley, John T. "The 1964 Election in Wyoming." *Western Political Quarterly* 18, no. 2, "The 1964 Elections in the West" (June 1965).

Hochschild, Adam. *King Leopold's Ghost*. Boston: Houghton Mifflin, 1998.

Holzinger, Phoebe. "The Eagle Killings." Murie Audubon newsletter *Plains and Peaks* 38, no. 6 (August–September 2004).

Honan, William H. "The Art of Oratory in the Senate of the United States." *Esquire*, May 1969.

Hughes, Ken. *Chasing Shadows: The Nixon Tapes, the Chennault Affair, and the Origins of Watergate*. Charlottesville: University of Virginia Press, 2014.

Ibach, Kim, and William Howard Moore. "The Emerging Civil Rights Movement: The 1957 Wyoming Public Accommodations Statute as a Case Study." http://www.uwyo.edu/robertshistory/civil_rights_movement .htm, accessed March 16, 2015.

Irvine, Van. *Anybody Can Be Slow*. Thermopolis WY: Irvine, 1989.

Johnson, Lady Bird. *A White House Diary*. New York: Holt, Rinehart and Winston, 1970.

Johnson, Lyndon Baines. *The Vantage Point*. New York: Holt, Rinehart and Winston, 1971.

Karnow, Stanley. *Vietnam: The First Complete Account of Vietnam at War*. New York: Viking, 1983.

Karpan, Kathleen M. "A Political History of Jack R. Gage." *Annals of Wyoming*, Fall 1976.

Kennedy, John F. *Profiles in Courage*. New York: Harper and Row, 1955.

Kissinger, Henry. *World Order*. New York: Penguin, 2014.

Lacouture, Jean. *Ho Chi Minh: A Political Biography*. New York: Random House, 1968.

Lankford, Nelson D. *The Last American Aristocrat: The Biography of Ambassador David K. E. Bruce*. Boston: Little, Brown, 1996.

Larson, T. A. *History of Wyoming*. Lincoln: University of Nebraska Press, 1965.
———. *History of Wyoming*. 2nd ed. Lincoln: University of Nebraska Press, 1990.

Lederer, William J. *Our Own Worst Enemy*. New York: Norton, 1968.

Lederer, William J., and Eugene Burdick. *The Ugly American*. New York: Norton, 1958.

Logevall, Fredrik. *Choosing War: The Lost Chance for Peace and the Escalation of War in Vietnam*. Berkeley: University of California Press, 1999.

Lyon, Peter. *Eisenhower: Portrait of the Hero*. Boston: Little, Brown, 1974

MacLysaght, Edward. *Irish Families, Their Names, Arms, and Origins*. 3rd ed. New York: Crown, 1972.

Manchester, William. *The Glory and the Dream: A Narrative History of America, 1932–1972*. Boston: Little, Brown, 1973.

Marable, Manning, and Leith Mullings, eds. *Let Nobody Turn Us Around*. Lanham MD: Rowman and Littlefield, 2000.

Mason, Mary Kay. *Laramie: Gem City of the Plains*. Dallas: Curtis Media, 1987.

Matthews, Donald R. *U.S. Senators and Their World*. New York: Norton, 1973.

McCullough, David. *The Path between the Seas*. New York: Simon and Schuster, 1977.

McGee, David. "A Family Affair." *Reporter Magazine*, March 9, 1967, 43–48.

McGee, Gale W. McGee, "A China Policy for the United States," *South Atlantic Quarterly* 53, no. 3 (June 1954).

———. "After Panama: Some Lessons and Opportunities in the Aftermath of Canal Treaties Debate." *South Atlantic Quarterly* 78, no. 1 (Winter 1979).

———. "A Debate Resumed." *American Scholar: A Quarterly for the Independent Thinker*, Spring 1950.

———. "Early Cold Wars." *Current History: The Monthly Magazine of World Affairs*, June 1950.

———. *The Responsibilities of World Power*. Washington DC: National Press, 1968.

McGovern, George. *Terry: My Daughter's Life and Death Struggle with Alcoholism*. New York: Villard, 1996.

———. *A Time of War, a Time of Peace*. New York: Random House, 1968.

McNamara, Robert S. *In Retrospect: The Tragedy and Lessons of Vietnam*. New York: Times Books–Random House, 1995.

Mendelsohn, Jack. *The Martyrs: Sixteen Who Gave Their Lives for Racial Justice*. New York: Harper and Row, 1966.

Miller, Merle. *Lyndon*. New York: G. P. Putnam's Sons, 1980.

Morgenthau, Hans. *Politics among Nations: The Struggle for Power and Peace*. New York: Knopf, 1948.

Mulloy, D. J. *The World of the John Birch Society*. Nashville: Vanderbilt University Press, 2014.

Newton, Jim. *Justice for All: Earl Warren and the Nation He Made*. New York: Riverhead, 2006.

Nicholas, Lisa J. *Becoming Western: Stories of Culture and Identity in the Cowboy State*. Lincoln: University of Nebraska Press, 2006.

Official Report of the Proceedings of the Democratic National Convention 1960. Edited by Paul A. Smith and Richard E. May. Washington DC: National Document Publishers, 1964.

Okihiro, Gary Y. *Storied Lives: Japanese American Students and World War II.* Seattle: University of Washington Press, 1999.

Payne, Robert. *The Rise and Fall of Stalin.* New York: Simon and Schuster, 1965.

Pearson, Drew. *Drew Pearson Diaries, 1949–1959.* Edited by Tyler Abell. New York: Holt, Rinehart and Winston, 1974.

Piereson, James. *Camelot and the Cultural Revolution: How the Assassination of John F. Kennedy Shattered American Liberalism.* New York: Encounter Books, 2007.

Purdum, Todd S. *An Idea Whose Time Has Come: Two Presidents, Two Parties, and the Battle for the Civil Rights Act of 1964.* New York: Henry Holt, 2014.

Rippy, J. Fred. *Bygones I Cannot Help Recalling: The Memoirs of a Mobile Scholar.* Austin TX: Steck-Vaughn, 1966.

Risen, Clay. *The Bill of the Century: The Epic Battle for the Civil Rights Act.* New York: Bloomsbury, 2014.

Roberts, Phil, ed. *Readings in Wyoming History.* Laramie: Skyline West, 2004.

Rosenstone, Steven J., and Raymond E. Wolfinger. "The Effect of Registration Laws on Voter Turnout." *American Political Science Review* 72, no. 1 (March 1978).

Sale, Kirkpatrick. *The Green Revolution: The American Environmental Movement, 1962–1992.* New York: Hill and Wang, 1993.

Schlesinger, Arthur M. *The Vital Center.* Boston: Houghton Mifflin, 1949.

Schmitz, David F., and Natalie Fousekis. "Frank Church, the Senate, and the Emergence of Dissent on the Vietnam War." *Pacific Historical Review* 63, no. 4 (November 1994).

Schrecker, Ellen. *No Ivory Tower: McCarthyism and the Universities.* New York: Oxford University Press, 1986.

Sheehan, Neil, E. W. Kenworthy, Fox Butterfield, and Hedrick Smith. *The Pentagon Papers as Published by the New York Times.* New York: Quadrangle Books, 1971.

Sinclair, Barbara. *The Transformation of the Senate.* Baltimore: Johns Hopkins University Press, 1990.

Sholokhov, Mikhail. *And Quiet Flows the Don.* New York: Alfred Knopf, 1934.

Sorensen, Theodore C. *Kennedy.* New York: Harper and Row, 1965.

Stossel, Scott. "Sargent Shriver and the Birth of the Peace Corps." *Peace Corps Online Magazine.* http://peacecorpsonline.org/messages/messages/2629/2024714.html, *accessed March 17, 2015.*

Strober, Gerald S., and Deborah H. Strober. *Let Us Begin Anew: An Oral History of the Kennedy Presidency.* Perennial, 1964.

Sullivan, Rosemary. *Stalin's Daughter: The Extraordinary and Tumultuous Life of Svetlana Alliluyeva*. Harper, 2015.

Swanson, Frederick Harold. *The Bitterroot & Mr. Brandborg: Clearcutting and the Struggle for Sustainable Forestry in the Northern Rockies*. Salt Lake City: University of Utah Press, 2011.

Talbot, David. *Brothers: The Hidden History of the Kennedy Years*. New York: Free Press, 2007.

Tang, Nhu Truong. *A Vietcong Memoir: An Insiders' Account of the Vietnam War and Its Aftermath*. New York: Vintage Books, 1986.

Terasaki, Gwen. *Bridge to the Sun*. 1958. Rockaway OR: Rock Creek Books, 2012.

Thomas, Evan. *Being Nixon: A Man Divided*. New York: Random House, 2015.

Thompson, Larry Clinton. *Refugee Workers in the Indochina Exodus, 1975–1982*. Jefferson NC: McFarland, 2010.

Thonsenn, Lester, ed. *Representative American Speeches, 1964–1965*. New York: H. W. Wilson, 1965.

Toffler, Alvin. "A Freshman's Washington Merry-Go-Round." *Pageant,* May 1959.

University of Wyoming Trustees. October 24–25, 1947, Minutes of Meetings. http://www.uwyo.edu/trustees/board-meeting-archives/1940–1949-minutes/1947-board-of-trustees-meetings.html.

U.S. Senate, Committee on Foreign Relations. "Study Mission to Southeast Asia November–December 1962." Washington: Government Printing Office, 1963.

U.S. Department of State. *Foreign Relations of the United States, 1961–1963*. Vol. 4, *Vietnam, August–December 1963*. http://history.state.gov/historicaldocuments/frus1961–63v04/d332.

U.S. Senate Historical Office, "Joseph R. McCarthy: A Featured Biography." http://www.Senate.gov/artandhistory/history/common/generic/Featured_Bio_McCarthy.htm.

U.S. Senate, Committee on Commerce. "Civil Rights-Public Accommodations." Report of the Committee on Commerce on S. 1732. Washington: Government Printing Office, July 1963.

Weiner, Tim. *One Man against the World: The Tragedy of Richard Nixon*. New York: Henry Holt, 2015.

White, Theodore. *The Making of the President 1964*. New York: Atheneum, 1965.

White, William S. *The Citadel*. New York: Harper and Brothers, 1957.

Wildavsky, Aaron. *Dixon-Yates: A Study in Power Politics*. New Haven: Yale University Press, 1962.

Williams, Robert. *Negroes with Guns*. New York: Marzani and Munsell, 1962.

Woodward, Bob. *The Last of the President's Men*. New York: Simon and Schuster, 2015.

Wooster, Martin Morse. "Too Good to Be True." *Wall Street Journal,* April 1, 2005. http://www.wsj.com/articles/SB111232604205595288, accessed June 25, 2015.

Wyoming Tales and Trails. "Bill Nye and the Boomerang." http://www.wyomingtalesandtrails.com/laramietpris2.html, accessed on January 8, 2015.

Zelizer, Julian E. *The Fierce Urgency of Now.* New York: Penguin, 2015.

Zimmer, Louis B. *The Vietnam War Debate.* Lanham MD: Lexington Books, 2011.

Index

Photographs are indicated by P with a numeral.

antiwar movement (*continued*)
230–31; in Vietnam, 195; work by
Thomas in, 19. *See also* nonviolent
strategy; Vietnam War
apartheid, 243
Apollo 8 (space ship), 206
Appropriations Committee. *See*
U.S. Senate Appropriations
Committee
Armed Forces Committee. *See* U.S.
Senate Armed Forces Committee
Armstrong, Hepburn T., 69
The Arrogance of Power (Fulbright), 219
assassinations: of Anastasio Somoza,
292; of John F. Kennedy, 5, 48,
149, 153, 155–57, 212, 268; of Mal-
colm X, 153, 179, 212; of Martin
Luther King Jr., 153, 157, 211, 212;
of Medgar Evers, 212; of Robert F.
Kennedy, 153, 212
Atlas missile program, 61

Baker, Bobby, 104, 105, 110
Baker, Howard, 16
Baker, Loraine. *See* McGee, Loraine
Baker (wife)
Baker, Madge, 16
"balance of power" principle:
applied to the Senate, 100; as his-
toric U.S. precept, 45; McGee on,
24, 44, 45, 132, 181, 190, 203, 220.
See also domino theory
bald eagles. *See* eagle slaughter
Balewa, Alhaji Sir Abukabar Tafawa,
120–21
Ball, George, 209, 244
Barlett, Ruhl, 252
Barnett, Ross, 115
Barrett, Francis, 140

Barrett, Frank: 1952 senate campaign of, 60–61, 70; 1958 senate
campaign of, 67, 68–69, 73–79,
84, 278, 314n13; gubernatorial
campaign of, 36, 39; obituary
of, 82; political career of, 36, 68;
Robertson scandal with, 80–82; as
sore loser, 89
"Barrett Helped Compromise a Sen-
ator's Tax Case" (Pearson), 80–82
Bartlett, Ruhl, P22
baseball, 60, 76
basketball, 14, 16, 154, 168, 172
Battle of Stalingrad (1942–43), 54
Beaver, Wendell, 233
Beck, Mike, 194–95
Becker, Keith, 234
Becoming Western (Nicholas), 273, 278
Bedont, Attilio, 218
Bell, Tom, 233
Benes, Vaclav L., 41
Benson, Ezra Taft, 78
Berlin Conference (1884), 120
Berry, James P., 218
Birch, John, 132–33
birds. *See* eagle slaughter; pheasant
hunting
black citizens, violence and discrim-
ination against. *See* civil rights
movement; racial violence
Black Panther Party, 153, 198–99
Blount, Winton, P3, 227
Bolivia, 292–93
Borah, William, 193
Bork, Robert H., 255
Borman, Frank, 206
Bostwick, R. R., 198
Bowers, D. W., 188
Bowles, Chester, 44

Church, Frank, P2; as 1960 convention leader, 114; 1962 Cuba trip of, 144; as chair of Select Committee on Intelligence Activities, 260; friendship with McGees of, 88; reputation of, 101; Vietnam War debates of, 181, 182–84, 186, 300

CIA (Central Intelligence Agency), 121, 222, 260

"Citizenship in a Republic" (speech by Roosevelt), 4, 299

Civil Rights Act (1964), 3, 4, 86, 160–62, 302

civil rights movement: acts of civil disobedience, 141, 179, 191–92; legislative bills on, 3, 4, 86, 138, 142, 160–62, 193, 302; Little Rock High School integration, 60; racial violence during, 138–41, 153, 162–63, 179, 190, 211–12; and Senate Rule 22, 96–97

Clark, John B., 37, 70

Clay, Cassius, 167, 184, 202

Clay, Henry, 100

Clean Air Act (1963), 3, 302

clearcutting practices, 233–37

Clements, Earle, 68

Clinton, Bill, 225, 251

Coad, Arden, 215–16

coal. See mining industry

Cody Enterprise, 137

Colby, William, 260

Collingwood, Charles, 185

Colson, Charles, 236

Commerce Committee. See U.S. Senate Commerce Committee

Committee on Human Rights for the Western States, 139

Common Sense (publication), 305n13

communism: antiwar activity by, 187–88; in China, 38; loyalty reviews of, 31, 77; McGee's essay on, 44–45; and Oppenheimer, 102; in South America, 131; U.S. policy in Southeast Asia against, 148–53; UW "Red Scare" investigations, 31–34, 72, 270, 305n13; in Vietnam, 124–25. See also Red Scare

Congo, 121

Congress for Racial Equality (CORE), 138

"Congress Project" (Nader), 248, 249

conscientious objection, 19–21, 187–88, 215. See also antiwar movement

conservative extremism, 167–68, 300. See also John Birch Society (JBS); Republican Party

Constellation (aircraft carrier), 170

Conwell, Ralph, 34, 71–72, 76–77

Cook, Dick, P11, 91, 92, 272, 311n3

Cooper, Betty, P11, 18, 91, 292

Cooper, Charles, 179

Council for a Livable World, 175, 231–32

Council on Environmental Quality, 235

Council on Foreign Relations (CFR), 43–44, 63

Counts, George, 31

Cox, Archibald, 255

credibility gap, 218, 220. See also distrust and secrecy of government

Cromwell, Oliver, 9–10

Cronkite, Walter, 1, 283

C. Turner Joy (ship), 170

Cuban missile crisis, 144–45

Cuban Revolution, 144

Cunningham, Jack, 252

Haig, Alexander, 256, 259
Haldeman, Bob, 221–22, 255, 257
Halverson, Richard, 297
Hamilton, Alexander, 85
Hamilton, Bruce, 233
Hampton, Fred, 198
Hang 'Em High (film), 254
Hansen, Cliff, 71, 123, 162, 166, 241, 266–67, 271
Harding, Warren, 102
Harriman, Averill, 44
Harrison, William Henry, 36, 37, 163, 166, 281, 326n31
Hart, Gary, 263
Hart, Phil, P7, 2, 89, 90
Hartke, Vance, 90
Harvey, Paul, 135–36
Hatch Act (1939), 250
hate-crimes legislation, 193
Hathaway, Stan, 175, 213, 241, 261–64, 279
Hay, John, 45
Hayden, Carl, 119, 146
health care reform, 3, 4, 142–44, 173, 174–75, 268, 302
Herschler, Ed, 69
Hickey, J. J., 87, 111, 113–14, 122–23
Hickey, Winifred, 87
Hicks, Granville, 44
High Country News, 279
hiking, 126, 233
Hill and Knowlton, 294
Hilsman, Roger, 152
Hinckley, John T., 35, 178
Ho Chi Minh, 124–25
Hodges, Ralph, 236
Hoffa, Jimmy, 254
Honan, William H., 100
Hook, Sidney, 41, 72

Hoover, Herbert, 101
Hoover, J. Edgar, 48, 101, 188. *See also* FBI (Federal Bureau of Investigation)
House of Representatives. *See* U.S. House of Representatives
Hoyt, Palmer, 177
Hruska, Roman, 78
Huergo, Marcelo, P5
human rights policies in Latin America, 286, 287, 291–93
Humphrey, George Duke, 30–31, 32
Humphrey, Hubert, 86, 96, 173, 213, 214
Hunt, H. L., 80, 135
Hunt, Lester (senator), 46, 91, 106, 127, 309n27
hunting, P17, 12, 25–26, 177, 202
Huntington, Burt, 177
Ibach, Kim, 140

Idlewild International Airport, 48
Illinois, 21–22
Indochina Refugee Panel, 294–95
Indonesia, 146–47
Inglis, David, 104
Inouye, Daniel, 181
insecticide poisoning, 296
Institute on International Affairs (University of Wyoming), 40–42
Internal Revenue Service (IRS), 80, 81, 222
Interstate and Foreign Commerce Committee. *See* U.S. Senate Interstate and Foreign Commerce Committee
Iowa State College, 20
Irvine, Van, 237–38, 239

isolationism: of Barrett, 73, 74, 75;
and McGee's co status, 19–20;
McGee's evolving ideas on, 14,
22–24, 180–81, 224; Rippy on, 23–
24; of Wyoming, 84
Izaak Walton League, 226

Jackson, Henry, 54, 117
Jackson, Otis, 197
Jacoby, Glenn J. "Red," 154
Japanese American internment and
reintegration, 17–18, 303
Jaworski, Leon, 257
Jenkins, Walter, 113
Job Corps, 175
John Birch Society (JBS), 132–38,
165, 167–68, 174, 201, 300
John F. Kennedy International Airport, 48
Johnson, Lady Bird: at Kennedy's
inauguration, 126; on LBJ's 1964
candidacy, 173; McGees and Wyoming visits of, 109, 169, 171–72; at
McGee's funeral, 297
Johnson, Lyndon B., P2; 1960 presidential candidacy of, 107, 109,
112–17; 1964 presidential candidacy of, 173, 177–78; appointments
by, 90–91, 101, 194, 204–5; on civil
rights legislation, 160; conspiracy theory about, 157; description
of McGee by, 205; at Kennedy's
inauguration, 126; McGee's relationship with, 1, 107, 109–10,
158, 184, 187, 210; and McGee's
work on Judiciary Committee,
47; Medicare legislation by, 173;
presidential acts by, 4, 169, 193,
226; presidential swearing-in of,
157; refusal of second full term,

209–10; on Senate Rule 22, 96,
97; on Strauss, 104; in support of
McGee's campaigns, 79–80, 91,
163–64; and Vietnam War, 157,
158–59, 169–71, 185–86, 221, 222
Johnston, Felton "Skeeter," 94
Joint Committee on Atomic Energy,
102–5
Jones, Dick, 271, 279
Jones, Paul, 92
Jordan, Hamilton, 289
Judiciary Committee. *See* U.S. Sen-
ate Judiciary Committee

Karpan, Kathy, 122–23, 137
Kaunda, Kenneth, 120
Keating, Kenneth, 2
Kefauver, Estes, 78
Kelly, Venita, 59
Kendall, Del, P11
Kennan, George, 44
Kennedy, Jacqueline, 126
Kennedy, John F., P1, P6; 1960 presidential candidacy of, 107, 109,
110–12, 115–18; on Appropriations
Committee, 90; assassination of,
5, 48, 149, 153, 155–57, 212, 268;
on civil rights legislation, 138,
141–42; on conservative extremism, 167; on Cuban missile crisis,
145; health care reform of, 142–
44; inauguration of, 125–26; on
McGee, 1, 99, 100; and McGee's
work on Judiciary Committee, 47;
meeting McGee's parents, 11; on
Norris, 13; Peace Corps by, 4, 5,
121; political positions of, 108–9;
presidential acts by, 4; on railroad
strike, 145–46; Southeast Asia
policy of, 149–53; in support of

McGee, Gale William, other work:
1956 tour of Soviet Union, 47,
49–59, 63; 1956 visit to Germany, 48–49; as bulletin editor,
17; career overview of, 1–4, 299–
302; as CFR fellow, 43–44, 63;
early teaching positions of, 15–17,
18–19, 20; at Hill and Knowlton
firm, 294; on Indochina Refugee
Panel, 294–95; at Moss McGee
Associates, 294; as OAS Ambassador, P15, 1, 4, 286–93; Rumsfeld nomination of, 260–61; UN
ambassador appointment consideration, 1–2, 204–5, 209, 285; as
UN delegate, 243
McGee, Gale William, political opinions of: "An Academic Looks
at Vietnam," 187; "The American Hunger for Sudden Performance," 44–45; on balance
of power principle, 24, 44, 45,
132, 181, 190, 203, 220; "A China
Policy for the United States,"
42; commencement speeches,
64, 203, 213, 311n11; "A Debate
Resumed," 39–40; Denver Post editorial, 26, 70; early views on war
of, 19–21, 23–25; on foreign policy, 46, 63–65, 186–87, 224, 289;
"Forgotten Men," 13–14; "The
Founding Fathers and Entangling Alliances," 24; isolationism,
evolving ideas on, 22–24, 180–81;
list of early papers, 23; maiden
congressional speech of, 99–100;
newspaper articles about, 34–35,
70, 162; on North Korean, 207–
8; oratorical skills of, 63, 99–101,
106; "Prospects for a More Toler-

able Co-existence with the Soviet
Union," 43; The Responsibilities
of World Power, 150–51, 219, 220–
21, 309n5; "A Survey of Foreign
Efforts to Ally with the United
States, 1789–1919," 23
McGee, Gale William, as university
professor: at Iowa State College,
20; at Nebraska Wesleyan University, 16–17, 18–19, 303; at Notre
Dame University, 20–21; salary of,
16, 31; and textbook investigation,
31–34, 72, 270; at University of Wyoming, 1, 25, 26–27, 29–31, 47, 303
McGee, Gale William, as U.S. senator:
1950 consideration to run, 35–37,
309n26; 1958 campaign of, 66–83,
108; 1958 election of, 1, 2, 5, 83–84,
86; 1959 Vietnam trip and hearing
on, 127–28; 1960 presidential campaign and, 107, 109, 110–14; 1960
trip to Africa, 34, 119–22; 1962 trip
to Asia, 146–48; 1962 trip to Cuba,
144; 1963 trip to South America,
131; 1964 campaign of, 163–69,
173–78; 1966 trip to Asia, 199–200;
1970 campaign of, 229–32; 1970
party debates by, 229–30; 1973 trip
to China, 245–47; 1976 campaign
of, 1, 3–4, 5, 266, 270–84; Carter's
support of, 2, 290; and civil rights
movement, 109, 138–41, 161–63,
199; conflicts with Fulbright, 62,
128, 194, 196, 200, 219; correspondence on Vietnam War, 190, 197,
202–3, 208–9, 215–16, 218; correspondence with constituents on
federal regulations, 248–49, 275–
76; correspondence with constituents on Nixon's impeachment,

McGee, Gale William (*continued*)
255, 260; correspondence with
constituents on race relations,
211; correspondence with constituents on spending, 92–93; Cuban
missile intel of, 144; environmental work by, 234–40, 302; Ford's
support of, 1–2; on health care
reform, 143, 302; and John Birch
Society, 132–38, 165, 167–68, 174,
201, 300; Johnson's campaign
support of, 79–80, 91, 163–64;
Johnson's relationship with, 1,
107, 109–10, 158, 184, 187, 210; on
Judiciary Committee, 46–47; Kennedy's assassination and funeral,
155–56; Kennedy's support of,
1, 77, 108, 125–27; meeting with
Khrushchev, 62; and mining legislation, 265–67; Morgenthau's
debate with, 200–201; on Nixon's
pardon, 260; Nixon's relationship with, 1, 281, 300; office staff
of, 91–92; Panama Canal debates
of, 288–90; passing of Civil Rights
Act, 160–62; passing of Voting
Rights Act, 4, 193; on Post Office
and Civil Service Committee, 223,
226–27, 250, 275; on racial violence, 191–93; relationships with
other senators, 88, 95–96; salary of, 71, 93, 226, 275, 315n22;
Strauss appointment fight, 101–
6; swearing-in ceremony, 88–89;
transition of life to, 86–88; USAID
investigation, 131–32, 301; on USS
Pueblo capture, 207–8, 301; Vietnam War debates and speeches
of, 181–90, 195–96, 203–4, 219,
244–45; visit to Panama Canal
Zone, 288; on voter registration
reform, 250–51, 302; on Watergate scandal, 253–58
McGee, Garton (father), P6, 10–12
McGee, Joel (grandfather), 10
McGee, Loraine Baker (wife): P8,
P11, P18, P20; 1956 trip to Germany, 48–49; 1956 trip to Soviet
Union, 49–59; 1959 trip to Africa,
34, 119–22; 1973 trip to China,
247; 1979 trip to Bolivia, 292;
and campaigns, 65, 66, 174, 283;
courtship and marriage to Gale,
14–16; death of, 298; as Gale's
nurse, 177, 247–48, 296; homes
of, 11, 22, 29, 43, 72, 93; as host
of Eleanor Roosevelt, 41; and
Jackie Kennedy, 108; at Kennedy's assassination and funeral,
155–56; Lazy G ranch of, 251–52,
296; as mother, 19, 22, 28–29, 66;
Soviet reports by, 49, 50, 57, 63,
64; transition to Washington life,
86–88; at Tricia Nixon's wedding,
253; and voter reform, 251; as welcoming to Nisei students, 18–19
McGee, Lori Ann (daughter), P20,
7, 66, 94, 254
McGee, Mary Gale (daughter), P20,
66, 156, 187, 213–14
McGee, Max (brother), 11, 297
McGee, Robert (son), P20; adult
life of, 128, 251, 297; birth and
early life of, 29; campaign assistance by, 66, 74, 77; at Kennedy's
funeral, 156
McGhee, Harvey (great-
grandfather), 10
McGovern, George, P2; and Council for a Livable World, 231–32; on

Witzenburger, Edwin J., 119–20
Wold, John: 1964 senate campaign of, 168, 169, 172–76, 178; 1970 senate campaign of, 230, 232; as Wyoming's 1970 Man of the Year, 225
Women's Republic Clubs, 12, 38, 71, 101
women's rights, 223
Woods, Rose Mary, 256
World Order (Kissinger), 268
World Series games, 60, 76
World War II: and balance of power, 181; effects on educational enrollment, 20, 30; Japanese American following, 17–18; Pearl Harbor attack, 17, 19, 20, 21, 204; visible landscape scars from, 48, 49, 54
Wyoming: 1958 Senate campaign of, 83–84, 312n11; 1960 presidential campaign and, 107, 111–13, 116–17; 1963 legislative resolutions in, 166–67; 1970 Man of the Year, 225; black population and civil rights in, 138–41, 162–63; clear-cutting practices in, 233–37; cultural symbolism of, 272–74, 278; descriptions of Laramie, 26–27, 28, 29; eagle slaughters in, P10, 234, 237–40, 263, 280; environmental concerns of, 225–26, 233, 240–43; equal rights laws in, 223; geography of, 28; and Hathaway's nomination, 261–64; history and statehood of, 30; Kennedy and issues of, 126–27; Kennedy's visit to, 107, 118–19, 153–54; Lady Bird Johnson's trips to, 169, 171–72; McGee's relationship with, 1, 3, 6–7, 25, 63–65, 249, 280; mining industry of, 79, 264–67, 277; reclamation projects of, 164; right-to-work law in, 166–67, 178; voter registration in, 251
Wyoming Democratic Party: conventions of, 107, 118–19, 257; history of, 178; and labor laws, 166; Senate campaigns of, 36–37, 69, 84; on Vietnam War, 203, 229. *See also* Democratic Party
Wyoming Eagle, 35, 76, 83, 228
Wyoming New Democratic Coalition, 228, 230
Wyoming Republican Party: 1950 voting turnout of, 69, 312n11; criticism of, 37; history of, 4, 66, 178; and labor laws, 166; Senate campaigns of, 77–78. *See also* Republican Party
Wyoming State Journal, 281, 282
Wyoming State Tribune, 61
Wyoming Stockman-Farmer, 163, 164

Yates, Eugene, 103
Yellowstone National Park, 157
Young, Andrew, 285
Young, Stephen, 131
Young Democrats Clubs, 122, 174
Young Republicans Club, 12, 13

Zhou Enlai, P16, 246–47

Some Other Titles in the ADST's Book

Mongolia and the United States:
A Diplomatic History
Jonathan Addleton

Toussaint's Clause: The Founding
Fathers and the Haitian Revolution
Gordon S. Brown

Intervening in Africa: Superpower
Peacemaking in a Troubled Continent
Herman J. Cohen

Born a Foreigner: A Memoir of
the American Presence in Asia
Charles T. Cross

Inventing Public Diplomacy:
The Story of the United States
Information Agency
Wilson Dizard Sr.

Raising the Flag: America's First
Envoys in Faraway Lands
Peter D. Eicher

"Emperor Dead" and Other Historic
American Diplomatic Dispatches
Peter D. Eicher, ed.

Diversifying Diplomacy: My Journey
from Roxbury to Dakar
Harriet Elam-Thomas

Behind Embassy Walls: The Life and
Times of an American Diplomat
Brandon Grove

Economic Diplomat: A Life in the
Foreign Service of the United States
Deane R. Hinton

American Ambassadors: The
Past, Present, and Future of
America's Diplomats
Dennis C. Jett

The Architecture of Diplomacy:
Building America's Embassies
Jane C. Loeffler

Escape with Honor: My Last
Hours in Vietnam
Terry McNamara, with Adrian Hill

Vietnam and Beyond: A Diplomat's
Cold War Education
Robert H. Miller

Witness to a Changing World
David D. Newsom

Plunging into Haiti: Clinton, Aristide,
and the Defeat of Diplomacy
Ralph Pezzullo

Ellsworth Bunker: Global
Troubleshooter, Vietnam Hawk
Howard B. Schaffer

Losing the Golden Hour: An Insider's
View of Iraq's Reconstruction
James Stephenson

The Anguish of Surrender:
Japanese Pows of World War II
Ulrich Straus

Abroad for Her Country: Tales
of a Pioneer Woman Ambassador
in the U.S. Foreign Service
Jean Wilkowski

For a complete list of series titles, visit adst.org/publications.

Other works by Rodger McDaniel

Dying for Joe McCarthy's Sins: The
Suicide of Wyoming Senator Lester
Hunt (Wordsworth, 2013)

The Sagebrush Gospel
(Wordsworth, 2014)